Penguin Education
Modern Economics Texts

The Economics of Capital Budgeting

Michael Bromwich

Michael Bromwich

The Economics of Capital Budgeting

Penguin Books

Penguin Books Ltd,
Harmondsworth, Middlesex, England
Penguin Books
625 Madison Avenue, New York, New York 10022, U.S.A.
Penguin Books Australia Ltd,
Ringwood, Victoria, Australia
Penguin Books Canada Ltd,
41 Steelcase Road West, Markham, Ontario, Canada
Penguin Books (N.Z.) Ltd,
182–190 Wairau Road, Auckland 10, New Zealand

First published 1976

Made and printed in Great Britain by
Richard Clay (The Chaucer Press) Ltd,
Bungay, Suffolk
Set in Monotype Times

To my parents

Contents

Preface

This book tackles the problem of the allocation of investment funds within the firm, that is: what total finance should the firm employ, what specific investment projects should it undertake, and how should it fund these projects? There is a tendency both in practice and in books in this area to concentrate on project appraisal (the second question). However, all three questions are intimately related, and a discussion of any one commits us to a discussion of them all.

The objective is to summarize, from an economist's point of view, the analytical research of approximately the last ten years and to outline the controversies and gaps in the existing literature. The emphasis will be on 'why we do it' rather than 'how we do it', since the fundamental need is for a normative theory at the individual-firm level. However, the lack of an operational theory (and therefore a meaningful theory) in various areas will be highlighted.

This volume is meant to be useful to both undergraduates and postgraduates in economics and business studies, who need an analytical introduction to the literature of capital budgeting. It should also appeal to those taking management diplomas and accounting examinations who are not satisfied with the 'cook book' approach of their required texts. Finally, it is hoped that all those in business who wish to understand the theoretical foundation of capital budgeting will find their needs met by this book.

No previous knowledge of project appraisal or business finance is necessary, but some acquaintance with economics and the elementary use of graphical techniques is useful. No mathematical ability is required, but a facility to manipulate algebraic formulae will help, as will a passing acquaintance with accounting. Here and there a little knowledge of linear programming and probability theory is useful.

Many people have given me valuable advice on earlier drafts of this book; especially helpful were J. Arnold, B. V. Carsberg, C. Tomkins and C. M. E. Whitehead. The remaining errors are, of course, my responsibility. I would also like to thank W. T. Baxter and H. C. Edey for unstintingly giving me their wise counsel for many years.

My inadequate thanks also go to Mrs Evans, Mrs Pritchard, Miss Oxley and Mrs Robertson who were unfortunate enough to type parts of many incomprehensible drafts of this book.

1 Capital Budgeting and Decision Making

Introduction
Capital budgeting defined

Economics is concerned with the allocation of scarce resources between alternative uses so as to best obtain objectives. Capital budgeting concentrates on these allocations over time; on decisions which involve current outlays in return for expectations of future benefits. Investment decisions, which are the concern of capital budgeting, involve such choices as: for the individual – house buying and the purchase of consumer durables; for the firm – investment in plant, research and development and advertising; for the government – the construction of roads, of a Channel tunnel, and space research. All three entities are faced with an infinite number of possible investment opportunities to be financed out of a limited amount of funds. This book outlines an analytical framework which guides the way to the optimum set of investment projects for the firm. Although we concentrate on decisions made by the firm, the same principles apply, with modification, to those of individuals and of public agencies.

Capital-budgeting theory seeks to provide a body of analysis giving answers to the following three questions:

What specific investment projects should the firm accept?
What total amount of capital expenditure should the firm undertake?
How should this portfolio of projects be financed?

These three decisions are closely related. The problem is not simply one of deciding which investments to finance with a given amount of funds for the amount of borrowing and the volume of shares issued are variables within the firm's control. Thus decisions about project choice and the acquisition of funds, ideally, must be made simultaneously. Similarly, a yardstick for project acceptance cannot be set without considering the cost of funds to the enterprise, and this cost will be influenced by the characteristics of the investment opportunities available to the firm.

For our purposes, then, capital budgeting is defined as covering all three questions. This and the next two chapters are introductory but contain essential material for the understanding of the remainder of the book. Chapters 4 and 5 examine in detail various alternative methods of project appraisal. The following chapter focuses on the cost of funds, and chapters 7 and 8 discuss the central issue of financing policy – the choice between debt and equity. The complications of the dividend decision are then considered. The amendments necessary to allow the theory to deal with the situation where the firm has access to but a limited amount of funds are considered in the following two chapters. Uncertainty impinges on all the above issues and its implications are dealt with in the last part of the book, where chapters 12 and 13 deal with methods of allowing for the uncertainty associated with any project considered in isolation. The final two chapters outline the methods available to treat the uncertainty associated with the firm when taken as a whole.

Reasons for interest in capital budgeting

Developments since the Second World War have stimulated the search for criteria, or systematic decision rules, for project appraisal. Rapid economic growth and technological progress have vastly increased the investment opportunities available to firms having only limited funds. Rapid technological advance has tended to increase the lag between decision making and the benefits of these decisions. It has also increased the necessary size of capital commitments and caused the rate of technical and product obsolescence to increase. Thus correct project-appraisal decisions are increasingly crucial. Mistakes are not easily recouped, for most capital investments are highly specific and have little value in alternative uses. Often the only possibility is to abandon and start again.

Similarly, technical progress has made industry more capital intensive and thus investment decisions increasingly determine the long-term framework in which the firm operates. The firm's future operating and product strategies are often severely constrained once the factory is built.

The increasing complexity of modern industry has forced top management to delegate much of the analysis necessary for project appraisal to staff specialists. This makes imperative the provision of sound comprehensible decision rules for investment decisions. The growth of decentralized decision making has added stimulus to this need. A set of decision rules for investment which are understood and accepted as rational by all within the firm are essential in this context.

Theoretical developments have made possible the partial fulfilment of this need. Thus the problem of comparing receipts obtained at different times seems to have been solved. Advances in economic forecasting, econometrics and budgetary control have made the prediction and measurement of receipts and costs easier. But for many problems concrete solutions have not yet emerged. Dominant among these is the lack of a sound theoretical or operational way of handling the problem of uncertainty.

However, this book is written in the belief that some of the problems have been solved sufficiently well to ensure that the analysis presented generates better decisions than those obtained using any other method.

It can be argued that the uncertainty surrounding the estimates on which capital budgeting is based renders useless anything other than rough rules of thumb. But such rules often amount to ignoring the difficulties. Perhaps the strongest advantage of the analysis in this book is that the difficulties of investment appraisal are squarely faced. Even when we cannot give complete answers, the suggested approach encourages the spelling out of hypotheses and assumptions (model building) and this helps to clarify the problems discussed.

Model building allows us to step back from the confusion of reality and to think through the effects of various assumptions one by one, thus deriving many otherwise unobtainable predictions, which can be subjected to empirical test.

Choice and the decision-making process

Earlier, it was said that investment appraisal involves a choice between alternatives. A review of the components of the decision-making process in general is likely to help in defining the scope of capital budgeting. A consideration of a general model for decision making also gives a bird's-eye view of some of the problems of project appraisal.

The components of the general decision model

It is generally accepted that any decision has the following elements (Alexis and Wilson, 1967, chapter 3):

1 A set of choice alternatives (in capital budgeting, the available projects).

2 A set of outcomes or pay-offs associated with each alternative (the net benefits from the projects). Outcomes may be certain – the selection of any alternative leading uniquely to a specific pay-off; or they may be uncertain – any one of a number of outcomes being associated with any specific decision.

3 A number of states of the environment (for example, inflation and depression would be two alternative states), whose occurrence determines which of several possible outcomes is obtained from any decision alternative. Where certainty prevails, the outcome of a project is known and therefore only one state of the environment is possible.

4 Goals or objectives which the decision-maker seeks to achieve (for example, the maximization of profits).

5 Criteria derived from these general objectives which enable us to rank the various alternatives in terms of how far their pay-offs lead to the achievement of the decision-maker's goals.

6 Constraints on the alternatives which the decision-maker may select; examples are government policy on mergers, and top management directives not to engage in certain types of business.

7 The decision-maker.

These components together constitute a general model of decision making, shown diagrammatically opposite.

					states of the
decision alternatives	X_1	X_2	X_3	... X_n	environment
pay-offs	Y_{11}	Y_{12}	Y_{13}	... Y_{1n}	E_1
	$\vdots$	$\vdots$	$\vdots$	$\vdots$	$\vdots$
	Y_{m1}	Y_{m2}	Y_{m3}	... Y_{mn}	E_m

decision rule: maximize Y_{ij}

The decision alternatives, for example, the potential projects in capital budgeting, are represented by X_1 to X_n. The possible pay-offs from each decision alternative (the net receipts from each project, for example) are represented by the Ys. The actual pay-off for each project is the actual Y obtained, and is dependent on which state of the environment prevails. Thus, if the project represented by X_3 is selected, any outcome from Y_{13} to Y_{m3} is possible depending on the state of the environment that occurs. Our aim is to choose projects (Xs) so that total pay-off (the sum of the Ys of the projects selected) is maximized. This decision must respect any constraints which may exist; for example, that only projects X_1 to X_J out of the total available projects can be considered.

In capital budgeting, at least, two separate types of decision can be distinguished. First, accept or reject decisions, where we seek to maximize total pay-off, however defined, by selecting all projects having a positive pay-off. Second, ranking decisions, which are of two types. The first concerns projects that are mutually exclusive. For example, alternatives must be ranked in order of profitability when selecting the optimal design for a dam. Ranking must also be undertaken where inputs such as labour, finance or management time are limited as lack of resources constrains the number of projects we can select. In this case we wish to choose those projects which maximize the benefits from using scarce resources.

The remainder of the book will put some flesh on this abstract model of capital budgeting. However, before proceeding, it is useful to examine the steps through which one must go to breathe life into our general model. A comparison of these steps with the capital-budgeting model defines the latter's area of interest.

To construct a decision model the following procedure must be followed. The first step is to recognize the problem concerned and to try to fix a boundary to the area of investigation. This may well be the most difficult part of the analysis for we tend to look only at narrow ranges of alternatives, determined by our past experiences and our present situation. There is some evidence that, not surprisingly, executives avoid long-term planning in favour of today's problems, thereby ensuring that the problems of tomorrow will be even more severe (Stewart, 1963).

This myopia means that it is essential for the firm to set up a formal mechanism for scanning its environment for opportunities and to give early warning of future problems. Fixing the problem boundary presents a dilemma. The wider the area investigated, the more likely it is that all the factors which impinge on the decision will be considered. But this widening is accompanied by both a rise in costs and a lengthening of study time. Thus, a value judgement is necessary when setting the problem's boundaries. Analysis, therefore, does not surplant judgement, but sharpens it and allows its better exercise. The mere setting down of the problem and the listing of its variables and the associated environmental factors should improve decision making.

The next stage in the process is to specify the objectives to be used to rank the pay-offs. Ideally, we are looking for a preference ranking which accurately reflects the goals of the organization. In practice, well-defined objectives seldom exist. For example, in the public sector, one would assume the goal is to maximize the welfare of the public. However, this is too hazy to be operational and we are forced to use proximate criteria, such as the increase in national income or the percentage change in income distribution resulting from project acceptance.

The use of partial criteria has the obvious danger that they may supplant the 'real' objective. For example, the criterion used by a supermarket in evaluating late-night opening on a Thursday was the increase in net revenue over a normal Thursday. This was not a good guide to profitability for it included, among other things, the sales normally made on other days which were transferred to Thursday.

Further, it is often very difficult to quantify the contribution of some sectors of the organization to the firm's goals, for example, expenditure on research and development or employee welfare. Often, however, some indication can be obtained by using an index other than cost. For example, in our supermarket example, increased labour turnover could serve as an index of employee dissatisfaction with late-night opening. The analyst is often forced to use proximate criteria, either to make the problem manageable or because of intangible elements. Again, managerial judgement is not supplanted by analysis, but rather the latter allows us to isolate crucial areas of concern and provides information which should improve decisions.

Another difficulty associated with defining objectives is that (within most organizations) several, often conflicting, goals may exist. For example, the maximization of sales revenue and of profits are conflicting objectives. Although only top management can reconcile the conflict, analysis can be a help by indicating the cost of an increase in sales volume in terms of profits foregone, that is, by showing trade-offs between the two objectives.

The next step in the decision process is to search for information to determine what environmental factors impinge on the project and what design alternatives are available. The search process may be expensive and may be biased. The literature reveals many projects which have been accepted on the basis of the preferences of managers rather than on how well the projects achieved organizational goals (Cyert, Dill and March, 1958). Formal planning procedures may encourage greater attention being given to the efficiency of the search function.

The listing of decision alternatives is not simple as alternatives may not be obvious. It is not immediately clear that deterrence and shelters are competing solutions to defence from nuclear attack and the analyst may therefore mistakenly concentrate on finding the 'best' type of shelter. This highlights the concept of different levels of goals. Attempts to use lower-level partial criteria, such as finding the 'best' type of shelter, ignoring higher objectives, such as safety from nuclear attack, may lead to non-optimal solutions. A criterion used in the Second World War to evaluate the results of anti-submarine warfare was the number of submarines sunk for a given sum of money spent on ships and other resources. However, this ignored other methods of rendering submarines inactive, for example, bottling them up in harbour, which may have been cheaper. Thus, proximate criteria must fit into the objectives above them. They should indicate an improvement only if this achieves an improvement in a higher-level objective.

After problem formulation and the search phase, there follows the process of evaluation. Here the first step is to build a model of the problem; that is, to describe the various alternative projects by developing hypotheses about the relationships between each one, and its possible environments and likely pay-offs. Such hypotheses allow us to make predictions about the outcome of selecting any given project when any specific environment obtains.

Models are used extensively in science, and range in type from physical scale models, such as those used in wind tunnels, through symbolic representations of chemical structures to mathematical models. It is fashionable to pretend that the use of models in business is new, but when budgeting, accountants are simply producing arithmetical models of the firm. Indeed, the balance sheet is merely a symbolic model of one aspect of the organization.

The use of models is very important in economics. The dominant model in microeconomics is that of the firm in perfect competition. Even with this simple model many assumptions have to be made. The most important of which are: that the output of each firm in the industry and its demand for factors is too small to allow it to influence selling or factor prices, that there is free entry into the industry and that all firms, whether or not in the industry, have equal knowledge about the industry's future profits. Using these assumptions, we can say that the profit-maximizing output is that where marginal cost equals price, and by using the model, we can predict the effects on the firm's output if, say, a tax per unit of output was imposed.

Thus the major advantage of models, which are simplifications of reality, is that they allow us to make predictions and obtain decision rules which may otherwise be unobtainable. For example, the firm cannot decide between two competing factory designs by building both and then using only the best one.

The essence of model building is abstraction, and the weakness and the strength of model building is that all models are simplifications, hopefully reflecting only items relevant to the decision. For example, a scale model of an aircraft may be sufficient for testing in a wind tunnel, but a full-scale mock-up may be needed for testing the ease of maintenance and service. Both of these models may abstract from the plane's weight but for other purposes this factor may be the only relevant one.

In the social sciences, testing the predictions obtained from models is often very difficult and expensive, and indeed may be impossible. We must often rely on past experience and tests utilizing past results. That is, we are forced to ask the question: how well does the model explain relevant past data? Additionally, we may be able to use the results of similar models as guides. In capital budgeting, models are used to try to explain the relationships between the various alternative projects, the possible alternative environments and the firm's objectives.

After building the model we must plug in forecast values for variables within the organization's control and for the various states of the environment. Such forecasts may be deterministic, that is, they are assumed certain to occur, or they may be uncertain, where any one of several estimates may appear. The problem of uncertainty is one which we will have to consider in detail later.

The final stage in the decision-making process is to select the alternatives which give the maximum pay-off according to the criterion we are using. More generally, models may be used not to select specific projects but rather to provide general decision rules, such as if you wish to maximize profits in perfect competition, produce that volume where marginal cost equals price. This is the way models will be used in this book; to produce general decision rules which, if followed in appropriate conditions, will maximize profits (defined in a specific sense).

It should be appreciated that the need to exercise judgement is present throughout the whole procedure and that each stage in the process interacts with the others. There is no clear point where one finishes and another begins. It is frequently the case that the specification of the original problem is radically altered by information generated by later stages of the analysis. This gradual crystallization of the issues may be the most rewarding part of the whole process.

Our discussion of the decision-making process is summarized in Figure 1.

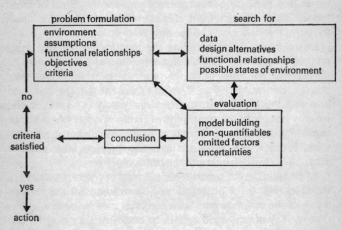

Fig. 1 Steps in decision making

The decision-making process and capital budgeting

A comparison of the capital-budgeting process and the general decision model allows us to define the area of interest of project appraisal, and as a by-product highlights some of the important problem areas ignored by capital budgeting.

Much of the above decision process is ignored by capital budgeting as normally defined. It is usually assumed that the projects to be appraised represent the best investments available to management, that is, the search for opportunities has already been done. In yes/no decisions it is usually hypothesized that each project represents the optimal way of achieving its specific goal. Moreover, it is often assumed that no better project than those currently available will appear in the future. Capital budgeting is, therefore, really only useful late in the decision process, in the evaluation stage.

Problem perception and the search process are viewed as needing the use of other types of analysis. The recognition of strategic problems and the search for opportunities are usually regarded as the concern of the corporate planning function. This latter, by helping to generate the company's long-term objectives and by fixing the long-term area of company activity provides, at least, the general setting for capital budgeting. The firm often must act now if it is to be in a sound position in (say) ten years' time. But management are unlikely to be able to forecast accurately this far ahead and therefore cannot use the precise criteria of capital budgeting. Heavy reliance may therefore have to be placed on intuition and past experience. Even if it were possible to apply capital-budgeting models to every possible project, the expense and the length of time necessary for such an exercise would make it impractical. Corporate-planning techniques, therefore, place emphasis on proxy objectives which it is believed are easier to forecast than the data required for capital-budgeting models. Thus, these former techniques should be relatively less expensive and time consuming in use.

Briefly, such methods involve setting subsidiary objectives which, if realized in the long-term, should ensure that the firm's overall goals are likely to be achieved (Ansoff, 1968). With these general criteria, which may be qualitative rather than quantitative, the company's economic environment is searched for opportunities likely to satisfy these targets. These opportunities, adjusted for the forecast abilities of competitors to take advantage of them, are then matched with the resources the company has (or will have) with current plans, in an attempt to highlight corporate strengths and weaknesses. Strategies are then evolved to exploit the former and remedy the latter. The process of making these general strategies operational is a major source of projects for appraisal.

Similarly, little attention has been paid in the capital budgeting literature to the search for proposals to solve current problems. It is normally assumed with accept or reject decisions that earlier preliminary appraisals have shown that each project represents the optimal way of achieving a specific aim. But yes/no decisions involve a preliminary ranking of those mutually exclusive alternatives, which satisfy a given objective. However, as the same principles govern all ranking decisions, the optimization of individual projects will not often be explicitly referred to in this book.

The search process has been ignored in the literature partly owing to the lack of an analytical theory and partly because it has been regarded as the job of engineers and management. However, that these groups normally generate much of the basic data on which investment appraisal depends seems to be leading to the idea that the search process for decision alternatives should, at least in its final stages, be conducted by interdisciplinary teams. This trend should be encouraged, for the most sophisticated project-appraisal techniques will not rescue the firm from poor project generation. Although little is known about search, that is no reason to say there is no point in trying to improve project-appraisal techniques. First, because a more rigorous approach to the latter, calling for a detailed listing of decision alternatives and a careful comparison of alternative projects, may encourage a more thoughtful attitude to project generation. Second, 'correct' appraisal techniques are not demonstrably more expensive than the rules of thumb currently used and do give better results.

The second major area of the decision process ignored by capital budgeting is that of the setting of goals and acceptance criteria. Some variants of the economist's profit-maximization objective are normally used (often unquestioningly) in the project-appraisal literature. A fierce controversy about both what corporate objectives are, and what they ought to be, is currently raging among social scientists. In the next chapter the implications of this debate for capital budgeting are examined.

2 Objectives

Introduction

Our review of the decision process highlighted the crucial role of objectives in decision making. Models constructed with a specific objective in mind may be of little use in attaining some other goal. A project may be very acceptable to a firm which seeks to maximize profit but be rejected by a company aiming for maximum growth in sales revenue. Thus, we must be very clear about the objectives we are assuming before proceeding to construct models for project appraisal.

There is little agreement in the academic literature about what the objectives of firms are or what they ought to be. Central to economics is the assumption that firms seek to maximize profits. This goal has been suggested on several grounds. There is the legal argument that the equity holders are the owners of the firm which, therefore, should be run for their benefit by trustee managers.

More importantly, since Adam Smith, economists have argued that under certain very restrictive conditions, profit maximization by the individual entrepreneur, who is assumed to receive all the profits, leads to the maximization of overall economic welfare. This thinking is basic to our free-enterprise system; by doing the best for yourself, you are unconsciously doing your best for society. The theory underlying this invisible-hand philosophy is very complex and can be touched on but briefly.

Owners of firms when attempting to maximize profits wish to achieve the largest excess of revenues over costs. These costs result from competitive bidding for scarce resources in factor markets. The prices offered for a factor will depend on the revenue the bidding firms expect to receive from using the input. This revenue will be determined by the price of the goods to be produced using the factor. Such prices reflect those consumer desires that are backed by money. The way in which consumers spend their incomes establishes a set of prices for final goods that reflect the values placed on commodities. Prices in the final-goods market therefore represent the value the economy places on the various goods and services that are available. The bids offered for factors depend on the prices that exist in the final-goods market. The bidding process thereby ensures that factors are employed by those whom society thinks will use them in the most worthwhile way.

The price generated for any input by the factor market applies to all the units traded. This price just equates factor demand and supply and will be equal to the expected revenue to be obtained from using the last, or marginal, unit traded. Additional input at this price would be unprofitable, for the revenue that could have been obtained from using the input would not cover its cost. All those firms that do obtain factors will employ them on products that are deemed, at least, as valuable as the commodity which is produced by the marginal unit of the factor. All such enterprises are therefore manufacturing products that are considered more valuable than the goods that would have been produced by those organizations that were denied factors by the bidding process. Thus, the invisible hand guarantees that factor prices will reflect the value of the output sacrificed by allowing any given firm to use the inputs it requires. The costs faced by entrepreneurs are opportunity costs reflecting the revenue obtainable from factors in their best alternative use.

Thus firms, by seeking to maximize revenue over and above these opportunity costs, should be maximizing the economic welfare of society.

Further, the profit-maximization system has a built-in control device which ensures that in the long run the allocation of resources reflects society's preferences as expressed in the market place. Profits greater than those regarded as normal attract new entrepreneurs into the industry and this competition ensures that excess profits are removed. Thus we have a purely automatic system which, providing everyone is looking after himself, ensures the optimal economic welfare for society.

But this millennium is not easily achieved. Indeed, it has been suggested that its attainment should not be our aim, for the market system reflects only those wishes which are backed by money and ignores major social problems, such as the distribution of income. Further, the market system cannot easily cope with the benefits or costs of an action which fall not on those taking the action but on others. Industrial pollution, which is currently the centre of much attention, is an example of such a cost. For both these reasons the government interferes with the working of the price system so as to mitigate the adverse effects of strict adherence to the invisible-hand philosophy.

Another argument raised against profit maximizing is that the control mechanism referred to above may be impeded due to imperfections in the market, such as barriers to entry which imply the presence of monopolies and oligopolies (where an industry is dominated by a few firms). Such imperfections may also mean that market-factor prices no longer measure opportunity costs. Government intervention would again be necessary to remedy these market imperfections. However, government activity may not always make for the better working of the system. For example, price and wage restraint, though perhaps worthwhile for other reasons, may prevent the market price of factors reflecting their opportunity costs.

However, government clearly plays an important role in our economic system. To the extent that it is successful in ensuring the smooth working of the market system and remedying its weaknesses, the above arguments against profit maximization lose force. But even if the government fails, it is questionable whether individual firms should endeavour to do what they can to plug the gap.

Such actions, unless accompanied by similar ones from other firms, are likely to lead to bankruptcy. For example, one firm in an industry may attempt to stop the pollution it causes by investing in costly equipment, thereby increasing the price of its output. Unless all other firms in the industry take similar action, customers of the socially-conscious enterprise may switch to the new, relatively cheaper goods produced by its competitors. Our firm's actions would become viable only if consumer tastes altered so that they were willing to pay a premium for goods produced in a way that did not cause pollution. Similar results could be expected even if a whole industry moved towards using pollution-free equipment. Without a change in consumer behaviour, demand would be transferred to other commodities. Thus pollution control cannot easily be left to the industrial sector, and government action is really required to deal with the problem. For these and other reasons, some people would argue that curing the problems associated with the invisible-hand system must be the responsibility of the government. In addition, even if it were possible for the industrial and commercial sectors to take direct action to, say, redistribute income, many would consider that these are not the appropriate agencies to make value judgements for the community as a whole. Such matters are seen as being a governmental responsibility.

If we agree that firms are free to disregard those social consequences of their actions which cannot be dealt with by the market mechanism, then profit maximization is still important; not as a way of achieving overall economic efficiency, but rather as the efficiency criteria for individual firms. With this view, by following profit-maximization decision rules the firm will obtain the greatest economic value from the factors it uses. It will, in this way, be seeking to maximize the added value of its output and therefore to use its resources in the most efficient way. This may not lead to the optimal welfare of society if the government has not adopted the necessary economic and social policies.

Thus, with this view, profit maximization is regarded not as a way of achieving overall economic efficiency, but rather as an efficiency objective for the individual firm which, assuming that no substantial imperfections exist in the factors or final-goods market, maximizes the creation of new wealth by that firm. Looked at in this light, profit maximization says nothing about who receives the new wealth thus created. This is in contrast to the 'classical' view which assumes that all profits ought to go to the firm's owners. The majority of the criticism of profit maximization has concentrated on this latter point (Cyert and March, 1963, chs. 3–6).

Other possible objectives

Both in the academic and business world there is a growing dis-
enchantment with the idea that the firm's aim should be the
maximization of the equity-holder's wealth. This objective has
been criticized both from a normative viewpoint, that is, what
companies ought to do, and from a positive one, that is, what
companies do. Most critics take as their point of departure the
estrangement between owners and managers. It is argued that the
manager has become the dominant decision-maker in the firm,
partly because of the wide spread of stockholding, which means
that no individual shareholder or group of individuals can necessarily make their views on company policy prevail, and partly due
to the inadequate information for decision making provided to
shareholders. Thus, with this view, the aims of management have
become dominant, and goals which reflect their prestige, such as
the maximization of sales revenue or being research and development leaders, have partly superseded the profit goal (Cohen and
Cyert, 1965, chs. 16–17).

Similarly, it has been argued that the firm is a coalition of
various different groups – equity-holders, employees, customers
and suppliers – each of whom must be paid a minimum to get him
to participate in the coalition. Any excess benefits after meeting
these constraints are seen as being the subject of bargaining between the various groups. Often, however, it is not clear that
prestige goals and the results of bargaining are in conflict with
profit maximization. For example, giving management large
fringe benefits may lead to greater efficiency. In the same way it
is not clear whether investments to boost worker morale lead to
profit maximization.

Further, given certain restrictive conditions, following profit-
maximization rules as efficiency criteria will lead to the largest
pool of benefits to distribute among the various participants in
the bargaining process. The assumptions necessary for this to be
true are quite complex but roughly require that all participants in
the bargaining process value profits in the same way. This requires
that all participants can be treated as if they were affected in the
same way by taxation and market imperfections. This means,

among other things, that they all face the same opportunities for borrowing and lending and are all either willing to take the same type of risks or are equally free to use the capital market to diversify away risk which they dislike. Such conditions are unlikely to apply in the real world. However, the same assumptions are required to justify measuring a firm's efficiency by its value added. As yet, no more meaningful way to evaluate efficiency has been proposed.

In reality the bargaining process does not occur formally at the end of the year, rather it proceeds informally throughout the year via individual action rather than by face-to-face bargaining. The bargaining process is not overt and its results emerge from day-to-day decisions taken within the limits of existing constraints. For example, management often assume that shareholders expect at least the same dividends as last year, and that decisions can be faced with management's own goals in mind once this constraint is satisfied. Bargaining is likely to come into the open only if such constraints are not respected.

Moreover, many of the side payments resulting from the bargaining process are not made in monetary terms; for example, equipment for research could be a side payment to the research director. Thus in many situations, it is difficult for anyone to know whether profit-maximizing behaviour is being attempted. Finally, although most of the results of bargaining can, in theory, be evaluated in terms of money dividends diverted from shareholders to other groups, often, information sufficient for such calculations is not available. All these difficulties weaken the argument for the narrow view of profit maximization.

Of course, some groups may have objectives which are not consistent with profit maximizing. Management (probably the most powerful member of the coalition) may wish, for prestige reasons, to maximize sales revenue, subject to constraints imposed by other members of the firm. Other members of the coalition may force the firm to accept financing opportunities which are not optimal for the equity-holders. Similarly, the risk attitude of the coalition may differ from that of the equity-holders.

In this situation, even our narrow concept of profit maximization as leading to the largest fund of benefits to be bargained over, may be inappropriate. This is because some participants may regard an increase in the pool of benefits as being achieved at the expense of their own goals and may not regard the extra benefits they obtain as adequate compensation. For example, maximum profits and maximum annual growth in sales revenue are unlikely to be achieved at the same output level. Managers with the latter goal may not regard the extra profits achieved at the profit-maximizing volume as adequate compensation for failing to meet their goal. This is likely, for it is not clear how their share of extra profits can be used to allow them to obtain their goal.

The criterion used in this book: maximize shareholders' welfare

Notwithstanding the above, in most of this book we assume that firms seek to maximize profits which, as will be shown, is equivalent to seeking the maximization of the equity-holders' welfare. Most of the reasons for making this assumption have already been indicated, so we shall just briefly repeat them here. The first is because many objectives which seem to conflict with profit maximization may in fact be subsidiary to it. Second, equity-holders, as a group in the bargaining coalition, should know how much the pursuit of other goals is costing them. Moreover, in the last resort, management is supposedly at the mercy of the shareholders. If it persistently fails to meet minimum profit constraints, it may be replaced or the firm subjected to a takeover bid. Further, prestige-seeking managers may adopt the market value of the firm's shares as, at least, a partial indicator of their performance.

Finally, and perhaps most importantly, the argument that profit maximization decision rules can be used as efficiency criteria, abstracting the distribution of benefits, seems to have much force. This is especially so, as no more meaningful way to measure efficiency has been suggested nor has any alternative goal been found which more effectively promotes the long-run welfare of society or the firm.

However, it is possible that the theories which suggest that firms do not maximize profit but rather have several objectives are correct. Indeed, there is already some empirical evidence that this is so. However, often the objectives that conflict with profit maximization can, in fact, be incorporated into the models used in this book. This possibility arises because it is often argued that people do not aim for the maximum possible level of any objective, but rather will be satisfied if a target level is obtained. (Simon, 1959, gives a good explanation of this view.) This approach allows us to build models that maximize profits subject to first fulfilling the target levels of other goals. This does assume either that all the aspirations of the members of the firm can be achieved simultaneously, or that some mechanism for reconciling goal conflict exists.

Different firms will be made up of people with different goals. Thus the constraints on our profit-maximizing models will differ between firms and recognition of non profit-maximizing objectives may require a unique capital-budgeting model for each enterprise. Thus profit maximizing is adopted in this book partly because we have nothing to put in its place and partly because of its believed generality.

The technical objections to profit maximization

As yet we have not provided an operational (i.e. usable) definition of profit maximization for the firm. Normally profit maximization is assumed to apply to the long run as projects will contribute profits through time and not just in one year. Thus we must devise some means of comparing profits received at different times. This is a purpose of discounting, which will be explained in chapter 4.

Similarly, we have to take account of the uncertain world in which we live. An operational definition of profit must enable us to decide between two options, such as: £200 with certainty, or £1000 if things go right but nothing otherwise. Some suggestions as to how this may be done are examined in later chapters.

Further, to make our objective operational, we need to be more precise about what we mean by profits; do we mean net profit before tax, current profits, or all the future profits expected from a project? The meaning of profits will be defined more precisely in the following chapter, where the accountant's profit figures will be found to need adjustment. But briefly, and anticipating this discussion, profits will be taken to mean the time- and risk-adjusted net cash flows received from a project throughout its life; that is, the positive change in the firm's cash balances over time, resulting from the project. The valuation of such cash flows will be dependent on the time of their receipt and the predicted uncertainty of their achievement. Cash flows will therefore have to be adjusted for these factors. We can use this definition to examine several different objectives that have been suggested as leading to profit maximization.

Does the maximization of profits mean that we should adopt the course of action giving the largest absolute profit? This is not a viable criterion, for by issuing new shares and investing the proceeds in low-yielding bonds, the firm can increase its absolute profits, but at the expense of earnings per share.

The maximization of earnings per share has been suggested as the criterion by which projects should be appraised. This measure suffers from all the difficulties associated with the accountant's profit concept. In addition, it implies that the market value of shares are a function only of earnings. One has but to look in the financial newspapers to see that dividends seem to play a large part in the valuation of companies.

Obviously shareholders are interested in the return on their investment (profits/equity value) and the maximization of this has frequently been suggested as the objective for a company trying to maximize equity-holders' wealth. However, the numerator of this measure is an accounting antifact and subject to all the vagaries and conventions of financial reporting. Moreover, the measure suffers from a fundamental defect, for it can be increased by reducing its denominator as well as increasing its numerator (profits). Indeed, the measure can be maximized by restricting the firm's activity to its single highest-yielding project. This is not to say that the investment necessary for any project is irrelevant but rather it cannot be taken into account using the simple calculation above.

Finally, all the above objectives and their variants, of which there are many, make no allowance for uncertainty or the timing of receipts. Thus the individual, who we have in mind, must make his own adjustments for these factors.

The criterion used for project appraisal must, if maximization of owners' wealth is the aim, include all the future expected receipts and outlays due to the project's acceptance, these having been made comparable over time and been adjusted for risk. However, it will become clear later that adjustments for risk raise many difficult problems, as individuals, due to the circumstances in which they find themselves, may value differently cash flows of a given degree of risk. Thus, for ease of exposition, the early part of this book will assume the existence of certainty. This allows us to concentrate our attention, in the first instance, on obtaining a clear understanding of some crucial matters free of the complications of uncertainty.

In our assumed world of certainty, wealth can be maximized by selecting all those projects whose time-adjusted incremental cash flows have values greater than (or equal to) that of the investment necessary to obtain them, providing that the cash flows are net of any incremental operating costs.

Each project selected in this way will increase the equity value of the firm, because it will yield increased dividends to equity-holders after meeting the commitments associated with its financing. If all available projects which fulfil this criterion are accepted, this will (under certainty) maximize the value of the firm. In this situation, this is merely the sum of the values of the enterprise's projects. Thus, selecting projects in this way is equivalent (under certainty) to maximizing the market value of the firm's shares. This is therefore the basic criterion which will be used to evaluate projects in this book.

Moreover, the maximization of stock values ensures that the equity-holders' economic welfare is at an optimal level. The approach adopted in this book guarantees this, providing that opportunities to borrow and lend and to buy and sell stock are open equally to all.[1] The maximization of stock values gives the equity-holder the largest amount of wealth. And, if the individual does not like the time pattern of the cash flows generated for him by the accepted projects, he can adjust them using the market. That is, he can translate the pattern of cash flows provided by the company to the one he desires by borrowing or lending and selling

1. This assumes that a perfect or near perfect capital market exists. As will be seen, adjustments to the argument are needed where this is not so.

or buying stock. Thus if the company currently provides him with cash in excess of his present needs he can re-invest these funds. By accepting projects so that the company's value is maximized, the firm will provide the equity-holder with the largest possible amount of wealth to adjust as he desires.

Above we have implicitly assumed a valuation model for shares. We assumed that the value of a company is a function of the net cash flows generated by its projects. Exactly how these cash flows are valued is the subject of much debate, for they can be defined either in terms of earnings or of dividends. In a world of certainty this distinction is irrelevant, for if all earnings are retained in the firm, the value of the company on liquidation increases by a known amount and share prices will be adjusted accordingly.

But in the real world, with uncertainty rampant, past dividends often form the basis of future expectations and therefore take on a greater significance. Our valuation model will assume that future dividends, adjusted for timing and risk, alone form the basis for share prices. In the final analysis, these (including any final liquidation distribution) are all the stockholders can obtain from their investment and therefore capital gains must be based on somebody's expectations of future dividends. The simplicity of this presentation hides many different problems and implicit assumptions. These will be gradually introduced and discussed throughout the book.

3 Techniques of Investment Appraisal-Decision Budgets

Introduction

Central to investment appraisal is the drawing up of budgets indicating the result of project acceptance. Any decision is only as good as the estimates of outlays and receipts on which it is based. This chapter examines the conceptual problems associated with estimating and argues that costs and receipts defined in terms of cash flows are most useful in decision budgets.

This argument, as was explained in the previous chapter, rests on the maximization of the equity-holders' welfare, which involves accepting only those projects which increase the market value of the company. Our valuation model assumes that this is based on the size, timing and risk quality of dividends. A project's contribution to dividends depends, in the last analysis, on its future cash flows, that is, the expected flow of receipts and outlays, following its acceptance. If the value of a project's time- and risk-adjusted receipts is greater than that of its outlays, its acceptance under our assumptions will cause an increase in the value of the firm. Thus decision budgets should set out the additional cash flows accruing to the firm if the project being considered is accepted. This is the approach to decision budgets advocated by the economist. However, data for project appraisal is normally provided by accountants who may not follow this approach when compiling their reports. We need therefore to examine these different approaches to decision budgets.

Decision budgets – the economist's approach

The economist is interested in choice between alternatives and therefore his approach to decision budgets has relevance for project appraisal. The economist's approach to decisions is to ask 'what difference does it make?'. His budgets will show the expected future cash inflows and outflows associated with any decision, the emphasis being on the incremental, or differential, effects of the decision. Such decision budgets therefore set out the expected changes in the firm's position following project acceptance.

This means that historical (past) costs have no place in decision budgets. They are, however, probably our major guideline to future costs. As an example of the irrelevance of past costs, consider the decision to sell your car now or in one year's time. For ease of exposition, we will assume that the decision concerning transportation next year can be taken independently of similar decisions in the future. This decision involves estimating the current second-hand market price of the car and deducting from this the incremental travelling costs incurred if it were sold. This figure should then be compared with the running expenses associated with keeping the car net of its disposal value at the year's end. The relevant facts for the decision are set out below, where it is assumed you will keep your driving licence whether or not the car is sold. It is also assumed that if the car were sold, the garage space freed could be rented out to someone else. The values of the cash flows are not adjusted to reflect their timing. This is partly because of the short time-span and small sums involved. But, more importantly, abstracting from the timing issue allows us to concentrate on a few crucial issues in the theory of decision budgets. The complications introduced by adjusting for the timing of receipts and outlays are considered in the next chapter.

Table 1 Keep or sell car

	Sell (£)	Keep for one year (£)	Difference (incremental cash flows) (£)
market price	+500	+25	+475
additional travelling expenses	−400	—	−100
running costs		−300	
driving-licence fee	−5	−5	—
garage space	+50	—	+50
net incremental cash flows			425

You should sell your car now as this gives the larger increase in today's wealth. For a firm faced with a like decision, selling the car will increase its net cash inflows, and therefore dividends, and will help to maximize its equity values.

That the car cost you £1000 a year ago and in selling it now you are losing £500 less the benefits of one year's use, is irrelevant. There is nothing that can be done to avoid this; the original price of the car is a sunk (past) cost and cannot possibly be affected by the decision. All you can do is to pick the best of the alternatives available now. To sell the car is still the best decision, whatever its original price. The driving-licence fee is an example of an irrelevant future cost. It remains the same whichever decision is taken and could be left out of the Table.

Table 1 deals only with the quantitative aspects of the decision and ignores the qualitative factors, such as the status aspect of owning a car or the convenience of doing so. These are left for the decision-maker to deal with. Such non-quantifiables are normally present in decisions and often can be weighed only by judgement. But, as will be shown later, often, after much thought, many such factors can be expressed on a non-monetary scale. Thus, labour morale might be quantified in an approximate way using figures for labour turnover. Even the above Table is useful in evaluating the non-monetary aspects of the decision, for if the car were not sold, the convenience of having it and/or the associated status aspect must be valued at over £425. It is important that the qualitative aspect of a decision should be made explicit.

Opportunity costs

Decision budgets should facilitate choice between various alternatives and therefore ought to reflect the other benefits lost when a given project is accepted. Such benefits are those from the projects sacrificed due to the acceptance of the proposal under consideration. If two projects A and B are mutually exclusive, that is, the acceptance of one precludes undertaking the other, the opportunity cost of accepting A is the foregone benefits from B and vice versa. In the decision concerning selling the car, we compared the two available alternatives and selected the one with the largest net cash flow. That is, we compared selling (net cash inflow

£550 − £405 = £145) with the opportunity of retaining the car (net cash outflow £305 − £25 = −£280). Thus, in decision budgets, the economist's 'opportunity cost' definition of cost should be used. The costs of any project should reflect the foregone benefits from the sacrificed next best alternative. Thus the opportunity cost of retaining the car is £425 (£145 + £280), the net cash flow arising from its sale.

As another example, consider a decision about which of three jobs to accept. All the projects used the same amount of a material K which is scarce and no substitute is available. The firm has just enough of K to do one of the three jobs and no more can be obtained.

The relevant information about each job is summarized in Table 2.

Table 2 Which job to accept

	Job X (£)	Job Y (£)	Job Z (£)	Historical cost (£)	Market price now (£)
surplus from job excluding cost of material K	1500	1200	1700		
material K				1800	1000

The market price of material K would, if the material were freely available, reflect its opportunity cost to society and to the firm. In this situation, by using the material for, say, job X, the firm foregoes only the opportunity of selling it on the market. None of the other jobs are affected by the decision, for more K can be bought for £1000. Note that the price paid for K in the past does not enter into the decision. But in our example no more K is available and therefore only one of the jobs can be done. If X is chosen instead of Y or Z the opportunity cost of using K is the higher of the receipts lost from not being able to accept either job Y (£1200) or Z (£1700). Similarly, if Z is chosen over X, then the opportunity cost of K is £1500. Obviously, job Z should be selected as this yields the highest surplus over its opportunity cost. If we produce Z, we forego the receipts from the job with the next highest surplus (job X), but obtain an additional contribution of

£200 (£1700 — £1500). If we undertake job X we lose £200 and we would lose £500 if Y were accepted. Thus, the opportunity cost of material K is £1700.

The economist's approach to decision making, in other words, looks at all available alternatives, for without alternatives costs cannot exist. It is a forward-looking approach with the emphasis on finding incremental costs, valued on an opportunity cost basis.

As has been pointed out by Gould (1962), in principle opportunity costs are unnecessary for decision making for to obtain them we must know the net cash flows from all the available alternatives. But if this information is available, the correct decision is obtained by selecting projects according to the size of their net cash flows and there is no need to calculate opportunity costs. Given the data in our example, job Z is obviously the best one and there is no need to work out its opportunity cost. However, this argument ignores the influence of the opportunity cost concept in forcing us to be forward looking, to examine all alternatives and to emphasize incremental costs. Moreover, as we shall see, the opportunity cost idea is essential when we are trying to measure costs in complex situations with many projects to choose from.

Strictly, it would be possible to proceed to a decision in such situations by setting out the cash flows for every possible combination of projects which is feasible, given the amount of scarce factors available. The best course of action would be that which did not infringe the constraints and yielded the largest set of net cash flows. However, such a procedure is expensive and impracticable even in relatively simple situations owing to the large number of combinations of projects that would have to be considered. In such circumstances an approximate procedure may yield worthwhile results. It may be possible to reach a decision by seeking to estimate the foregone cash flows for each factor if the input is used on a given project. The firm should accept all those projects which yield a surplus when the factors they use are valued in this way. An example utilizing this approach is given later in this chapter.

However, where several inputs are scarce not only is the number of combinations likely to be too large for all the alternative cash flows to be set out, but it may also be impossible to calculate the opportunity costs of using inputs on any given project. Fortunately, such complex decision problems are often amenable to linear (and other) programming methods, which as part of their solution yield opportunity costs for scarce inputs (Carsberg, 1969, especially chs. 2 and 4).

The opportunity cost of inputs. The market price of factors may not measure correctly their opportunity cost to the firm if these inputs are in short supply to the company. Here, imputed costs measuring the foregone benefits due to project acceptance must be used in decision budgets. For example, consider a project which uses material X. This material was bought a year ago for £400 but it is now obsolete and would therefore fetch only £100 if resold. However, if not used on this project it could be used on another job as substitute for a material which would cost £200. Using the opportunity cost concept, all we need to do to obtain a cost for material X is consider what alternatives are foregone if X is used on the project. Its historical cost is irrelevant for there are no available alternatives which allow it to be recovered. The only alternatives available are: to sell X for £100 or to use it as a substitute, which would save £200. The latter represents the greater sacrifice if the original project is undertaken and should be used in decision budgets to measure the opportunity cost of material X.

Sometimes no physical cash outlay will be associated with using a factor. For example, in our car decision, the £50 from the garage space may not be an explicit rental payment but rather an implicit estimate by the decision maker of the benefits he could obtain from using that space in other ways as, for example, a workshop. That is, the £50 is an 'imputed' measure of the opportunity cost of the space.

Decision budgets – the accountant's approach

It is well known that the so-called principles of financial accounting that are used in preparing company accounts may be inappropriate for decision budgets. This is not to say that they have no utility for other purposes, though much of the literature suggests that they are useful, in the main, only for stewardship purposes (Edey, 1963).

A brief review of the defects of conventional profitability calculations for decision-making purposes should help us understand the necessity of using the approach outlined in the last section when compiling decision budgets. It should also highlight the need for care when basing decisions on data prepared by more traditional accountants. The analysis below may be a little unfair on our 'straw man' accountant, for it assumes he is an accountant wedded to historical cost accounting, whereas there are many accountants who are attempting to apply the opportunity cost concepts discussed above. Moreover, the recent report of the Inflation Accounting Committee (The Sandilands Committee (1975), set up by the British Government), may well lead to the substitution of replacement costs for historical costs in accounting reports. Such a move may make routine accounting reports more useful for decision making. However, replacement costs do not always measure opportunity costs, and care will still be needed when interpreting accounting reports. It is believed that most management accounting systems currently in use have some of the characteristics reviewed below and have not yet been restructured to incorporate all the recommendations of the Sandilands report.

The first problem arises from the accountant's desire to base asset valuations on some objective basis. Accounting valuations therefore normally reflect the historical cost of the assets under consideration. A project analyst who adheres to the usual accounting principles could not incorporate opportunity costs in his reports. He would value current assets already owned by the firm at the prices paid for them in the past, even though their market prices had altered during the period the firm has held them. The cost and market-value rule does allow the accountant to adjust the valuation of items that have fallen substantially in value during this period. However, this approach is unlikely to be undertaken for the evaluation of individual projects.

Recall our example concerning using the scarce material K on any of three jobs (X, Y and Z). The traditional accountant would argue that K should be charged at its historical cost of £1800 to any job using it. This would indicate that none of the jobs were profitable. This is shown in Table 3.

Table 3 Which job to accept

	Job X (£)	Job Y (£)	Job Z (£)
surplus from job (excluding cost of material K)	1500	1200	1700
material K (historical cost)	1800	1800	1800
profit (loss)	(300)	(600)	(100)

The statement using historical cost to value material K overstates the cost of using K on any of the jobs. This is because the historical cost of K does not correspond to an alternative use of the material which is available to the firm. Further, it may well be that the accountant would still charge the historical cost to the job using the unit of K that is in stock, even though the firm could, if it wished, obtain more units of K at the existing market price of £1000. Again (according to the accountant) none of the jobs are worthwhile, whereas in this situation they all should be undertaken, for the opportunity cost of using any unit of K is the price that has to be paid for it now. This is also true of the unit in stock because it could be replaced at a cost of £1000.

Similarly, the traditional accountant may ignore opportunity costs when dealing with fixed assets if he includes depreciation based on historical cost in the cost of using these assets. The true economic depreciation caused by using any asset is measured by the decline in the asset's value resulting from that use. For example, assume that a machine that can be used only for one job could be sold now for £1500 and for £500 after being used for a further year. The opportunity cost of employing the machine is £1000. It is unlikely that depreciation computed in the conventional way will reflect this. The accountant seeks to apportion the historical cost of the machine over its estimated lifetime using simple rules which often do not measure the decline in the asset's economic value over time. Assume that the machine we have just discussed cost £6500 when purchased three years ago and was expected to have a five-year life span. The most simple depreciation method (the straight-line method) obtains an annual depreciation charge by dividing the price of the asset by its expected lifetime in years. In our case this gives an annual charge of £1300 relative to a true opportunity cost of £1000. According to the accountant, our machine will have a book value of £2600 at the beginning of the year we are considering, whereas it is now expected that it can be sold only for £1500. A naïve interpretation of the accountant's book-value figure would suggest we would lose money if we sold the asset for less than its book value or if we used it on a job which did not yield a surplus after meeting all costs other than depreciation of this latter amount. This would be the case even if only one job were available or if £1500 was the best price we could obtain for the machine. Thus, using historical cost depreciation may lead to incorrect decisions.

The investment appraisal models used in this book allow us to abstract from these difficulties for they do not incorporate an annual depreciation charge. As has already been indicated, the procedure used is to compare at the time of decision the value over the project's lifetime of its time-adjusted net cash inflows with the value of the investment outlay necessary for the project. The various methods for valuing a project's cash flows according to their time of receipt are discussed in the next chapter.

There is another difficulty associated with accounting profitability figures. These latter normally are calculated for a given time period, normally a year. This involves ascertaining the costs and revenues for that period, and adjustments have to be made for both costs incurred in one period but paid in other periods and sales made in one period but with the associated payment obtained in another period. The cash-flow models used in this book recognize events only when cash is received. The two methods may therefore give different pictures of the profitability of any given period and recognize the results of a given event at different times. This difference in the recognition of the timing of a given event means that when its value is adjusted for its time of occurrence, it will be given different values depending on which accounting method we are using.

In this book we will base our models on cash flows rather than accounting profits, partly because of the difficulties discussed in this section and partly owing to the lack of any clear agreement as to how accounting profits should be measured. However, far more important is the consideration that it is cash that allows dividend payments and we are assuming, at least for the time being, that it is these payments which determine the market valuation of a company's shares.

There is one further reason why the conventional accounting approach is not helpful for decision making. The accountant tends not to follow the concept of incremental costs. He will normally allocate fixed overheads (that is, those expenses which do not vary directly with output) on some arbitrary basis. He argues that items such as head-office expenses are just as essential to production as, say, material and labour costs, and therefore should be included in the cost of a unit of output. For decision making, at least, this argument has no strength. Fixed costs are, by definition, not incremental and therefore should not be included in decision budgets. At best, allocation of fixed overheads is confusing, and may lead to wrong decisions.

Consider the case of a departmental store deciding on its policy for next year. The accountant has provided the following budget, on the basis of which he urges that department C should be closed.

Table 4 Closure of a department

	Dept A (£)	Dept B (£)	Dept C (£)	Total (£)
sales	1250	2500	500	4250
less cost of sales	750	1800	250	2800
	500	700	250	1450
allocated fixed overheads				
heating (based on sq.ft)	120	150	120	390
rates (based on sq.ft)	100	125	100	325
supervisory salaries (based on number of employees)	50	70	30	150
	270	345	250	865
profit (loss)	230	355	—	585

The accountant has allocated heating, rent and rates and salaries, which are assumed to be fixed irrespective of activity. There is no obvious way to trace these directly to the department concerned; the first, could perhaps, be metered. Let us draw up a revised decision budget showing the effect of closing department C following the principle of what difference does it make?

Table 5 Closure of a department

	Store with department C (£)	Store without department C (£)
sales	4250	3750
less cost of sales	2800	2550
contribution to fixed overheads and profits	1450	1200
less fixed expenses	865	865
profit	585	335

As can be seen, total profit falls to £335 on closure. Closing the department means losing a contribution of £250 to overheads and profit, whereas the accountant's statement implied that we would lose nothing. We should only close the department if an alternative use for the space could be found that would give more than £250 towards overheads and profit. It is in this way that the allocation of fixed costs can be misleading. It treats fixed overheads as if they were variable with activity. In our example, allocation on a different basis might give department C a profit and one of the others a loss.

The above method is called the contribution approach and is used extensively by some accountants. It attempts to distinguish, for decision making, between fixed costs and those which vary directly with output. All decisions are evaluated by whether their expected revenue exceeds the associated change in variable costs. This net revenue is a contribution to fixed overheads and profits. If a project is expected to yield a positive contribution it should be undertaken at least in the short run.

The approach serves to overcome some of the problems of overhead allocation. But a word of warning, the so-called 'direct' costs (those varying with outputs) are not equivalent to the incremental costs referred to earlier. Direct costs are routinely generated by the accounting system, and what is regarded as a direct cost depends on the ease with which it can be traced to units of final output. The accountant, to make his work feasible, makes somewhat arbitrary classifications between fixed and variable costs, which may not be suitable for use in decision budgets. That is, some costs categorized as fixed may be changed by decisions and, indeed, some direct costs may not change at all. The major differences between the economist's and the accountant's approach are summarized in the following example.

Toys Ltd are considering whether to supply a large department store with toys. The contract will last for precisely fifty weeks. Their cost accountant submits the estimate below, which includes allocated overheads.

Table 6 Estimate for a contract

	£
Material	
x in stock at original cost	500
y ordered (contract price)	600
z to be ordered (current price)	1000
Labour	
skilled men – total wages £36 a week	1800
non-skilled men – total wages £20 a week	1000
foreman	1000
Machinery	
old machine – depreciation	500
general overheads	3600
total cost	10000
price offered	6000
loss	4000

The accountant advises that the job should not be taken. He submits the following information.

Materials. Material x is an obsolete material, for which very little could be obtained if it were resold. It can, however, be used as a substitute on another job for material costing £450, but material

x would need some adaptation before being used. This will cost £90.

Material y was ordered a year ago, but delivery was delayed and in consequence it now has a realizable value of £700. This material could only be used by Toys Ltd for this one job.

Direct labour. The requirements could be met by transferring skilled men from other departments. These men would add a total of £36 a week to the wage bill of the department making the toys. Their previous places will be taken by less skilled new employees costing in total £38 per week. They will be paid a basic wage of £33 per week in total and, to produce an equivalent amount, these new men will have to work overtime, at a total cost of £5 a week. The non-skilled labour would be specially employed. All work would be on a fifty-week contract. The foreman is on the staff, and would be retained at his existing wage whether or not the contract was accepted. If not needed on the contract he would be placed in a clerical vacancy, the salary for which is normally £10 per week.

Machinery. The machine to be used is obsolete and could not be used for any other job, but could be sold for £250. If used on the contract it will have no scrap value at the end of the year. The accountant's figures for depreciation represent one instalment of depreciation reckoned on the original cost of £5000. The machine was bought five years ago when it was thought to have a ten year life. The accountant argues that this purchase price must be recovered otherwise the firm will lose money.

General overheads. These are charged at 200 per cent on skilled labour and recover expenses such as rates, head-office expenses and the managing director's salary. None of these costs will be altered by the contract's acceptance. The toys produced will be stored in space in the factory that cannot be used for any other purpose.

Using our concept of incremental relevant opportunity cost, the accountant's table could be restated as shown in Table 7.

Using the incremental opportunity-cost approach our answer is different from that of the accountant. Examining the reasons for the different figures highlights the difference between the two

Table 7 Revised estimate using opportunity-cost concepts

	£	£	£
material x (alternative cost minus conversion costs)		360	
material y (realizable value)		700	
material z (current price)		1000	
			2060
direct labour			
total wages if job taken			
skilled men	1800		
unskilled replacements	1650		
plus overtime	250		
	3700		
non-skilled men at £20 per week	1000		
	4700		
less total wages if job not accepted			
skilled men	1800	2900	
Foreman (alternative cost)		500	
machinery (alternative cost)		250	
general overheads (not relevant to decision)		—	
total incremental cost			5710
price			6000
surplus to cover overheads and profits			290

approaches. Applying the opportunity-cost concept to material x, what alternatives are available? Only to use it as a substitute material, for it cannot be sold. If it were used as a substitute, the firm would save the market price of the other material *less* the necessary adaptation costs of £90, that is £(450 − 90). This is what is sacrificed if x is used on the contract. Its historical cost of £500 is irrelevant for this was paid in the past (it is a sunk cost) and has no bearing on the available alternative uses for x.

Similarly with material y, if it is used on the contract, what other alternatives are rejected? There is but one – to sell it on the open market for it cannot be used within the firm on any other job. Its contracted price has no relevance, for this is a committed cost that will have to be paid whether or not the new contract is accepted. Again, the correct cost for decision budgets is the value in the rejected best alternative use, in this case £700. This assumes a constant realizable value for material y. The cost of using material z is, of course, the money sacrificed to buy it.

Following our incremental-cost concept, the cost of labour is the extra cost incurred due to accepting the job; the cost of the replacement labour and overtime. The foreman's wages do not enter into the calculation as they are unaffected by the decision. There is, however, an opportunity cost of using him on the contract; the wages paid to fill the clerical vacancy.

The accountant has charged depreciation of £500 to the job. The firm's aim should be to maximize profit with the resources it has and thus only future alternatives are relevant. The purchase price of machinery is relevant only when making a decision to buy. Once the machine is bought this cost is no longer a decision variable (a variable within the firm's control), and is superseded by the future alternatives that are available at the time of the new decision. In the very simple case of Toys Ltd, the alternatives available are to sell the machine for £250 or to use it on the contract, thereby sacrificing the former amount.

General overheads are said to be fixed and therefore are irrelevant to the decision. This is not to say that covering overheads is unimportant, for if they are not met in the long run the firm will go bankrupt. However, the best way to avoid this is to accept all projects which cover or more than cover their associated opportunity costs, thereby ensuring the largest possible surplus out of which to pay overheads. Allocating overheads to all jobs within the firm on some arbitrary basis is merely confusing.

The cost of storage space is not included in our calculations for there is free space in the factory. However, if this had any alternative use, an imputed cost should be incorporated in our decision budget.

This example should make clearer our approach. The aim of decision budgets should be to include all the incremental costs, valued in terms of foregone alternatives. This is not to say that the accountant's costs never have utility, but merely to point out that they must be used with care in decision budgets.

Non-quantifiable costs and benefits

So far we have been dealing with costs and benefits which can be expressed in money terms. However, in the firm and, more especially, in the public sector, cost and benefits which are difficult to quantify may be important. These represent a major problem in using cost–benefit analysis to evaluate government investment. For example, the travelling time saved is often advanced as benefit from building a new railway or underground line. How can such savings be measured? A rough approximation may often be useful. Valuing the travelling time saved during business hours at the average hourly wage or salary rate may be such an approximate measure. Market research may yield useful clues as to how to value travel time saved during leisure periods. Similarly, within the firm, the effect of a project on labour morale may be crucial to its acceptance. Presently, morale is essentially non-quantifiable but some approximate indicators do exist; the rate of labour turnover, the number of complaints raised by union representatives and the frequency of disputes. Some of these measures can be quantified in money terms; for example, labour turnover. But in other cases we have to use scales other than cost and also use estimates, such as that although a project will add £50000 to profits, it will increase the number of minor labour disputes experienced in the first year of its life by 20 per cent. The decision-maker has the difficult job of weighing these estimates.

Normally, it is easier to quantify costs than benefits, but this is not always so. A useful device whereby costs but not benefits can be evaluated is to express benefits on some non-monetary scale and to aim to either minimize the cost of a fixed bundle of benefits or to maximize the benefits obtained for a given cost. For example, one of the aims in building a new railway line might be to cut the average journey time from A to B by, say, fifteen minutes. Given this goal, the analysis reduces to finding the design which minimizes the cost of achieving this objective.

Of course, such goals should not be accepted unquestionably; a new bus service might be a cheaper way of cutting journey time. Thus, prior to setting goals to be achieved by a new railway line, a comparison is necessary between this and other alternatives, such as increasing the speed of existing methods of transport by reducing traffic congestion. Here, it may be helpful to use schedules which quantify benefits on non-monetary scales. Figure 2 allows a comparison between the cost of time saved for a given journey by a new fast bus service and a new railway line.

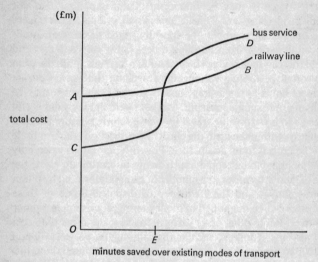

Fig. 2 Cost of time saved under alternative methods of transport

This diagram sets out some very useful information for the decision. First, the fixed cost of a new rail line (OA) is much higher than that of initiating a new bus service (OC) but variable cost of increased time saving by the former method (shown by the slope of the line AB) is much lower. Figure 2 also shows that additional fixed investment is needed for the bus service after E minutes have been saved, whereas no additional fixed investment is needed for the train service, at least within the traffic level being considered. Thus, a new bus service is cheaper if the aim is to achieve savings of less than E minutes, but if greater time savings are desired, a train service may be better. The decision could not be based only on this information, for many other factors, such as the effects of the two systems on congestion, must be considered. This brings us into the realms of cost–benefit analysis, which needs a book to itself. However, probably enough has been said to show that even where benefits or costs are not quantifiable, much can be done to aid the decision-maker. This section is also intended to highlight the need to spell out the impact of non-quantifiables on decisions.

External effects

The indirect effects of decisions must also be considered when estimating costs and benefits. These are discussed extensively in economic theory, where they are called external effects. These are defined as the benefits and costs generated by a decision which accrue to those other than the organizational unit making the decision. The classic example of an external cost is the pollution visited on the neighbours of a factory with a smoky chimney. The decision which gives rise to such pollution will normally be made by considering only the private costs and benefits, accruing to the decision-maker's organization. That social welfare could be improved by installing anti-pollution equipment will not enter into the decision calculus unless the decision-maker can charge for such social benefits. A divergence arises between social and private costs if he is unable to do so. Methods of closing this gap lie in the area of cost–benefit analysis and are beyond the scope of this book.

However, where the activities of one department impinge on other areas of the company, similar externalities may arise in the firm. Often decisions which are best from a departmental point of view may be suboptimal for the total firm. For example, in a firm with widespread plants, if one of these raises wages in response to local market pressures, this may cause a company-wide demand for similar increases. Wage policy is often centralized in an attempt to cope with this sort of difficulty.

All that is being said is that ideally all the effects of a project within the firm should be considered in project appraisal. However, few models are available to help with this problem. This is an area of capital budgeting in which judgement is still crucial both for recognizing and quantifying externalities and in deciding how to deal with them in decision making.

An example may help in understanding the *suboptimization* problem. Consider a divisionalized car firm which produces medium-price cars in one division and low-price cars in another. If pricing decisions are left to the divisions the interdependence of demand between the two types of car may be ignored. A price cut by the division selling cheap cars will affect not only competitors but also the firm's own medium-car division. Thus, the pricing decision must be made from the overall firm point of view. Within any divisionalized firm there may be many other decisions of this type. Transfer-price theory attempts to deal with this difficulty. No simple rules of procedure for avoiding the suboptimization problem in project appraisal can be laid down. But the use of a head-office project-appraisal department to survey all divisional proposals for 'external' effects may help.

4 Methods of Investment Appraisal

In the two preceding chapters, we assumed that the cash flows received from projects at different times had been made comparable. This chapter examines why such adjustment is necessary and how it may be accomplished. The approach will be to first examine, using a simple graphical analysis which should be familiar to economists, the theoretical framework underlying optimal investment decisions. Various methods of investment appraisal which allow for the timing of cash flows will then be examined in the light of the principles derived from this framework to see how far their use ensures optimal investment decisions.

Four assumptions will be made which allow us to abstract temporarily from many complex problems. First, that fractional parts of any project can be undertaken; secondly, that the cash flows expected to accrue from any investment are independent of decisions relating to any other project and, thirdly, that these cash flows are known with certainty; finally, that no firm or individual has sufficient funds to affect the price of funds in the capital market. These last two assumptions amount to saying that the capital market is perfect. This means that everyone can borrow or lend as much as they wish at the going rate of interest and that this rate is the same for everyone. Lenders will not need to make any adjustments to the interest rate to allow for the riskiness of projects when certainty is assumed. Furthermore, with these assumptions, both debt and equity yield an identical return and, therefore, there is no need to distinguish between them. Extending the analysis to cope with the situation when these assumptions are relaxed will be the major task facing us in later chapters.

The theoretical background
Time preference

Investment decisions involve foregoing present consumption in the hope of greater future consumption. To make investment choices the individual must therefore be able to value consumption opportunities occurring at different points in time. He needs to calculate either implicitly or explicitly a set of subjective exchange rates (prices) which express the relative value he places on opportunities to consume at different times. For example, if a man does not mind whether he possesses £100 worth of goods now or £110 worth next year, his subjective rate of exchange (his rate of time preference) for this particular choice is 10 per cent. Only with the aid of such rates can the individual make investment decisions which allow him to obtain his most desired pattern of consumption over time.

In the same way as the individual is assumed to be willing to consume additional icecream only if its cost in terms of other goods sacrificed falls as icecream consumption rises, we can postulate that the individual will, *ceteris paribus*, regard successive, additional opportunities for future consumption as progressively less valuable in terms of current consumption. Thus, if our man were offered a second choice between £100 now and £110 next year he may now choose the immediate goods, and prefer the future option only if it were increased to, say, £115; for the second choice, his marginal rate of time preference has increased to 15 per cent. Thus, it can be assumed that every individual has a schedule of time-preference rates and the specific rate for any choice will depend upon, among other things, the bundles of goods available now and in the future, the amount of each type of good already owned or consumed, his wealth and the expected pattern of his income over time.

Even Robinson Crusoe on his desert island needs to estimate his own rate of time preference. He requires this so that he can choose between using his time either to fish for his supper or to make fishing rods to increase his capacity to fish in the future, thereby obtaining extra future consumption. His problem is to choose, within the opportunities available to him, an optimal time pattern of consumption. The elements of this choice are shown in Figure 3, which uses a graphical analysis first suggested by Hirshleifer (1958).

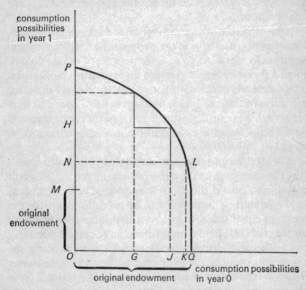

Fig. 3 Robinson Crusoe's investment opportunity curve

It is assumed that Crusoe will remain on the island for only two years and that he is deciding how much of his resources to devote to investment activities. It is assumed that any fishing rods made in the first year can only be used in the second and cannot be taken off the island when he leaves. Thus, no investment activities will be undertaken in the second year. He has an original endowment of resources (time) in each year which, if entirely devoted to consumption activities, will yield a given amount of consumption in that year. And his range of consumption opportunities, given this endowment, are shown by the curve PQ. This represents all the combinations of present and future consumption attainable by him. The horizontal axis OQ represents potential consumption in year 0 and the vertical axis OP shows that for year 1. The consumption he could obtain if he devoted all his labours in year 0 to consumption goods is shown by OQ. By foregoing all consumption in year 0 and using all his resources for investment he can increase his possible consumption in year 1 to a maximum of OP.[1]

Any point along the investment-opportunity curve indicates the total consumption available in the two years with a given amount of investment in year 0. At point L, for example, Crusoe would be foregoing KQ current goods in return for extra consumption next year of MN. His productive opportunities are ranked along the curve in terms of the consumption gained in year 1 over that foregone in year 0. At point L he obtains MN next year by investing KQ now. The incremental return he obtains from investing KQ is measured by $(MN/KQ) - 1$.[2]

The curve is drawn to represent diminishing returns to investment; as Crusoe moves up the curve he must forego more current consumption to obtain the same increment of consumption in year 1. Thus, starting from point L, he needs to invest current consumption equal to JK to obtain a first increment of future consumption of NH. But he must forego more current goods GJ to obtain a second identical increment. If the steps along the curve represent projects, the return per project falls as he moves up the curve. However, as we have assumed that fractional parts of projects may be undertaken, the slope of PQ at any point represents a marginal rate of return.

How does Mr Crusoe decide between current consumption and investment activities? He needs to rank the bundles of goods represented by PQ, and to do this he must subjectively construct

1. The kink in the PQ curve opposite M indicates that the endowment in the second year cannot be used to increase consumption in the first year; in more technical terms, that productive opportunities are not perfectly reversible. In the remainder of the book we will assume idealistically perfect reversibility of productive opportunities; that is, any investment opportunity offers the possibility of transforming goods in year 0 into year 1 goods and vice versa.

2. He invests KQ and receives a net return of $MN - KQ$ and his incremental return is given by

$$\frac{MN - KQ}{KQ} = \frac{MN}{KQ} - \frac{KQ}{KQ} = \frac{MN}{KQ} - 1$$

curves which link differing bundles of current and future goods, each of which give him equal satisfaction. These curves are normally called indifference curves in economic theory. In Figure 4 Crusoe is indifferent between all those bundles of goods lying on curve I. He has no preference between receiving the combination OC in year 1 and OD now (shown by point A) or that consisting of OE next year and OF now (point B). If he was originally at point B he would invest DF only if promised, at least, CE in the future. Thus the slope of the curve reflects his subjective time preference.

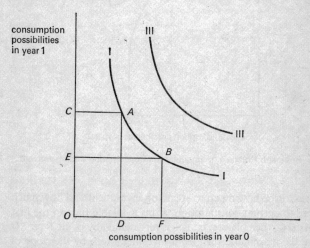

Fig. 4 Robinson Crusoe's consumption indifference curves

There is an infinite number of indifference curves of which curves I and III are examples. Each shows the various combinations of present and future consumption that yield a given level of utility. Movements to the right in the diagram represent increased utility. Crusoe's aim is to get on the most valuable indifference curve, the one furthest to the right, and thus obtain that pattern of consumption over time which he considers optimal.

By combining Figures 3 and 4, as in Figure 5, it is easy to

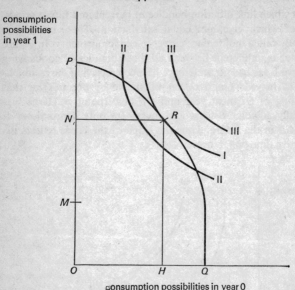

consumption
possibilities
in year 1

Fig. 5 Robinson Crusoe's optimal plan for consumption and investment activities

advise Crusoe how much to spend on investment and how much to give to current consumption. If his available time in the first year is OQ, then his best choice is represented by point R on PQ where the marginal return from investing, given by the slope of PQ, is equal to his rate of time preference. At this point he devotes time equivalent to OH this year to current consumption and invests HQ for a return of MN in year 1 (remember OM represents his original year 1 endowment).

No other allocation of time would give him a better combination of current and future consumption. Moving up PQ beyond R would mean that he was undertaking projects yielding future consumption less valuable than the current goods sacrificed to obtain it (the slope of PQ is less than $[<]$ the slopes of the indifference curves cutting PQ above R). If he stopped investing prior to reaching R he would be foregoing investment opportunities which more than compensated for sacrificed current consumption (slopes of indifference curves below R < slope of PQ).

This simplified example brings out some of the essential elements in allowing for time in investment decisions. In this elementary situation, the optimal pattern of consumption over time can be achieved by continuing to select investments until the marginal return from investment is equal to the individual's marginal rate of time preference. Following this decision rule guarantees that the decision-maker's welfare is maximized, provided that the latter's objective in making investment decisions can be expressed in terms of a desired consumption pattern over time.

The introduction of a capital market

The existence of capital markets introduces a second reason, intimately connected to the first, for placing a different value on money received at different points in time: a pound held now can be invested and will accumulate with interest to more than a pound in the future. The rate of interest represents a second possible opportunity cost of consumption. Now when the individual invests in productive opportunities, he foregoes not only consumption but also either sacrifices the interest he could have obtained by lending on the market or has to pay this rate on borrowed money.

A capital market can easily be introduced into our diagram, providing that we assume that everybody can lend and borrow at the same rate. The axes in Figure 6 now represent amounts of actual or potential income in years 0 and 1. The individual may be in a position where initially all his income is expected in either period one or two, as shown by OQ and OP respectively, or where some income is expected in both periods (point T).

The existence of a capital market introduces opportunities to borrow and lend additional to the physical investment opportunities (e.g. seed planting) depicted by PQ.[3] Borrowing and

3. The absence of a kink in PQ reflects our assumption of perfect reversibility. Productive opportunities are assumed to transform consumption in year 0 into year 1 consumption and vice versa.

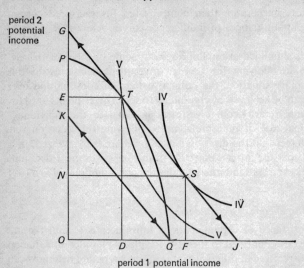

period 2
potential
income

period 1 potential income

Fig. 6 Optimal plan where there are lending and borrowing opportunities

lending opportunities can be represented in the diagram by lines like KQ and GJ which show what the individual could obtain by using the market (they are therefore called market lines). With our assumption of a perfect capital market, such lines serve to show the effect of either borrowing or lending; borrowing being represented by moving down the lines and lending by moving up them. For example, if an individual who starts with OQ this year lends he can get OK next year, which equals OQ plus interest ($OK = OQ + OQr$, where r is the interest rate expressed as a decimal). Thus the slope of KQ (OK/OQ) reflects the rate of interest ($OK/OQ = 1 + r$).[4] Any amount on the horizontal axis can be converted to its future equivalent by drawing a line with this slope and noting where it hits the other axis – lending OJ

4. $OK = OQ + OQr = OQ(1 + r)$,

hence $OK/OQ = 1 + r$

or $r = (OK/OQ) - 1$.

should return OG in the next period. Future money can be converted into current amounts in the same way; OG received next year is equivalent to OJ obtained immediately

$$(OG/(1 + r) = OJ).$$

Figure 6 is drawn so that a market-opportunity line represented by GJ is tangential to the investment opportunity curve PQ at point T. Here, the rate of return on the marginal investment (the slope of PQ) is equal to the market rate of interest (the slope of a market-opportunity line). The decision-maker starting with an initial endowment for the two years of OQ, invests DQ for a return of OE in the next period. Under our present assumptions, point T represents the best selection of physical investments. Investing beyond this point would mean accepting investments yielding lower returns than obtainable by lending on the market (the slope of $PQ <$ the slope of GJ). Ceasing investment prior to selecting all those projects represented by point T would mean foregoing returns greater than the rate of interest. Thus, optimal selection of physical investments is made if we accept all projects which yield a return equal to, or greater than, the rate of interest. This decision rule makes sense if the individual has to borrow to finance his investments. If he uses his own funds, the opportunity cost of investing is the rate of interest he could have obtained on his funds by lending.

However, the above decision rule merely tells us when to stop undertaking additional physical investment. It says nothing about how such investments should be financed. By borrowing on the basis of the future cash flows expected from the investments implied by point T, the individual can move down JG until he reaches a point, like S in the figure, which is on a higher indifference curve than is T. By using the market to adjust the pattern of cash flows he receives from productive investment, he receives cash flows of OF in year 0 and ON in year 1, which better reflect his time preferences. Thus, the overall investment optimum is reached in two stages.

First, all investments offering a rate of return at least equal to the rate of interest are accepted (point T in the figure), and then by borrowing or lending in the market, the cash flows thus obtained are adjusted to the most desired consumption pattern, as reflected by the indifference curves (point S, for example). Stage one covers the selection of investments, and stage two the financing of such opportunities to reach an optimal consumption position. Our individual, who has a high preference for current income, converts most of the future cash flows at T into current income totalling OF. The two-stage process guarantees that when the best selection of investments is made and the market adjustment process carried out, the investor's marginal-rate time preference will equal both the rate of interest and the marginal rate of return on investment.

The investor is only in equilibrium if these rates are the same and he will seek to equate all three rates (Porterfield 1965, Ch. 2). For example, consider an investor in the following position:

His marginal investment opportunity is to invest £100 now for a return of £115 next year – a return of 15 per cent;
On the consumption side, he is indifferent between consuming £100 now or £120 in year 2 – his marginal rate of time preference is 20 per cent;
The cost of borrowing in the market is 6 per cent.

The individual faced with these opportunities will borrow so that he can step up present consumption, thereby lowering his marginal rate of time preference, and will also borrow for investment reducing the return offered from further investment. These activities will stop only when all three rates are equal.

Capital-budgeting techniques will lead to the maximization of the shareholders' welfare, assuming that they wish to achieve their optimal consumption pattern over time, only if they aid the achievement of the equilibrium referred to above. Such techniques will do this only if they encompass both the optimal selection of physical investment and its optimal financing. That is, they must involve both a comparison between opportunities within the firm and those available in the market, and take into account the shareholders' consumption wishes. The remainder of this chapter examines how well these objectives are achieved by some of the more popular discounting techniques. Prior to this, it is necessary to explain the elementary mathematics of compound interest. A good alternative presentation of the necessary material is given in Merrett and Sykes (1963), chapter 1.

Discounting methods
The mechanics

In theory these are very simple, entailing merely an elementary knowledge of compound interest. In practice, the calculations may be quite complex, where for example, cash flows are not received at the end of each year as normally assumed by compound-interest tables. But the real difficulties lie in appreciating how discounting fits into the above conceptual framework. For the most comprehensive treatment of this see the earlier parts of Hirshleifer (1958).

Compound-interest techniques are probably most easily understood by first considering how money invested today will, because of interest, accumulate to a larger sum in the future. Suppose we have £100 today and can lend it and be certain of repayment with 10 per cent interest in one year. £100 lent at the beginning of a year will accumulate to £110 at the end: £110 is the terminal value of £100 invested at 10 per cent for a year. This can be written using symbols as

$$S = 100(1 + r) = 100(1 + 0 \cdot 10) = £110,$$

where S is the terminal value and r the interest rate, expressed as a decimal. If the loan is extended on the same terms, each extra year will result in another increment of $1 + r$. For example, £100 accumulates to £121 after two years. The general formula for the terminal value of £1 invested now for n years is

$$S = 1(1 + r)^n.$$

The terminal value of £1 invested for n years at a given rate of interest can be found in compound interest tables in the column headed $(1 + r)^n$.

The present value of a single sum

As £100 accumulates to £110 in one year if the interest rate is 10 per cent, it seems logical that the value placed on £110 to be received in one year under the same conditions should be

£100, that is, £100 = £110 ÷ (1·10). This recognizes that a £100 held now could be invested at the going rate of interest and be worth £110 at one year's end. Similarly, £121 in two years' time is worth £100 now; that is V = £100 = £$\frac{121}{(1\cdot10)^2}$, where V stands for the present value of £121 accruing in two years' time. Thus the formula for the terminal value of £1 invested for n years with interest rate r can be rearranged to tell us the present value of S received in n years' time, that is,

$$V = \frac{S}{(1+r)^n}.$$

Any present value can, by definition, be turned into a terminal value by multiplying it by $(1+r)^n$; for example, £100$(1+r)^2$ = £121. The present value of £1 to be received n years in the future with a given interest rate is shown in compound-interest tables in the column headed v^n.

All we need to do to find the present value of a set of cash flows received in different years, is to reduce the cash flow received in each year to its present value and add. For example, suppose unequal cash flows S_1, S_2 and S_3 are to be received at the end of 1, 2 and 3 years respectively, and the interest rate is r. The total present value of these cash flows is

$$V = \frac{S_1}{(1+r)} + \frac{S_2}{(1+r)^2} + \frac{S_3}{(1+r)^3} = \sum_{i=1}^{i=3} \frac{S_i}{(1+r)^i},$$

where in the right hand expression $\sum$ is a sign indicating the summing of all the Ss; in our case from S_1 to S_3. The figures below the Σ sign indicate that we must start adding at S_1, and those above that we must stop at S_3. We shall see later that this is a useful shorthand expression.

The present value of an annuity

The above cash flows were of unequal value and their present values had to be looked up individually. However, sometimes cash flows are constant for every year; that is, $S_1 = S_2 = S_n$.

Such a series of constant cash flows is called an annuity. The present value of an annuity is given by the formula

$$V = \frac{S\{1 - (1 + r)^{-n}\}}{r}.^5$$

The present value of £1 per year received for n years with a given interest rate is shown in compound-interest tables by the $a_n r$ column. The terminal value of an annuity is given by the $S_n r$ column in the tables and is the result of multiplying our expression for the present value of an annuity by $(1 + r)^n$. Two other useful columns in the tables are that headed a_n^{-1} which gives the amount which must be received each year, if an annuity is to have a present value of £1 at the going interest rate, and that headed S_n^{-1}. This latter gives the constant amount that must be paid into a sinking fund each year if the fund is to have a terminal value of £1. This column might be used if we wished to invest sufficient money per year over an asset's life to ensure that funds are available

5. The seemingly complex formula given above is easily derived. Consider the series

$$V = \frac{S_1}{(1 + r)} + \frac{S_2}{(1 + r)^2} + \cdots + \frac{S_n}{(1 + r)^n}, \qquad \qquad 1$$

where $S_1 = S_2 = \cdots = S_n$. Multiplying both sides by $1/(1 + r)$ gives

$$\frac{V}{(1 + r)} = \frac{S}{(1 + r)^2} + \frac{S}{(1 + r)^3} + \cdots + \frac{S}{(1 + r)^{n+1}}. \qquad \qquad 2$$

Subtract 2 from 1

$$V - \frac{V}{(1 + r)} = \frac{S}{(1 + r)} - \frac{S}{(1 + r)^{n+1}}.$$

After the subtraction only the initial term of the first series and the last term of the second series remain. Multiplying this expression by $1 + r$ gives

$$V(1 + r) - V = S - \frac{S}{(1 + r)^n}$$

and by simplifying, we obtain

$$V + Vr - V = S\left\{1 - \frac{1}{(1 + r)^n}\right\}.$$

This can be written as

$$Vr = S\{1 - (1 + r)^{-n}\} \quad \text{since} \quad \frac{1}{(1 + r)^n} = (1 + r)^{-n}.$$

Our original expression then follows by dividing throughout by r.

to replace the asset when it has to be scrapped. If an annuity goes on for ever, it is called a perpetuity and the formula for its present value simplifies to S/r, for the $(1 + r)^{-n}$ factor in our earlier formula becomes insignificant as the life of an annuity becomes very long.

Net present value

All methods of investment appraisal which allow for the time value of money are based on compound-interest principles. The net present value method involves calculating the present value of a project's cash flows, both positive (receipts) and negative (outlays). A project has a positive net present value if the present value of its cash inflows exceeds that of its outflows. This can be written in a general form

$$NPV = \sum_{i=1}^{t=\infty} \frac{S_t}{(1 + r)^t} - I_0,$$

where S_t represents net cash inflows in each year from 1 to ∞ and I_0 the investment outlay assumed to be made at the project's start. It is assumed that the project will have an infinite life; thus the cash flows are summed from $i = 1$ to $i = \infty$.

As will be explained below, with the assumptions made earlier, all projects having a non-negative net present value should be accepted. As an example, assume that a firm is offered the chance to invest £1000 for returns of £500, £1000 and £200 at the end of the 1st, 2nd and 3rd year respectively of the project's three-year life. Assume also that the firm can lend or borrow at 5 per cent. The present value of the project's cash inflows is calculated as

$$\text{present value} = \frac{£500}{(1 \cdot 05)} + \frac{£1000}{(1 \cdot 05)^2} + \frac{£200}{(1 \cdot 05)^3}.$$

These values can be found from compound-interest tables using the v^n column, and are calculated thus:

present value of cash inflows:

$$£500 \times V^1 0 \cdot 05 + £1000 \times V^2 0 \cdot 05 + £200 \times V^3 0 \cdot 05$$
$$= (500 \times 0 \cdot 9523) + (1000 \times 0 \cdot 9070) + (200 \times 0 \cdot 8638)$$
$$= 476 + 907 + 173 = £1556.$$

The project's inflows have a present value of £1556 and deducting the present value of investment (£1000) necessary to undertake the project gives the project a net present value of £556. The project should be accepted according to the net present value decision rule.

The meaning of net present value

With our assumptions a project's positive net present value measures the increase in the value of a firm's equity which would occur once the market knew of the project's acceptance. It represents the increase in potential present consumption that the project makes available to equity holders, after any funds used are repaid with interest. For example, assume that the firm finances the above investment by borrowing £1000 on the market at 5 per cent; the loan repayment and interest to be met out of the project's proceeds as they occur. The pattern of cash outlays and receipts this implies is shown in Table 8.

The equity-holders thus receive £422 at the end of year 2 and £200 at the end of year 3. These payments have a present value of £556 (as the reader should check). That the project's net present value measures the increase in current consumption made possible by its acceptance is seen more clearly if we imagine the firm borrowing £1556 and immediately paying out £556 to equity-holders. This could be done and the loan plus interest still be repaid by the end of the period as shown in Table 9.

Similar reasoning shows that the firm should accept the proposal if it intends to use its own funds to finance the project. If it rejected the project it could either pay out the £1000 as a dividend on which the shareholders could earn no more than 5 per cent, or it could itself invest for no greater a return. This is so because in a perfect market there is always money available to undertake any opportunity yielding more than the interest rate and thus all such opportunities will be taken up. This means that there is no available opportunity to invest given funds in projects offering yields greater than the interest rate.

Moreover, consumption opportunities cannot offer any greater return, for otherwise investors would not be willing to maintain the existing yield rate on the firm's shares. Thus a project with a

Table 8 Pattern of cash flows assuming loan repaid out of project's proceeds

Year	Loan outstanding at beginning (£) 1	Interest accrued at 5% (£) 2	Total amount owed before repayment (£) 3 (=1+2)	Proceeds from project (£) 4	Loan outstanding at year end (£) 5 (=3−4)	Proceeds to shareholders (£) 6 (=4−3)
1	1000	50	1050	500	550	–
2	550	28	578	1000	–	422
3	–	–	–	200	–	200

Table 9 Pattern of cash flows assuming net present value paid out immediately

Year	Loan at beginning (£)	Interest (£)	Total amount owed before repayment (£)	Proceeds from project (£)	Payment to shareholders (£)	Payment to creditor (£)	Loan at year end (£)
1	1556	78	1634	500	556	500	1134
2	1134	56	1190	1000	–	1000	190
3	190	10	200	200	–	200	–

positive net present value covers the opportunity cost of both internal and external funds. Its acceptance, therefore, makes the shareholders better off. Looking at it another way, the net present value of a project is the price at which the firm (and its shareholders) could sell the opportunity to undertake the project to someone else and be no worse off.

It should be noted that a specific valuation model is implied in our argument. In earlier chapters we assumed that shareholders valued the company on the basis of its future dividend flows. It is obvious that these flows should be discounted to allow for time. Thus in our model, the value of the firm on the market (V_0) becomes the sum of the firm's expected dividend flows discounted to the present at the going interest rate. By accepting all projects which have a positive net present value, we ensure that V_0 is maximized, for, with our assumptions, the value of the firm is merely the total present value of the cash dividends from all its projects. We can write this as

$$V_0 = \sum_{i=1}^{i=n} \frac{D_{1i}}{(1+r)^i} + \sum_{i=1}^{i=n} \frac{D_{2i}}{(1+r)^i} + \cdots + \sum_{i=1}^{i=n} \frac{D_{mi}}{(1+r)^i},$$

where the first term on the right is the total present value of the dividends expected from project 1 (denoted by the subscript 1) and the last is present value of dividends expected from the mth project. The total of these give the value of the firm. Accepting any project with a positive net present value merely adds another $\sum D_i/(1+r)^i$ element to the right-hand side of the valuation equation and thereby increases the value of the firm. Thus abstracting from uncertainty, the value of the firm depends on (is a function of) the size of its dividend stream and the interest rate used in discounting. How r is found will be explained in chapter 6.

The net present-value concept can easily be introduced into our earlier theoretical framework and into our earlier figures. In Figure 7 the market lines, such as GJ, are lines of constant present value ($J = G/(1+r)$). The net present value of any selection of investments shown in Figure 7 can be shown using simple geometry.

Assume that the firm is originally at point OQ with all its

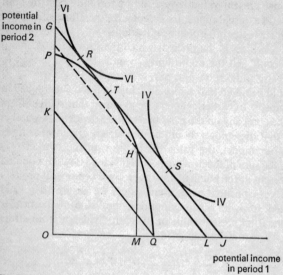

Fig. 7 Graphical presentation of NPV rule

income expected in the first year. It could invest these funds in the productive opportunities shown by PQ. The net present value of points on this curve can be calculated by drawing through any point (say H) both the market line HL cutting it and the vertical line HM connecting it with the horizontal axis. That segment of the horizontal axis lying between M and the intercept L of the market line HL with the horizontal axis measures the gross present value from accepting the investments shown by point H. The net present value of this selection, QL, is obtained by deducting from the segment ML, which represents the gross present value of the project, the present value of the required investment outlay, MQ.

The length of the net present-value segment QL can be extended by continuing up the productive opportunity curve from H to point T. This movement would lengthen the net present-value segment of the horizontal axis by LJ. Similar constructions show that further movements up PQ would reduce the size of the net present-value segment and would mean accepting projects with negative net present values. Thus accepting all projects with a net present value equal to or greater than zero would lead us to that selection of productive investments which was earlier shown to be optimal, point T.

But the net present-value rule says nothing about the second stage of optimal investment decisions, that is, using the market to convert the cash flows generated by the optimal selection of investments to the investor's desired pattern. The net present-value rule does not help the firm in seeking to give shareholders their desired pattern of cash flows over time (Hirshleifer, 1958). But this need not concern the firm, providing that everybody can borrow and lend at the going rate of interest (e.g. there is a perfect capital market). The firm by following the net present-value rule makes the 'best' investment choice and if, as we will assume, it pays out the cash flows implied by this choice, each shareholder can borrow or lend, using these dividends, to obtain his desired pattern of cash flows. He can, by following the market lines, obtain his optimum pattern of income over time. If the individual's indifference curves are represented by curves like VI in Figure 7, he will lend and move up GJ from point T to R. If, on the other hand, the investor's preferences are represented by curves like IV, he will borrow on the market until he reaches point S. Thus the firm does not need to be concerned about the subjective time preference of its equity-holders, provided that everyone can borrow and lend at the same rate. The complications which arise with imperfect markets will be discussed later.

A numerical example of how the individual can adjust the cash flows he receives from a firm may help to understand this point. Assume that the firm in our earlier numerical example pays off the loan in the first two years, distributing nothing to equity-holders in the first year of the project's life and £422 in the second year and £200 in the third year. If the equity-holders would rather have one immediate payment of £556, they can borrow this sum at 5 per cent, and use the later cash flows from the firm to repay the loan. The mechanics of this transaction are shown in Table 10.

You should check that the equity-holders can use the market to

Table 10 Conversion of one set of cash flows
into another more desired set

Year	Loan at beginning (£)	Interest (£)	Payments to equity-holders from firm (£)	Payments by equity-holders to creditors (£)	Loan at year end (£)
1	556·0	27·8	–	–	583·8
2	583·8	29·2	422	422	191·0
3	191·0	9·0	200	200	–

obtain any other pattern of cash flows having a present value of
£556 by trying one or two examples.

Some practical difficulties with the NPV rule

If we temporarily relax our assumptions, it is clear that the simple
presentation above abstracted from three very important issues.
In the real world the capital market is imperfect; often individuals
do not have equal access to the market; some may be unable to
borrow at all. The firm's equity-holders may therefore not be
able to adjust their dividends to the pattern they most desire.
Further, individual equity-holders probably face different interest
rates, and these latter often differ for borrowing and lending.
Thus the firm cannot assume that all payout patterns are equally
preferable. Moreover, it is unlikely that the firm can produce a
pattern of cash flows that will please everyone. As will be explained
in a later chapter on dividend policy, the current theory is of
little help to the firm. Probably all the firm can do is to follow
the net present-value rule and have a consistent payout policy,
thereby attracting like-minded shareholders. The point to remember is that the net present-value method pays no attention to
the problem of aiding shareholders in obtaining via the capital
market, their optimal consumption pattern over time, and thus
its use does not guarantee that the equity-holder's welfare is
maximized. Management have to consider separately shareholders' preferences for income over time. Some suggestions as to
how this might be done are presented in chapter 9.

The second real-world difficulty is that of imperfect knowledge
and uncertainty. For example, assume that our firm intended to
pay out £422 and £200 respectively in the second and third years
of the project. Anyone seeking to borrow on these amounts must

know about these plans and must persuade creditors that they will actually come to fruition (at least, with a certain probability). This may give rise to another difference between shareholders, other than the one referred to above, as different shareholders and the people who supply them with funds may have very different views of a specific company's projects. Conditions of certainty and perfect knowledge do not apply in practice, and later chapters will deal with uncertainty in detail. The point to remember, however, is that the net present value method as so far presented, only produces optimal solutions under conditions of certainty and perfect knowledge.

In defence of our naïve model, it may be claimed that it is sufficiently near the truth to give useful predictions about the effects of a project on the market value of the firm. Moreover, our model, especially when adjusted (as far as we are able) for uncertainty, does embody what are normally accepted in the literature as the aims of equity-holders. The firm, by using the net present-value rule, is doing the best it can for shareholders who have these aims and are not subject to substantial capital rationing, even though because of uncertainty and imperfect information they may not know this. The latter two factors may mean that the capital market will use approximate-valuation models. For example, share values could be based on some weighted average of past dividends. But in the long run, a firm using the net present value rule for selecting investments will produce a better performance judged by such a weighted average than it would using most other project-appraisal techniques. However, uncertainty may mean that the market uses a set of valuation principles which are in direct conflict with those we are suggesting. The use of the net present-value method will not then be optimal. Several such models have been suggested, but there is no empirical evidence that stock-market valuations depart so far from the basis used in this book. Whatever their limitations, the simple models we have used so far do, at least, isolate some crucial variables that must be considered in project appraisal.

The firm itself can partially plug the information gap by issuing cash-flow budgets to shareholders, together with some indication of the degree of certainty attached to these forecasts.

But until most companies do this, the best the firm can do is probably to follow a consistent policy of maximizing share values via net present-value models (adjusted for uncertainty) and hope this pleases the majority of its equity-holders, who are, after all, free to sell their stock if it does not.

A third real-world difficulty exists. Shareholders may have very different marginal tax rates and this will affect the amount each individual has to trade in the market. Again, the firm can only adopt a consistent policy favoured by a specific type of equity-holders.

In sum, the valuation model based on net present value assumes that all net cash flows from a project are paid out as dividends and such cash flows are known with certainty and can be traded in a good capital market. These assumptions also apply, in general, to the naïve version of the internal rate of return method of appraisal to be discussed later. By using these models we should get an idea of the general principles involved, although there are difficulties in real-life application. In later chapters, some indication will be given of how far we can cope with the problems that arise once our assumptions are relaxed. The next few sections deal with other methods of taking time into account in project appraisal.

Net terminal value

It has been shown that a present-value figure can be turned into a terminal value by merely multiplying it by $(1 + r)^n$ (see p. 64). Thus, accepting all projects which have a positive net present value is equivalent to accepting all those with a positive net terminal value. Both decision rules lead to the same result. The net terminal-value method may be easier to use where the rate of interest is expected to vary within any year of a project's life (as explained in Porterfield, 1965, ch. 3).

Internal rate of return

To find the net present value of a project we discounted the project's cash flows by a given interest rate. Alternatively, we could seek to find the rate of interest which equates the discounted value of a project's cash flows to the discounted value of its necessary investment outlay. That is, we could find r in the equation

$$\sum_{n=0}^{n=\infty} \frac{I_n}{(1+r)^n} = \sum_{n=0}^{n=\infty} \frac{D_n}{(1+r)^n}.$$

The left-hand side of this equation represents the discounted value of the investment outlays for the project made at any time from the beginning of year 1 until infinity. Similarly, the right-hand side stands for the discounted value of the project's net inflows over the same period. The rate of interest which equates the two sides of the expression is represented by r and is called the project's internal rate of return. This rate is the maximum rate of interest which the firm could afford to pay if the project were to be financed by borrowed funds and the project's cash flows as they appeared were used to repay the loan and interest. If this rate were paid, the shareholders would be made neither better nor worse off by the project's acceptance. The firm would just break even on any project financed in this manner. Thus the internal rate of return for any project represents the maximum rate of interest that can be paid to finance a project without causing harm to the shareholders. All this is only true with our assumptions of a perfect capital market and certainty which allow us to treat debt and equity as equivalent and to abstract from the dividend-policy question.

Shareholders would neither gain nor lose if the project used in previous examples which has an internal rate of return of approximately 35 per cent were financed by a loan bearing interest at this rate. This is shown in Table 11.

The firm could borrow the initial £1000 and pay interest of

Table 11 Pattern of cash flows when financed by loan at 35 per cent rate of interest

Year	Loan at beginning (£)	Interest at internal rate of return of 35% (£)	Total owed before payment (£)	Proceeds paid to creditors (£)	Loan at year end (£)
1	1000	350	1350	500	850
2	850	298	1148	1000	148
3	148	52	200	200	–

35 per cent on the outstanding loan and just break even. The decision rule for project acceptance follows logically from this: undertake all projects with an internal rate of return greater than or equal to the cost of borrowed money. Similarly, the firm, if it were using its own funds to finance the project, should proceed if and only if the internal rate of return from the project were at least equal to the return it could get from lending on the market (assuming no capital rationing). Thus a knowledge of the firm's cost of capital (the firm's lending and borrowing rate) is just as essential to the internal rate of return method as it was to the net present-value method. The cost of funds merely enters the process at a different stage.

To calculate an internal rate of return, it is necessary to solve what may be quite a complex mathematical expression (a polynomial in n), but computer programmes are available for this task. Sometimes, however, the solution can be obtained by trial and error. As an instance of the approach, let us determine internal rate of return of the project in our numerical example. This can be done by plugging various rates of interest into the present-value formula until the equation for the internal rate of return is satisfied. We have to find a discount rate which exactly equates the present value of the cash flows from the project to the present value of its initial outlay. This can be determined using the v^n column of the compound-interest tables. Using a 10 per cent rate gives the cash flows a value of £431 in excess of the initial investment. The project's internal rate of return is thus larger than 10 per cent. A higher rate must be tried, say 40 per cent. This gives a negative value of £60 to the cash flows, net of the original investment. This trial and error procedure is continued until the rate of return which just equates the two is found. In the example, this rate is approximately 35 per cent (as you should check).

It will now be shown that the internal rate of return method leads to that selection of investments which was earlier demonstrated to be optimal. In Figure 8 the market rate of interest (the firm's cost of capital) is represented by the slope of the lending and borrowing line, $G/J = -(1 + r)$. For the simple two-period case, the internal rate of return is that rate which, when used as a discount rate, equates the value of sacrifices in the first year to the present value of gains in the second year. It has already been shown that the slope of the investment-opportunity curve at any point measures the incremental return from the marginal project at that point. For example, the marginal return at point T is

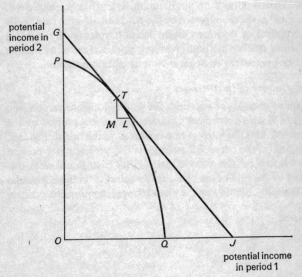

Fig. 8 The internal rate of return decision rule

approximated by $(MT/LM) - 1$. The internal rate of return of a project involving a sacrifice of LM in return for MT is given by r in the expression $LM = MT/(1 + r)$. Rearranging, it can be seen that this is identical to $r = (MT/LM) - 1$. Thus the internal rate of return in the two-period case is measured by the slope of the investment-opportunity curve.[6]

6. But, as will be explained in the next chapter, this equivalence between the internal rate of return and the marginal rate of return of a project does not hold for multiperiod projects. Many of the theoretical weaknesses of the internal rate of return method introduced in the next chapter stem from this (Hirshleifer, 1958).

The internal rate of return decision rule says that you should select investments in order according to their internal rates of return until the internal rate of return of the marginal project equals the firm's cost of capital. The firm is advised to move up the investment-opportunity curve PQ until its slope (the internal rate of return) is equal to that of the market line and thus the firm will reach point T on our diagram. The projects selected will be the same as those suggested by the net present-value rule. Thus for accept/reject decisions both decision rules give the same results. But neither method gives any guidance as to the market operations necessary to achieve a consumption optimum.

The equivalence of the two rules

The equivalence of the two rules for yes/no decisions can be seen in Figure 9, where a project's net present value is plotted on the vertical axis and the interest rate is shown on the horizontal axis. Any point on the curve RX represents the project's net present value (shown on the vertical axis) if its cash flows were discounted by the rate of interest directly below it on the horizontal axis. Thus, discounting by the rate OB gives the project a positive

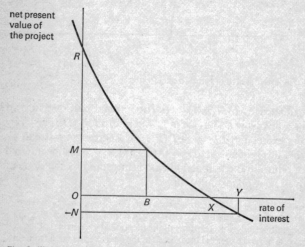

Fig. 9 Illustrating the equivalence of IRR and NPV rules

present value of *OM*. Similarly, the project has a negative present value of *ON* if the interest rate *OY* is used.

The net present-value curve will slope downward for a normal project; one whose pattern of cash inflows and outflows takes the form of an outlay, or series of outlays, followed only by inflows. The degree of curvature will depend on the pattern of the project's cash flows over time.

The net present-value rule says to accept the investment if it has a positive net present value, in our case, if the interest rate lies between *O* and *X* (e.g. between, say, zero and 8 per cent). The project has a negative present value at interest rates greater than *X* and should be rejected. The internal rate of return of the project is that discount factor which reduces its net present value to zero. This is represented in the diagram by the point *X* where the *RX* curve cuts the horizontal axis. The present value of the project's inflows equals that of its investment outflows at this rate of interest and the project has a zero net present value. Thus the internal rate of return rule also leads to accepting the project if the discount factor is less than or equal to *X* (the internal rate of return).

However, as will be shown in the next chapter, in more complex situations there are reasons for preferring the net present-value method. One argument for using the internal rate of return method can, however, be disposed of now. It has been suggested that as this method produces a rate of return, a concept with which businessmen are familiar, it will be more easily accepted than the net present-value method. But the rate of return understood and used by businessmen may be the accounting rate of return (book profits over book investment) and although the internal rate of return does belong to the same family, it is a second cousin at least twice removed (Solomon and Laya, 1967). There is some danger that businessmen may treat the internal rate of return as identical to an ordinary accounting rate of return without being aware of its rather distinctive character.

Other discounting methods

The procedures suggested above are by no means the only possible discounting methods. The annuity method can be used where the annual net cash flows from a project can be treated as being constant over time and involves computing the annuity which, if received over the project's life, would have a present value equivalent to the project's investment outlay. Any opportunity having annual net cash flows greater than this annuity should be accepted. For a full discussion of this method see Merrett and Sykes (1963, pp. 39–42).

Another method involves dividing a project's discounted net cash inflows by the present value of its investment outlay, thus obtaining a discounted benefit–cost ratio. The acceptance rule using this method is to undertake all projects having a ratio equal to, or greater than, unity. If the ratio is less than this, the present value of the outlay for the project exceeds the value of its net cash inflows (it has a negative net present value) and therefore the project should not be undertaken. This is more fully explained in Quirin (1967, ch. 3). The above two methods when used correctly, will normally give the same answer as the net present-value method, but see page 107. There are some advantages in using benefit–cost ratios when ranking decisions are involved. The reason for this will be explained in later chapters.

Discounting and risk

One final argument has been put forward for discounting – to allow for risk. It is suggested that some percentage should be added to the discount rate to cover risk. If the firm's cost of capital is 5 per cent, then, say, 10 per cent should be added to this for a very risky project and perhaps 3 per cent for a less risky one; giving total discount factors of 15 per cent and 8 per cent respectively. Many risk patterns are possible and a treatment which takes these specifically into account might be preferable. Such approaches will be outlined in chapters 12 and 13.

Inflation and capital budgeting

Another use of inflated discount rates arises with one suggested method for dealing with expected general price-level changes. This requires that the cash flows of each year are expressed in the money values reigning in that year and discounted by an appropriately adjusted discount rate. This latter incorporates not only both the time preference of the suppliers of funds and their view of any given firm's risk (see chapters 12 and 13) but also an additional factor to protect their funds from the effects of inflation. This latter factor may not equal the rate of expected general price level change, for it seems unlikely that the suppliers of funds can fully protect themselves from inflation. Chapter 6 explains that management always face difficulty when attempting to estimate the return required by fund suppliers. This task is made more difficult in this inflationary environment (see Wilkes, 1972). Another approach to dealing with expected inflation when appraising projects is to estimate for all elements of the project's cash flows, their value in terms of the money values in the year they are received or paid out and then to discount these items so that they are all expressed in terms of the money values reigning at the time of decision. This conversion of each individual element of a project's cash flows in each year into real terms requires management to forecast how each element will be affected by expected price level changes. Some elements may be expected to increase faster than the expected change in the general price level, say, wages; others may rise by less (e.g. debenture interest). The final step with this approach is to discount these real cash flows by a discount rate incorporating elements reflecting only the project's risk and the time preference rates of fund suppliers.

For more on all this see Bromwich, 1969. Both the above approaches are rather simple minded, but a full discussion of these matters requires a detailed investigation of the inflation accounting debate which is beyond the scope of this book. Moreover, the correct theoretical treatment of inflation requires recognition that it is just one type of uncertainty and can be dealt with adequately only by using the methods examined in the final chapters in this book.

The appraisal techniques so far presented in this chapter by no means exhaust all those used in practice. However, those so far explained, or variants of them, are the major methods used in practice to take account of the time value of money. The last section of this chapter examines the limitations of some appraisal procedures which do not involve discounting.

Non-discounting methods

In the business community non-discounting methods probably hold sway. A British survey, admittedly based on a very small sample, found that under half of the respondents used any of the methods outlined so far in this chapter. Similar results have been obtained in America (Istvan, 1961). This may be partially due to the feeling that without a reasonable theory of search for new investments, little is gained by using sophisticated appraisal techniques (see chapter 1, pp. 20–22). However, discounting techniques probably need little extra information over conventional techniques and as they take into account the differing values of cash flows received at different times they should produce better results.

The businessman's attitude may be also affected by the dominance of the firm's information system by accountants, who in general have not been trained in the techniques presented in this book, and whose professional attitudes may possibly militate against their acceptance. There are signs that accountants are aware of their weaknesses in this area and are trying to remedy their deficiencies. For example, the examinations of most of the professional accounting bodies have been amended to include project appraisal and elementary operations research.

Another factor acting against the acceptance of discounting methods is that they probably are not easy to understand. Moreover, their correct use really requires a thorough knowledge of the difficult conceptual framework introduced earlier in this chapter. Indeed, it is believed that the clearer understanding of the essential elements of investment decisions which follows from an appreciation of the theoretical basis of capital budgeting is the most important gain coming from the application of the appraisal methods advocated in this book. The remaining sections of this chapter deal briefly with some popular project-appraisal techniques which do not take account of the timing of cash flows.

The payback method

This is a method of investment appraisal used by many firms. The payback period is the time projects have to run before their original investment is returned. The necessary calculations for three different projects are shown in Table 12.

Table 12 The payback method

	Projects		
	X (£)	Y (£)	Z (£)
a Outlays (at beginning of year 1)	−1000	−1000	−1000
b Receipts			
year 1	600	600	200
year 2	400	200	200
year 3	–	200	600
year 4	–	–	400
c Payback (time by which b = a)	2 years	3 years	3 years

The decision rule is to accept any project having a shorter payback than some target period. This target period varies considerably from firm to firm, and no clear guideline exists as to how it should be set. This is in contrast to our previous methods where the rate of interest served as the cut-off rate. Moreover, it is not easy to see how a payback cut-off rate can be related to our assumed objective of maximizing shareholders' wealth. The payback method pays no attention to cash receipts obtained after the payback period. The payback for both projects Y and Z above is three years, but this ignores the extra £400 earned in the fourth year by Z. Thus short-term projects are favoured, and not all the factors relevant for appraisal are included. Moreover, the method pays no attention to the value of money received at different times. For example, if the target payback was two years, then only project X would be acceptable even though it has a negative net present value at any positive discount rate and a zero internal rate of return. Only project Z may be worth while when time preference is taken into account.

The payback method is both easy to calculate and to understand. But this surely does not compensate for the wrong decisions to which it may lead. One claim for the payback method is that it allows for risk to be easily taken into account, by shortening the cut-off period for more risky projects. This procedure has advantages where the firm has little information about

the cash flows in later years of a project's life, for the method
assumes that no such cash flows will be obtained. However, in
general, most firms probably do have some notions about future
cash flows and it may be better to try to incorporate these into
the analysis. Methods for doing this will be examined when we
deal with uncertainty. The usefulness of using payback methods
to allow for risk is considered further in chapter 12. Payback may
be a useful appraisal device for the firm that is expecting liquidity
problems, provided that cash flows rather than accounting
figures are used in its calculation. Accepting projects with short
payback periods should help to overcome cash shortages.

The accounting-return method

There are many appraisal techniques which use some variant of
the rate of return. Generally, these do take account of a project's
earnings over its lifetime and therefore they represent an improvement over the payback technique. Often, the return per pound of
investment is calculated (total accounting profit over necessary
investment). Another approach is to divide the average profit per
year by the project's total investment. To illustrate the weaknesses of these approaches we will use an apparently sophisticated
version of the average return per year method.

The project in Table 13 gives gross profits of £1000, £3000 and
£5000 in its first, second and third years for an investment of
£8000.

Table 13 An accounting-return method

	Gross profits	Depreciation	Net profit or (loss)	Value at start	end	Average investment
year 1	1000	2666	(1666)	8000	5334	6667
year 2	3000	2667	333	5334	2667	4000
year 3	5000	2667	2333	2667	–	1333
average			333			4000
average return 333/4000 = 8·32 per cent						

The first step is to deduct depreciation from the gross profits.
This means that the original cost of the project has to be allocated in some arbitrary manner, to each year of its life. In the

example, straight-line depreciation is used. This allocates an equal charge to each year. Thus the yearly cash flow pattern is distorted; in what sense will a loss be made in year one? The average value of the machine in the first year is obtained by taking an average (£6667) of its values at the beginning and end of the year. The average value over three years is £4000, i.e. $\frac{1}{3}$(6667 + 4000 + 1333). One variant of the accounting-return method is calculated by expressing the average income of £333 as a percentage of this average investment. The project will only be accepted if this rate of return (8·32 per cent) exceeds some target rate. But again, it is not clear how this target rate should be defined.

The method shown, apart from incorporating the distorting effects of the arbitrary allocation of depreciation, and the use of accounting profits, shares a weakness of all variants of the accounting-return method. It fails to take time into account, for it weighs all profits equally, irrespective of when they are received. Further, the method shown may fail to take into account the duration of receipts. It may not distinguish between a project returning £5000 for one year and another earning £5000 for ten years, as both have the same average yearly proceeds.

The figures used in calculating both the payback and the accounting return often may not be based on the incremental cost principle. For example, accounting profit including allocations of fixed overhead might be used rather than cash flows, in calculating a project's rate of return. This is just an example of the general point that in contrast to discounting methods, there would seem to be no generally agreed way of defining receipts and expenditures to be used with non time-adjusted methods. In practice, different concepts are used, including profit before or after tax, and profit before or after depreciation.

None of the above methods takes any account of time preference and if this is thought to be important they should be rejected in favour of either the net present-value or the internal rate of return method. The next chapter offers some guidance as to which of the latter is more likely to lead to optimal decisions.

5 Internal Rate of Return Versus Net Present Value

In the previous chapter it was shown that, given the assumptions of certainty, perfect capital markets and both complete divisibility and independence of projects, the decision-maker using project-appraisal methods based on either the net present-value or internal rate of return concepts would accept all those investments which increased shareholders' welfare. That is, the use of either method would lead him to select that set of projects which gave shareholders the maximum net present value to trade in the market when seeking to optimize the utility of their consumption stream over time. This chapter examines the claim that the net present-value method is the theoretically superior method. It will be shown that the net present-value concept is more directly related to our assumed objective of maximizing the utility of consumption over time, and can be applied to a wider range of investment decisions.

The first section of this chapter considers, in some detail, the performance of the two methods in a variety of situations requiring accept/reject decisions. The following sections deal with decisions which necessitate the ranking of projects. It will be shown that the two methods may give different rankings to the same set of projects and that neither ordering is necessarily optimal in all circumstances.

Accept and reject decisions

In chapter 4 it was shown that knowledge of a project's net present value is sufficient in simple accept/reject situations to ensure decisions which lead directly to the maximization of the present value of the stream of cash flows received by shareholders. In contrast, the internal rate of return concept is not directly related to our objective, and appraisal methods based on this

concept make economic sense only because in simple accept/
reject situations they lead to the same decisions as the net
present-value method. Knowledge of a project's internal rate of
return is neither necessary nor sufficient for optimal investment
decisions. The familiar diagram below may help the understanding of this point. Consider a firm whose plans involve
accepting those projects represented by point B on the investment

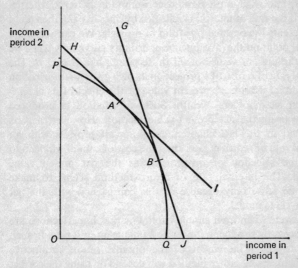

Fig. 10 Reliance of the IRR method on information other than marginal
returns

opportunity curve PQ. Now assume that it has been suggested
that the company should also undertake those additional proposals which would take it to point A on PQ.

We cannot decide whether to accept these additional investments on the basis of a simple comparison between the internal
rates of return of the respective marginal projects at A and B.
That portfolio A's marginal project has a lower internal rate of
return than that of portfolio B does not in itself lead to any
decisions. To advise the decision-maker we must know what
opportunities are foregone if the extra investments are accepted.

The rate of interest represents the opportunity cost of accepting *A* or *B* if funds are freely available in the capital market. The choice of *A* or *B* (and indeed, any other point on the investment opportunity curve) depends on this rate. If the rate of interest is such as to produce market lines like *HI*, then the projects represented by point *A* have the highest present value, and thus yield the largest amount of funds for shareholders to convert, via the market, into their most desired consumption pattern. Alternatively, if the rate of interest is reflected by lines like *GJ*, then point *B* represents the optimal portfolio of projects. We can select the optimal point on the investment opportunity curve only when we know the present values of all those points like *A* and *B*. The internal rate of return of a project on its own gives no information about either a project's present value or the effect of its acceptance on shareholders' wealth. Such information is produced directly using the net present-value method. However, as was explained in the last chapter, accepting all projects with an internal rate of return greater than the cost of capital will lead to the same selection of investments as the net present-value method. The internal rate of return method seems to make economic sense only because of this consistency with the net present-value model.

However, when even simple capital-market imperfections are introduced, there may no longer be a unique interest rate. In such situations the achievement of the optimal set of productive investments using either method will depend on using the correct definition of the cost of capital.[1] The next section considers, as an example, the adjustments necessary to the net present value method if it is to give correct decisions in the presence of some simple capital market imperfections.

Accept and reject decisions with imperfect capital markets

Once we step outside our world of complete certainty where everyone can borrow and lend at the going rate of interest, we encounter *capital rationing*. This term will be used to describe

1. Chapter 10 explains that although a theoretically correct definition of the cost of capital for capital rationing situations exists, it often may not be possible to quantify this in any meaningful way in practical situations.

any situation where there is a limit on the ability of individuals or firms to obtain as much capital as they wish at the going rate of interest. Later chapters deal specifically with investment appraisal in these circumstances. However, one type of capital rationing can be dealt with now; that where a different rate of interest is charged for borrowing to that which can be obtained when lending.

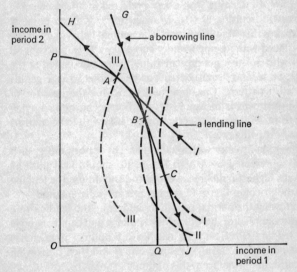

Fig. 11 Optimal investment selection where borrowing and lending rates differ

Differing borrowing and lending rates can easily be incorporated in our earlier diagrammatic analysis (Figure 11). Again PQ is the investment opportunity curve but now there are two market rates of interest, and thus two sets of market lines. One set is for borrowing (like GJ) which investors can move down in the usual way; the other set of lines, of which HI is characteristic, reflects lending opportunities. The investor moves up a lending line as he increases the amount of funds he puts on the market. The gap between the two interest rates is indicated by the differing slopes of the lines; the borrowing line is steeper reflecting the assumed higher cost of borrowing.

A lending line *HI* is tangential to *PQ* at *A* and a borrowing line *GJ* is tangential at *B*. It is clear that an investor, facing the situation represented in the diagram, should move towards point *C* by proceeding down the borrowing line from *B*. Moving along the lending line from point *A* moves him away from his optimal position for *A* intersects with a less preferred indifference curve (III) than that cutting *B* (II). Moving upwards from point *A* merely makes this situation worse. The optimal behaviour for the investor faced with an opportunity curve like *PQ* is to accept all projects with positive net present values when discounted at the borrowing rate, and then to borrow on the market so as to get his desired cash pattern. The opportunity cost for the investor of further investment is measured by the borrowing rate; moving from *B* towards *A* involves accepting projects with lower returns than the borrowing rate.

However, an investor with a different set of opportunities, such as those represented by *MN* in Figure 12, should lend until he reaches his highest indifference curve and should use the lending rate as the discount factor in the net present-value method.

By following the normal procedure and using the lending rate as the discount factor, he will achieve point *A* and can then move up the lending curve until he reaches the optimal indifference curve at point *D*. Ceasing investment at *B* and then borrowing would move him away from this optimum.

Firms do not have enough information to construct the figures we have discussed. However this should not stop them obtaining a productive optimum (points *A* or *B*), which is all our two appraisal methods achieve. This theoretical solution can be obtained by using the following decision rule. First, accept all investments which have a positive net present value at the borrowing rate. Funds should be borrowed on the market if the firm does not have sufficient internal funds to finance all these investments (following this rule will get the firm to point *B* in both Figures). Second, if the firm still has internal funds left after this operation, it should accept all projects with a net present

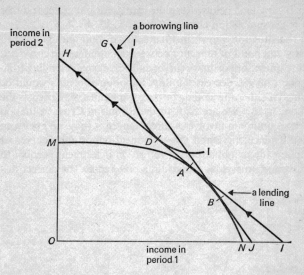

Fig. 12 Optimal investment selection where borrowing and lending
rates differ: lending rate operative

value when discounted at the lending rate.[2] Finally, any surplus
funds remaining after this should be lent on the market.

Internal funds may be exhausted prior to accepting all projects
with a positive net present value when using the lending rate as
the discount factor. In this situation, projects must be ranked in
some way. The firm should proceed down this ranking until its
funds are exhausted. This is an example of a second type of
capital rationing, which may be called *absolute* or *strong* capital
rationing, where the firm has but a limited amount of funds to
use for investment in one or more time periods. How such a
situation may come about when borrowing and lending rates

2. This abstracts from the dividend decision which is examined in chapter 9.
Shareholders may prefer the firm to pay dividends rather than to invest in
projects with a positive net present value at the lending rate. But by
following our rule the firm is making the best choice from its set of
investment opportunities. If shareholders have better opportunities they
may, if they wish, sell their shares.

differ is explained below. Absolute capital rationing due to other factors is examined in chapters 10 and 11.

In the situation shown in Figure 13, an optimum is reached directly at a point of tangency between an indifference curve and the investment-opportunity curve; and borrowing or lending from any point on *KL* decreases utility. Suboptimal results would be obtained if either the lending or borrowing rates were used as the discount factor. We are back in the Robinson Crusoe situation where an optimum involves a direct tangency (point *E*) between an indifference curve and the investment-opportunity curve. At this point the marginal rate of return on investment is equal to the investor's marginal rate of time preference. The correct dis-

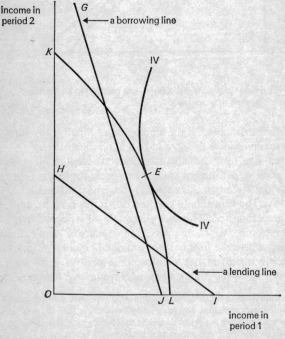

Fig. 13 Optimal investment selection where borrowing and lending rates differ: neither rate operative

count factor to use in order to select all those proposals represented by the EL segment of the investment-opportunity curve would be the return of the marginal project at E. By comparing the slope of the productive-opportunity curve at E with those of the two market lines shown in Figure 13, it can be seen that the correct discount factor will be lower than the borrowing rate but higher than that obtained by lending. The exact rate can be found only after the optimal selection of productive investments has been made. However, we really want the discount rate to aid us in arriving at this decision.

It is possible to suggest an approximate decision rule: accept all projects with a positive net present value at the borrowing rate. If there are then insufficient internal funds to undertake all projects acceptable at the lending rate, projects must be ranked in terms of their contribution per unit of scarce funds. Funds should then be allocated to the best projects in this ranking until finance is exhausted. The best way to construct such a ranking will be examined in an elementary way in the following sections. The absolute capital rationing problem will be examined more intensively in chapters 10 and 11.

The preceding sections can be summarized firstly as saying that in perfect capital markets and in some imperfect ones, both appraisal methods normally give the same accept/reject decisions. In imperfect markets the choice of the right market rate (lending or borrowing) to use as a discount factor or standard of comparison, is very important. Finally, in some capital-rationing situations, incorrect results may be obtained if either the borrowing or lending rates are used. Here, to obtain an investment optimum, projects have to be ranked in some way.

Ranking projects

Ranking is necessary in at least two situations. First, when choosing between mutually exclusive methods of achieving an objective. Such choices are quite common, and are met, for example, in the selection of either a factory location, or the best type of machine to do a specific job. Indeed, it was argued earlier (chapter 1) that alternative ways of achieving any given end should always be examined prior to the final accept/reject decision on any specific project. Only the winner of such a contest should be subjected to the full rigours of appraisal. If this view is accepted, then almost every capital-budgeting decision within the firm involves a ranking decision. Second, as was suggested above, ranking is also necessary in some capital-rationing situations.

The difficulty with ranking decisions is that the two appraisal methods discussed in this chapter may yield differing orderings when applied to the same set of projects. The internal rate of return ranking runs downwards from the project with the highest internal rate of return, and the net present-value method orders projects in terms of their net present values at a given discount rate. This latter ranking may depend on the discount rate used; certain projects may be preferred with low rates and others with higher rates.

The mechanics of the two ranking methods are illustrated in Figure 14, which is similar to one introduced earlier (see Figure 9),

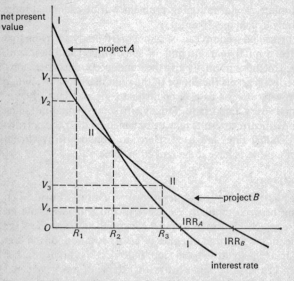

Fig. 14 Different rankings given by NPV and IRR methods

where the curves labelled I and II represent the net present values at differing interest rates of two different projects. It will be assumed that only one of the projects can be undertaken because of either mutual exclusiveness or the presence of capital rationing.

The present-value rule would advise accepting project A if the company's cost of capital was below R_2, and project B if it were higher. With a discount factor of R_1, projects A's net present value is greater than that of project B ($V_1 > V_2$), but if the discount factor is R_3, project B's net present value (V_3) exceeds that of the other project (V_4). The different rankings given to the projects by different rates of interest arise because of a difference in the time patterns of the cash flows of the two projects. At lower rates of interest, project A with more of its receipts received later in time is preferred. Such later cash flows become less valuable with high discount factors, and as the interest rate increases, preference will switch to project B with its larger earlier cash flows.

The internal rates of return of the two projects are given by the points where curves I and II intersect the horizontal axis, and are shown by IRR_A and IRR_B respectively. At these points the present value of the projects' cash inflows will equal that of their investment outlays. The internal rate of return method in contrast to the net present-value methods always ranks project B above project A because of the former's higher internal rate of return.

A numerical example may clarify the nature of the conflict in the rankings given by the two methods. The choice is between projects P and Q and the discount factor is assumed to be 10 per cent.

Table 14 Ranking by NPV and IRR

	Project P(£)	*Project Q* (£)
Outlay	—9000	—9000
proceeds		
year 1	3000	6000
year 2	5000	4000
year 3	6000	3000
net present value	2367	2014
internal rate of return (approximate)	22·5%	24%

The internal rate of return method favours project Q, but the net present-value approach selects project P. This different ordering arises because the 10 per cent discount rate used with the net present-value model values more highly the later cash flows of project P than does the much higher internal rate of return of this project. This latter rate, as will be emphasized below, can be regarded as serving, in some sense, as the discount rate with the internal rate of return method.

In our example, by keeping the size of the investment outlays the same for both projects, we abstracted from another difficulty with the internal rate of return model. The internal rate of return concept is an average, whereas net present value is an absolute amount. The internal rate of return of £1 invested for one day for a return of £2 is 100 per cent and the method would therefore signal that this option was preferable to one offering a 25 per cent return on £10 over the same period, even if the two options were mutually exclusive.

The following sections examine the question of which method of ranking (if either) should be used by a firm intent on maximizing its equity-holders' wealth. However, as preparation for this, it is useful to look first at the differing assumptions which underlie the two models.

Re-investment rates

Implicit in the net present-value method is the assumption that any positive net cash flow occurring during a project's life can be re-invested at a rate of interest equivalent to that used as the discount factor. This is best seen by accumulating the cash flows from a project to some terminal date and then finding the present value of this amount. Table 15 does this for the project used as an example in the last chapter, which for an immediate outlay of £1000 yielded £500, £1000 and £200 in years one, two and three respectively. The project has a net present value of £556 when discounted at 5 per cent.

The net present value arrived at in this way would have been different if the intermediate cash flows had been assumed to be re-invested at any rate other than 5 per cent.

The same implicit assumptions are made where the firm rather

Table 15 Re-investment assumptions of
the net present-value method

Year	Proceeds (£)	Interest received if proceeds re-invested in		Terminal value of total cash flows at end of year 3 (£)	Present value at time O of the terminal value (£)
		2nd year (£)	3rd year (£)		
1	500	25	26	551	476
2	1000	–	50	1050	907
3	200	–		200	173
total				1801	1556
less original investment					1000
net present value					556

than using its own funds, as was assumed above, finances a
project by a loan. Here the firm could use the project's intermediate cash flows to repay the loan used to finance the initial
investment. In a perfect capital market, this is equivalent to re-
investing, because redeeming the loan reduces the firm's future
interest costs by the same amount as would have been gained
from re-investment. If the project's first-year cash flows were paid
out to creditors, future interest payments would be reduced by
£25 in the second year and £26 in the third year. It can be shown
similarly that the net present-value method assumes that any
additional investment (net cash outflows) necessary during a
project's life will be financed at a rate of interest equal to the
discount rate.

The internal rate of return method makes a different implicit
assumption about the rate earned on intermediate cash flows. It
assumes that all a project's proceeds can earn a return equal to
the project's internal rate of return. This is shown in Table 16,
where it is assumed that our project is financed by a loan of £1000
at a rate of interest of 35 per cent (the project's internal rate of
return). The loan is to be repaid at the project's end and interest
is to be paid out of the proceeds as they accrue.

Thus the firm will break even only if the cash flows of £150 and
£650 are retained in the business and re-invested at a rate of
35 per cent to accumulate to £1150 at the end of year 3. This is
not surprising, for the internal rate of return method attempts to
find an interest rate which will equate the present value of a

Table 16 The re-investment assumptions of the internal rate of return method

Year	Project cash flows (£) 1	Loan out-standing (£) 2	Interest paid at 35% (£) 3	Cash flows retained in business (£) 4 = (1 – 3)	Interest on retentions in 2nd yr (£) 5	Interest on retentions in 3rd yr (£) 6	Terminal value of retentions (£) 7 = (4 + 5 + 6)
1 beg.	–	1000	–	–	–	–	–
1 end	500	1000	–350	150	52	71	273
2 end	1000	1000	–350	650	–	227	877
3 end	200	–	–350	–150	–	–	1150
							–150
balance available at end of project to repay loan							1000

project's proceeds with that of its investment outlays; that is, to find an average yearly rate of return which just equates the two. Thus, using the internal rate of return method for ranking is equivalent to assuming that any intermediate cash flows from a project will be re-invested to earn the project's internal rate of return, whereas the net present-value method hypothesizes that such cash flows will earn only interest equal in value to the discount rate.

The re-investment assumptions of the net present-value method seem to make economic sense where, as assumed by our earlier diagrammatic analysis, everyone can borrow and lend at the going rate of interest. In this situation, given certainty, any project offering a return greater than the market rate of interest will always be accepted, for such projects can always be financed by borrowing on the market. Thus the existence of intermediate cash flows does not make possible the acceptance of any additional project yielding more than the market rate of interest. The use of intermediate cash flows merely means that the firm can finance such projects without borrowing on the market and thus in a perfect capital market, intermediate cash flows when re-invested will earn only the going rate of interest.

This re-investment assumption is merely a specific application of the net present-value model's general assumption that the discount rate reflects the opportunity cost of capital. Discounting at the going rate of interest recognizes that with a perfect capital market the benefits sacrificed by accepting any specific project are measured either by the cost of borrowed funds or by the interest foregone if internal funds are used. For example, the opportunity cost of the project in our numerical example is £1157 which is what £1000 of retained earnings would accumulate to over three years, if invested at 5 per cent. The project has a terminal value of £1801 and yields a surplus of £643 (present value £556) over this opportunity cost and therefore should be undertaken.

Using the internal rate of return method is equivalent to employing a project's internal rate of return as the discount factor for that project. This amounts to assuming that by undertaking any project the firm foregoes the chance to earn that project's internal rate of return on both the capital tied up in the project and its intermediate proceeds. For example, it is equivalent to assuming that if the project shown in Table 16 was not undertaken, the funds thus released could be invested at 35 per cent. But, as already emphasized, in a perfect capital market, the opportunity cost of undertaking any specific project is measured by the going cost of funds which bears no obvious relationship to the internal rate of return of any non-marginal project. The internal rate of return method gives sensible answers for accept/reject decisions because it is used in conjunction with the opportunity cost of funds. But the opportunity cost of funds does not enter into the internal rate of return method when it is used for ranking. The choice between two mutually exclusive projects is made solely on a comparison of the projects' internal rates of return.

Mutually exclusive investments

With a perfect capital market, the net present-value method leads to the best choice between mutually exclusive investments. For example, if the projects introduced earlier (*P* and *Q*) were mutually exclusive, the net present value ranking would suggest that *P* should be accepted. This is correct with a perfect capital market. The internal rate of return method overlooks the key difference between projects *P* and *Q*, which is that if *Q* were accepted, we could, assuming it were feasible, switch to *P* by investing £3000 of the cash flows obtained from *Q* in year one and thereby receive an extra £1000 in year 2 and an extra £3000 in year 3. This would increase our present wealth by £353 (the difference between the net present values of projects *P* and *Q*).

The incremental method

The last section gives a clue as to how the internal rate of return method can be used to choose correctly between mutually exclusive projects. The correct comparison between *P* and *Q* should not be in terms of average yearly yields but rather in terms of cash flow differences between the two projects. That is, using *Q* as a base, the incremental investment to obtain *P* should be compared with the consequent incremental cash flows. The question is having accepted Q, would we get a better return from P? The switch to P entails foregoing £3000 in year 1 in return for extra cash flows of £1000 and £3000 in years 2 and 3 respectively. The internal rate of return on this pattern of cash flows is 18 per cent. This is greater than the cost of capital and therefore P is better than Q and should be accepted. This is shown in the table below.

Table 17 The incremental-yield method

	P (£)	Q (£)	Difference (£)
outlays	9000	9000	–
proceeds			
year 1	3000	6000	−3000
year 2	5000	4000	+1000
year 3	6000	3000	+3000
internal rate of return			18%

The correct procedure when using the internal rate of return for choosing between mutually exclusive projects is to compute the incremental rate of return between pairs of projects. This may be quite a complex procedure for pairs of projects will have to be compared and the winner of each contest compared with the victor of another duel, and so on. In contrast, the net present-value method allows us to reach a decision immediately.

Ranking with absolute capital rationing

This situation occurs where, in any time period, the firm either does not have access to more than a specific amount of funds irrespective of the rate of interest it is willing to pay or does not wish to invest more than a certain amount. This means that accepting any specific project may entail foregoing the return from another project offering a greater return than the market rate of interest. In this situation the opportunity cost of the capital tied up in any specific project will be higher than the market rate of interest, and the existence of intermediate cash flows may allow investment at a higher rate than the market cost of funds. This does not render the net present-value method useless. It calls for a redefinition of the discount rate so that it measures correctly the opportunity cost of investment. This cost may vary from year to year reflecting the expected relative scarcity of funds at any time. Thus, if the discount rate in years 2 and 3 of our usual example was expected to be 7 per cent, its net present value becomes

$$\frac{£500}{(1 \cdot 05)} + \frac{£1000}{(1 \cdot 05)(1 \cdot 07)} + \frac{£200}{(1 \cdot 05)(1 \cdot 07)^2} - £1000 = £553.$$

The following table shows what assumptions are made about the re-investment of cash flows when the discount rate changes over the project's life.

Table 18 Re-investment assumptions where discount factor changes

Year	Proceeds (£)	Interest if re-invested at		Terminal value at end of year 3
		7% 1st yr	7% 2nd yr	
1	500	35	37	572
2	1000	–	70	1070
3	200			200
total				1842
present value[a]				1533

[a] Obtained by using $1842/(1 \cdot 05)(1 \cdot 07)^2 = £1533$

The ability of the net present-value method to cope with multiple discount rates over time is one of its advantages over the internal rate of return method. The latter involves a comparison of an internal rate of return with but a *single* cost of capital.

However, in a capital-rationing situation, the internal rate of return of the last accepted project may provide an approximation to the opportunity cost of funds. But it can be only approximation, for the real opportunity cost is the benefit foregone due to the project's acceptance – the foregone return from the marginal project.[3] For example, accepting project Q when ranking using internal rates of return is equivalent to assuming that the oppor-

---

3. Hirshleifer (1958, Section 3) shows that only in the two period case can a project's internal rate of return be equated with its marginal return.

tunity cost of capital is 24 per cent. Precisely correct decisions will be made only if this opportunity cost is explicitly estimated and used as the discount factor in the net present-value model.

Whether either method's assumptions about the opportunity cost of capital are correct in any specific situation is an empirical matter and will be discussed further in chapters 10 and 11. However, it can be argued that the assumptions implied by the simple net present-value method are not likely to be realistic in situations of absolute capital rationing. But the method is flexible and easily adjusted to include multiple discount rates over several years. This is not possible with the internal rate of return method.

Technical difficulties with yield method

There are other difficulties associated with the internal rate of return which also stem from its method of calculation. The first of these occurs where we are considering projects whose cash flows do not follow the conventional pattern of an outflow, or series of outflows, followed by a series of inflows. For example, some projects may involve outlays both at their beginning and end. Such projects may be quite rare, but one example is that of projects which have positive abandonment costs, such as old buildings which must be demolished at the end of the project. To undertake the project at all the firm must accept the cost of demolition at its end. Less rare instances of non-conventional cash flows are likely to appear where the incremental yield method is used to rank mutually exclusive projects, e.g. several net outflows may appear in the differential series of cash flows generated by the method. Projects which have non-conventional cash flow patterns may have multiple rates of return. For example, the cash flow series, $-£1000$, $+£2550$, $-£1575$ has internal rates of return of 5 per cent and 50 per cent. This is shown in Figure 15 where the net present value curve intersects the horizontal axis twice.

Multiple rates appear because several different interest rates may equate the present value of a project's cash inflows to the present value of its initial outlay. This occurs because different interest rates may give differing values to each and every

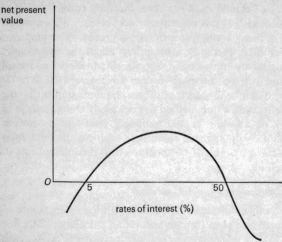

Fig. 15 Multiple rates of return

component of a project's cash flows; very high interest rates will give a low value to all but a project's near cash flows, whereas very low rates treat all cash flows as of nearly equal value. Thus as the interest rate tends to zero, the present value of a project will approach the algebraic sum of its undiscounted cash flows and will be negative if this is negative. In our example, at all interest rates below 5 per cent, the project's negative third term outweighs its positive middle term and generates a negative present value. With a cost of capital greater than 5 per cent, the positive second term in the cash-flow pattern will be less sensitive to changes in discount rate than the third term. With these rates of interest the present value of the project's cash inflows will outweigh that of the two negative cash flows and give the project a positive net present value. If the discount rate continues to rise, the project's negative third term will become insignificant but the positive cash flows (the second term) will fall in value faster than the negative first term. Thus, at some specific rate of interest the value of the negative terms will exactly offset that of the positive second term and the net present-value curve will again intersect the horizontal axis.

Where multiple rates of return exist there seems to be no mathematical or economic grounds for specifying any one of them having value of more than −100 per cent as the 'internal rate of return' for all are the roots of a single polynomial equation (Quirin, 1967, pp. 53–7). Several procedures have been suggested which allow the internal rate of return method to be used with projects that have non-conventional cash flows (for example, Wright, 1963). The net present-value method is not affected by these problems and, *ceteris paribus*, it would seem to be best to use this method, especially as the adaptations necessary to render the yield method useful can be quite complex.

A final disadvantage of the internal rate of return method for both accept/reject decisions and ranking decisions, is that it may not be possible to derive a meaningful internal rate of return for some patterns of cash flows (Hirshleifer, 1958, Section 3).

Practical reasons for preferring the internal rate of return

Some writers, whilst admitting the theoretical difficulties of the internal rate of return method, have suggested these are outweighed by its practical advantages (see Merrett and Sykes, 1963, ch. 5). They argue that as rates of return are more easily understood by businessmen, they may prefer internal rates of return measures to those utilizing the net present-value concept. This is, of course, an empirical question, but there is a danger that the apparent similarity of the internal rate of return to the ordinary accounting rate of return (accounting profits divided by 'book' investment) may be rather misleading and generate incorrect decisions.

It has been argued that the internal rate of return method allows the analyst to avoid measuring the firm's cost of capital (Merrett and Sykes, 1963, p. 150); the analyst merely generates the internal rates of return of the projects under consideration and leaves it to management to decide on an appropriate cut-off rate for the project. Thus the cost of capital is not ignored. It merely enters the decision-making process at a different stage.

Much stronger is the claim that internal rate of return allows management to adjust for risk or at least see how much 'elbow room' over the cost of capital is offered by a risky project

(Merrett and Sykes, 1963, ch. 5). For example, if the internal rate of return of a risky project is estimated to be 60 per cent then, it can, perhaps, go quite badly wrong and still yield a reasonable return. A net present value being an absolute amount cannot be easily used to gauge how much room for manoeuvre there is with a risky project. However, discounting for risk, which is what this approach amounts to, may not be the best way of treating risk. It will be argued later that, wherever possible, a more explicit treatment of risk is to be preferred.

In sum, the net present-value method is to be preferred to the internal rate of return method for ranking mutually exclusive projects where a good capital market exists, because the former's implied assumptions normally make more economic sense. Moreover, the internal rate of return measure suffers from some technical defects, that is, some patterns of cash flows may have no internal rate of return at all or have several such rates.

The net present-value model generates an absolute measure but with absolute capital rationing relative profitability is often crucial. For example, if we have a limited sum of money to invest, it may be better to concentrate on small 'richer' projects, giving a higher contribution to net worth per unit of scarce funds, rather than accepting larger projects with higher individual net present values but having, in combination, a lower total net present value. A project's internal rate of return may give some approximate idea of relative profitability, though as will be explained in later chapters, there exist other methods which yield theoretically correct results in situations of absolute capital rationing.

Some authors, to overcome the problems associated with using the net present-value method in absolute capital-rationing situations, have suggested that rankings should not be in terms of absolute net present values but rather in terms of discounted benefit–cost ratios, which are obtained by dividing the present value of a project's net cash inflows by the present value of its investment outlays. It is argued that the use of the latter for ranking is more likely to lead to optimal investment decisions in terms of our objective, for such an ordering emphasizes the relative profitability of projects. Again, it will be suggested later that even these methods will lead to suboptimal decisions in many capital-rationing situations.

Net present value versus discounted benefit–cost ratios

Rankings produced using benefit–cost ratios may be different from those obtained with either the net present-value or internal rate of return methods. That the orderings produced by the net present-value method and discounted benefit–cost ratios may differ is shown by Schwab and Lusztig (1969), and illustrated using a variant of their analysis in Figure 16. The present value of a project's investment outlays at a given interest rate is shown on the horizontal axis, and the present value of the project's cash inflows using the same interest rate is shown on the other. A 45° line through the origin connects all projects with a benefit–cost ratio of unity; along this line the present value of a project's inflows equals its investment cost. For example, the project represented by point E on the 45° line requires an outlay of OC_1, in return for cash flows having a present value of OF. The project has a benefit–cost ratio of unity, for OF is of the same length as OC_1 ($OF/OC_1 = 1$). The slope of the line connecting any point to the origin measures a project's benefit–cost ratio. For example, the slope OA is given by OG/OC_1, where OG is the present value of the project's inflows and OC_1 the project's original outlay.

Both of the projects shown by points A and B have a positive net present value for they both have benefit–cost ratios greater than one; they lie to the left of the 45° line OJ. Using the net present-value rule, the project represented by point B would be chosen over that shown by A, for the former has a higher absolute net present value ($C_2B - OC_2 > C_1A - OC_1$). This is shown in the diagram by the greater length of line JB relative to AE. As C_2J is drawn of equal length to OC_2, the segment JB indicates project B's net present value. Similarly, AE represents the net present value of project A, because C_1E is of the same length as OC_1. The ranking is reversed using benefit–cost ratios; the line from the origin through A has a steeper slope (representing a higher benefit–cost ratio) than that through B.

A numerical example of this situation is given in Table 19

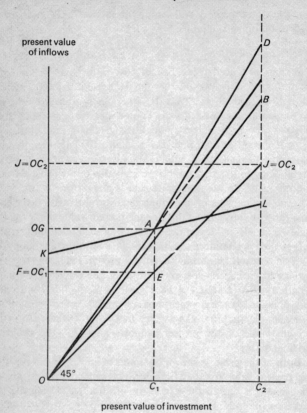

Fig. 16 Ranking via NPV and discounted benefit–cost ratios

where each project shown requires an immediate outlay in return for a cash inflow at the year end. The table shows the project's net present values and discounted benefit–cost ratios using a discount factor of 10 per cent.

If projects E and F were mutually exclusive, the net present-value method would select F. The benefit–cost procedure would advise opting for E, for in terms of the diagram, it lies on a steeper line through the origin.

Table 19 Rankings via net present values and benefit–cost ratios

Projects	Cash inflows (£)	Present values of inflows (£)	Investment (£)	Net present value (£)	Benefit–cost ratio
E	715	650	500	150	1·30
F	1100	1000	800	200	1·25
H	500	455	300	155	1·51
F–E	385	350	300	50	1·16
F–E invested at 10%	330	300	300	–	1·00

If A and B in the diagram are mutually exclusive projects, then to choose B as prescribed by the net present-value rule is optimal providing that a perfect capital market exists. Accepting project A rather than B makes available funds equal to $C_1 - C_2$ for other use, but by our assumptions these could be invested only at the discount rate. In the one period case, such opportunities can be represented in the diagram by a set of lines (of which KL is an example) which have absolute slope equal to $1 + r$, where r is the interest rate. Excess funds allow us only to move along KL to point L which has a lower present value than B. In terms of our numerical example, accepting E rather than F saves £300 of our investment funds, but these can be invested only at 10 per cent and would yield the cash flows shown in the last line of Table 19. The fourth line of the Table indicates that if the £300 were invested in project F it would return more than the market rate of interest (£385 rather than £330) and would contribute an extra £50 to the firm's present worth.

This supremacy of the net present-value ranking does not necessarily apply in absolute capital rationing, where, for example, our funds are limited to C_2 in the diagram. If the discount rate used to obtain net present values is defined in the usual way, as a market rate of interest, then we may overlook the fact that by accepting A rather than B we free funds which may be invested in a project with a benefit–cost ratio like that represented by the line $A - D$. Accepting such a project would enable us to achieve points like D which have higher present values than B. In terms of our numerical example, in an absolute capital-rationing situation selecting E rather than F may allow us to invest in a project like H which yields a considerably higher return on the £300 released than does F.

This advantage of benefit–cost ratios applies only if the net present-value method is used naïvely; that is, if we simply select projects in order of their absolute net present values. Both the net present-value and benefit–cost procedures would give the same answer if we compare every combination of projects that could be financed by C_2; both rules would prefer a combination of projects A and D to project B alone. Using the net present-value rule in this way would lead to selecting projects E and H in our numerical example assuming that only £800 were available for investment. However, ordering in terms of benefit–cost ratios has the advantage that it simultaneously ranks projects and tells us which should be accepted.

Thus at least with absolute capital rationing in one time period, selecting projects in order of their benefit–cost ratios until the funds constraint is met is preferable to selecting in order of net present values.

The search for a simultaneous ranking and acceptance method is doomed to failure where fractions of projects cannot be undertaken. Where discontinuities occur it is not possible simply to proceed down a ranking until the funds constraint is met. Here we are forced to look at the net present values of all feasible combinations of projects. For example, assume we have £1000 to spend, and have a choice between three projects, one returning inflows having a present value of £1000 for an investment of £800, another yielding £650 for £500, and a final project which returns £600 for £500. In the Table below these projects are ranked using both net present values and benefit–cost ratios.

Table 20 Ranking with discontinuities

Project	Present value of cash flows (£) (1)	Investment (£) (2)	Net present value (£) 3 = (1–2)	Benefit/Cost ratios 4 = (1/2)
1	1000	800	200	1·25
2	650	500	150	1·30
3	600	500	100	1·20

Naïve use of the net present-value rule would lead to the acceptance of project 1, whereas the benefit–cost ratio approach would advise the acceptance of project 2 if used in a similar way. The correct choice is the one which maximizes total net present value. This can only be found by comparing the net present value of all feasible combinations. In our case, we should accept projects 2 and 3, which give a net present value of £250 against that of £200 obtained with project 1 alone.

6 The Cost of Capital

Introduction

Given our earlier assumptions and abstracting from capital rationing, the maximization of net worth can be achieved by using either the net present value or the internal rate of return decision rule. Both rules depend heavily on the correct definition and measurement of the cost of capital. This latter is used in the net present-value approach to discount a project's cash flows, and should represent the opportunity cost of the funds used to finance a project. With the internal rate of return method, the cost of capital serves as the cut-off rate, or the standard of comparison against which to gauge a project's internal rate of return.

The cost of capital represents the cost of funds used for a project and should be defined in the same way as all other costs; as an opportunity cost. The cost of capital may be obtained from the market or may have to be imputed. For example, the use of retained earnings does not entail any payments by the firm, but as will be shown later, their use does involve shareholders foregoing opportunities and therefore is not costless. Moreover, as with other inputs, the market price of funds may not measure their opportunity cost where funds are scarce. Further, <u>the use of any given type of finance may cause the cost of other funds to rise.</u> Such increases are not reflected in the market price of the funds being raised, and have to be separately taken into account when defining the cost of capital.

In project appraisal the cost of capital serves as a cut-off, or hurdle rate, which must be 'cleared' by acceptable projects. Ideally, its use automatically sets the size of the firm's total investment budget, for only projects with returns equal to or greater than this rate should be accepted. Following this policy will lead to the maximization of shareholders' wealth, for only projects which increase the firm's net present value will be accepted.

It is perhaps more apt to describe the cost of capital as the required rate of return on projects but the term cost of capital is firmly entrenched in the literature and therefore will be used in this book. The term 'cost of capital' does emphasize how the required rate of return is derived and reminds us that this latter must normally be set with reference to the market conditions which prevail at the time when the firm wishes to use funds. This does not mean that the cost of capital is unaffected by what the firm does but rather that it is not entirely within the firm's control.

The cost of capital under certainty

The role of the cost of capital is generally agreed on in the literature, but a controversy exists over how it should be defined and therefore about its measurement. In a world of certainty and perfect markets, no such problems exist. It has previously been shown that the rate of interest serves as the cost of capital in this situation, and represents the market rate of exchange between present and future money. There is no difference between the costs of debt and equity for there are no risks to be borne. The profitability of any project depends on the conditions prevailing in the capital market as reflected by the rate of interest which regulates the demand for and supply of funds. The desirability of projects thus depends on the market rate of interest; a project being acceptable at some rates but not at others. The rate of interest, like any other price, thus serves an allocative role. It continues to fulfil this function in an uncertain world, but the unique rate is replaced by a family of interest rates, each associated with differing degrees of uncertainty.

The cost of capital in an uncertain world

Here the returns expected from a project or firm are uncertain and thus, it is normally assumed that the cost of funds in the market reflects not only the time value of money but also the risk inherent in their use by any specific firm. Some authors give different meanings to the terms 'risk' and 'uncertainty'. They will, however, be used in this book as if they were synonymous. Varying degrees of risks are attached to different types of funds. The risk associated with borrowed funds (debentures, etc.) is normally less than that with equity shares; debentures often have contractual guarantees as to payment.

Most of the major problems to be faced when measuring the cost of capital spring from the existence of uncertainty. One task is to ascertain the cost of capital for each type of finance. However, the cost of different financing instruments should not be looked at in isolation; the use of different types of funds may have different effects on equity-holders' wealth. Thus, there is a need to consider whether for any firm there is an optimum mix of different types of funds which if used to finance its planned capital projects would maximize the unit market price of equity shares.

The cost of capital problem can be attacked in two stages. First, we can endeavour to derive a cost for each type of finance, ignoring any effect its use may have on the price of other funds. Then, we can examine the effects of using different mixes of funding instruments. The remainder of this chapter is addressed to the first question. This is unrealistic, but allows us to isolate more easily many factors which partially determine capital costs. The next two chapters tackle the question of whether there exists an optimal capital structure for the individual firm.

Measurement problems still remain even if we restrict ourselves to obtaining the cost of specific types of funds, for this task brings us face to face with the problem of valuation under uncertainty. For example, to obtain the cost of ordinary shares we have to assume that the market uses a specific valuation model. How stock is valued is subject to debate. All that can be done in this book is to review critically the various cost of capital models that have been suggested in the literature. However, our objective should never be forgotten: to derive discount factors which can, in an uncertain world, serve the same role as did the rate of interest under certainty and thereby lead to the maximization of shareholders' wealth.

The cost of equity capital

The use of share capital has no accounting cost. The use of equity by a firm does not involve any outlays which an accountant would normally call costs. However, equity-holders expect either dividends or capital gains from their investments and such expectations give rise to an opportunity cost of capital. Equity funds should only be used if the return from a project covers this cost. Equity financing arises from two major sources; new issues on the stock market, and retained earnings generated by the retention of profits within the firm. In the following discussion we will ignore what may, in practice, be crucial issues, such as how the control of a firm could be affected by a new stock issue.

New issues

Ideally, we wish to find a cost of capital the use of which guarantees that projects will be financed by new issues if, and only if, their acceptance would not reduce the value of the firm's existing equity. In our earlier model the market value of shares depended on the discounted sum of the future dividends expected by investors. The market value of the firm was assumed to be given by:

$$V_0 = \sum_{1}^{\infty} \frac{D_i}{(1 + k)^i}.$$

V_0 is the value of the company, the sum of the value of its shares on the stock exchange. The expected dividends for the ith year are represented by D_i, i representing the year in the future when the ith dividend is to be received, and $(1 + k)$ is the discount factor. The sign to the left of D_i is a summation sign which says we must add together the present values of all the dividends expected to be received from now to infinity. The total expression says that the current value of the firm in the market place is assumed to depend on the present value of all expected future dividends. The cost of capital, which is what we are trying to find, is represented by k and is crucial to the valuation model. If it changes, so may the portfolio of projects the firm should accept.

The dividends in the model are merely estimates and can be

wrong. For ease of presentation, it will be assumed that the dividends expected from the firm in each year in the future are all regarded by investors as having the same degree of riskiness, and that all the firm's investment proposals also possess this degree of uncertainty.[1]

The dividends expected from different firms may have different degrees of uncertainty attached to them by the market. The market may allow for this by increasing the cost of capital demanded of risky firms; the greater the perceived risk of the firm, the higher its cost of capital. Thus, in our model, k takes into account not only time preference but also the relative risk attached to the firm. That is, k is made up of a rate i reflecting time preference, and a rate q which allows for the relative risk attached to the dividends of a specific firm. Some writers have suggested that for investment appraisal there are better methods of risk adjustment and the cost of capital used in project appraisal should be net of its risk element. The case for this will be examined later, but the various costs of capital discussed in the next three chapters will include a risk element.

It will now be shown that the equity cost of capital should be defined as the minimum rate of return (including a risk allowance) that must be obtained from a project to ensure the maintenance of the value of existing equity. The rate which fulfils this condition is that at which the market capitalizes the firm's future dividends; that is, k in our general formula on page 115. A simplified example may make clear the reasoning behind this claim.

Let us assume that a company is financed solely by 5000 shares having a market value of £2 each. Further, assume that the dividends of the company are expected to be £1000 a year for ever. The market capitalization rate for the firm is therefore 10 per cent. This can alternatively be put by saying that the market expects a 10 per cent annual yield from this particular stock; that is, the market is willing to pay £10 to obtain £1 of the

1. This assumption will be explained more precisely in later chapters after the necessary statistical concepts have been introduced. A knowledge of the material covered in chapters 12 and 13, although not necessary, should make it easier to follow this chapter and the two succeeding ones.

firm's annual dividends. The firm does not retain any of its net cash flows because its cash depreciation allowances are assumed to be just sufficient to maintain expected dividends. Now assume that the firm is considering whether to undertake a project costing £5000 which is to be financed by a new equity issue and which is forecast to return net dividends of £500 per year of the same risk quality as the presently expected dividends. To ensure that the existing equity-holders do not lose by the project's acceptance, the firm's value must rise to at least £15000 (original capital £10000 + £5000 cost of project) following the project's acceptance. We need to find the minimum rate the project must earn to give the firm this value. The market should use the same capitalization rate in valuing both new and old dividends, for they are assumed to be of the same risk quality. With this capitalization rate the firm must pay out dividends of at least £1500 per year to justify a market value of £15000. The new project must therefore add £500 per year to net dividends if it is to be acceptable. The project just contributes this amount and therefore the firm should be indifferent about its acceptance.

The firm's cost of capital will only be correctly defined if its use ensures that our appraisal methods give identical advice as to the project's acceptability. Using the market capitalization rate as the cost of capital gives the project a net present value of zero and therefore fulfills this condition.

That 10 per cent is the correct discount factor to use in our example can easily be shown. Any project yielding less than £500 a year would have a negative net present value at this rate and should be rejected. Any project contributing more than £500 per annum would have a positive net present value and should be accepted. Consider as a second example whether our firm should undertake a project which costs £5000 and returns £600 a year into perpetuity. This has a present value of £1000 with a 10 per cent discount rate and should be accepted. If the market knew of the project's acceptance and believed the firm's cash flows estimates, then, in an efficient market, the firm's total equity would rise to £16000. £5000 of this sum represents the value of the new shares which are necessary to finance the project. Thus the value of the existing equity would rise by £1000. This increase in the value of the firm's equity is measured by the project's net present value utilizing a 10 per cent discount rate. Using the market capitalization rate as the cost of capital therefore yields the correct decision.

The exact distribution of the increase in value between old and new equity-holders will depend on the price of the new issue. To do the best it can for existing shareholders, the firm should issue the new shares at a price which implies a 10 per cent yield; 2273 shares should be offered for sale at a price of £2.20 each.[2] This price will ensure that the whole of the project's net present value will go to the existing shareholders in the form of capital gains. This is the ideal price and the price of the new shares in the stock market will only approximate to this because of uncertainty and the existence of transaction costs.

The above arguments are summarized in the table below, where the first project discussed which yields annual dividends of £500 in return for an investment of £5000 is labelled project A. Project B is the second project which requires the same investment but generates annual dividends of £600.

In our example we used the simplifying assumptions that both the firm and the two contemplated projects yielded constant future dividends and that the firm did not plough back any of its net cash flows. These assumptions form the basis of one proposal for measuring the cost of capital: that k should be equal to the constant dividends per year (d) divided by the current market value V_0, that is, $k = d/V_0$. Our valuation formula becomes:

$$\left[k = \frac{d}{V_0} \right] = \left[V_0 = \frac{d}{k}. \right]$$

It is worthwhile listing the large number of implicit assumptions which made it possible for us to both derive this formula for the cost of capital and to suggest a general way of measuring it.

2. Obtained using:

$$\frac{\text{total value of firm after issue less required finance}}{\text{number of shares prior to new issue}}$$

$$= \frac{£16000 - £5000}{5000} = \frac{11}{5} = £2.20.$$

Table 21 The cost of new equity issues

the company's situation before accepting either project A or B		£
market price of shares before the new issue		2
total number of shares before the new issue	5000	
1 market value of firm		10000
2 expected yearly dividends before the new issue		1000
3 cost of capital and capitalization rate (3 = 2/1 × 100) 10%		

project A	
cost	5000
expected annual incremental dividends to infinity	500
necessary minimum market value of company after new issue and accepting the project (£10000+£5000)	15000
4 total future earnings per year necessary to guarantee this value, if capitalization rate is constant	1500
5 required dividends from project to avoid dilution of existing equity value (5 = 4−2)	500
net present value of project using capitalization rate as discount factor	0

project B	
cost	5000
expected annual incremental dividends to infinity	600
market value of company if accepted	16000
less part due to new equity-holders	−5000
less market value of existing equity before new project	−10000
gain to existing stockholders	1000
net present value of project using the capitalization rate as discount factor	1000

These are:
1 That the incremental dividends from the projects under consideration are of the same risk quality as the existing expected dividend stream. The cost of capital to the firm would probably rise if the projects under consideration were relatively more risky.
2 That the new issue of shares does not for any other reason cause the cost of capital to rise.
3 That the firm's dividends expectations have been communicated to and accepted by the equity market. This is of crucial

importance, for if the market did not know of or did not believe the firm's estimates of the incremental dividends from either of our projects, the market price of the shares might fall when the new issue was announced, rising again only when the market had somehow or other been convinced of the correctness of the firm's forecasts.

4 That only equity finance is used. If not, the effects, if any, of the new issue on the cost of other funds would have to be considered.

5 That a dividend valuation model is used.

6 That there are no issue expenses for new shares.

These assumptions really amount to ignoring most of the difficulties in estimating the cost of capital, and thus the model should not be thought of as a completely practical tool for measuring the cost of capital. It serves, rather, as a framework which can be used to isolate some of the key variables affecting the cost of capital. An examination of these assumptions highlights some of the theoretical weaknesses of the cost of capital concept and some of the controversies surrounding its use.

By assumption one, the discount rate includes an element for risk. However, different shareholders may have different views as to both expected future dividends and their riskiness. Thus, management will be forced to use a cost of capital which they hope will be broadly applicable to all equity-holders; thereby attracting those who like their policy and causing those with different views to sell their stock.

The question as to how the market formulates its future expectations of dividends has not yet been answered in the literature. We abstracted from this problem by making assumption 3, but management when estimating the cost of capital must try to put themselves in the market's position. Investors have only rough guides as to a company's future earnings and must, when estimating future dividends, rely heavily on past dividends and accounting profits, adjusted to allow for any other information they have, such as directors' forecasts. Our rules will not necessarily lead to maximization of the market value of a firm's shares if the equity-holders base their forecasts entirely on, say, last year's accounting profit. This is so, even though by using our approach the firm would be doing what many think shareholders should logically want. How the firm is to proceed when shareholders use rules of thumb methods of evaluation is not clear.

The valuation model based on dividends has been criticized and a model based on earnings advocated instead. However, retained earnings will be of benefit to the shareholder only if they lead to capital gains and such gains must, at least in the long term, be founded on expectations of future dividends (including a liquidation dividend). Moreover, with uncertainty, shareholders may be forced to rely heavily on past dividends as guides to the future and thus may use something like our model. Another reason for preferring a dividend approach to valuation is that where the investor has difficulty in borrowing or lending to obtain his desired income stream, dividends may be crucial to the achievement of his desired consumption pattern. This is especially so if he does not wish to sell his share to realize capital gains.

The use of the dividend model as presented has two disadvantages. It may lead to using the current dividend/price ratio as the cost of capital. This is wrong, for it is future dividends which are important. It should also be noted that using the popular price/earnings ratio as a basis for valuation implies all the assumptions listed above except that these now apply to earnings rather than dividends. Second, our model does not allow for growth in dividends. This latter point will be discussed in the next section. One word of warning should be noted; many other models for obtaining the cost of capital have been suggested but only variants of the one above, including both its properly formulated earnings and growth equivalents, are defensible, given our assumptions about the firm's objective.

The cost of retained earnings

Retained earnings are a major form of finance for many companies. Such retentions may lead to growth in both cash flow earnings and in dividends. Our simple model with its constant dividends is therefore no longer useful. Similarly, the investment analysts' price/earnings ratio can no longer be used as a basis for obtaining even an approximation as to the cost of capital.

Retained earnings, like equity funds, have no accounting cost but do have an opportunity cost. If the company retains cash flows then the equity-holder foregoes the return he could have obtained if these funds were paid out. He receives, instead, higher dividends in the future. Only projects whose expected extra future dividends at least cover these foregone opportunities should be financed by retained earnings. The cost of equity reflects the return shareholders would obtain if cash flows were paid out as dividends. It is the return expected from new shares both in the company and similar firms, and therefore measures the returns foregone by equity-holders due to investing in the project rather than in the next best market or consumption alternative. If this were not so, the market would not be willing to subscribe for the company's shares on the existing yield basis. Thus, only projects which have a positive net present value when discounted at the cost of equity capital should be financed by retentions. This decision rule temporarily ignores the impact of personal taxation.

As an example, assume that our earlier projects were to be financed by retained earnings. This would mean the equity-holders foregoing dividends of £5000. If these were paid out, shareholders could expect to earn a 10 per cent return by investing in companies of equal risk. Thus, neither project A nor B should be accepted unless it generates at least this return. The equity cost is therefore the correct discount factor to use for retained earnings.

This approach, however, can only be used as a guideline, for different shareholders may be subject to different tax rates and may therefore have conflicting dividend preferences. An equity-holder whose marginal tax rate is 40 per cent can only invest 60 per cent of every pound of dividends he receives. That is, by retaining profits our firm is forcing him to forego opportunities to earn 6 per cent per year. He may therefore prefer earnings to be retained, providing the firm has projects which have positive net present values when discounted at this rate. Given sufficient other people in a similar situation, such a policy will cause the value of the firm's stock to rise; if our equity-holder sells his shares, he will obtain relatively higher returns in terms of capital gains, assuming that these gains are not taxed or are taxed at a lower rate than dividends.

But the tax position of individual equity-holders may differ and thus each may have a different cost of capital. The lucky individual (or, more probably, institution) which does not pay tax will, under our assumptions, require a return of 10 per cent from the firm. But those subject to income tax would prefer the use of lower discount rates; the exact rate preferred by any individual will depend on the rate of tax he faces.

It has been argued in the literature that where shareholders are subject to differing tax rates the correct discount rate to use is that based on the preferences of tax-free individuals (Quirin, 1967, pp. 107–9). All those equity-holders who are subject to tax will have lower costs of capital than this, and therefore using this rate will ensure that all accepted projects cover the minimum requirements of all shareholders, and that at least the tax-free ones are made better off. This assumes that firms face, at least, the same opportunities as the tax free investor; that is, in our example, that the firm can earn at least 10 per cent on retained earnings. This ought to be the case, for such opportunities should be available on the market even if funds cannot be re-invested within the firm at this rate. But those equity-holders subject to income tax could, provided that capital gains are taxed at a lower rate, be made better off if the firm used a lower cost of capital. Thus, management when deriving a discount rate to use for retained earnings has somehow to weigh the conflicting interests of shareholders.

Some writers have suggested that the firm should use the tax-free cost of capital adjusted by a factor reflecting the weighted average of the equity-holders' marginal tax rates. But the information required for this calculation may be considerable, the computation of the weighting factors involving a knowledge of the marginal tax rate of each investor in the firm.

Solomon (1963, pp. 53–5) has suggested that to overcome the difficulty of conflicting interests, the minimum cost of retained earnings should be equated with the returns that the firm could obtain by investing on the market. That is, funds should be retained only if they return at least as much as external investments of equal risk quality. (Such investments have a return equal to the rate required by tax-free individuals.)

Such returns measure the opportunity cost of using cash flows within the firm. In a reasonably competitive market, external opportunities should offer a return equivalent to the cost of capital of equity funds for the firm being considered, for opportunities which are exactly similar in terms of risk and profit should sell at the same price on such a market. By using this external criterion we have shifted our attention from the opportunities foregone by equity-holders to the external opportunities foregone by the firm itself when it retains funds. With the external-yield approach, we are supposedly freed from trying to assess the impact of taxes on different equity-holders.

The external-yield criterion is not universally accepted. It should be remembered that both it and the tax-free rate provide only a minimum cost of retained earnings for one group of equity-holders. If a substantial majority of the firm's equity shareholders have the same marginal rates of tax, the firm can do better for them by explicitly taking tax effects into account when quantifying the cost of capital. In fact, the investors in any particular firm may well be of quite a similar type because firms normally have consistent dividend and retention policies and therefore tend to attract those investors with similar desires.

So far all we have done is arrive at a formulation for the cost of retained earnings and have not made any comments about whether or not dividends should be paid nor in what amount. These matters will be taken up later (chapter 9).

Growth in dividends

Above we assumed that the same amount of dividends were expected to be received in each year in the future. This enabled us to derive the formula:

$$k = \frac{d}{V_0}.$$

This formula can be adjusted to allow for dividends which are expected to grow at a specific rate per year (say g). Such expectations would give a forecast dividend stream, starting from the existing dividend (d) of:

$$V_0 = \frac{d}{(1 + k)} + \frac{d(1 + g)}{(1 + k)^2} + \frac{d(1 + g)^2}{(1 + k)^3} + \cdots + \frac{d(1 + g)^{n-1}}{(1 + k)^n}.$$

(The element $(1 + g)$ is raised to the power $n - 1$ as the dividends are assumed to grow only from the second year.) Again, we wish to find k, the cost of capital. It can be shown that the above formula condenses to $V_0 = d/(k - g)^1$, which, by rearrangement, gives $k = d/V_0 + g$.

Thus, where dividends are expected to grow at a specific rate each year, the cost of capital, k, is given by the reciprocal of the normal price/dividend ratio *plus* the growth rate, g, expressed as a percentage. The former is easily obtained but it may be rather more difficult to forecast the growth rate expected by investors on the margin. Given this, however, ascertaining the cost of capital is quite straightforward. For example, if a firm's stock is selling at £20 with an annual dividend of £2 per share which is growing by 3 per cent per year, then the equity cost of capital is:

1. This can be done by multiplying both sides of the above expression by $(1 + g)/(1 + k)$. By subtracting this expression from the earlier one we obtain:

$$V_0 - V_0 \frac{(1 + g)}{(1 + k)} = \frac{d}{(1 + k)} - \frac{d(1 + g)^n}{(1 + k)^{n+1}}.$$

This can be simplified by multiplying throughout by $(1 + k)$, giving:

$$V_0(1 + k) - V_0(1 + g) = d - \frac{d(1 + g)^n}{(1 + k)^n}.$$

Multiplying this out gives:

$$V_0 + V_0 k - V_0 - V_0 g = \frac{d(1 - (1 + g)^n)}{(1 + k)^n}$$

which equals:

$$V_0(k - g) = \frac{d(1 - (1 + g)^n)}{(1 + k)^n}$$

Thus:

$$V_0 = \frac{d[1 - (1 + g)^n/(1 + k)^n]}{(k - g)}.$$

The term in square brackets on the right becomes insignificant when the number of years over which the dividends are expected to be received is very large. Thus the present value of a stream of dividends growing at a rate g into perpetuity is given by the expression: $V_0 = d/(k - g)$. The cost of capital can be found by rearrangement: $k = d/V_0 + g$.

$$k = \frac{2}{20} \times 100 + 3 = 13 \text{ per cent.}$$

This growth in dividends comes about because a fraction, say b, of the earnings (net cash flows) per share is re-invested at a rate of return, r, and therefore, dividends will grow by the amount br per year. This becomes clear if we express the above formula in terms of earnings rather than dividends. The formula becomes $k = E_0(1 - b)/V_0 + br$. The numerator of the first expression on the right becomes $E_0(1 - b)$, where E_0 is the current earnings of the firm and the factor $(1 - b)$ is the amount of the earnings paid out by the firm. The proportion of earnings retained by the firm is represented by b, and r is the return obtained on these earnings.

This model has been criticized (Bodenhorn, 1959) basically because we normally visualize the amount of funds ploughed back into a business as depending on the opportunities available to the firm. It seems unlikely that there will always be just sufficient opportunities offering a constant return of r to absorb a given proportion of retained earnings each year, and that the absolute amount of such opportunities will increase by the required proportion each year. Growth models which allow the proportion b and r to vary have, however, been formulated.

Moreover, there is something disturbing about a model which allows the market price of a share to be made infinite. The price of the shares would be infinite if in our earlier dividend growth model k and g were equal. If this were so, the right-hand side of our valuation equation would have an infinite value, that is $d/(k - g) = d/0$. Thus if r were greater than k, the firm could obtain an infinite price for its stock by an appropriate choice of b. However, this result can be avoided by assuming, as many people believe, that r is a decreasing function of b, the payout ratio. In this situation the return which can be obtained from further investment falls as the proportion of retained earnings is increased in an attempt to make stock prices infinite. Alternatively, it can be assumed that as current investment is increased, the cost of capital will rise thus ensuring that the denominator in our expression cannot become zero. This increase in the cost of capital might occur because re-investment is seen as shifting dividends further into the risky future (see chapter 9 for more on this).

The cost of non-cash items

All our models involve cash flows, and therefore depreciation – a non-cash expense – has no relevancy in these models. Depreciation is normally deducted from accounting profits on the income statement. Such profits are not used in our cash-flow based models. The difference between the financial-accounting approach and our cash-flow approach is explained in Table 22, where a firm starts the year with new fixed assets of £20000 financed entirely by equity. During the year cash expenses were £5000 and sales revenue was £6000. The net cash flow during the year was therefore £1000. Depreciation on a straight line basis is assumed to be £2000 per annum.

Table 22 Cash flow versus accounting profit

	Cash flow	Accounting profit
sales revenue	£6000	£6000
less cost of sales	−5000	−5000
less depreciation	–	−2000
increase in shareholders' funds	£1000	−£1000

the company's balance sheet, using the usual accounting conventions, is:

equity shares	£20000	fixed assets at cost	£20000
less loss for year	1000	less depreciation	2000
			18000
		cash	1000
	£19000		£19000

Using our cash flow concept it is clear that £1000 has been generated during the year, and therefore any project financed with this money should be evaluated using the cost of retained earnings as the discount rate. That depreciation, as such, is irrelevant can easily be seen by substituting any number for the

£2000 depreciation. For example, let us assume that depreciation for the year was £10000. The accounting loss would be £9000 and the balance sheet would become:

Table 22(a)

equity shares	£20000	fixed assets at cost	£20000
less loss	9000	less depreciation	10000
			10000
		cash	1000
net worth	£11000	total assets	£11000

The amount of cash generated during the year is still only £1000. If cash profits, net of depreciation, comprised the data provided for investment appraisal, then depreciation would have to be added back to obtain the cash flows.

The cost of long-term debt

Long-term loans and debentures are normally expected to have a lower cost than equity shares, for their interest payments are normally less uncertain. Moreover, in the event of non-payment, creditors often have legal rights and may even enforce the liquidation of the company. The contractual rate on fixed-interest capital does not measure the cost of debt for such funds may sell at a premium, or discount, on their nominal prices. The correct rate to use is the effective rate of interest which is found by equating the market price of debt to the present value of the interest per year *plus* any final amount due at maturity. That is, to find the cost of debt capital we have to seek the internal rate of return (the effective rate of interest) which equates the value of the annual payments to debenture-holders (the Qs in the formula below) *plus* any final repayment (Q^*) to the current market price of the debentures (I). We have to find k_d in the expression:

$$I = \sum_{1}^{n} \frac{Q_i}{(1 + k_d)^i} + \frac{Q^*}{(1 + k_d)^n}.$$

Interest on debt is a tax-deductable expense to the firm and this must be allowed for when computing the cost of debt funds. In the case of perpetual bonds, for example, k_d is given by: $k_d = Q_t (1 - t)/I$, where Q_t is constant, and t the corporate tax rate.

Risk and the debt market

The debt market may be assumed to allow for risk in the same way as equity-holders, by including a risk premium in the discount rate. This premium should be just sufficient to ensure that creditors are indifferent between a risky transaction and a loan assumed to be default free (government stock, ignoring inflation). The debt market will set its cost of capital for a risky loan so as to give on average the same return as it would receive on safe money. Risky ventures which are successful will return more than this rate and the resulting surplus can be used to absorb the losses of interest and principal from unsuccessful ventures. Thus, provided the risk premium for each venture is set correctly, the supplier of debt funds will expect to earn on average the default free rate of interest. There is, in other words, a divergence between the promised return from a loan and the return expected, on average, by creditors. The cost of capital for debt which we derived above is in fact the promised return required on funds by the debt market.

It has been argued that as creditors expect to receive, on average, the expected rate, this is therefore the cost of capital the firm should plan to pay. However, the general view in the literature is that this rate should normally not be used as the cost of debt because the promised rate on debt will have to be paid provided that the firm is a going concern and will not default if any specific project fails. In the long run we would expect that the promised rates required by the market would tend towards the expected rate. However, given the dynamics of the economy and the poor information available to debt holders, it would be reasonable to assume that there will normally be some divergence between promised and expected rates. For a more detailed treatment of the cost of capital under uncertainty, see Mumey (1969, chs. 1–5) who discusses other definitions of the cost of capital.

The cost of preference shares

In this book, preference shares will be treated simply as a special type of debt. This may seem strange as, strictly, preference dividends are allotments of profit to the firm's owners, who may not have any legal guarantee of receiving their dividends. However, the characteristics of preference shares are sufficiently similar to debt to allow them to be treated as such without any serious distortion. The nominal dividends on preference shares are known and there is a fair certainty of them being paid. If they are not, then preference shareholders may have similar rights to debenture-holders. Normally preference shareholders have no voting rights and are not expected to bear risk to the same degree as ordinary equity-holders. As preference shares are normally rather more risky than debt their cost of capital may be somewhat higher.

One difference between debt and preference shares is that payments to preference shareholders are not tax-deductible by the company. Thus calculations of the cost of capital of preference shares does not involve any adjustment for tax effects, whereas these effects are netted off in deriving the cost of debt.

The cost of short-term credit

This section has concentrated on the cost of long-term debt. This does not mean that short-term credit has no cost. The cost of a bank overdraft is normally the interest payable on it. Other short-term credit may have an imputed cost. Failure to take advantage of discounts for quick payment implies that the return from using funds in other ways exceeds the savings from such payments.

The cost of capital under capital rationing

All the above has been phrased in terms of external opportunity cost (that is, external to the company). Thus the cost of retained earnings was taken to be the dividends foregone by shareholders due to retention. However, under capital rationing, where funds are scarce, the use of capital may have an internal opportunity cost, reflecting alternative investments foregone. We shall return to this subject later (chapter 10).

7 The Cost of Combinations of Debt and Equity

This chapter discusses models which help to define and measure costs of capital where the firm is free to use a mixture of debt and equity. We will firstly consider the cut-off rate that should be used in investment appraisal where a firm uses a constant mix of debt and equity. Then, the situation where the firm can vary its leverage (the proportion of debt to equity in its financial structure) will be examined. No authoritative conclusions for these latter circumstances have yet emerged. There is disagreement about the effect of changes in leverage on the value of a firm. All these issues are taken up after the next section which introduces and describes some of the effects on equity values which the literature suggests result from changes in the debt/equity ratio.

Financial versus business uncertainty

So far in this book we have assumed that the cash flows in our models are either certain or subject to uncertainty about such general factors as economic and political trends, the degree of future technical change, and such specific factors as expected conditions in the markets for the firm's product. Such uncertainties are normally subsumed under the title of *business uncertainty*. The use of debt financing may bring with it additional risks to shareholders, which are normally categorized as *financial uncertainty*. The introduction of debt places onto already risky profits a fixed and prior charge, which often is contractually guaranteed. The need to meet fixed interest payments out of the firm's uncertain cash flows from operating may increase the variability of the residual earnings accruing to stock holders.

Moreover, if such interest is not paid, creditors may be able to force the firm's liquidation, thereby exposing shareholders to a potential loss of their whole stake in the firm owing to short-run liquidity problems. In addition, the use of debt sometimes brings with it restrictions on management's freedom; a debt agreement may limit the directors' ability to declare dividends.

Against this, some argue that the use of debt will increase the average return that shareholders can expect from the firm. The return required by the suppliers of debt finance is normally less than that expected by equity-investors owing to the lower risk normally borne by the suppliers of debt funds. Abstracting from financial uncertainty, existing shareholders should therefore obtain greater returns if a project is financed by debt rather than by relatively high-cost equity. For example, if the cost of debt is 8 per cent per annum and that of equity 10 per cent, shareholders gain the 2 per cent difference between these two rates if debt rather than equity is used to finance a given project.

The cost of capital when the debt and equity mix is unaltered

The financial uncertainty felt by equity-holders should be unchanged if additional amounts of debt and equity are issued in their existing proportions. In this situation our task is merely to find the cost of a mixture of funds of constant proportions.

To help the analysis, we will hold constant all other factors affecting the cost of capital by assuming that the firm, after meeting debt charges, pays out all its net operating cash flows, and that the earnings from any potential project are of the same risk quality as all the firm's other projects. Finally, so that we can use the perpetuity formula introduced earlier, we will assume that the earnings from any project are expected to be constant into perpetuity. In these circumstances we can, following Solomon (1963, chs. 7–9), distinguish three possible definitions of the cut-off rate for project appraisal. The first is the cost of debt which we derived in the preceding chapter (see page 128). The cost of debt when considered in isolation is given by the formula:

$$k_d = \frac{Q}{I}, \qquad\qquad 1$$

where k_d is the debt cost of capital, Q is the monetary amount of the fixed annual debt interest and I the market value of debt. Similarly, the preceding chapter indicated that using the earnings valuation model the equity cost of capital considered in isolation was given by k_e in the formula below:

$$k_e = \frac{E}{V_e}, \qquad\qquad 2$$

where E represents the net earnings per year going to equity which we are assuming are all paid out as dividends, and V_e the market value of the firm's equity.

Neither of these rates can be used directly to discount a project's total annual cash flows. The debt cost of capital does not allow for the higher cost of equity and the equity rate ignores the advantages, if any, of using debt.

Common sense suggests that a weighted average of the two rates should be used to discount a project's total cash flows. This weighted average, or overall cost of capital can be expressed as:

$$k_0 = k_d \frac{I}{V_0} + k_e \frac{V_e}{V_0}. \qquad\qquad 3$$

The average cost of capital is represented by k_0 and the equity and debt costs are respectively weighted by the proportion that debt (I) and equity (V_e) bear to the firm's total market value, which is represented, as usual, by V_0. This latter is merely the sum of the market values of debt and equity; that is,

$$V_0 = I + V_e.$$

A simple numerical example should help to clarify the concept. Should a firm accept a project which returns £15 per year for an outlay of £100 if it is to be financed, following the firm's usual policy, by equal amounts of equity and debt? Assuming that the costs of the equity and debt are respectively 8 per cent and 4 per cent, the weighted average cost of capital in this situation is given by:

$$k_0 = 0 \cdot 08 \times \frac{50}{100} + 0 \cdot 04 \times \frac{50}{100} = 6 \text{ per cent.}$$

The net present-value decision rule would recommend acceptance, for the project has a net present value of £150 when discounted at the firm's average cost of capital of 6 per cent. Using k_0 as the project appraisal cut-off rate will ensure that a project will be undertaken only if its acceptance increases or leaves unchanged the value of the firm's existing equity.

This can be seen by considering the dividends received by shareholders if our project is accepted. The project generates £15 per year prior to meeting the return required by creditors. This charge amounts to £2 a year (4 per cent of £50) and, therefore, shareholders receive net earnings of £13 per year. But, given our assumptions, the market value of the firm's shares should rise following the project's acceptance, provided that it returned anything over the minimum required by new equity-holders. This required return is £4 per year (8 per cent of £50) and thus the project generates a £9 surplus over the cash flows required by the new equity-holders. This represents a bonus for shareholders. The exact distribution of this bonus between new and old equity-holders will depend on the issue price of the new shares. This reasoning suggests that in the conditions being considered, any project having a net present value, when evaluating at the average cost of capital, should be accepted.

We could alternatively evaluate the project by appraising directly the net cash flows it makes available to equity-holders. Here, the opportunity should be accepted if, and only if, the equity cash flows it generates have a non-negative net present value when discounted at the equity cost of capital. This decision rule can be expressed using the internal rate of return model as: accept, if, and only if, the annual cash flows net of debt charges going to shareholders yield an internal rate of return on the equity investment in the project greater than or equal to the cost of equity. This can be expressed in symbols as, accept if:

$$(\bar{Y} - k_d I)/V_e \geqslant k_e. \qquad\qquad 4$$

The new symbol $\bar{Y}$ stands for the total yearly earnings from the project. The numerator of the expression on the left is the annual net equity cash flows, and the denominator, the amount of the project's outlay provided by equity. Plugging in the numbers from our example gives:

$$(£15 - £50 \times 0\cdot04)/£50 \geqslant 0\cdot08.$$

This yields: 26 per cent $>$ 8 per cent, and signifies project acceptance.

The costs of capital derived above have to be adjusted to allow for the tax advantages of debt (see Solomon, 1963, especially pp. 114–17). These accrue because corporation tax is levied on earnings after deducting debt interest (that is, on $\bar{Y} - k_d I$). The tax savings from debt going to equity-holders equal the debt charges multiplied by the firm's tax rate.

Where taxes are levied on profits net of debt interest, the total earnings going to stockholders are given by the formula:

$$(\bar{Y} - k_d I)(1 - t),\qquad\qquad 5$$

where t represents the marginal rate of corporate tax. Multiplying out this expression gives:

$$\bar{Y} - \bar{Y}t - k_d I + t k_d I.\qquad\qquad 6$$

This says, in a rather complex way, that the dividends received by equity-holders from the firm are equivalent to its total earnings net of corporation tax ($\bar{Y} - \bar{Y}t$) *less* the payments to debt holders ($k_d I$) *plus* the tax saving on the latter ($t k_d I$). Thus the equity cost of capital allowing for the tax saving from debt becomes:

$$k_e = \frac{(\bar{Y} - k_d I)(1 - t)}{V_e},\qquad\qquad 7$$

and this rate should be used in computing the after tax weighted average cost of capital, which becomes:

$$k_0^t = \frac{(\bar{Y} - k_d I)(1 - t)}{V_e}\frac{V_e}{V_0} + k_d \frac{I}{V_0}.\qquad\qquad 8$$

As these after-tax-cost-of-capital formulae are rather cumbersome, and as their use, in general, makes no difference of principle, most of the discussion in this book will ignore corporation tax.

Returning to our major theme, using the firm's existing weighted average cost of capital as the cut-off rate for project appraisal has the advantage of simplicity, but the assumptions which underlie the model should not be forgotten. For example, using the existing weighted average assumes that the acceptance of any project does not change the general riskiness of the firm. Adjustments will have to be made to our formula where this is not so. Further, a specific project may sometimes enable the firm to obtain cheaper finance and the discount factor used for the project should reflect the cost of these cheaper funds. The weighted average cost of capital, at least as presented here, cannot fulfil this role.

Further, in our formulae for the overall cost of capital, the market values of debt and equity are used as weights on the assumption that they directly relate to our assumed objective of maximizing the market value of equity. The use of book values as weights would be inconsistent with the formulas we used in chapter 6 to derive the individual costs of capital of debt and equity. Using the balance-sheet value of equity as a weight may considerably distort the importance of equity in a firm's financial structure if the market value of equity deviates significantly from its balance-sheet value.

However, the market's estimate of financial risk may be based on a study of balance-sheet values and the average cost of capital generated by our model may not reflect the return the market would expect from the company if these values differ substantially from market values. The mix of funds issued by the firm may be constant in terms of market values but may seem to represent increased leverage if book values alone are considered. Another difficulty with our formula is that market values may well fluctuate considerably from day to day. This can be partially overcome by using some average of market values over time in our formula.

Finally, the weighted average cost of capital will give correct advice only when the firm keeps approximately constant the proportions of debt and equity it issues. Changes in these proportions may mean that the financial risk of the business as perceived by the market alters, and this may cause changes in the cost of funds to the firms. The definition and measurement of costs of capital in the face of changes in financing mix is the subject of both the remainder of this chapter and chapter 8.

The cost of capital where the mix between debt and equity alters

Alterations in capital structure may cause changes in the cost of funds to a firm. The cost of debt may rise as the proportion of debt in a firm's capital structure is increased. The risks of not being paid the required interest or not having capital repaid may become substantial, at least, when the debt proportion reaches high levels. Similarly, as already explained, we would expect the cost of equity to rise with leverage owing to increased financial uncertainty. However, although the literature is unanimous about the existence of financial uncertainty, there is little agreement about its exact effect on the rate of return required by equity-holders.

One view is that as the proportion of debt in a firm's financial structure is increased, the cost of equity will always rise so as just to offset any advantages flowing from the lower cost of debt funds relative to equity. This implies that a firm's average cost of capital will remain constant whatever its degree of leverage.

The simplest version of the opposing view, which is normally labelled the 'traditional view' is that as leverage is increased from a low level, financial uncertainty is at first felt to be unimportant and causes little or no change in the costs to the firm of equity or debt. Thus, it is argued that shareholders reap the full advantage of the relatively low cost of debt when only a little leverage is used. However, supporters of the traditional view argue that the financial uncertainty felt by equity-holders will rise with leverage if the proportion of debt used by the firm is increased above a certain level. They therefore expect the cost of equity also to increase with leverage. They hypothesize that if the leverage process is continued, this rise in the cost of equity will eventually be such as to offset exactly any advantage flowing from debt. It is argued that both debt and equity costs may rise very substantially reflecting the riskiness of high leverage if yet more debt is raised after this point (or range) is reached. With this view, the value of a firm and, therefore, its average cost of capital will be affected by the amount of debt in its financial structure.

This is really a debate about valuation; one school suggests that the total value of the firm is unaffected by leverage, and the

other predicts that the debt and equity mix used by the firm can
affect its value. No one has yet succeeded in refuting the predictions of either model, at least to the satisfaction of that
model's supporters. All that can be done in this book is to present
the various arguments and seek to explain the issues involved.

The 'traditional view'

There is, in fact, no such thing as the traditional view and what is
described in this section is a 'straw man' serving to bring out the
essential points of most variants of the theory.[1] To simplify the
analysis, we shall assume that an entirely equity-financed
company, which pays out all its constant net cash flows as dividends, is gradually swopping equity for debt. We will assume that
this process is carried out by costlessly withdrawing shares and
replacing them by an equivalent amount of debt. This may be
impractical (and in the United Kingdom is illegal without permission of the Court) but allows us to hold constant all other
factors influencing the firm's value, such as the size of its dividend
stream and business risk. We have also abstracted from the
dividend decision by assuming a payout ratio of 100 per cent,
and will, for the time being, assume a taxless world.

Assume that the company starts the swopping process with
10000 shares, each worth £1, and that the firm earns £1000 per
year, all of which it distributes to shareholders. Its equity cost of
capital is thus 10 per cent when there is no debt in its financial
structure.

Now let 2000 units of stock be replaced by an equivalent
amount of 5 per cent debt. The annual income going to equity-
holders falls to £900 {£1000 − (5 per cent of £2000)}. These
stockholders who remain in the company after the exchange share
between them an extra £100 – the difference between the £200
the company previously paid on the withdrawn stock and the
£100 return required by the substitute debt. If no financial uncertainty is felt by equity-holders at this level of leverage, the

1. Probably the best presentation of this view of leverage is Schwartz (1959);
see also Robichek and Myers (1965, Ch. 3). The early part of the latter
book covers in a more rigorous way the same material as in this and the next
two chapters.

total value of the firm's equity is £9000, for the dividends received by the remaining shareholders will still be capitalized at 10 per cent. Using £2000 worth of debt has increased the total value of the company to £11000. In this situation, the firm's weighted average cost of capital must decline from its original 10 per cent level, for the firm's equity cost is constant and lower-cost debt is being used to replace relatively expensive equity. The gain to those shareholders who did not have their shares withdrawn is found by calculating the value of the company's shares after the transaction; the shares, under our assumptions, increase in value from £1.00 to £1.125 each.

Financial uncertainty will sooner or later cause the cost of equity to rise if the swopping process is continued. But the traditional view is that this rise will not immediately be sufficient entirely to offset the gains flowing from using extra debt and, thus, the value of the company will continue to rise with leverage. As an illustration, assume both that our company continues to exchange equity for debt until it has £5000 of debt in its financial structure, and that with this debt/equity ratio perceived financial uncertainty causes the equity capitalization rate to rise to 12 per cent. In this situation, the annual income to shareholders is £750 (£1000 − 5 per cent of £5000). The value of the company's remaining equity is found to be £6250 and the total value of its debt and equity is £11250. Thus, leverage can increase the total value of the firm even though the cost of equity rises with leverage. In our example, increasing debt by £3000 causes the price of the remaining shares to rise to £1.25 per share. This implies that the cost of extra debt, including its effect on the equity cost, is still lower than the cost of equity. The overall cost of capital must therefore still be declining with leverage. Calculations show that our firm's average cost of capital is approximately 9 per cent with £5000 of debt in its capital structure.

If the swopping process is continued, the next stage, according to the traditional view, is that where the cost of equity rises so as to offset exactly any gain from using debt. This will mean that the company's total value will be stable in the face of increasing leverage. As an example, assume that £11250 is the maximum value our company could obtain via increased leverage and that a debt level of £6000 lies within the region where extra debt makes no difference to this value. The firm's equity cost with this level of debt would be approximately 13·34 per cent and would exactly offset any gains from using the last increment of debt (that is, the increased cost of equity owing to employing the extra increment of debt (1·34 per cent × £5250) would be equal to the gains from this increment of debt. This is found by taking the difference between the cost of the marginal increment of equity withdrawn and the cost of the substitute debt ((12·0 per cent–5 per cent) × £1000).)

Traditionalists view further increases in debt which take the firm outside its region of optimal leverage as causing the cost of both debt and equity to rise sharply. Such rises would cause the total value of our firm to decline. Assume that our firm has debt to the value of £7000 in its financial structure and this causes the debt cost to rise to 6 per cent and the equity cost to 16 per cent. The value of the firm's equity would fall to £3625 ({£1000 − 6 per cent of £7000}, capitalized using the 16 per cent cost), and the company's overall value would fall to £10625.

The traditional view of the effects of increasing the debt/equity ratio are summarized in the diagrams below. In Figure 17(a) the costs of debt and equity are graphed against increased leverage. Figure 17(b) illustrates the effect of leverage on the overall value of the company. Some traditionalists would argue that the

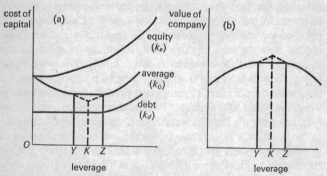

Fig. 17 The traditional view of leverage: (a) Cost of capital and leverage, (b) the value of the company and leverage

average cost of capital is minimized not over a region of leverage ($Y - Z$ in the diagrams) but rather at a specific point (as shown by K). This view would produce a 'U' shaped average cost of capital curve, as shown in the diagrams by the dotted line.

The traditionalists' range (or point) of optimal leverage may differ between industries and between firms in the same industry. This is because the variability of net equity cash flows after meeting debt charges depends, in part, on the business uncertainty associated with the firm's operating cash flows. This will depend on both the characteristics of the specific firm and the industry in which it operates. Firms and industries whose business uncertainty is regarded as relatively low should be able to use greater degrees of leverage than those operating in areas of higher risk. The use of debt by firms and industries in the former category is less likely to cause shareholders to perceive increased financial uncertainty because a given level of debt will have a smaller effect on the variability of their cash flows than on those of relatively more risky firms and industries. Similarly, the use of debt is less likely to lead to the insolvency in the former firms and industries.

The alternative view: the Modigliani and Miller hypothesis
Introduction

A contrary argument has been presented by Professors Modigliani and Miller.[2] They suggest that in a taxless world the value of a company is independent of its financial structure. They start from the basic view that in economic equilibrium, two identical goods should sell for the same price. They then argue that the discounted market value of a stream of cash flows should depend after discounting on only the size of the stream and the estimated business uncertainty attached to it. Thus, two series of cash flows which are identical in size and business uncertainty should sell for the same price. Modigliani and Miller argue that the distribution

2. Their argument was first presented in Modigliani and Miller (1958) and further elaborated in Modigliani and Miller (1963) and Miller and Modigliani (1966). Most of the major papers contributing to the controversy are contained in Archer and D'Ambrosio (1967) – see especially the two papers by Durand (1952) and (1959), and Modigliani and Miller's reply to the latter, Modigliani and Miller (1959).

of cash flows between debt and equity should not affect the total value of a company. In their view, using differing mixtures of debt and equity merely changes the distribution as between debt and equity of the business uncertainty associated with the firm.

If two businesses, identical in all but their use of debt, are to sell at the same prices, their average costs of capital must be identical at all levels of leverage. This is because the value of the companies will be the same only if their identical total earnings are capitalized using the same weighted average cost of capital. That the weighted average cost of capital is to remain constant in the face of leverage changes implies that any advantages in using relatively low-cost debt must be completely offset by increases in the cost of equity. Modigliani and Miller deny the existence of a profitable area of leverage, such as that shown in Figure 17. They argue that companies engaging in leverage immediately move to the $Y - Z$ region of this diagram and never move out of it.

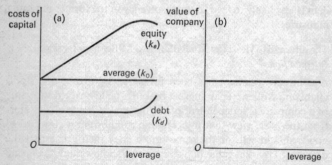

Fig. 18 M. and M.'s view of leverage: (a) Cost of capital and leverage, (b) value of the company and leverage

Figure 18 highlights the differences between Modigliani and Miller's theory and the traditional view. As Modigliani and Miller believe that, abstracting from the effects of tax, the value of a company is invariant with leverage, the value of the firm when graphed against leverage in 18(b) is shown as a straight line, as is the overall cost of capital in 18(a). This implies that the cost of equity capital must rise as shown in 18(a), so as to always just offset any advantages flowing from the use of debt funds. The equity cost of capital will increase at a constant rate with leverage, provided that the cost of debt does not rise with leverage. If debt charges do increase as high levels of leverage are reached, the cost of equity will increase less rapidly because there will be less gains from debt to offset in this situation.

In Modigliani and Miller's view no capital structure is optimal; any degree of leverage is as good as any other. Modigliani and Miller's special contribution is to suggest a market mechanism which ensures that their view is correct, given certain assumptions and abstracting from the effects of taxation. Before examining this contribution in some detail, it is useful to examine the implications of the two opposing views of the effects of leverage for project appraisal.

Implications for the cost of capital to be used in project appraisal

The firm's constant weighted average cost of capital can be used as the discount factor if we accept Modigliani and Miller's argument and assumptions and hold constant all other factors acting on the firm's value. This rate should, *ceteris paribus*, be easier to forecast than the equity cost of capital which, according to Modigliani and Miller, will change with alterations in financial structure.

On the other hand, if we adhere to the traditional view, there is no escaping a difficult forecasting job for the firm's overall cost of capital will be sensitive to changes in the debt/equity ratio. How such forecasts are to be made is not clear. This is especially so, as complex and time-consuming empirical studies have failed to produce any definitive evidence about the effect of leverage on costs of capital. Such studies are made especially difficult as the traditional theory does not presently offer any theoretical basis for quantifying the effects of leverage on the cost of capital. It merely gives qualitative predictions about the shape of the weighted average cost of capital curve. The following sections analyse in some depth the hypothesis that the value of the firm is invariant with leverage.

Modigliani and Miller revisited

Modigliani and Miller do not deny that there may be short-term advantages accruing from the use of debt, for example, where the debt market underestimates the rate of price change. However they show that given their assumptions, no long-term advantages flow to equity-holders from the relatively low cost of debt as compared with that of equity. They do this by demonstrating that in equilibrium two companies which are identical except for their financial structure will have the same total value (see Modigliani and Miller, 1958).

The necessary assumptions

It is essential to examine the assumptions of Modigliani and Miller's model, for much of the academic debate has concerned the 'real-life' validity of this model.

Modigliani and Miller base their valuation model for shares on earnings rather than on dividends but, as will be explained in chapter 9, this does not matter because the model can be recast in terms of dividends without affecting the results.

Moreover, for ease of presentation, they assume that a firm's average earnings are expected to be constant from year to year and to continue to infinity. This assumption allows them to use simple perpetuity formulae in their presentation. Again this does not matter; a growth trend in earnings (or dividends) can be introduced into their model without upsetting the results.

The existence of uncertainty means that the definition of the yearly earnings used by Modigliani and Miller is quite complex for they attempt to treat uncertainty explicitly. In this situation, the actual earnings obtained by the firm in any one year will be any one of several possible earnings figures, and each such figure for any year may be combined with any one of several possible outcomes for each of every other year. Thus with uncertainty, a given set of assets may be expected to yield any one of several income streams over time. Each possible stream will generate an average income per year which may be different from that associated with all the other possible cash flow streams expected to flow from the given set of assets. Modigliani and Miller assume that a probability of attainment can be assigned to each possible set of cash flows and therefore also to the average annual income for each stream. This probability of obtaining a stream's average yearly earnings reflects the joint likelihood of the occurrence of each and every one of the yearly cash flows making up that stream.

These concepts are illustrated in Figure 19, where all the possible average yearly incomes, serving to summarize all the potential cash flow streams that a given set of assets can yield, are plotted on the horizontal axis. The probability assigned to each

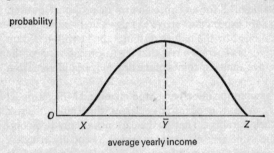

Fig. 19 Probability distribution of average annual earnings from a specific set of assets

average annual cash flow is plotted vertically. These probabilities are expressed as decimals, and must add up to unity, for by definition only one average annual income will actually appear. The curve connecting the average incomes and their probabilities is continuous, for we are assuming that the set of assets concerned can yield an infinite number of cash-flow streams. Further, it is assumed that the cash-flow streams from the assets are such as to yield only average yearly incomes falling within some range, such as that shown by OX to OZ on the diagram's horizontal axis.

Modigliani and Miller assume that the earnings figure used in the investors' valuation model for any firm is the average (mean value of the probability distribution) of all the possible average incomes per year that may be generated by the firm's assets (that is $\bar{Y}$ in the diagram). The earnings figure used by investors for valuing any set of assets (or any specific firm) is the average of all the yearly average incomes associated with all the possible cash-flow streams that might be generated by the assets under consideration. This former mean value is found by weighting each of the possible average incomes by its probability of attainment and summing these averages for all cash-flow streams. This mean value of all the possible average incomes per year will be represented by $\bar{Y}$ in all the succeeding formulae. It will stand for the investors' estimate of the firm's or project's constant yearly earnings. Modigliani and Miller also assume that all investors agreed about the value of $\bar{Y}$ for any specific firm or project. However, shareholders are expected to arrive at this value by making estimates which must, by the nature of things, be heavily based on past earnings data. There is a risk that the true mean value of the possible average annual incomes of the firm may be different from its estimated value ($\bar{Y}$).

The next assumption underlying Modigliani and Miller's model is that firms can be grouped into risk classes which reflect the risk quality of their earnings. That is, the earnings of any two companies in the same risk class are regarded as equally risky. A pound of the earnings of any firm within a specific risk class is assumed to be a perfect substitute for a pound of earnings from any other company in this risk class. Modigliani and Miller assume that the average earnings of firms in the same risk class are perfectly correlated and that their earnings will differ only because of differences in the size of firms. This assumption allows Modigliani and Miller to argue that all such firms will be expected by the market to yield the same overall return (k_0) per pound of funds; that is, all firms in the same risk class will have the same weighted average cost of funds, abstracting from the possible effect of leverage.

Modigliani and Miller prove their theory using a capital market where there are no impediments to trading; this may be taken to imply that all investors behave rationally[3] and have

3. In seeking to achieve our assumed objective of maximum net present worth. Recent studies using mathematical models of a type beyond the level of this book have shown that this set of assumptions can be substantially reduced; see, for example Stiglitz (1974). Modigliani and Miller's original assumptions are retained here because it is believed that this eases the understanding of their theory.

equal costless access to the capital market. This latter assumption ensures that individuals and firms can both borrow and lend at identical rates for the same purpose. Finally, it is initially assumed that no corporation taxes exist. Modigliani and Miller defend the use of restrictive assumptions of this type as being necessary to allow us to come to grips with the problem of leverage, but believe that the existing empirical evidence shows that relaxing these assumptions does not confound their theory.

The propositions

Modigliani and Miller prove three propositions using these assumptions.

1 The total market value of a company is independent of the amount of debt in its financial structure

The acceptance of proposition 1 implies two corollary hypotheses about the behaviour of a firm's overall weighted average cost of capital (k_0) in the face of changing leverage. The first of these is that the company's overall cost of capital will be unaffected by changes in its debt/equity ratio. In a situation where a firm's earnings are constant over time, this cost is given by dividing the firm's annual earnings ($\bar{Y}$) by its total market value (V_0). Only if its two constituent elements are unaffected by leverage will it be unchanged by leverage. In Modigliani and Miller's model, the firm's total annual earnings are held constant by definition and the constancy of market value follows directly from proposition 1, as, therefore, does the invariantness of the firm's overall cost of capital.

The second hypothesis which follows from proposition 1 is that the weighted average cost of capital of a levered firm (k_0) must equal the equity cost of an unlevered company in the same risk class (k_e), irrespective of the degree of leverage used by the firm with debt in its financial structure. The equity cost of an unlevered firm is found by dividing its constant yearly earnings ($\bar{Y}$) by the market value of its equity (V_e), that is:

$$k_e = \bar{Y}/V_e.$$

The overall cost of capital of a company, which is identical with the all-equity firm except that it has some debt in its financial structure, is found by dividing its identical earnings figure ($\bar{Y}$) by the total value of its debt *plus* equity (V_0). If proposition 1 is accepted this latter value must be the same as the total value of the all-equity company, and our second subsidiary hypothesis follows, that is:

$$k_0 = \bar{Y}/V_0 = k_e = \bar{Y}/V_e.$$

It can be shown that if proposition 1 is accepted, this equivalence of the overall cost of capital of a levered company with the equity cost of an all-equity company is maintained even though the firms have different sized annual earnings, provided that they are in the same risk class.[4]

2 As leverage increases, the equity cost of capital of a levered corporation (k_l) will always rise just sufficiently to offset advantages flowing from the lower cost of debt relative to equity.

The equity cost of a levered firm (k_l) is given by dividing the firm's total yearly cash flows ($\bar{Y}$) net of debt charges (represented by $k_d I$, where I equals the total value of the firm's debt and k_d the effective rate of interest) by the market value of the firm's equity (V_e). This can be expressed symbolically as:

$$k_l = (\bar{Y} - k_d I)/V_e. \qquad\qquad 9$$

Accepting proposition 1 we can use this definition to prove the second proposition. Proposition 1 says that the combined value of the debt and equity of a levered firm must have the same value as an otherwise identical all-equity company. This can be alternatively stated as asserting that the identical annual income of the two companies can be derived by multiplying the market value of the levered firm by the equity cost of capital of the unlevered

4. Assume that, the size of the income stream of an unlevered company differs from that of a levered firm in the same risk class by a given factor α, which is larger than 1. It follows from proposition 1 that the former's value will differ from the latter's by the same factor, that is, if the total value of the levered company is V_0 then the value of the all-equity firm will be $V_0\alpha$. This means that the equity cost of the unlevered firm is given by: $\alpha \bar{Y}/\alpha V_0$ which, by cancellation, simplifies to $\bar{Y}/V_0$ which is the formula for the overall cost of the levered firm.

firm. That is, the income of both firms ($\bar{Y}$) can be obtained by multiplying the equity and debt values (V_e and I) of the levered company by the unlevered company's equity cost (k_e), that is,

$$\bar{Y} = (V_e + I)k_e. \qquad \qquad \textbf{10}$$

If this expression for the firm's annual income is substituted into our earlier formula for the equity cost of capital of the levered firm (expression **9**), we get:

$$k_l = (k_e\{V_e + I\} - k_d I)/V_e. \qquad \qquad \textbf{11}$$

Expression **11** simplifies to:[5]

$$k_l = k_e + (k_e - k_d)I/V_e. \qquad \qquad \textbf{12}$$

This final expression for the levered company's equity cost of capital states that this cost is equal to the equity cost of the all-equity company plus a premium related directly to the proportion of debt used by the company. At any level of leverage this premium will be just sufficient to absorb any benefits from using relatively low-cost debt. Such gains are equal to the difference between the all-equity cost of capital and the cost of debt weighted by the proportion of debt in the company's financial structure, that is,

$$(k_e - k_d)I/V_e.$$

These gains are therefore identical to the premium which will be required by equity-holders in a levered company if proposition 1 is accepted.

3 A firm which wishes to maximize its equity-holders' wealth should use as its cut-off rate for project appraisal the unlevered cost of equity for its risk class (k_e) or, more practically, its own existing weighted average cost of capital.

5. Multiplying out the first element on the right hand side of the expression, $k_e(V_e + I)/V_e$, and substituting this into expression **11** gives:

$$\frac{k_e V_e}{V_e} + \frac{k_e I}{V_e} - \frac{k_d I}{V_e}.$$

The V_e terms in first element disappear, and collecting together all the terms containing I gives the expression we want, that is:

$$k_e + (k_e - d)I/V_e.$$

The third proposition follows directly from the other two, both of which imply that the cost of equity increases as more debt is raised. Using either of the above costs of capital takes this into account, whereas the effects of financial uncertainty are not allowed for by the cost of debt and are not reflected correctly by the cost of equity which reigned prior to any change in financial structure.

This proposition does not mean that the weighted average cost of capital which reigns at any specific time can be used unthinkingly as the cut-off rate. Rather it asserts only that the types of funds used for any project are irrelevant to its acceptance. In their analysis Modigliani and Miller hold constant all other factors which may affect this cost, such as expected changes in interest rates and in the cost of unlevered equity streams. Moreover there may be reasons which are not incorporated in Modigliani and Miller's model for preferring specific types of finance; for example management might prefer equity finance because they may have to accept some restrictions on their freedom of action before they can use debt funds.

As propositions 2 and 3, which are the interesting ones for project analysts, hinge crucially on the first one, we will now investigate a simple proof of that first hypothesis.

A simple proof of proposition 1

Consider two firms E and L, both in the same risk class, and with expected earnings of £1000 per year. Firm E is financed entirely with equity and has a value of £10000 (V_e), and therefore an equity cost of capital of 10 per cent. Firm L uses debt, having a market value of £4000 and an effective interest rate of 4 per cent. Supporters of the traditional hypothesis might expect firm L to have a greater total value (V_L) than firm E, provided that the former's proportion of debt was regarded as acceptable. Let us assume that the levered firm's total market value is £12000, which implies that the value of its equity is £8000. Modigliani and Miller argue that a market process they call 'arbitrage' will in time act to eradicate this difference in the overall values of the two firms. Equity-holders in firm L, the over-valued company, would sell their shares, borrowing simultaneously so that their personal investment portfolio had the same leverage as company L ($4000/8000 = \frac{1}{2}$), and invest their funds in the unlevered corporation and show a gain.

For example, a shareholder who held 25 per cent of the stock of firm L could sell his shares for £2000, and by borrowing £1000 at 4 per cent give his own portfolio the same leverage as that of company L. With these funds he could buy £3000 worth of shares in firm E and his total yearly income after paying interest charges of £40 would be £260. With his original holding in company L he obtained a net annual income of £210; that is, one quarter of £840 (£1000 less debt charges of £160). He thus gains £50 by indulging in 'arbitrage'. Moreover as his interest payments are the same, Modigliani and Miller argue that the risk he bears is, in some sense, unaltered.

The mechanics of the 'arbitrage' process for our example are shown in the table below.

Table 23 The 'arbitrage' process

Original holding in L		New holding in E	
value of shares	£2000	£3000	
gross annual income	250 (£1000/4)	300	
debt charges	40 (4% of £4000/4)	40 (4% of £1000)	
net income	£ 210	260	
		less net income from L	−210
		'gain from arbitrage'	£ 50

The new holding in E is financed by:	
selling original holding holding in L	£2000
borrowing in same proportions as L (4/8)	£1000
buying shares in E	£3000

The sale of shares in the levered company associated with the 'arbitrage' process will depress the value of these shares, and thus the total value of the two companies will be equated, if the process continues long enough. It can be shown that the same process would work to increase the total value of a debt-financed company if this were undervalued by the market as compared with an identical but all-equity company (see Fama and Miller, 1972, ch. 4). In either case, the 'arbitrage' process will continue until no further gains can be made – that is until the total values of the levered and unlevered companies are identical. Thus the 'arbitrage' process ensures that the total value of levered and unlevered firms in the same risk class will only differ by a factor reflecting the differing size of their cash flow streams. Modigliani and Miller's proposition 1 must hold after the 'arbitrage' process has been carried through to its conclusion. 'Arbitrage' also guarantees that the overall cost of capital of the levered firm will be the same as the equity cost of the unlevered company. For example, in our case both E and L have the same total annual earnings $\bar{Y}$, and therefore at the end of the 'arbitrage' process their values will be equal, that is, $(V_L = V_E)$, and thus k_0 must equal k_e for otherwise $\dfrac{\bar{Y}}{V_e}$ will not equal $\dfrac{\bar{Y}}{V_L}$.

Thus the 'arbitrage' process provides a mechanism that ensures that Modigliani and Miller's proposition 1, and therefore their other propositions, will be true in equilibrium, given their assumptions. This view is contrary to that held by the 'traditionalists' who believe that judicious leverage may benefit equity-holders.

The next chapter reviews this academic debate and briefly surveys the contribution that empirical research has made towards resolving the argument.

8 Optimal Capital Structure – The Debate

The real world difficulties of the Modigliani and Miller propositions

Two competing theories should be judged on the correctness of their predictions for the real world. Unfortunately the evidence currently available has not generated a clear refutation of the predictions of either leverage theory. Most of the academic attacks on Modigliani and Miller's propositions have therefore been directed towards showing that their assumptions are so far removed from the 'real world' that their theory cannot yield useful predictions (see, for example, Durand, 1959). This is a task which can be successfully prosecuted only by the production of empirical evidence refuting Modigliani and Miller's theories. However, a review of the criticisms that have been levelled against Modigliani and Miller's assumptions is useful, for it highlights the points which must be considered in further research and in the practical business of deciding the make-up of a firm's financial structure.

The introduction of taxes

One criticism of Modigliani and Miller is that their simple model postulated a tax-free world. However, Modigliani and Miller have shown that in their framework, the existence of taxes on corporate earnings means that the weighted average cost of capital will no longer be invariant with leverage, but will decline continuously as debt is added to a firm's financial structure.[1]

If we accept Modigliani and Miller's conclusions about the effect of leverage in a tax-free world, the only advantage flowing from using debt funds arises because interest is deducted from a company's annual earnings prior to computing its tax liability. The effect of this tax saving on the overall cost of capital of a

1. They dealt with the effects of tax in their first article (Modigliani and Miller, 1958) and altered their views in Modigliani and Miller (1963).

levered firm can best be shown by firstly adapting the Modigliani and Miller model to allow for the effect of corporate income taxes, abstracting from the tax-deductibility of debt.

The value of an all-equity company is given in these circumstances by the formula $V_e = \bar{Y} - t\bar{Y}/k_e$, where t is the marginal rate of corporation tax. This expression simplifies to $V_e = \bar{Y}(1 - t)/k_e$. The value of an identical but levered firm could be written as $V_0 = \bar{Y}(1 - t)/k_0$, and Modigliani and Miller's conclusions for a tax-free world still hold.

We have already seen in the preceding chapter that if interest is tax deductible, a firm using debt will pay less tax than if it were solely equity-based (chapter 7, p. 135). This tax saving will equal the firm's annual debt charges ($k_d I$) multiplied by the tax rate t, that is, $k_d I t$. Thus, the value of a levered corporation can be found by adding the discounted value of the tax savings from debt to the value of an otherwise identical all-equity company ($V_e = \bar{Y}(1 - t)/k_e$). This gives the value of the levered company as:

$$V_0 = \frac{\bar{Y}(1 - t)}{k_e} + \frac{tk_d I}{k_e}. \qquad\qquad 1$$

However, it has been argued (Solomon, 1963, pp. 114–17) that the tax savings on debt are more certain than equity payments, for the former accrue whenever debt charges are paid. Thus such savings might be capitalized not at the equity cost of capital but rather at the same rate as debt payments. This means the value of a levered company is given by:

$$V_0 = \frac{\bar{Y}(1 - t)}{k_e} + \frac{tk_d I}{k_d}, \qquad\qquad 2$$

which, simplified, becomes:

$$V_0 = \frac{\bar{Y}(1 - t)}{k_e} + tI. \qquad\qquad 3$$

The introduction of debt increases the value of the firm to its equity-holders by tI, and its weighted average cost of capital must fall gradually as the proportion of debt in its financial structure is increased. Each extra increment of debt raises the value of the firm, by the increase it causes in the total tax savings going to equity-holders. The overall cost of capital (k_0) must decline reflecting this.

The tax deductibility of debt charges does not necessarily mean that a company should use as much debt as possible in its capital structure for there may be disadvantages flowing from the use of debt funds not taken into account by Modigliani and Miller. These will be considered later.

Market imperfections and personal risk

At the heart of the 'arbitrage' process are the assumptions both that individuals and corporations have the same access to capital markets, and that the risk associated with personal and corporate borrowing is identical. It has been argued that both assumptions are so far removed from the 'real world' as to render impossible the 'arbitrage' process. Further, it has been suggested that engaging in arbitrage is not costless, as assumed by Modigliani and Miller, and that this cost may impede the 'arbitrage' process.

Corporations may have a higher credit standing than individuals because of their greater size and therefore the greater 'perceived' certainty of their ability to pay interest. This may mean that if firms can borrow at lower rates than individuals, the 'arbitrage' process cannot be relied upon to eradicate any differences in the values of firms due to differences in their leverage. Against this, it has been argued by Modigliani and Miller that there is some evidence that the relevant rate of interest for 'arbitrage' is approximately equivalent to the interest rates charged to corporations. This may reflect the fact that when an individual borrows he does not have the protection of limited liability, and his whole personal wealth therefore stands behind the loan. Moreover, it has been suggested that borrowing on personal account is not the only way by which 'arbitrage' can occur. A similar result can be obtained by alterations in the overall leverage of personal investment portfolios.

There are several reasons for believing that because of risk, corporate and personal leverage are not perfect substitutes for the individual. In our example of the 'arbitrage' process, the man who holds £2000 worth of stock in the levered company has the advantage of limited liability. Once he switches to the unlevered company he can still lose his total investment but he will also be liable for his debts. Even though a total loss is unlikely, he may be forced to meet debt charges out of other income or capital if the unlevered firm has a bad year.

There is an additional risk associated with the 'arbitrage' process, for Modigliani and Miller envisage this as being carried out by borrowing on the margin. This involves obtaining funds by pledging as a security the holding which one hopes to buy. The individual may be required to make up the value of this pledge if the holding falls in value. This may place additional risk on the individual who 'arbitrages' because this process involves enlarging his investment portfolio. In the United States, margin borrowing is subject to severe restrictions. It has been argued that these restrictions, together with the personal risks of borrowing, may render the 'arbitrage' process inoperative. But it may be that, as suggested above, changing the leverage of individual investment portfolios serves as an adequate substitute.

Further, only some investors need be active to guarantee Modigliani and Miller's results and not all investors will need to resort to margin borrowing for this purpose. However, opponents of Modigliani and Miller deny that sufficient investors are willing, or able, to indulge in 'arbitrage' to guarantee the real world applicability of Modigliani and Miller's propositions. In England the managers of institutional funds could if they wished 'arbitrage' by changing the leverage within their own portfolios. That they do not seem to do so has been cited as an argument against Modigliani and Miller's view.

It has also been suggested that if there were advantages to be had from 'arbitrage', firms could themselves profitably indulge in this type of operation. For example, if the stock of firms with 50 per cent debt in their financial structures was selling at a premium, companies could increase their market value by altering their financial structure to reflect this level of leverage. There would thus be little opportunity for individuals to profit by 'arbitrage'.

With this view the lowest cost of capital can be obtained by adopting whatever capital structure is fashionable at any time and the cost of capital therefore becomes heavily dependent on the financial structure of firms. Modigliani and Miller answer this by saying that, even assuming away the institutional difficulties of firms altering their funding mix in this way, no one will gain from this practice in the long run. They seem to argue that the premiums attached to any specific capital structure are short-run phenomena, and, therefore, the only investors who would gain from firms altering their debt/equity ratios to attract such premiums are those who sell their shares at the temporary inflated price reigning whilst the market is not in equilibrium. Modigliani and Miller suggest that it would be incorrect for the firm to use the lower overall cost of capital which reigns whilst a premium exists as its project-appraisal cut-off rate. Once the demand for any particular financial structure is satisfied the market will revert to valuing the returns from the firm's projects at the higher long-run cost of capital. If the projects did not yield, at least, this rate, their acceptance would cause the firm's value to fall.

The above paragraph serves to remind us of the long-run equilibrium orientation of the Modigliani and Miller propositions. For example, they probably would not deny that the equity-holder could gain from the use of debt in the short run if the market underestimated the degree of future inflation when subscribing to a fixed interest loan. In these circumstances, the real burden of debt will decrease as prices actually rise and debt will be cheaper than expected in real terms. But within Modigliani and Miller's framework, market forces should work to ensure that in equilibrium everybody, including creditors, will have the same average expectation of future price changes.[2] This is not to deny that firms can exploit what they consider to be errors in the market's long-run expectations about rates of interest and overall costs of capital. Such mistakes by the market can make the use of a specific type of financial structure profitable to shareholders.

Modigliani and Miller's model does not incorporate such possibilities; they argue that speculation against the capital market may not be a legitimate function of a manufacturing

2. This refers only to a type of partial equilibrium because it is not clear that inflation can exist with equilibrium in the money, goods and factor markets.

company. This view does not rob the investor of potential gains, for the individual could, if he wished, speculate about correctness of market expectations by changing the leverage of his own portfolio.

Modigliani and Miller are fully aware that market imperfections and other factors not included in their model could favour the traditional position. However, they are not convinced that such factors affect their predictions. No amount of argument will settle this essentially empirical question. But before reviewing the empirical evidence, we need to look at a theoretical difficulty associated with the Modigliani and Miller model.

Extreme leverage: a theoretical difficulty with the Modigliani and Miller model

This difficulty can be best introduced by means of an example. Assume that an all-equity company is abruptly transformed into one financed purely by debt. In this situation rational debt holders would require, at least, the return obtained by shareholders, for they would bear the same risk as did the equity-holders. Indeed, debt-holders, if they are relatively more concerned about risk (are more risk averse) than the original equity-holders, may require a higher reward for bearing this risk.

This extreme example suggests that the cost of debt is likely to rise if a company engages in what is regarded as excessive leverage. This rising cost of debt would sooner or later cause the firm's overall cost of capital to increase with leverage, even in the unlikely event of the cost of equity not rising. Traditionalists would argue, however, that no firm that wished to maximize its shareholders' wealth would operate in this high debt region for equity financing would be at least as cheap, and raising additional funds using a constant mix of debt and equity would be even cheaper. The traditional view of optimal leverage is that no rational firm ought to increase its leverage beyond the point where its marginal cost of debt, defined to include any consequent changes in equity costs, is equal to its weighted average cost of capital.[3]

3. For a more general conclusion, see Robichek and Myers (1965), pp. 48–9.

Modigliani and Miller seem also to accept that the cost of debt will increase with excessive leverage but still maintain their proposition 1 and hypothesize that a firm's weighted average cost of capital will be constant even with extreme leverage. This will occur with rising debt costs only if equity-holders perceive less financial uncertainty at high levels of leverage. If this is the case the premium over the cost of a pure equity stream that shareholders in a levered firm require to protect themselves from financial uncertainty will grow at a decreasing rate with leverage. If leverage becomes so extreme as to cause the cost of debt to equal or exceed the cost of a pure equity stream, the constancy of the overall cost of capital can be maintained only if the return required by equity-holders actually falls. This seems to imply the illogical position that equity-holders regard their shares as increasing in value as the company becomes more highly levered, even though this subjects them to greater risk. This cannot be so if we assume risk aversion.

Modigliani and Miller are aware of these difficulties, but argue that the whole thing is of little interest, since, in practice, companies do not carry leverage to such extremes. However, to ensure the general applicability of their theory, they argue without elaboration that firms using high degrees of leverage attract risk-seekers (that is, gamblers) who are willing to accept a lower than normal return for bearing a specific degree of risk in return for the prospect of high earnings. Such earnings are possible if a highly-levered firm successfully services its debt.

Again the argument between Modigliani and Miller and the 'traditionalists' is about assumptions; this time about attitudes to risk. Thus, it is essential to see what light the currently available evidence sheds on the debate.

The empirical evidence

The real world 'facts' are by no means conclusive – evidence favourable to one or the other theory has been produced, only to be criticized by supporters of the other view. Some very difficult problems must be solved before any conclusive empirical refutation of either theory can be obtained. This is because the subject of concern is the market valuation of firms and the raw material for any such investigation is the market's estimates of the future prospects of firms. Further, many factors impinge on the market values of firms, such as changes in expectations and the effects of overall economic policy. Both of the theories we want to test are concerned only with the effect of leverage on a firm's value, and therefore hold all such factors constant. Thus historical data must be selected so that all factors affecting the valuations of companies, other than leverage, are held constant. Alternatively, the influences of factors other than leverage must be removed from the raw data.

The difficulties of obtaining empirical evidence

This latter process represents a major difficulty in empirical analysis, for such adjustments to historical data can only be approximate and may therefore bias any answers obtained. However, many of the approximations which can generate bias in empirical work are gradually being recognized and adjustments suggested.

Multiple regression analysis can be used to isolate the effects of each of the factors affecting the value of a firm. However this technique is difficult to use where many of the variables concerned are interdependent and their relationships not well understood. This situation exists where the subject of concern is the market value of firms. For example, a strong relationship has been found between share values, dividends and pay-out rates. However, it is not clear whether dividends are an important factor in share valuation because they are valued in themselves or because they give clues about future earnings.

A more specific problem associated with the testing of Modigliani and Miller's models is that the data have to come from companies in the same risk class. No clear rules for defining risk classes have yet been presented, and our earlier definition of risk classes is not easy to use in practice. Moreover, such a measure may well be misleading if the market, when placing companies into different risk classes, allows for factors (such as liquidity) not covered in our models. Researchers have often opted to use data from narrowly-defined sets of similar businesses. However, there may be insufficient variation in the financial structure of such firms to allow a clear test of either hypothesis.

An almost intractable problem for empirical analysis is that the researcher is forced to use imperfect measures, such as trends in historical data, to represent expected future earnings. Further, he will often have to use accounting data which, however useful it is for other purposes, may produce bias in empirical work.

All these difficulties are gradually being overcome as the methodology of empirical investigation progresses, but they do mean that the results of such work must be treated with caution, and that any findings are almost always subject to, at least, academic debate.

Specific studies

In their first article, Modigliani and Miller (1958) studied American data for forty-three electrical utilities and forty-two oil companies. They used cross-section analysis which involves the comparison at a specific point in time of the values of different companies in the same risk class with differing degrees of leverage. Modigliani and Miller would expect such firms to have the same overall cost of capital. Time-series analysis, which involves comparisons of the same company over time as it alters its financial structure, would probably be more appropriate for the theory but raises many seemingly intractable problems. In comparisons over time, allowance has to be made for more exogenous factors affecting value than where the comparison involves different companies frozen at a specific point of time.

In their study Modigliani and Miller used each firm's historical after-tax rate of return, computed using the company's total market value, as an approximation for the firm's weighted average cost of capital. They sought to ascertain the relationship between the firms' overall costs of capital and their leverage. They found that the average costs of capital of the firms in their sample were approximately identical, irrespective of leverage. This does not sit well with their after-tax predictions, which suggest that a firm's weighted average cost should decline gradually with leverage.

In their study Modigliani and Miller also sought to examine the effect of leverage on the equity cost of capital. They did this by computing the historical rate of return to equity for each firm using market values and comparing this with the degree of leverage used by that firm. The findings supported their view that the equity cost of capital rises with leverage so as to offset the advantage of low-cost debt; the cost of equity was higher for more levered firms. The data even showed signs of the predicted decline in the rate of growth of the cost of equity at high levels of leverage.

It is not surprising that this study has been criticized; it was one of the first attempts to obtain empirical evidence on a highly controversial issue. The data used by Modigliani and Miller have been criticized. First, it has been argued that Modigliani and Miller's sample contained firms in more than one risk class; the characteristics of the firms from the oil industry in their sample differed considerably, both in terms of products manufactured and in marketing areas. Second, it has been suggested that the range of leverage covered in their electrical utility sample was insufficient to allow the traditional curve to emerge (see Weston, 1967).

A different type of criticism came from Barges (1963) who suggested that Modigliani and Miller's use of market values in computing rates of return could produce a bias in favour of their theory. Barges attempted to overcome this difficulty by using book values. He was aware that the use of accounting figures can also produce bias and tried both to adjust for this and to test for bias in his work with data from department stores and the cement industry. He could find no indication that his results were biased by his data. His findings tended to support the traditional view by suggesting that the weighted average cost-of-capital curve was of the traditional 'U' shape.

Both Modigliani and Miller and Barges tried to reduce the contamination of their results by factors other than leverage by using observations from industries where such factors had historically been relatively stable. For example, by using only large electrical utilities Modigliani and Miller were able to ignore the effect of the size of firms on the cost of capital. An alternative approach is to use regression analysis to estimate explicitly the effects of other factors and to adjust for their effects prior to considering leverage. Weston used this approach in his study of the electrical utility industry (1963 and 1967). Prior to investigating the effect of leverage, he estimated and adjusted his data for the effect on the cost of capital of expected growth in earnings. As previously explained, expected growth introduces an additional factor into the valuation equation, e.g. gives the valuation equation the form $V_e = D/(k_e - g)$. Using the non-growth model, $(V_e = D/k_e)$, in statistical analysis ascribes to leverage that part of the value of the company due to growth expectations. For example, the effect of leverage on the overall cost of capital may be obscured if for some reason growth expectations are increasing at the same time as extra leverage is causing the overall cost of capital to rise. In this situation, the resultant rise in g may mask any change in the cost of capital arising from increased leverage.

Forecast future growth in earnings should be measured by the market's expectations that the firm will invest in projects yielding a return above the cost of capital. In his statistical analysis, Weston was, however, forced to use as an approximation the historical growth rate in earnings for his sample over the ten years prior to his study. His results should, therefore, be used with caution for such figures are only imperfect indicators of expected future growth.

Given this, Weston found that when the influence of growth was removed, leverage was negatively correlated with the overall cost of capital; that is, the cost of capital declined as leverage increased. He also found that after removing the effect of growth, the cost of equity did not increase with leverage, at least in the ranges he was studying.

Weston's findings do not necessarily refute Miller and Modigliani's theory, for they forecast a declining overall cost of capital with leverage when corporate taxes are taken into account. Weston found that in his sample a 1 per cent increase in leverage caused the overall cost of capital to decline by 0·25 per cent. Whether such a decline is too large to be explained purely by the effects of taxes is not clear. Further, Weston's results are relatively weak, since growth and leverage together only explained approximately 50 per cent of the variations in the costs of capital of the firms he studied.

The most sophisticated empirical attack on the problem of leverage is contained in a later paper by Miller and Modigliani (1966). Using complex econometric techniques, they tried to explain the total value of each firm in a sample drawn from the US electrical utility industry in terms of:

Their yearly earnings capitalized using the equity cost of an unlevered company in the same risk class;
The size of the firm; and
The growth potential of the firm's earnings.

They adjusted the value of the firms in the sample to abstract from the benefits flowing from the tax-deductibility of debt and obtained equations explaining these adjusted values in terms of the three above variables. To test their hypothesis that leverage has no effect on the values of companies, they added a variable representing leverage to their equations. Modigliani and Miller would predict that altering their equations in this way would not add to their ability to explain corporate values. In their view, they have already removed the only effect of debt by adjusting the values of their sample to allow for its tax advantage. They suggest that their findings confirm this claim.

The statistical techniques used by Miller and Modigliani in their second study (1966) represent a considerable step forward in the use of econometric techniques in business finance. For example, they used special techniques to avoid bias flowing from measurement errors in their data. These errors arise because the raw material of Modigliani and Miller's theoretical model is the market's expectations of future corporate earnings, whereas historical-earnings figures had to be used in their empirical investigations. However, the methodology of their study has been criticized. There have been suggestions that their estimates are still not free from built-in biases favouring their hypothesis. Moreover, it has been pointed out that the data they used came from an industry which is subject to considerable governmental regulation. Gordon (1967) has suggested that if Modigliani and

Miller's findings are amended for this, their results might support the traditional hypothesis. Further, it has been suggested again that Modigliani and Miller's sample does not have a wide enough spread of leverage levels to allow a cost of capital curve of the traditional shape to emerge.

Given the above difficulties of cross section analysis, it may be useful to suggest a test similar to that of the 'survivor' technique used in measuring the effects of economies of scale. This general approach utilizes the traditional economic hypothesis that in the long run all firms will be forced to use optimal methods of operation if they are to survive. This would suggest that we could expect firms to gravitate towards a specific debt/equity ratio over time if one financial structure were clearly optimal. We could implement the 'survivor' technique by studying the changes over time in the financial structures of firms in the same risk class. If Modigliani and Miller are correct (ignoring taxation effects), such changes should be random, whereas the traditional view of leverage would be supported if we could detect a movement by firms towards a specific financial structure. Although this approach seems a worthwhile possibility, it has many difficulties of its own. For example, there may be other factors than leverage forcing firms to adopt a specific debt/equity ratio.

Conclusions

It is not clear that any direct empirical refutation of either theory will ever be forthcoming, for the opposing theories tend to differ in their qualitative predictions only in the presence of extremes of leverage. Moreover, it has been suggested that, even if we accept Modigliani and Miller's arguments, the overall cost-of-capital curve will turn upwards with extreme leverage if shareholders are risk-adverse. With this view, we would expect the empirical evidence to show that firms in the same risk class cluster around the bottom of a slowly declining average cost-of-capital curve. It could be argued that such evidence, rather than supporting Modigliani and Miller, merely shows that firms are seeking the bottom of the traditional 'U'-shaped curve. It may be possible to discriminate between the two theories only if we could obtain data from many otherwise almost identical firms with a wide range of financial structures (including, at least, one all-equity firm). With such information, we should be in a better position to say whether the slope of the overall cost-of-capital curve was greater than that which could be justified purely by the tax-deductibility of debt.

That sophisticated versions of the opposing theories can give similar qualitative predictions does not mean that considering them is a waste of time. Traditionalists would expect the overall cost-of-capital curve to be much steeper and would expect its optimal level to be lower than would supporters of the Modigliani and Miller school. Thus, the former would view deviations from the optimal capital structure as more expensive than would the latter.

Moreover, the two views suggest very different decision rules for project appraisal. Modigliani and Miller's supporters would argue that a firm's existing weighted average cost of capital, adjusted for the tax effects of debt, might be used as the cut-off rate for project appraisal, whereas traditionalists see no escape from the difficult task of forecasting the effects of different financing methods on the average cost of capital which is expected to reign after a project's acceptance.

The debate is thus important and, as yet, unresolved, though Robichek and Myers (1965, pp. 40–44) have suggested a possible way of reconciling the two camps. They accept Modigliani and Miller's view that the only advantage of debt is its tax-deductibility, but argue that when a high proportion of debt is used by a company, the variability of its earnings net of debt charges will be large. They suggest that this may mean that in some years after paying interest the firm may not generate enough earnings to allow re-investment sufficient to meet its shareholders' future income expectations. It is possible that the value of the firm may decline with leverage if the use of high proportions of debt makes likely interruptions to a firm's re-investment plans. This suggests to Robichek and Myers that there may be an optimum level of leverage even if we keep the Modigliani and Miller hypothesis. But, in fact, this reconciliation of the traditional view with that of Modigliani and Miller is achieved only by denying Modigliani and Miller's assumption that the risk quality of the earnings of highly levered and unlevered firms in the same business are identical.

Throughout this chapter has run the implicit assumption that dividends and retained earnings are valued equivalently by investors. This assumption is subjected to scrutiny in the next chapter, which deals with the third element of the investment, finance and dividend-decision trio.

9 Dividend Policy

Controversy reigns over the whole area of dividend policy. On one side are those who say that a firm's policy concerning the proportion of net earnings paid out to shareholders does not affect its share price. Others argue that the market values a pound of current dividends more highly than the equivalent amount received in the form of either capital gains or more distant dividends. The debate, as in the subject generally, is about the valuation model used by the market. The arguments are of great complexity, and all that can be done in this book is to review the basic elements of the opposing views. The empirical evidence so far produced has yielded no conclusive refutation of either hypothesis.

A simplified approach

We could, following Porterfield (1965, ch. 6), side-step the whole issue by suggesting that a firm which wishes to maximize the wealth of its existing shareholders should pay a current dividend *if* and *only if* the value of its shares, including any dividend, after the declaration of the dividend is not forecast to fall below that reigning prior to the declaration. That is, a dividend should be paid if:

$$V_1 + D_0 \geqslant V_0, \qquad\qquad 1$$

where V_1 is the forecast market price per share excluding the contemplated dividend (the ex-dividend price) after the declaration of the dividend, V_0 the market price reigning immediately prior to this and D_0 the contemplated dividend.

This approach can be used only if the firm knows the factors considered by investors when seeking to value its equity. Thus, this decision rule assumes that the valuation debate has been

resolved. However, an examination of Porterfield's decision rule
allows us to concentrate on several important issues whilst avoiding the valuation debate (which will be taken up later). Thus, for
the time being we will assume that a dividend valuation model is
used to arrive at the prices of shares; that is, we will assume that
V_1 is obtained by calculating the present value of all the firm's
future dividends. We will further simplify the analysis by
assuming that the market value of the firm after a dividend
declaration will be identical to that which will reign when the
dividend is actually paid. It is possible that these two values might
differ. If this were the case a decision would have to be made as
to which value to use in the model – Porterfield prefers the after-
payment price.

The major purpose of Porterfield's decision rule is to allow for
the fall in the ex-dividend value of a firm's shares which normally
occurs when the market obtains knowledge of a dividend. This
decline results because the new dividend has to be financed and
the cost of the funds used, *ceteris paribus*, will cause a reduction
in the level of later dividends. Thus, the lower value of the firm
after a declaration (V_1) reflects the lower level of all future
dividends other than the payout under consideration.

It will be shown later in this chapter that the size of this fall in
the ex-dividend value of the company will depend on how the
dividend is to be financed. Share values may also fall after a
declaration because this causes the discount rate applied to a
company's future cash flows to alter. This happens if the new
dividend changes the view that investors hold of the business
uncertainty attached to the company. Moreover, the size of an
announced dividend may cause investors to alter their forecasts
of the amount of future dividends. This may cause the ex-
dividend value of the company to change by more or less than
the value of the forthcoming dividend.

A re-arrangement of Porterfield's decision rule tells us the size
of the optimal dividend. This decision rule can be expressed as
saying: pay a dividend if its positive effect on the wealth of shareholders is at least equal to the fall it causes in the firm's ex-
dividend value, that is if $D_0 \geqslant V_0 - V_1$. It follows that the size
of a current dividend should be increased until the marginal

increment in the dividend equals the consequent marginal decline in the ex-dividend value of the firm. This can be stated alternatively as: increase the dividend under consideration until $D_0 = V_0 - V_1$.

The above suggests that before we can decide whether a dividend payment is in the best interests of shareholders we need to know the type of valuation model that they use and also the amount of dividends they expect in each year in the future. The firm and the equity market may have different views as to the size of likely dividends in future years. This would mean that the announcement of a dividend may have a different effect on market values to that suggested using our models. How the firm is to ascertain the views of equity-holders concerning future dividends is not clear, especially as such forecasts might differ between investors. It may be that all a company can do is to follow a well publicized pay-out policy and hope that investors use this in their forecasts.

However even the assumption that investors use a dividend valuation model, and that the firm somehow knows the content of investors' forecasts does not extricate us from all the difficulties surrounding dividend policy. Three major questions still remain:

1 Should the opportunities available to equity-holders outside the firm be taken into account when formulating dividend policy?

2 Should the personal tax position of shareholders influence dividend decisions?

3 Should the existence of capital rationing (scarcity of funds) within the firm have an effect on the size of optimal dividend payouts?

Outside opportunities

At first sight, it might seem reasonable that dividends should be distributed to allow shareholders to take advantage of any investment opportunities they have which yield a higher return than investment in the firm. Similarly, it might be argued that the firm should release funds so that its equity-holders can indulge in any consumption opportunities which they value more highly than the cash flows from the firm's investment projects. However, it can be shown that distributing funds to give equity-holders access to attractive outside opportunities will not lead to the maximization of their wealth, provided that the company's shares are freely tradeable on the stock market.

In earlier chapters we saw that, in the absence of capital rationing and uncertainty, a firm will, *ceteris paribus*, maximize the wealth of its shareholders by following the net present-value rule for investment decisions. Similarly, it has just been suggested that optimal dividend policy involves announcing and paying a dividend only if the ex-dividend market value of the firm's equity plus the dividend itself is at least equal to the equity value reigning prior to knowledge of the dividend. It will now be shown that the firm will maximize the present worth of its equity-holders' investment by following these two rules simultaneously.

An investor who does not like the cash-flow pattern generated in this way could, in a perfect market, obtain cash to undertake his preferred alternatives, either by borrowing on the basis of later cash flows from the firm or by realizing part or all of his shares on the market. Even in an imperfect capital market, the latter method of obtaining funds is still available to the equity-holder.

Deviations from the optimal dividend policy, which release funds from the company so that the equity-holder can invest in his outside opportunities, will cause a decline in the value of the firm's shares. Such reductions will cause the equity-holder's total wealth, including that from his outside opportunity, to fall below that obtainable if the optimal dividend policy had been pursued and the investor had sold his shares. This is because a dividend in excess of the optimal amount will have to be financed and the cost of this will cause the value of future dividends to fall by more than the amount of the contemplated dividend. Moreover, the cost of such finance cannot be met by accepting additional projects yielding returns greater than the cost of their finance, for all such opportunities will have already been accepted using the net present-value investment decision rule.

Thus, any deviation from these optimal decision rules will cause the value of the investor's shares to fall from the optimum. Thus if the firm's dividend policy is altered to allow the shareholder to indulge in outside opportunities, the value of his shares plus the outside investment financed from dividends will be lower than if the investor had realized his shares at their maximum value. Adherence to our decision rules would ensure that the shareholder disinvested the minimum possible amount to pursue his more profitable outside opportunities. Moreover, such behaviour ensures that the investor's residual investment in the company has the highest possible value. Following our optimal decision rules allows the equity-holder to reap the benefit of his outside investments, whilst maintaining the value of his residual investment in the company at its maximum, and thereby ensuring that his total wealth is also maximized.

A numerical example may help in understanding this point. Assume that a shareholder requires £100 to take advantage of an opportunity outside a firm of which he owns all the 500 issued shares. These have a market value of £1 each and are expected to pay an annual dividend of £0·1 each. The outside opportunity yields an immediate return of £200 but the firm's optimal dividend policy does not generate sufficient cash to allow its acceptance. If the shareholder realizes £100 of his shares, his total wealth after taking advantage of the outside opportunity will equal £600, the value of his remaining shares plus the money obtained from the outside opportunity (£400 + £200).

Now assume that the company arranges to borrow at 15 per cent sufficient money to pay out the £100 as an extra dividend. His total wealth will now be found by adding the value of his shares after the dividend payment to the receipts from the outside opportunity. The total annual dividends from the company will now be £50 *less* the debt interest of £15, assuming the cost of capital does not change. The value of the company after the extra dividend can be found by capitalizing the new annual dividends at 10 per cent. This yields a value of £350 for the 500 shares and the shareholders' total wealth is reduced to £550 (£200 + £350).

Our conclusion that the outside opportunities available to equity-holders should not influence dividend policy holds only if the investor is free to buy and sell shares on the market. This he may not be able to do where the shares involved are not traded on a recognized market. Similarly he may not wish to sell his shares either because of a temporary depression in the market or because such sales make him liable to relatively high short-term capital gains tax.[1] In such situations, dividends are no longer merely one element of the shareholder's total wealth but become, perhaps, the shareholder's only source of funds. As a result, the existence of alternative opportunities outside the firm becomes important and must be taken directly into account by management, for dividends may be the only funds available to shareholders. However, different investors will probably have access to a variety of outside opportunities and may also differ both in their willingness to sell shares and in their tax positions. Here, it seems that all the firm can do is to follow a consistent policy (say, one that pleases the majority of its existing equity-holders – the literature gives no guidance as to how such preferences can be ascertained) and hope to attract like-minded investors.

Dividend decision and capital rationing

As will be explained in the next chapter, projects should be accepted according to their relative impact on shareholders' wealth if the firm cannot obtain unlimited funds at the going market rate (or rates). In this situation using funds for dividends means foregoing projects. Thus, dividends should be paid only if they lead to a larger relative change in equity-holders' wealth than any projects sacrificed owing to their payment.

Taxes

In most countries dividends are subject to personal tax, and the dividend model we have used so far in this chapter must be amended to incorporate the effects of taxation. In this situation, the value of a company will be based on investors' estimates of future dividends net of tax and thus V_0, the value of the company, is given by:

$$V_0 = \sum \frac{D_i(1 - t)}{(1 + k^t)^i}. \qquad 2$$

1. This was the position with capital gains tax in the United Kingdom until recently (see the next footnote).

The symbol t represents the marginal rate of tax on dividends (D_is). The discount rate (k^t), which measures the opportunity cost of capital, is also net of tax. The levying of taxes on dividends does not alter the decision rules discussed so far, provided that all the equity-holders face the same marginal rate of tax. Conflicts of interest between equity-holders as to the cost of capital the firm should use for project appraisal will emerge where personal tax rates differ. We have already seen that the literature tends to support using the rate of return required by tax-free individuals as the cost of capital in these circumstances (chapter 6, p. 122).

A further conflict of interest is likely to arise from the policy in most countries of taxing dividends more heavily than capital gains.[2] In this situation, equity-holders will obtain only $(1 - t)D$ from any dividend payment (D), whereas if the same amounts were received in the form of capital gains, they would receive $(1 - c)D$ where c is the marginal rate of tax on capital gains. Retentions would be preferred if c were smaller than t. More generally, equity-holders who are subject to both income and capital gains tax would prefer re-investment provided that the realizable capital gains net of tax are at least equal to the after-tax dividend $(1 - t)D$ which could have otherwise been declared.

However, with uncertainty there is no guarantee that retaining D will necessarily generate an equivalent amount of capital gains. This may mean that £1 of capital gains is regarded as less valuable than £1 of dividends. In this case, retentions will be preferred only if they promise larger after-tax capital gains than the equivalent foregone after-tax dividends. The amount by which the promised net of tax capital gains must exceed the amount obtainable if the same sum were paid out as dividends will depend on the investor's attitude to risk and on his forecast of how much capital gain will be generated by £1 of retentions.

Shareholders may have different preferences as between current dividends and capital gains reflecting both their differing individual tax positions and their differing estimates of the amount of capital gains that any given amount of retentions

2. The current situation in the United Kingdom is that capital gains are taxed at lower rates than income for those who pay the standard rate of income tax, or above.

will yield. Again, it would seem that all a company can do is select a consistent payout policy which satisfies the majority of its shareholders, and let investors adjust to this by buying and selling shares.

The valuation debate

If we wish to use the above theoretical framework as a guide (which is all it can be) in making dividend decisions, we must attempt to ascertain whether the market views £1 of dividends and £1 of earnings as equivalent. There are two camps. One argues that in a tax-free world, the market is indifferent between receiving a specific sum of money in the form of dividends or capital gains; the other suggests that dividends are preferred to capital gains for a variety of reasons. Predominant among these is the suggestion that dividends to be received shortly are valued more highly than either the more distant dividends or capital gains which flow from retentions because current dividends are regarded as more certain.

The irrelevancy argument

The central tenet of the irrelevancy argument as presented by Miller and Modigliani (1961) is that the market capitalizes net operating earnings, and, thus, is indifferent as to whether these are distributed as capital gains or as dividends. Miller and Modigliani first show that this proposition holds in a world of certainty and perfect markets, and then suggest that their hypothesis holds even when these assumptions are relaxed.

The dividend decision with certainty and perfect markets

In chapter 4 (p. 53) it was shown that in these circumstances the firm's dividend policy automatically followed from its investment plans. It was also explained that if the equity-holder did not like the cash-flow pattern implied by this optimal investment plan, he could use the market to adjust this pattern to any other having the same net present value. Thus, the market valuation of a firm depended entirely on the size of its yearly operating cash flows.

The irrelevancy argument with uncertainty

An example will be used to explain how Miller and Modigliani extend this argument to an uncertain world. To do this they use the same general assumptions as for their capital structure theory. Consider an all-equity firm with a cost of capital of 10 per cent, which is expected to pay out a constant yearly dividend of £100. Assume that this firm has an opportunity to accept an additional project requiring an outlay of £100 for returns of £15 per year into perpetuity, the first instalment of which is to be received in one year's time. These returns are of the same risk quality as the company's other projects. This project should be accepted, for it has a net present value of £50 when discounted at the equity cost of capital reigning at the time the outlay is to be made. The total value of the firm should therefore increase by £50 immediately the market knows of the project's acceptance. If dividend policy is irrelevant, it should be possible to show that, abstracting from taxes and new issue expenses, this increase will accrue irrespective of whether the project is financed by a new share issue or by re-investment. The former procedure would allow the current dividend, which we will assume is due immediately, to be paid, whereas the latter would involve its cancellation. If it can be demonstrated that the value of the firm is the same under the two alternatives, this would show that dividends and capital gains are regarded as of equal value, at least, with our assumptions.

If the current dividend were not paid, the value of the company would be obtained by calculating the present value of £115 received in perpetuity, the stream starting one year in the future. Thus V_0 is given by applying the perpetuity formula to both the old and new dividends (D_i and D_p respectively), that is:

$$V_0 = 0 + \frac{D_i}{k} + \frac{D_p}{k} = £0 + \frac{£100}{0 \cdot 1} + \frac{£15}{0 \cdot 1}$$
$$= £0 + £1000 + £150 = £1150 \qquad 3$$

Now let us assume that the project was instead financed by an additional share issue to new investors thereby allowing the current dividend to be paid to existing equity-holders. If the firm's dividend policy were irrelevant, the value of the firm using this financing alternative should be the same as that reigning when the current dividend was withheld.

The value of the company to the existing equity-holders if a new issue were made is the sum of the current dividend (D_0) and the expected yearly dividends without the project (£100 per year), together with the new project's dividends ($D_p = £15$ per year) net of the return required by the new equity-holders (D_n). This is shown in the formula below, which gives the value of the company after the new issue is made and the project accepted as:

$$V_0 = D_0 + \frac{D_i}{k} + \frac{D_p - D_n}{k}, \qquad\qquad 4$$

and plugging in our assumed numbers this becomes:

$$V_0 = £100 + \frac{£100}{0\cdot1} + \frac{£15 - D_n}{0\cdot1}. \qquad\qquad 5$$

The value of the company to the existing shareholders will be the same under the two financing alternatives only if the amount paid to the new shareholders is £10 per year, thereby giving the third term on the right a present value of £50. This will result only if the new equity-holders require the same rate of return (use the same discount rate) as the existing investors. Using this 10 per cent discount rate in the above formula gives V_0 the same value as was obtained when retentions were used for the project:

$$£1150 = £100 + £1000 + £50.$$

Thus, given our assumptions, the choice between dividends and retentions is irrelevant, providing that all investors use the same discount factor for the firm. Such an assumption would seem reasonable, for the risk characteristics of the business are unaltered in the above example. It does, however, assume that the amount of current dividend payments does not cause investors to revise their expectations concerning future profitability. Further, in an uncertain world, different investors are likely to have different views about the company prospects. It could be argued that existing shareholders are likely to be more optimistic and therefore that new investors might require a relatively higher return from the company.

Finally, let us assume that the project is financed by a debt issue. In this case dividend policy is irrelevant only if the marginal cost of the loan (its specific cost plus its effect, if any, on the return required by equity) is exactly 10 per cent. This would be so only if either Modigliani and Miller's capital structure theory were correct or if company leverage was such as to place it in the traditionalists' region of optimal leverage. Remember that Modigliani and Miller argue that using relatively low-cost debt increases the risk felt by equity-holders who therefore raise their required rate of return so as to offset exactly any gain from using debt. Thus, in these circumstances Modigliani and Miller's view of dividend policy is dependent on the correctness of their capital structure theory, and it may be that the dividend policy controversy will not be resolved until the capital structure debate is settled. The next section reviews the arguments of those who suggest that share values are sensitive to how the fruits from investing in a company are distributed.

The dividend capitalization view

It should be clearly understood that the debate is not about whether investors use dividends or earnings figures in their valuation models. It rather concerns whether a given sum of money is valued differently when distributed as current dividends or as capital gains via retentions. It can be shown that for a specific firm the use of either a dividends or earnings valuation model will give the same result, provided that identical amounts of dividends and earnings are valued equally by the market. For example, Gordon's dividend growth model, which was introduced in chapter 6 (see p. 124), will give a firm the same value when correctly reformulated in terms of earnings. Recall that the dividend version of this model when used to derive the equity cost of capital (k_e) was given by:

$$k_e = \frac{D_0}{V_e} + g, \qquad\qquad 6$$

where D_0 represents the current dividend of an all-equity firm and V_e is the current market value of the firm's equity. The expected growth rate in dividends (g) is made up of two elements: b, the percentage of earnings retained each year, and r, the return on these retentions. These are both held constant for all years in the future in simple versions of the Gordon model. Re-arranging the above formula and explicitly incorporating these two constants gives the value of the company as:

$$V_e = \frac{D_0}{k_e - br}.$$ 7

However, the current dividend (D_0) is equal to the firm's yearly earnings ($\bar{Y}$) less the proportion of these earnings which are re-invested (b). Plugging these symbols into the above valuation formula gives the earnings equivalent of the Gordon model, that is:

$$V_e = \frac{(1 - b)\bar{Y}}{k_e - br}.$$ 8

Both models applied to the same company will give it an identical value, provided that the same discount rate is applied to dividends and earnings. This ensures that the denominators and therefore the values yielded by the two formulations must be the same for they both have the same numerator. Strictly, neither model uses a pure dividends or earnings approach. For example, to use the dividend version of the model we must know the percentage of earnings a company intends to retain per year. Given that dividends and earnings models yield identical values for a given firm, those financial writers who believe that a firm's dividend policy does affect its value have attempted to show that a specific amount of dividends is regarded by the market as more valuable than the same amount of earnings. If this could be established it would destroy the equivalence of the two valuation approaches.

The discount rate argument – the riskiness of distant dividends

The dividend policy of a company would affect its value if investors were risk-averse and thought that dividends in the far future were more risky than those to be received shortly. With these assumptions, re-investment by pushing dividends further into the future makes them more risky. This affects the valuation of retentions, for the capital gains flowing from them ought to be based on the market's valuation of the future dividends to be generated by re-investment. Gordon's acceptance of this view is one reason why he supports a valuation model of the type associated with his name.[3]

Gordon believes that the risk attitude of investors will ensure that the discount rate will rise for each successive year in the future reflecting that the perceived uncertainty attached to dividends increases in direct proportion to their futurity. This allows Gordon to avoid the difficulty, alluded to in chapter 6, whereby his model could give a share an infinite value if the firm's retention rate was chosen so as to make the expected future growth rate in dividends ($g = br$) equal to the discount rate.

Modigliani and Miller would probably reply in answer to Gordon that the riskiness of a company depends only on the uncertainty associated with its operating cash flows. With this view, distant dividends are more uncertain only because the distant earnings which generate them are more risky. The uncertainty attached to such earnings will be the same whether they are distributed as dividends or as capital gains, and thus the payments of dividends cannot alter the value placed on a company by investors. Opponents of Modigliani and Miller have in answer suggested that another reason for applying a higher discount rate to later dividends is that the market prefers a given amount of current income to a sum, having the same present value, received in the future via retentions.

The discount rate argument

We have already seen that preferences for current income should not normally result in dividends being given a higher value than retained earnings. Even if investors cannot borrow or lend on the market, they ought to be able to obtain their desired income pattern by changing the size of their shareholding. However, supporters of the dividend capitalization view reiterate the point made earlier that in the 'real world' investors may not be willing to sell their shares to realize capital gains, because with uncertainty, stock prices may fluctuate and at times be temporarily

3. See Gordon (1962, ch. 5) and also his article on the same topic (1963).

depressed. Moreover, it may be regarded as inconvenient (and costly, if we take transaction costs into account) to make marginal changes in stockholdings. It is argued that such difficulties can produce a preference for current dividends over future earnings. Only empirical evidence can tell us whether these factors are significant enough to invalidate Modigliani and Miller's theory.

Modigliani and Miller suggest that these phenomena will not, in any case, generate a systematic preference for dividends over capital gains. They agree that some investors may prefer dividends for such reasons but point out that other investors may not be so affected and will therefore have different preferences between capital gains and dividends. Modigliani and Miller therefore suggest that in the long run each firm's dividend policy will attract a specific 'clientele' of investors. They recognize that if the market has preferences for any particular payout policy it will pay firms to meet this demand in the short run, but argue that the familiar 'arbitrage' will in time erode away any preferences for a specific dividend policy.

Other arguments against irrelevancy

Critics of the Modigliani and Miller theory also cast doubt on their assumption that all potential investors agree about each company's risk class and prospects. Investors may have access to different information and/or may evaluate differently the same information. For these sorts of reasons, existing equity-holders may be more optimistic than potential investors who may therefore require the promise of a higher return before they will buy a company's securities.

It has been argued, similarly, that dividend payouts may be valued not only in themselves but also as indicators of future profitability. With uncertainty and limited information, dividends may have to be given considerable weight in forecasting. Thus, it is suggested that alterations from past dividend policies may be taken by the market as a public statement that the firm's future profitability has changed.

Modigliani and Miller noted these effects but did not include them in their model. They assert that increased current dividends merely produce expectations of increased future earnings. It is these latter expectations which cause the market to revise equity values.

A final argument against Modigliani and Miller's position was introduced in chapter 6. This is that reinvestment might be preferred by the market if a lower rate of tax were levied on capital gains than on dividends. Modigliani and Miller claim they can find no evidence that low payout shares sell at a premium, which is what we would have expected if tax effects were important.

A view about whether the above objections to Modigliani and Miller's position act to make dividends more important to investors than earnings can be formed only by looking at the real world evidence.

The empirical evidence

The data currently available have not enabled the question to be resolved. This is hardly surprising given the variables we are trying to measure.

The theoretical models of dividend policy, introduced above, use concepts such as market expectations of future earnings and dividends, and the uncertainty attached to such forecasts. These cannot be observed directly in the practical world. Most empirical workers have therefore endeavoured to explain historical share prices over time using historical approximations to these concepts. For example, the historical trend in dividends is often used as a substitute for their expected growth rate in the future. Errors in the measurement of the true explanatory variables may bias the result of empirical studies. Modigliani and Miller claim that most of the evidence supporting the view that dividends are deemed by investors to be more valuable than earnings actually flows from the measurement errors introduced when historical earnings are used as a proxy for 'true' earnings.

Moreover, all the variables entering into our models are closely interrelated and the empirical unscrambling of their separate effects entails solving many statistical difficulties.

One of the most comprehensive empirical attacks on the dividends versus earnings question has been made by Gordon and is recorded in several articles and a book. (See, for example,

Gordon, 1962, p. 165 ff.) Using sophisticated versions of his dividend valuation model, he seeks to express in quantitative terms the correlation between share prices and six variables. These are:

The firm's current dividend yield;
The expected growth rate in dividends as implied by their historical growth rate;
A measure of historical earnings instability – to cope with uncertainty;
Leverage;
An index of liquidity; and
A measure of firm size.

He claims his studies give strong support for the dividend hypothesis and also suggests that company size, liquidity and historical stability of earnings all help to explain share prices. Benishay (1961) has produced evidence supporting these findings with regard to company size and the variability of earnings.

Gordon's model has been subject to debate in the literature. Some of these criticisms have already been mentioned (p. 126). One is that it reverses the logic of investment decision-making, which suggests that the payout ratio, which Gordon assumes is stable, should depend, at least in part, on the investment opportunities available to the firm. Against this, there is some evidence that, in practice, firms do tend to maintain a constant payout rate. Moreover, his assumption that there will be a sufficient supply of projects with a given average return (r) to absorb exactly a constant proportion of the firm's earnings (b) may be true only by chance. Gordon, though a strong supporter of dividend valuation models, recognizes that some of the criticisms of his work may be valid and therefore does not regard the dividend policy question as closed.

Gordon's statistical methods have also been questioned. It has been alleged that his model may not be free of measurement errors of the type explained earlier. Moreover, his definitions of some of his independent variables may introduce bias for their definition has to be based on share values, which are the dependent variables we are trying to explain. More serious is that when Keenan (1970) sought to reproduce Gordon's results with different data he found that though, in general, the signs of his correlation coefficients supported Gordon's findings, their magnitude varied between samples. From this Keenan argued that little of a quantitative nature could be said about the effect of dividends on share valuation using Gordon's model.

Modigliani and Miller have produced evidence supporting their irrelevance of dividends argument, which thus conflicts with the findings obtained by Gordon. Miller and Modigliani argue, in their second study (1966) that if unadjusted earnings data are used in empirical work, a bias is produced which tends to give spurious support to the dividend hypothesis. They suggest that a better measure of expected earnings is obtained by constructing a special earnings figure using sophisticated econometric methods (the method of instrumental variables; see Johnston, 1963, ch. 4.) They obtain their earnings figures by regressing the value of the firm on several causal factors such as current dividends, the firm's size, the growth rate of its assets, and its debt/equity ratio. They claim to obtain from this exercise an earnings figure which does not introduce bias into their empirical work. They then seek to find the correlation between share prices and six variables; (1) the tax rate, (2) the level of debt, (3) their measure of expected income, (4) the size of the firm, (5) its rate of growth, and (6) its risk class. Modigliani and Miller claim that their procedure purges dividends of their informational content about future earnings. When this effect is attributed to future earnings, which in their view is where it belongs, they found no evidence that dividend payouts affect share values. As yet, no reconciliation of the differing empirical findings is possible, though most of the existing studies do tend to support the dividend hypothesis.

Some would argue that the unsatisfactory nature of the empirical work in this field, and in the financial area generally, is the result of an incorrect approach to share valuation models. The method used by most researchers has been to tackle separately one part, or a sub-part of the investment, financing and dividend decision trio which together determine share values. It has been argued that such partial attacks on the valuation problem are unlikely to be successful, for all three decisions – investment, financing and dividend – impinge both on each other and on the supply of funds. Thus, all these decisions should ideally be considered together. It is claimed that partial theories which encompass but one aspect of financial management can only be misleading. To overcome this, several attempts have been made to synthesize the existing partial theories into a more general theory of equity valuation.

Probably the most well known of these is that by Lerner and Carleton (1964) who argue that as with all other goods, the equilibrium price of equity depends on demand and supply considerations. They therefore see share prices as being determined jointly by demand factors, as reflected by the investment opportunities facing the firm, and by supply considerations, such as the required return on equity and dividend policy. They envisage the firm as choosing its retention rate on the basis of two models. One represents the equity valuation model which the firm believes is used by investors. This model is postulated to be similar to that suggested by Gordon, except that the cost of capital is explicitly taken to be a function of both the riskless rate of interest and the firm's risk class. Further, the return from reinvestment is assumed to depend on the amount of earnings retained by the firm. With this model, the firm when choosing a specific retention rate (dividend payout) commits itself to providing a given return on investment. The second model (the demand for funds model) yields the return the firm can expect from any given amount of reinvestment. As in the supply model, Lerner and Carleton envisage that the return from reinvestment falls with increased retentions.

The mathematical equations which represent these two models can be solved simultaneously to give the retention rate which yields the highest possible price for the firm's shares. Note that for a solution to emerge the estimated effects of retentions must be identical in both models. That is, the assumptions actually held by investors about the effect of retentions by the firm, must be correctly reflected in the supply of funds model and must agree with the assumptions used in the demand model.

Lerner and Carleton argue that this must be so in economic

equilibrium. Work on general models is, as yet, in its early stages but does promise that we may, in time, be able to deal with complex problems such as the dividend decision in a general way whilst simultaneously considering the other two elements of the investment, financing and dividend decision trio. Unfortunately, the relationships between the various financial variables subsumed by this type of total theory are so complex that no real empirical tests of the results generated by these models have yet been proposed.

A word of warning – imperfect information

So far in this book we have proceeded on the basis that management communicate the expected effect of their policies to the market and that these communications are believed by investors. If this assumption is not valid, at least as an approximation, it is unlikely that following the theory in this book will lead to optimal results for investors. For example, management may accept a project with a very high net present value but share prices will stay constant if the market is not persuaded of the project's worthwhileness. Indeed, share prices may well go in the opposite direction to that predicted by our theories if communications from management are disbelieved. In the context of this chapter, there is no point in the firm pursuing an optimal payout policy unless the market is told of this intention, accepts that the policy is optimal, and believes it will be carried out.

We know little about either the valuation models that investors actually use, or how they make the estimates necessary for such models. What we do know suggests that only crude approximations to the models used in this book are employed. For example, in a different context, Clarkson (1965), when studying banking trusts, found that the managements of these trusts used crude inventory models to determine what stocks to buy and sell. More fundamentally, Simon has expressed grave doubts about whether human goal-seeking behaviour can be realistically described by maximizing models of the type used in this book (see, for example, Simon, 1959). However, although there is a need for much research in this area, as far as is known, no alternative to assuming that investors act as if they were maximizing present worth has yet been proposed which yields better real-world predictions.

However, it is clear that, whatever models investors use, they have to rely on very imperfect information to generate their estimates. This may render inaccurate the predictions obtained using the models described. Several writers have suggested that this difficulty could be partially overcome if firms issued budgets showing the cash flows which they expect to obtain in the future. Until such budgets are forthcoming the market must base its forecasts mainly on historical information, such as that contained in balance sheets and income statements, together with such bits of information as can be gleaned from documents like directors' reports and interim earnings statements. Such statements and reports often give little information on which to base forecasts, and normally refer only to the company as a whole.

Such statements therefore do not, in general, yield many clues as to either the make-up of a firm's existing or future project portfolio, or the profitability of individual projects. Thus the models in this book should not be thought of as precise practical tools for investment appraisal, but rather as means of isolating and thinking about those financial variables which are crucial to decisions, almost irrespective of either the type of valuation models used by the market or the type of information the market is forced to use in formulating forecasts.

Moreover, provided that the market values profitability, widely defined, firms using our decision rules should in the long run produce a better performance than those who do not. For example, even if investors judged a company on its current reported profits, following our decision rules should increase its value, for the results of this policy would be reflected in the firm's conventional income statements in due course. Thus, in practice, equity values will not rise immediately on the acceptance of a project with a positive net present value but rather will increase gradually. The lag will gradually reflect the time necessary for the project's incremental 'profitability' to show up in the firm's conventional financial statements. The effect of the project on corporate profitability will only approximate the project's net present value because of the distortion introduced by factors such as accounting conventions. But even this rise in share values will occur only if the market uses published historical information to appraise profitability.

Several studies suggest that the market does take into account such information when arriving at share values. These studies look at the effect on share prices of a specific item of information. Fama's work (Fama, Fisher, Jensen and Roll, 1969) indicates that, as our theory would suggest, the market places a value on stock splits only because it is believed that future dividends per share will not be reduced in direct proportion to the split. Fama suggests that on the knowledge of a split the market reacts as if this were tantamount to increased future dividends per share but quickly adjusts share prices downwards if such expectations are not realized. If this type of finding were shown to be general, it could be argued that the market reacts approximately as our theory suggests but with a lag reflecting the time span between, say, a project's acceptance and its impact on the firm's reported earnings. Thus a firm following our decision rules will be doing the best it can for its equity-holders. The validity of our decision rules for the real world therefore depends on how well stock-market prices 'reflect' available information. If such information is fully reflected then the market is said to be efficient. The weight of the evidence so far available suggests that the stock market is approximately efficient. This subject is very complex and cannot be further pursued here. But clearly research in this area has many important implications for capital budgeting and may in time cause adjustments to the theory expounded in this book. The best simple introduction to the theory of efficient markets is probably Brealey (1969). A very good survey of the existing literature is Fama (1970).

The next chapter analyses some decision rules that have been suggested for use when the firm is subject to some limitation on the amount of funds it has available for investment in any period.

10 Capital Rationing

In this chapter we investigate the implications for capital budgeting of relaxing our assumption that the firm can obtain unlimited amounts of any specific type of funds if it pays the existing market rate for such funds. The term *capital rationing* is normally applied to situations where the supply of funds to the firm is limited in some way. Thus, the term encompasses many different situations, ranging from that where the borrowing and lending rates faced by the firm differ to that where the funds available for investment by the firm are strictly limited. The first sections of this chapter examine the various types of capital rationing, for each may require different adjustments to be made to the investment appraisal models we have previously discussed. Moreover, capital rationing may either be enforced by the capital market (external capital rationing) or may be internal to the firm and result from managerial policy. The different characteristics of external and internal capital rationing are compared and contrasted in the first part of this chapter, the remainder of which is addressed to the situation where there is an absolute limit on the amount of funds which the firm can invest in a given period.

No clear-cut optimal decision rules exist for many capital-rationing situations and all that can be done is to review the various approximate methods of solution that have been proposed as practical methods of attack.

Types of capital rationing[1]

A condition of 'strong' external capital rationing is said to exist where the market places an absolute limit on the amount of finance it is willing to make available to a firm in a given time

1. For a full discussion of these and an assessment of the ability of existing theory to deal with each type, see Amey (1972).

period. It has been suggested that this form of capital rationing arises because the market, rather than raising the interest rate to a firm regarded as risky, may simply refuse to supply funds beyond limits which it considers safe (see Baumol and Quandt, 1965). 'Weaker' cases of external capital rationing may also reflect the market's uncertainty about a firm.

Our first example of 'weak' external capital rationing is where the rate the firm pays when borrowing differs from that obtained when lending. This difference in rates may reflect the relatively higher risks thought to be attached to the firm's borrowing, or may be solely due to differing transaction costs for borrowing and lending. Our second example of 'weak' external capital rationing is where the cost of capital required from the firm in a given period increases, reflecting the perceived increased risk of default, as the firm raises its demands for funds.

All three forms of external capital rationing are likely to be present in the short run. The total supply of funds cannot adapt instantaneously to meet changes in the demand for financing, and in the short run some method of rationing funds between firms may be necessary. This rationing may take the form of either charging higher interest rates as the demand for funds increases or the placing of a limit on the absolute amount of finance available to any specific firm.

Further, certain types of financing may not be available to firms in the short run. A new equity issue cannot be mounted overnight. The use of other types of funds in the short run may be relatively expensive in terms of their effects on equity values. For example a hastily mounted equity issue may reduce the value of existing stock, for prior to a new issue, the firm's performance has to be such as to convince investors that they will obtain their required return in the future. Similarly, if the market is temporarily depressed, such an issue may harm the existing shareholders.

Market imperfections and information lags may also result in some form of capital rationing being temporarily placed on firms. For this type of reason, we would expect the firm's short-run average cost of capital to rise at an increasing rate with additional demands for finance in the short run. Moreover, at some point in the process, the firm may come up against an absolute limit on the amount it can raise of some types of finance.

These rising costs of capital which accompany demands for extra finance should not be confused with those of chapters 7 and 8 which were occasioned by leverage changes. The alterations in the cost of capital considered in this chapter arise because the firm, by increasing the amount of finance it uses, changes the market's view of its risk class, at least in the short run. This will affect the cost of funds to a company even though it does not change its leverage.

There is little reason to believe that the factors, resulting in a weighted average cost of capital which rises rapidly with increased borrowing until some absolute limit is reached, are anything other than temporary phenomena. The supply and demand for funds should adjust over time and thereby resolve any temporary imbalance in the funds market unless persistent imperfections are present in the capital market. With this view, a firm can escape most of the difficulties of short-term external capital rationing by avoiding excessive demands on the market in any one period. This is especially so if its calls on the market are staggered so as to give investors time to ascertain the profitability of its project portfolio. Thus, it is often argued that, *ceteris paribus*, a firm's average real cost of capital should not differ substantially between periods provided that the firm stays within the same risk class, and carefully plans its financing policy. With this view, external capital rationing is of little significance to the firm, at least in the long run (see Baumol and Quandt, 1965).

This is not true of internal capital rationing, for there is evidence that some top managements pursue a policy of limiting the amount of funds available for investment in any one period. Later in this chapter it will be shown that such policies are not generally in the equity-holders' best interests. However, there are several situations where internally imposed fund constraints may be sensible.

Such restrictions may stem from a desire to avoid the difficulties attached to trying to raise what the market regards as excessive amounts of finance in any period. A divisionalized company may place limits on the amounts available for divisional investment in any one year in the hope that the corporate demand for funds will thereby be restricted to those sources having a cost approximately equal to the firm's long-run average cost of capital. Such a policy would be optimal for equity-holders provided that opportunities which are acceptable using expensive short-term funds do not disappear when their acceptance is postponed until they can be financed from 'normal' sources. Equity-holders gain from this procedure by avoiding the payment of the relatively 'expensive' rates required by the suppliers of short-term finance.

Similarly, it may be sensible for top management to impose fund constraints on divisional management if the firm's share-holders are averse to the higher risk of insolvency which may be associated with servicing relatively expensive short-run funds. Again, equity-holders would benefit if more normally priced finance were used, provided that the projects acceptable using expensive short-term funds are not lost owing to delay. In this situation, none of the cash flows from accepted projects would have to be diverted to maintaining the existing market price of the firm's shares in the face of the higher cost of capital required by the existing equity-holders if expensive short-term funds are used. A later section of this chapter deals briefly with the situation where net present values of projects are affected by postponement.

Weingartner (1963) has suggested that internal limits on divi-sional investment may also serve to motivate subordinates to produce the type of projects preferred by top management. For example, it could be argued that the search for high-yielding projects would be encouraged if funds were deliberately limited and divisional management instructed to maximize their division's cash flow net of the firm's cost of capital. However, a capital, rationing policy of this type would not be optimal for equity-holders if it resulted in the rejection of low-yielding projects with a total net present value greater than that obtained from the high-yielding projects found only because of the constraint.

Internal capital rationing becomes more defensible where fac-tors other than finance are in short supply. Short-run scarcities of managerial talent (see Penrose, 1959) or other resources, such as technical personnel, may mean that the firm cannot undertake all available projects having a positive net present value at the market cost of capital. In this situation the aim should be to accept those projects which yield the highest net present value per unit of the scarce resource. However, placing an absolute constraint on investment will not necessarily encourage the achievement of this objective, for the original outlay required by a project is unlikely to bear any close relationship to the amount of any scarce resources other than capital required by the project. This is especially so, where more than one factor is in short supply, since these scarce inputs may differ in kind and therefore in the relationship they bear to the project's original outlays. Mathematical programming is probably the most satisfactory way of handling the allocation problem in these circumstances but, as will be pointed out in the next chapter, this approach has difficulties of its own.

The constraints on funds which are actually observed in practice, may not have been imposed for any of the above reasons. Such limitations often seem unrelated to the achievement of any of the more usual corporate objectives. One popular rule of thumb is to restrict the investment funds available in any year to the amount of the previous year's accumulated *book* depreciation allowances plus any addition to reserves made in that year. Such constraints will not be in the equity-holders' best interests if they inhibit the firm from accepting investment opportunities having positive net present values after paying the going rate for their finance.

Lorie and Savage (1955) have suggested that such rules of thumb are not significant in the long run. They argue that the pressures of a profit-orientated economy will, in time, force top management to relax such constraints. In such an economy, a firm which sought to maintain artificial constraints on investment funds would either not yield sufficient profits to survive, or would be taken over by firms seeking to maximize their net present worth using the procedures described in this book.

This notwithstanding, there is little reason to doubt that many firms do persistently enforce a capital rationing policy. Such policies may simply represent attempts to make investment decisions manageable in face of practical difficulties. The organizational complexities of large firms may mean that investment decisions are rendered feasible only by using simple, but arbitrary, rules.

Thus, the practical use of some of the models in this book may have to wait upon advances in our understanding of organizational behaviour.

In this next section we begin a more detailed examination of capital rationing by analysing some of the 'weaker' types of external capital rationing. Internal capital rationing is taken up again later in the chapter.

External capital rationing
Different borrowing and lending rates

Chapter 5 (pp. 88–93) presented rules for accept/reject decisions in this situation, and suggested a solution to the problem of which of the two possible discount rates (the lending and borrowing rates) should be used for project appraisal. It was shown that this choice depended on whether the opportunity cost of further investment was represented by the cost of borrowing or the interest from foregone lending opportunities. The borrowing rate should be used as the discount factor in project appraisal where further investment requires increased borrowing and the lending rate used where investment is financed by foregoing lending on the market.

Rising costs of capital

In this situation, the marginal cost of funds rises with the amount of finance employed. The marginal cost of extra finance is the specific cost of such funds together with their effect on the cost of all the other finance used by the firm; that is, the market cost of the funds used, *plus* the return necessary to compensate the suppliers of the firm's existing finance for any additional risk they see arising from the contemplated method of financing. It is usually argued that only projects which cover both elements of the cost of extra finance should be accepted by the firm.

However, where projects are considered sequentially, their acceptability will depend on the cost of capital reigning at the time they are considered. A project that is acceptable if considered early in the year when the cost of capital is relatively low may be unacceptable later, when a higher cost of capital obtains. This problem does not arise in the framework of our earlier diagrammatic analysis (see, for example, chapter 5, pp. 88–93), where it was assumed that all projects had been ranked in terms of their incremental return prior to any financing decisions. If we work our way up this ranking (the productive opportunity curve) sequentially over time, the projects accepted at lower rates of interest would also be the best at higher rates.

Our theoretical model suggests a practical procedure for deciding which projects to accept where opportunities appear sequentially over time and the cost of capital to the firm increases with the demands for finance in any given period. Although at the beginning of any period we cannot predict what specific projects will appear during its span, we might be able to forecast the general types of opportunities likely to be available and the approximate profitability of each such class. Similarly, we might be able to estimate approximately the total financing necessary for the expected amount of projects in each category together with the types and amounts of financing opportunities likely to be available during the year.

With this information we can, following Porterfield (1965, ch. 6), rank the project classes in terms of their relative profitability and the financing sources in terms of their cost. How such orderings can be constructed will be taken up later in this chapter but given such a ranking, the firm can approximate our theoretical solution by matching the 'best' project classes with the 'best' sources of finance. This procedure will yield a discount rate for each project class which will reflect the optimal method for financing the projects from that class during the year. Actual projects submitted for decision during the year should be accepted only if they have a net present value using the discount rate applicable to their general class. This procedure should ensure that funds are kept available for projects whenever they occur throughout the year and that all projects are financed in the optimal way. Thus, a project will be accepted at the beginning of the year only if it is thought unlikely to displace a better project which may arise later in the year. The optimality of this procedure depends on the accuracy of the estimates made at the beginning of the year. The discount rates used may have to be recast as time passes and as the firm learns about the actual conditions it faces during the year.

This process of attempting to match project classes and financing sources at the beginning of the year may also give the firm an indication of the types of projects it could most profitably seek to discover during the year. The suggested method yields only approximate solutions and requires a lot of information. It is not clear what the firm should do if such information is not available.

Above, we defined the marginal cost of any specific type of finance as including the compensation for any effect its use has on the current cost of other funds utilized by the firm. However, the current use of a specific type of funds may also affect the market's expectations of financial risk in future periods. This may cause the cost of other finance to increase in later periods. No real analysis of this situation has yet been undertaken in the literature. All that can be suggested is that some attempt be made to forecast the effects of current financing decisions on the cost of future funds, and that the discount rate used by the firm be adjusted to reflect such effects.

The strong case of capital rationing – an absolute limit on investment funds

The remainder of this chapter considers situations where funds for investment are strictly limited in the current period, after which they are freely available at the going rate of interest. It has already been suggested that only if the firm is going through a liquidity crisis will the market impose a limit on funds. Even if some financing sources do limit their lending to the firm, other funds will be forthcoming providing that the firm is willing to pay a high enough price. Thus, it is usually argued that most examples of a complete constraint on funds result from managerial decisions.

The effects of an absolute limit on funds can be shown using the diagram opposite, where the amount of capital used by the firm in the period is shown on the horizontal axis and the average cost of capital on the vertical axis. The supply of funds forthcoming at different costs of capital (prices) is shown by the SS curve. The increasing slope of SS as the amount of funds employed rises reflects the higher marginal cost of each extra increment of funds. The other line in the diagram (BB) represents the usual demand curve for funds. Projects are ranked along it inversely in order of diminishing profitability; any point on this line shows the funds needed to finance those projects which have a positive net present value, when discounted at the cost of capital shown horizontally opposite on the Y axis (OK funds will be demanded when the average cost of finance is OY).

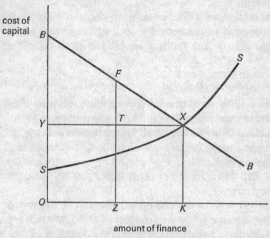

Fig. 20 The demand and supply of capital: the capital-rationing case

With these assumptions, a firm wishing to maximize its equity-holders' wealth should utilize that amount of funds indicated by the intersection of the demand (BB) and supply (SS) curves. In our case, the firm should raise OK funds and finance those projects represented by the BX segment of BB. Accepting those projects represented by BX gives the greatest increment in net present worth. Each project to the left of X has a positive net present value when discounted at the relevant cost of capital (OY), and the marginal project has a zero net present value at this interest rate.

Thus, following our decision rule will ensure that the marginal project accepted just covers its cost and that all other projects accepted yield a return over and above their financing (shown by the area enclosed by the line *YXB* in the diagram). If management imposes a constraint on finance so that investment cannot exceed, say, *OZ*, equity-holders will forego the net present values from those projects represented by *FX*. The cost to equity-holders of such a policy is represented in the diagram by the area *TXF*, which represents the excess returns over the average cost of capital of the foregone projects.

In the next section we will investigate the decision rules which have been suggested as theoretically optimal in the face of an absolute constraint on the funds available for investment in a given year.

Capital rationing in a single period – the theoretical solution

Although unlikely to be of general applicability, this case does serve to lead into more difficult capital rationing problems. Moreover, the practical solutions suggested for the one-period case are of interest because many of the more sophisticated methods suggested for dealing with multi-period capital rationing are not yet fully operational. These more advanced techniques will be dealt with in the next chapter.

The formal solution for the one period case can be illustrated using the diagrammatic analysis of chapters 4 and 5. We will use the same assumptions as earlier: (a) complete divisibility of projects, (b) certainty, and (c) the equivalence of the borrowing and lending rate. In addition, in the early part of this section, following Hirshleifer, we will assume that the firm and its equity-holders are subject to identical capital limitations. We shall also generally assume that equity-holders either cannot or do not wish to sell their shares in the company.

Recall that with the first three of these assumptions, the productive opportunity curve (*PQ*) in Figure 21 ranks, according to their incremental returns, all the projects which could be undertaken during the year. In the absence of a capital rationing constraint, the firm should seek to move up *PQ* to the point of tangency (*S*) with a present value line (*NM*), whose slope reflects the going rate of interest. The firm or its shareholders should then borrow to reach the highest indifference curve (*I*).

A capital constraint means that the firm cannot borrow, and

thus cannot move along that part of the market line shown by *SM*. We will assume that the limited amount of resources available for investment at the beginning of the year is shown by the horizontal distance between K_0 and Q.[2] This puts us back in a Robinson Crusoe situation where the optimal investment pattern is given by a direct tangency between PQ and an indifference

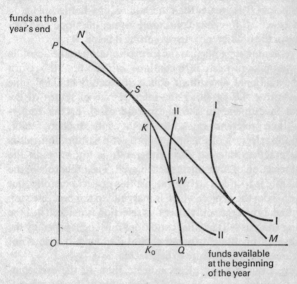

Fig. 21 Optimal investment behaviour under capital rationing

curve (II), reflecting the equity-holders' time preference rate. This is shown by point *W* in our diagram. The firm could, if it wished, still lend on the market. However, lending in a capital-rationing situation is only optimal if the funds constraint is ineffective – it would mean that the firm did not have sufficient projects earning a return greater than the going rate of interest to absorb its limited funds.

The diagram shows that with our assumptions, investing up to

2. Strictly, the axes of the diagram should be shifted so that K_0 becomes the origin of the diagram, and $K_0 Q$, the initial part of the horizontal axis which represents the firm's original endowment.

point W is optimal from the equity-holders' point of view. Movements beyond W involve foregoing consumption opportunities valued more highly than the returns from further investment, i.e. the slope of PQ above $W <$ the slope of the indifference curves cutting PQ above W. However, the firm should not cease investment prior to point W being attained. The return obtained from projects below W is greater than the value equity-holders place on the consequential foregone consumption; i.e. the slope of $PQ >$ the slope of the indifference curves cutting it below W.

This reasoning suggests that the formal solution to the absolute capital-rationing problem is to continue to invest until the return from the marginal investment equals the equity-holders' time preference rate. Using either the internal rate of return of the marginal investment (in the one period case), or the equity-holders' time preference rate at this point as the discount factor, leads to the selection of the optimal project portfolio. But this is of little practical interest, for neither rate is known until the optimal selection of investments is achieved. The usual role of the discount rate is to aid in arriving at just this project portfolio, but the return from the project which is marginal to the best selection of investments emerges only after this selection is made. Thus the foregoing analysis tells us what conditions must be satisfied by the optimal set of investments under capital rationing, but does not suggest how such projects are to be selected.

However, our analysis does indicate that, in these circumstances, following, say, the normal formulation of the net present-value rule would not necessarily lead to the best selection of projects from the equity-holders' point of view. The net present-value method would advise the firm to move up PQ until the constraint is encountered at point K, which is inferior to point W. This failure of the net present-value model results because the market rate of interest understates the opportunity cost of capital; it does not measure correctly either the foregone return from investment or the equity-holders' time preference rate in a capital-rationing situation. The market rate of interest is likely to reflect the opportunity cost of capital for the firm only if investors are aware of the firm's capital-rationing policy, together with its likely investment opportunities and its final choice from these projects; that is, if investors have solved or guessed the solution to the firm's investment problem.

The situation becomes even more complex if we relax our assumption that the firm's equity-holders are subject to the same capital constraints as the firm. There would seem to be no obvious reason why the equity-holders should face the same limit on borrowing as the firm. It is not clear that the project selection represented by point W is optimal if the individual equity-holder is free to borrow on his own account.

This is demonstrated in Figure 22, where the firm is assumed to be subject to capital rationing and has chosen what was shown earlier to be the optimal set of projects for this situation.

The individual equity-holder who has access to the capital market, will be able to move down the market line cutting PQ at W, and thereby reach a higher indifference curve than that tangential at W. But W may no longer represent the best selection of projects for such equity-holders. If the firm continued to accept projects until it encountered its funds constraint (point K), this

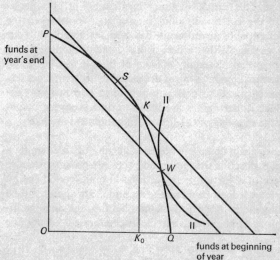

Fig. 22 Optimal investment under capital rationing where shareholders can borrow

would enable the equity-holder to borrow down a higher market line than that cutting point W. This will enable him to reach a higher indifference curve than that tangential at W. This selection of investments is optimal for the shareholder who can borrow on the market, for ceasing investment prior to the fund constraint being encountered would place him on a lower net present-value line.

The firm would arrive at the correct selection of projects for the equity-holder who could use the market if it used the slope of the investment opportunity curve at K as its discount rate. It should not use the market rate as the discount rate in this situation because the net present-value model merely advises the firm that all projects lying along the SQ segment of the productive opportunity curve should be undertaken. It gives management no advice as to which projects from this population should have scarce funds devoted to them. The net present-value model would select the optimal choice of projects (those lying along KQ) only if the slope of the productive opportunity curve at K were used as the discount rate. This formal solution is again not of practical interest because the correct discount rate emerges only when the optimal selection of investments has been achieved. But our analysis does suggest that a firm with a capital-rationing policy should not disregard its equity-holders' abilities to use the capital market when making investment decisions. A problem faces any firm which seeks to allow for its equity-holders' borrowing opportunities. Such opportunities are likely to differ between individuals and the interests of the firm's equity-holders[3] are likely to conflict.

Finally, we again come back to the difficulty of ascertaining a discount rate reflecting true opportunity cost. In order to produce the analogue of a curve like PQ at least in multi-period capital rationing, knowledge of this rate is required. This point will be taken up more fully in the next chapter, but the ranking of multi-period projects will be sensitive to the discount rate used, and the

3. The situation becomes even more obscure if we assume that equity-holders who do not like the firm's capital rationing policy can sell their shares. Little has yet been written about this situation (see Elton, 1970), but allowing this possibility may not change any of our conclusions.

correct ranking will be achieved only if a discount rate approximating to the opportunity cost of capital is used. The conditions that this discount rate must satisfy are known, but, as has been said, this *correct* rate only emerges when the optimal set of investments is known.

The above discussion highlights the fundamental difficulty associated with using the market rate as the discount factor. We indicated earlier that the market rate would advise us to select all those projects lying to the right of S on the line PQ in Figure 22. A choice amongst these projects is impossible unless a ranking like that along PQ exists. Net present values using the market rate give no indication of the projects on which limited funds are best employed. Only by discounting at the unknown opportunity cost of capital can we ensure the achievement of the optimal set of projects.

Our theoretical approach suffers from yet another major practical difficulty. To obtain our solutions, the firm must be able to order projects, and combinations of projects, according to their marginal returns. In practice, constructing anything like a productive opportunity curve will mean examining an impossibly large number of combinations of projects, even with but a moderate number of potential investment opportunities. Moreover, it is not clear what criteria should be used to obtain such a ranking. In the single-period case, ranking the projects by their internal rates of return yields an ordering in terms of marginal returns. But where a project spans several time periods its internal rate of return is a type of average and does not involve marginal comparisons. Hirshleifer has shown that a correct formal method of ordering multi-period projects by their incremental returns does exist, but it is not clear how the concept involved can be made operational (1958).

Thus our theoretical solutions for capital-rationing situations do not yield operational decision rules, although they are very useful in terms of isolating critical variables and in deriving the conditions which must be satisfied if optimal investment decisions are to be made. Most writers have, therefore, been forced to suggest approximate decision rules for use in situations of capital rationing (see Quirin, 1967, ch. 9, and Lorie and Savage, 1955).

None of these solutions is fully satisfactory for they all involve deviations from our formal optimum.

Some practical suggestions for dealing with one-period capital rationing

For the time being we will proceed on the assumption that any investment opportunity not undertaken in the period of capital rationing will be lost to the firm forever. In general, where but one resource is scarce in any specific period, the objective of a firm which wishes to maximize the net worth of its equity-holders should be to utilize the scarce factor so that each unit of the factor yields the highest possible net present-value return. Thus, where funds for investment are the limited resource and are insufficient to finance all those projects having a positive net present value when discounted at the market cost of capital, the aim should be to select those projects which generate the largest incremental increase in share values per unit of finance.

At least three methods of ranking have been suggested for the purpose of selecting such projects. These are that investment opportunities should be ordered: (a) in terms of their absolute net present values, (b) with reference to the ratio the present value of their net cash flows bears to the scarce funds they require (profitability ratios) and (c) via their internal rate of returns.

The procedure is the same for all three methods; the decision-maker moves down each ranking accepting projects until the available funds are exhausted. In terms of the previous analysis, the objective of the three rankings is to derive simultaneously the equivalent of an investment opportunity curve (PQ) and the optimum selection of projects.

These three ranking methods, when applied to the same set of projects, may yield different recommendations about those which should be accepted. The remainder of this chapter is devoted to comparing and contrasting the three methods to see which gives results that most nearly approximate to the maximization of equity-holder net worth in the face of a funds constraint in any one year. It will be assumed for the time being that the benefits from any one project are unaffected by whether other projects are accepted or rejected; that is we are assuming away any mutually exclusive or contingent projects.

Ranking in terms of absolute net present values will normally give incorrect results, for this procedure would suggest the selection of a set of large projects, each with high individual net present values but having in total a lower net present value than a combination of smaller projects, which, on average, yield a higher net present value per £ of scarce funds. For example, this ranking method, if used in a crude way, would favour a project yielding a net present value of £101 for an investment of £1000, over two other projects both yielding a net present value of £90 for an investment of £500, even though these latter utilize more profitably scarce funds.

This point is brought out more clearly in the detailed example below, where we assume that the firm's funds are limited in the first year to £8000, after which capital is freely available at the market cost of capital of 5 per cent. The projects currently available to the firm, together with their receipts and net present values when discounted at the going cost of capital, are shown in Table 24. Projects A, B, and C have constant annual receipts for five years. Project D returns nothing in the first two years of its life and £2000 per annum for the following years. Project E yields no receipts in the last three years of its life. The projects are assumed to be lost for ever if not undertaken immediately.

Table 24 Projects ordered in terms of absolute net present value

Projects	Total investment required: all in current year (£)	Annual net receipts in years (£)	Net present value at 5% (£)	Ranking via net present values
		1 to 5		
A	1000	300	300	5
B	4000	1000	330	4
C	2000	700	1030	1
		3 to 5		
D	4000	2000	940	2
		1 to 2		
E	5000	3000	578	3

All the projects have positive net present values when discounted at 5 per cent and all would be acceptable if money were freely available at this cost. As funds are limited to £8000 the projects must be ranked. In the Table they have been ordered in terms of their absolute net present values. We will assume that the projects are divisible – that is, we can undertake, say, 80 per cent of a project and receive 80 per cent of the net present value in return. The absolute net present value criterion would suggest accepting projects C, D and part (2/5ths) of E. If the projects were not divisible this latter instruction could be regarded as a direction to search for a smaller version of E. The suggested combination has a net present value of £2201; made up of £1030 obtained from C, £940 from D and £231 from E.

That this selection is not optimal can be shown by calculating the ratio of the present value of each project's net cash inflows to the investment necessary to finance the project. These 'profitability' ratios are used to rank the projects in Table 25 below, where the projects are also ordered according to the net present value they return per £ of scarce resource, calculated by dividing the fourth column of Table 24 by the second.

Table 25 Projects ranked by 'profitability' ratios

Projects	'Profitability' ratios	Rank	Net present value per £ of scarce funds	Rank
A	1·300	2	0·300	2
B	1·083	5	0·083	5
C	1·515	1	0·515	1
D	1·235	3	0·235	3
E	1·111	4	0·111	4

Both methods will give the same ranking and advise us to select projects C, A, D and 20 per cent of E. This project portfolio yields a total net present value £2386. Thus, using either ratio is preferable to ranking according to absolute values. That these 'profitability' indices yield the best use of the scarce funds can be checked by substituting any other of the available projects for any of those in our selection.

Our earlier theoretical analysis of capital rationing suggests that these ratios may yield incorrect advice if the market cost of capital is used as the discount rate in their calculation. It was suggested that a correct solution could be obtained in capital rationing situations only if the opportunity cost discount rate was used. To allow us to investigate some of the effects of using the opportunity-cost discount rate, assume that the rate that reflects foregone opportunities in our example is known to be 15 per cent. Using this rate in our calculations generates the revised table shown below:

Table 26 Projects ranked by 'profitability' ratios using the opportunity-cost discount rate

Projects	Present value of flows using 15% rate	'Profitability' ratios	Ranking
A	£1006	1·006	2
B	£3352	0·838	5
C	£2346	1·173	1
D	£3452	0·863	4
E	£4877	0·976	3

Several interesting things happen to our rankings with this new discount rate. For example, the rankings of D and E have been reversed, reflecting the heavier weight now given to earlier cash flows. These changes occur because in a capital-rationing situation the opportunity-cost discount rate reflects the foregone opportunities associated with any investment decision more accurately than the market rate. With a funds constraint, the acceptance of any investment means foregoing the return from the next best project. This lost return is the opportunity cost of undertaking the accepted project. The cost of capital used in ranking should reflect this for the selection of projects may, as in our example, be sensitive to the discount rate used.

Normally the opportunity-cost rate will be higher than the market rate, for a capital-rationing situation is, by definition, one in which all projects acceptable at the market rate cannot be undertaken. Thus, the return from the best foregone investment will be higher than the market rate.

Reworking our example using an assumed opportunity-cost

discount rate highlights the fact that investment in specific projects not only forecloses other projects, but also means that funds cannot be distributed to equity-holders. This latter foregone opportunity becomes important only when equity-holders are also subject to capital rationing, and cannot, or do not wish to, sell their shares. In this situation dividends enter directly into their welfare calculations and accepted projects should generate an annual return greater than the equity-holders' time-preference rate. With our revised calculations, several projects are rejected because they do not yield a return equal to the assumed time-preference rate of 15 per cent. The firm is advised to undertake projects C and A only and pay out the remaining £5000 to equity-holders. The market rate does not allow for this latter type of foregone opportunity because its use normally involves assuming that equity-holders can obtain funds at the market rate of interest.

The literature on capital rationing mainly abstracts from the situation where equity-holders are subject to capital rationing and do not want to sell their shares, presumably on the grounds that such situations are rare. Most writers have therefore concentrated on seeking a ranking method which measures the cost of foregone projects more accurately than do those methods which involve using the market cost of capital as the discount rate.

For example, Quirin (1967, ch. 9) has suggested that the best technique for measuring foregone project opportunities is to order projects according to their internal rates of return and to proceed down this list until the funds constraint is reached. However, the internal rate of return of a project is an imperfect measure of its marginal yield in all but the one-period case. Its use in multi-period capital rationing will involve deviations from our theoretical solution. Moreover, it should be remembered that the internal rate of return method has some technical defects (see pp. 103–5) which are not shared by appraisal methods based on the net present-value concept. However, it is worthwhile indicating what advice ranking via internal rates of return gives the decision-maker in our example. The projects and their internal rates of return are shown opposite.

The decision-maker is now advised yet again to choose A and C, and, in addition, project E. This choice yields a net present

Table 27 Projects ranked according to their internal rates of return

Projects	Approximate internal rates of return	Ranking	'Profitability' ratios ranking (5% discount rate)
A	15%	2	2
B	7%	5	5
C	22%	1	1
D	11%	4	3
E	13%	3	4

value of only £1908, when a 5 per cent discount rate is used. This different advice arises because the internal rate of return ranking reverses the order of projects D and E as compared with the profitability index using a 5 per cent discount rate. The reversal occurs because of the heavier weight given to the earlier cash flows of project E by the higher discount rate (13 per cent rather than 5 per cent), implied by the internal rate of return method, which, by definition, involves discounting a project's cash flow by its internal rate of return.

It has already been stated that with perfect capital markets there are several strong reasons for using variants of the net present value appraisal method. The choice of appraisal technique is not so clear under capital rationing. Lorie and Savage (1955, pp. 229–39) suggest that as our assumed aim is to maximize the net present value obtained, the internal rate of return portfolio should be rejected because it yields a lower net present value – £1908 – than obtained when using a profitability index based on the net present value method – £2386. Whilst we may agree with their objective, we cannot side-step the question of what discount rate should be used to obtain net present values under capital rationing? We have argued that, under capital rationing, the foregone return of the next best project is best approximated by ranking via internal rates of return (see Quirin, 1967, pp. 177–81).

However, it is possible that ranking via internal rates of return will understate the opportunity cost of the foregone project. This is likely, for a project's internal rate of return is a type of average taken over the project's whole span. The method is equivalent to discounting all projects' cash flows by that project's internal rate of return. But with one-period capital rationing, the opportunity cost of capital differs from the market cost of capital only for the year in which finance is limited.

We are assuming that a project is lost forever if rejected in the year of capital rationing, therefore the whole of the project's net benefits should be imputed to the year in which finance is limited. This objective can be achieved by discounting back to the end of the first year the project's cash flows in all years other than the first, using the market cost of capital. To calculate the return lost if the project is not accepted, it is necessary to find the internal rate of return which equates the present value of the project's cash flows at the end of the year of capital rationing together with that year's cash flows to the initial investment. The internal rate of return found in this way will be higher than the project's normal internal rate of return.

Quirin suggests another argument for using the internal rate of return ranking which is that it selects those projects which have relatively high cash flows in early years. The acceptance of such projects acts to reduce financing constraints in later periods. This is a good argument where the constraint is thought likely to exist in future years and is market-imposed owing to economy-wide conditions rather than reflecting dissatisfaction with, say, the firm's liquidity position. In the latter case, efforts should be devoted to rectifying the root cause of the situation. However, if the constraint is internally imposed it seems strange to advocate that management should in project appraisal adopt a method designed to mitigate a constraint which they imposed in the first place.

The preceding suggestions are of little use where either investment opportunities can be accepted only in their entirety, or where the results of projects are interdependent. In these cases, we normally have to examine all feasible combinations of the available projects. For example, in our illustration the profitability index computed using the market rate as the discount rate suggested a project portfolio consisting of C, A, D and a part of E. If E has to be undertaken in its entirety, it may well be that a combination of projects which exactly exhaust the constraint is preferable to the selection of C, A, and D, which leaves £1000 unused. The only way to check is to examine the yields of all feasible combinations of projects.

Capital rationing in a single period – conclusions

In sum, the current theory is of little help, even in the simple case of one-period capital rationing. It tells us the conditions that have to be satisfied if an optimal investment policy is to be pursued, but it does not yield any clear decision rules. The practical choice is between profitability indices using the market rate as the discount factor, and ranking via internal rates of return. It may well be that in our simple case with capital scarce in only one year, the internal rate of return ranking method more closely approximates the return from the best foregone project. Alternatively, management can try to estimate a discount rate which they think measures foregone opportunities. This rate could then be used in calculating net present value profitability indices. This might well be what some companies are attempting to do when they set target rates of return under capital rationing.

The postponability of projects

So far we have assumed that all investment opportunities would be lost forever if not undertaken in the year of capital rationing. It is likely that the acceptance of some projects could be postponed until a later period. Quirin (1967, pp. 181–5) has suggested that the possibility of postponement should be taken explicitly into account when dealing with both single- and multi-period capital rationing. In the former case the approach is to compare the present value of each project if it were commenced in a year of capital rationing with that obtained if it were delayed for, say, a year. We should accept those projects which give the highest net present-value contribution per scarce unit of funds, bearing in mind the effects of deferral, which may affect differently the potential projects. Let us assume that all the projects in our example other than project E can be postponed till later, project E being lost for ever if not accepted in the year of capital rationing.

The left hand side of the table opposite shows the optimal plan, abstracting from the effects of postponement. Plan 2 shows the present value obtained if project E is undertaken in its entirety and project D postponed to allow this. The higher value of plan 2 shows that it pays to delay project D for one year.

Table 28 The effect of project postponement

Plan 1: Projects selected according to profitability index using 5 % as the discount factor:		Plan 2: Postponement of D to allow the acceptance of E:	
	Net present value £		Net present value £
Projects commenced in year 1:		Projects commenced in year 1:	
C	1030	C	1030
A	300	A	300
D	940	E	578
20 % E (assuming divisibility)	116		1908
	2386		
Projects commenced in year 2:		Projects commenced in year 2:	
B (net present value discounted for one year)	314	D (net present value discounted for one year)	893
		B (net present value discounted for one year)	314
	2700		3115

The above procedure can be generalized. We should attempt to calculate the net present-value loss from the deferment of each project. This can be done by deducting from the net present value of the project if undertaken immediately that obtained if it were postponed until next year. To obtain a relative measure, such losses should be divided by the necessary investment for each project to obtain an index of postponability.

Deciding which projects to postpone gets more difficult when capital rationing is expected to extend over several periods. The general consensus in the literature is that mathematical programming ought to be used in this situation. This is the subject of the next chapter. This does not mean that our simple analysis is of no practical use. The information requirements of programming models are considerable, and few firms use programming models for capital-budgeting decisions. Moreover, our crude approaches do highlight some of the problems to be solved before more sophisticated methods can be used. For example, the discount rate used should reflect opportunity costs but it is not yet clear how foregone opportunities can be quantified prior to selecting the best set of investments. Finally, this chapter has shown that the choice between the net present value and the internal rate of return methods of appraisal is not as clear cut as, perhaps, it seemed in earlier chapters.

11 Capital Rationing and Mathematical Programming

Introduction and overview

With multi-period capital rationing, the capital budgeting problem becomes one of maximization subject to the fund constraints of each year. This can be viewed as a mathematical programming problem and several authors have suggested the application of mathematical programming to situations of capital rationing. The pioneer was Weingartner (1963) but see also Baumol and Quandt (1965).

Programming techniques do not require a preliminary ordering of investment opportunities along a project opportunity curve as did the diagrammatic treatment in chapter 10. Programming calculations generate such a ranking implicitly. The use of mathematical programming frees us from one of the difficulties of our earlier analysis.

Further, programming is a very powerful computational tool for dealing with situations involving an examination of many combinations of projects. It becomes clear that such a tool is needed to obtain optimal solutions for multi-period capital rationing when we recall the quite sophisticated techniques needed to achieve, even, an approximate solution in the one-period case.

Moreover, programming models generate internal opportunity costs (dual values or shadow prices) which enable us to evaluate the opportunity cost of the funds constraint for any period, and to estimate which of these constraints could most profitably be relieved. Programming in its more sophisticated forms enables us to solve simultaneously, at least in a conceptual way, the investment, financing and dividend problems, so that the best use, in terms of our objective, is made of both scarce funds and any other factors that may be in short supply.

The use of mathematical programming in capital budgeting is

not restricted to capital-rationing situations. The technique should be useful whenever management are trying to make optimal financial decisions in the face of restrictions on their freedom of action; such as, that dividends must not fall below a certain level, and that no more than, say, 10 per cent of accepted projects can be of the cost-reduction type.

However, the time has not yet arrived when optimal financing and investment decisions can be obtained merely by pressing a computer button to activate a programming model. Such notions lie in the future partly because of the amount of data needed by the models, and partly owing to the existence of unsolved theoretical problems. Prominent among the latter are (a) the adaptation of programming to deal with uncertainty (see, however, Peterson, 1969, ch. 15) and (b) the definition of the correct discount rate for capital-rationing situations.

However, there seems no doubt that the future lies with programming models. Our investigation will be in two parts. First, a simple two-period capital-rationing problem will be examined with the aid of linear programming. This example is constructed along the pattern of those used in simple introductions to linear programming (see Baumol, 1965, Ch. 5). (It is hoped that any difficulties with the presentation of linear programming in this chapter may be quickly resolved by reference to such books.) However, the chapter is also meant to help the reader who has no previous knowledge of these techniques to appreciate the benefits of using programming in project appraisal. The model used in the next section is, therefore, highly artificial and is not meant to be of direct use in dealing with real world capital-rationing problems.

The final section of this chapter continues our journey into the future by examining some of the adjustments necessary to render our simple programming model operational in complex rationing situations extending over several time periods.

Capital rationing and linear programming: a simple example

We are going to consider the case of a businessman who has decided to start a company which will hire out cars and trucks to other companies. He has estimated that the business will last three years and that all hiring agreements will be of this length and will be signed at the beginning of the period. He is certain that he can hire out as many cars and trucks as he wishes at his standard fee. All such fees are paid to him in a lump sum at the end of the third year. The net present values contributed by each car or truck rented out under these agreements are £200 and £500 respectively. All the vehicles he intends to use must be bought at the beginning of year one. Trucks cost £400 each, of which £100 must be paid at the end of year one and the balance at the end of the second year. Cars cost £300 each, £200 being due at the end of the first year and the remainder at the end of the second. The businessman estimates that his available funds will be £40000 in year one and £30000 in year two; that is, he is subject to capital rationing.

We will assume that the decision-maker's problem is to purchase that number of cars and trucks which maximize the net present value he receives from the venture, given his limited funds. He would be unwise to concentrate solely on one type of vehicle. Cars are a relatively expensive use of money in year one, as compared with trucks, and the latter are relatively expensive in terms of second-year funds. This can easily be illustrated by studying the effects of concentrating on trucks. The maximum number of trucks that can be purchased is 100. This number of trucks completely absorbs all the second year funds $\left(\dfrac{£30000}{£300} = 100 \right)$, and yields a total net present-value of £50000. Such a policy will not be optimal for an arbitrarily chosen combination of 150 cars and 50 trucks yields £55000 in net present-value terms and yet does not infringe the businessman's constraints.

We will solve this simple example by linear programming, and use our solution as a jumping-off point for further discussion. The word 'linear' means that the costs and revenues per unit will remain constant whatever the number of vehicles bought or hired out. This amounts to assuming that, for example, the businessman neither obtains nor gives quantity discounts and that the rental fees per vehicle are constant for any volume of business; that is, these fees do not have to be lowered to encourage demand. More generally, linearity means that all the variables in a problem, such as the amount of funds used, are assumed to vary directly with changes in the decision variables (in our case, the number of cars and trucks) and that the per unit variation for each factor will be constant over all levels of any decision variable.

There is, in fact, no need to use programming to solve our simple problem for Lorie and Savage (1955) have suggested an easier approach. However, their method does suffer from some defects which make it inappropriate for more sophisticated problems.

The data of our example are summarized below:

Table 29 Data for a linear programming solution

| | Per vehicle | |
	Cars £00s	Trucks £00s
net present value	2	5
payment in first year	2	1
payment in second year	1	3
total cost (undiscounted)	3	4
funds available in year one £40000	–	–
funds available in year two £30000	–	–

The data in the table can be used to set up a linear programming model of the problem. The aim is to choose that mix of cars and trucks which maximizes the businessman's net present worth. Each car contributes £200 to this and each truck £500, and thus our objective can be expressed in programming notation as:

maximize $2c + 5t$,

where c is the number of cars bought and t is the number of trucks. For ease of presentation the coefficients are expressed in hundreds of pounds. The next step is to express the funds constraints in the form required by programming models. Each car bought requires a payment of £200 in the first year and each truck £100. The businessman cannot spend more than £40000 on these two types of vehicle in this year. Again, working in hundreds of pounds, we obtain:

$2c + t \leqslant £400.$

This expression says that the total amount spent on cars and trucks in the first year must be no more than £40000. Similarly, the limit on funds in the second year can be expressed as:

$$c + 3t \leqslant £300.$$

Finally, we must instruct the programme that it is impossible to buy negative quantities of vehicles, for otherwise if it were found that the purchase of one type of vehicle was unprofitable, the model would reason that buying negative quantities of this type of vehicle would be profitable. This difficulty can be avoided by adding the restrictions that:

$$c \geqslant 0 \quad \text{and} \quad t \geqslant 0.$$

These non-negativity constraints allow only non-negative quantities of each vehicle to be purchased. Note that our model does not restrict c and t to being whole numbers and, therefore, allows the purchase of fractional parts of vehicles. There exists a method of programming called *integer* programming which generates answers only in whole units. Such answers are obtained at the cost of more complex calculations, together with extra difficulty in interpreting the economic meaning of the results obtained.

Our completed model is obtained by collecting together the above expressions thus:

The objective: maximize $2c + 5t$

Constraints: subject to: $2c + t \leqslant 400$

$$c + 3t \leqslant 300$$

$$c \geqslant 0, t \geqslant 0$$

The optimal number of cars and trucks can easily be generated by the usual linear programming methods (see Baumol, 1965, ch. 5). The graphical analysis below will be used to give some idea of the method of solution. The number of trucks is plotted on the horizontal axis and the quantity of cars on the vertical axis. The fund constraints can be charted in the following way. Abstracting from the payment required in the second year, 400 trucks could be purchased if all the £40000 available in the first year were spent on them. Alternatively, 200 cars could be obtained if the whole £40000 were concentrated on their purchase. The line connecting these two points shows all the combinations of cars and trucks which could be bought for £40000 (line AB). The constraint in the second year is represented by line CD which indicates all the combinations of the two types of vehicles which could be bought with the £30000 available in that year.

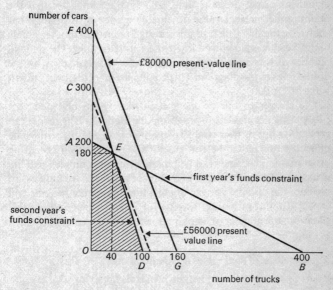

Fig. 23 Graphical solution of a linear programming problem

It is clear from Figure 23 that only a few combinations of vehicles satisfy both the constraints. For example, although there is money available in the first year to buy any combination plotting along EB, no funds are free for the necessary second payment. In fact, only those mixes of trucks and cars shown by the shaded area in the diagram (the feasible region) are available to the firm, given both fund constraints. Our aim is to select from these available choices of vehicles that combination which yields the largest net present value. With our simple example, this optimal solution can be found by plotting lines of constant net present value in the diagram (such as FG, which connects all mixes of vehicles yielding a net present value of £80000), and selecting that feasible combination of cars and trucks which lies on the highest line.

Given the linearity assumptions, all present-value lines will be parallel to each other, for each extra car or truck yields a constant increment of net present value. The diagram indicates that the optimum net present value obtainable by our decision-maker is shown by the line which passes through point *E*. All other points in the feasible region lie on lower present-value lines. The optimal number of cars is 180 and that of trucks 40; as shown by the dotted lines in the diagram. This combination yields a net present value of £56000.

The answer to our problem could have been obtained very easily using normal linear-programming methods. The reader can check that our answer could have been obtained only with some difficulty by trial-and-error methods. The benefits from using programming become readily apparent in more complex real life situations. For example, trial-and-error methods are unlikely to produce the optimal answer where a firm has ninety projects and expects capital rationing to reign for a ten-year period. In this situation, the number of combinations of projects can be regarded as infinite.

The usefulness of dual values in capital rationing

Apart from being able to handle problems involving a large number of possible combinations of variables with relative ease, linear programming models also automatically generate opportunity costs for the scarce resources involved. These opportunity costs are normally called the *dual values* or *shadow prices* of the limited inputs. In our case, they measure the total increase in net present value obtained if the constraints on funds in either of the two years could be relieved.

The precise meaning of dual values and their utility in capital budgeting is best appreciated by looking at the way in which they are generated by linear programming models. This requires us to investigate the computational processes of linear programming. A full explanation of the concept and meaning of dual values requires an understanding of some reasonably complex mathematics. The objective of this section of the chapter will, therefore, be restricted to trying to give an intuitive appreciation of the subject.

The derivation of dual values

It is easier to first consider how the shadow price of capital is derived in the single-period (or one-constraint) case. In this situation, the aim should be to maximize the contribution to our objective obtained per unit of the scarce funds when such funds are fully utilized. The net present value obtained, therefore, depends directly on the amount of funds available, for it is only this constraint which stops us achieving a larger net present value. Thus, we can argue that, in some sense, we owe all such returns to the amount of scarce funds employed. Using this type of reasoning, it can be argued that each unit of such funds is responsible for earning part of the firm's net present value. Alternatively, we can say that the company's total value would decline by a specific amount if it were deprived of one unit of capital. This sum measures the opportunity cost of such finance.

Where only one year's funds are scarce the opportunity cost per unit can be quantified by apportioning the firm's total net present value between the units of funds in such a way that their total value, when each unit is valued at this cost, just absorbs the firm's net present value. This process of apportioning the firm's 'profits' to units of scarce resource (or resources in linear programming) is described in the literature as 'imputing' the firm's 'profit' to the scarce factor. The 'imputation' is regarded as correct if the aggregate value of the scarce resource(s) when valued at its per unit imputed cost exactly exhausts the firm's total 'profits'.

A numerical example may make it easier to understand the process. To construct such an illustration we will treat our vehicle-renting example as a single-constraint problem by assuming that funds are freely obtainable at their market price in the second year. With this assumption, the decision-maker would buy only trucks, for they give a net present value of £500, in return for £100 of the scarce resources, whereas cars yield a smaller net present value per unit of scarce funds. The total number of trucks which can be produced if only the first constraint is binding, all other conditions remaining the same, is 400 (40000/£100). This number of trucks yields £200000 profit (in net present-value terms). Allocating this 'profit' over the 40000 units of scarce funds gives an opportunity cost of £5 per unit.

To check whether this is a correct measure of the opportunity cost of capital, we need to see whether the decision-maker's 'profit' is completely absorbed by the total amount of scarce funds when each unit is valued at this imputed cost. That this is the case is clear, for the value assigned to the total amount of scarce funds when each unit is priced at the imputed opportunity cost is £200000 which equals the net present value obtained from the optimal number of trucks. (That is, net present value $= 400 \times$ £500 = total factor cost $= 400 \times 100$ units of scarce funds at £5 each $=$ £200000).

Our opportunity cost can be obtained in another way by calculating the net present-value decline caused if one unit of scarce funds were denied to the firm. Each pound of funds in the first year allows the firm to buy one per cent of a truck. Thus, the benefits foregone when the total funds available in the first year are reduced by £1 is £5 of net present value (1 per cent of the £500 net present value contributed by a lorry).

The dual values of linear programming can be derived in exactly the same way by imputing the firm's optimal net present value over the scarce funds in the various periods, and they have the same meaning as the opportunity cost of funds in our one-period example. The imputation operation is, in this case, more complex, but an intuitive understanding of the process should help in grasping both the concept of dual values and the advantage of having these produced automatically.

In our two-period example, with the second constraint restored, producing the optimal number of cars gives net present-value 'profits' of £36000 (£200 $\times$ 180). This amount would be correctly imputed to the scarce funds in the two periods if the total funds used on cars, when valued at their opportunity cost, exactly absorbed this 'profit'. This condition can be expressed as an equation which says that the total value of funds used on cars in the first year when valued at their opportunity cost *plus* the total opportunity cost of the corresponding second-year funds must equal the total net present value obtained from cars. The total opportunity cost of funds, for each year, can be found by multiplying the number of cars in the optimal solution (180) by the number of units of that year's funds used per car valued at their presently unknown opportunity cost.

In the expression below, the first term on the left represents the total opportunity cost of funds used on cars in the first year and the second term is the equivalent expression for the second year. The symbols p_1 and p_2 represent the unit opportunity cost of funds in periods one and two respectively. Working in hundreds of pounds, and recalling that each car uses £200 of funds in year one and £100 worth in year two, our equation can be expressed as:

$$2p_1 (180) + p_2 (180) = £360.$$

Similarly, the total 'profit' from trucks will be correctly imputed if the values given to p_1 and p_2 allow the following equation to be met:

$$p_1 (40) + 3p_2 (40) = £200,$$

where 40 is the number of trucks in the optimal solution and p_1 and p_2 are defined in the same way as for the first expression. Thus, we have two equations and two unknowns and solving these two simultaneous equations gives shadow prices for funds in the two periods. This imputed value is found to be approximately £0·20 per unit of money in period one, and £1·6 per unit for period-two funds. These values could not be easily obtained by *a priori* reasoning.

Dual values reflect the effect of reducing constraints by one unit and rearranging the firm's operations to minimize the effect of this. Such opportunity costs are difficult, if not impossible, to estimate intuitively.

The meaning of dual values

With this background it should be easier to appreciate the usefulness of dual values. It can be shown that, in our case, these measure the incremental net present value obtained per pound of funds in either period, given that this money is allocated optimally between cars and trucks. They tell us how much it is worth paying over and above the market price for extra units of funds in either period. They also serve to measure the cost of capital rationing. In our example, it is quite clear that the businessman should concentrate on relieving the fund constraint in the second year, for such funds have much the highest shadow price.

The ratio of the shadow prices of any two years (p_t/p_{t-1}) represent the rate of exchange of scarce funds between years, and indicate the profitability of transfers between periods, where these are possible. In our example, such transfers are not allowed but, even here, the ratio of our dual prices serves to indicate the constraint that could be most profitably relieved.

Another use for the dual values is to help in appraising any investment projects which might be suggested as substitutes for cars or trucks. Such a substitution should be made only if it were found that the new project, say, motorboats, at least covered the cost of the scarce funds required when these are valued at their shadow price. For example, assume that each motorboat yielded a net present value of £100 in return for outlays of £50 in the first year and £100 in the second. This project should be rejected for the cost of the scarce funds used when valued at their shadow prices is £170 (50 × £0·20 + 100 × £1·6 = £10 + £160) and exceeds the net present value obtained per motor boat.

Our discussion of dual values assumes that only small changes to the optimal plan are envisaged, and that no substantial changes in the parameters (structural variables) of the model are likely. A major alteration in plans or a large change in the model's constraints may cause alterations in the optimal solution. The best approach in these situations is to rework the optimal plan which, with access to a computer, can be done easily.

The dual programme

Above, in order to make clear the economic meaning of shadow prices, we obtained dual values by first solving for the optimal amounts of cars and trucks that should be purchased. It is unnecessary to proceed in this way, for every linear programme can be recast so as to yield shadow prices. This revised model, which is normally called the *dual* programme, can be used initially and often is easier to solve than the original problem. Moreover, when computers are used for linear programming, they are often programmed to print out simultaneously both the optimal allocation of resources and the dual values associated with scarce factors.

The detailed formulation of dual programmes is beyond the scope of this book. A description of this and a good discussion of the economic meaning of dual values is contained in Baumol (1965, ch. 6). All that is necessary to follow the remainder of this chapter is to remember that a dual programme gives shadow prices directly.

In our example, it would do this by seeking to minimize the opportunity cost of the funds limitations in each year, subject to certain constraints. The majority of these restrictions are those which ensure that the opportunity costs generated by the programme must be such as to ensure that the total value assigned to the scarce resources will at least equal the total net present values obtained from the two types of vehicle.

The dual programme for our cars and trucks problem is set out below:

Minimize $\quad 400p_1 + 300p_2$
Subject to: $\quad 2p_1 + 1p_2 \geqslant 2$
$\qquad\qquad 1p_1 + 3p_2 \geqslant 5$
$\qquad\qquad p_1, p_2 \geqslant 0$

The first expression says that the objective of dual programme is to minimize the total opportunity costs assigned to the aggregate amount of funds in each of the two years. The first constraint imposes a restriction on the solution so that the opportunity cost of funds per car must at least equal the unit net present value obtained from the latter. The second constraint expresses the same condition for a truck. The last constraint says that the shadow prices generated must be non-negative. The first two constraints allow over-imputation; they merely say the solution cannot assign shadow prices which under-impute the net present value obtained from each vehicle. However, the optimal solution to the programme cannot yield opportunity costs which more than exhaust the net present values of cars and trucks. Such shadow prices would not be minimized, and the objective of the programme would not be satisfied.

Our simple example is very unrealistic and assumes away most of the difficulties of practical capital-rationing situations. A later section of this chapter investigates how some realism can be introduced into our model and examines some of the problems that this brings. However, our model is sufficiently complex to highlight a theoretical difficulty associated with using mathematical programming models in capital-rationing situations.

A theoretical difficulty associated with linear programming

The aim of our resource-allocation model was to maximize the total net present value obtained from leasing out cars and trucks. The net present value per vehicle is therefore crucial to the solution, as therefore is the discount rate used. Different discount rates may alter the net present values given to the firm's projects and therefore may cause changes in the optimal solution. Such present values normally are obtained in programming calculations by discounting the project's cash flows at the going market cost of capital.

However, our one-period analysis in the preceding chapter suggested that the use of this rate does not necessarily lead to the optimal selection of projects under capital-rationing conditions. In this situation, the correct discount rate, based on the opportunity-cost of funds, seemed to emerge only when the optimal set of investment opportunities had been selected. However, the achievement of this optimal project portfolio could be guaranteed only if this opportunity-cost rate were used as the discount rate for projects.

We encounter a similar situation with our programming model, for the solution to our capital-rationing problem may depend on the discount rate used to obtain the net present values in the model's objective function. The normal market rate would seem to be irrelevant where both the firm and its equity-holders are subject to capital rationing. This rate reflects market opportunities which are not available to the firm or its equity-holders. Moreover, our reasoning in the one period case suggested that where the equity-holder can borrow and lend, we may still need to use an opportunity rate. Only where investors have full knowledge of the firm's capital-rationing policy and its investment opportunities can the market cost of capital be expected to reflect the 'true' opportunity cost.

The sensitivity of the optimal solution to the discount rate used may also distort the shadow prices generated by the model and therefore rob them of some utility.

The literature gives little positive guidance as to what discount rate should be used in programming models, and little is known about the effect of incorrect rates on the optimal solution. Much theoretical work remains to be done in this area. However, Baumol and Quandt (1965) have suggested the use of a subjective discount rate based on maximizing the utility of cash withdrawals to investors. They substitute this aim for the objective of the maximization of net present worth. That the solution might lie this way is indicated by our graphical analysis of the single-period rationing case in the preceding chapter (p. 200). This suggested that the opportunity-cost discount rate could only be obtained with the knowledge of the investor's utility function (indifference curves). Baumol and Quandt go on to show that the opportunity-cost discount rate can be quantified providing that the relevant utility function and the opportunity set can be specified. Alternatively, and more usefully, they suggest the discount rate is simply the ratio of the utility of withdrawals in successive periods. This amounts to saying that management should use, as the discount rate, a subjective estimate, reflecting their guess at the equity-holders' time preference rate(s) in the face of capital rationing.

However, Weingartner (1966) suggests that the use of utilities introduces many problems. How can the utilities that share-holders attach to withdrawals be obtained? If preferences differ between equity-holders, whose utility function should be used? Weingartner's own solution involves the use of an estimated market cost of capital based on a specific pattern of future withdrawals by equity-holders. It can be shown that each different pattern of withdrawals implies a specific discount rate for the firm's overall cash flows. The pattern used should be that which maximizes the value of the firm on the market. The appropriate rate derived in this way can be used as the discount factor in our programming models. Carleton (1969) has suggested a similar solution to the problem, and argues that the dividend versus investment decision for the firm as a whole should be solved prior to using programming models. This procedure does yield a discount factor for the latter models. However, this approach (together with that of Weingartner) seems to abandon the simultaneous solution of the investment, financing and dividend problems which seems necessary for an optimal solution and is an attractive feature of programming approaches.

Others have contributed to the debate but it would seem that all that can be suggested is that the decision-maker should try to estimate the discount rate (or rates) which he expects to reign under capital rationing and use this in his programming calculations. He should test the effect of changes in this discount rate on the optimal project selection (e.g. he should use sensitivity analysis). Further theoretical development seems to wait on advances in our knowledge about investors' utility functions.

Extensions to the simple model

For the remainder of this chapter we will abstract from the discount-rate argument, and try to show how our simple linear programming model can be made more realistic. The first step is to recognize that most firms have more than two types of projects. Moreover, often the duplication of projects is not easy – two bridges cannot be built on the same site. This problem can easily be handled by specifying the programme so that one, or any finite number, of any specific type of project can be accepted. How this may be done is best shown using symbols.

Let us define x_j as a number which represents the proportion of jth project accepted in the final solution; x_j can vary from 0, representing the absolute rejection of the project, to $1 \cdot 0$, signifying its complete acceptance. Each project wholly accepted will yield a net present value which will be represented by the symbol b_j. Our objective, to maximize net present worth, can, therefore, be expressed in this notation as:

$$\text{maximize} \sum_{j=1}^{n} b_j x_j.$$

This simply requires the model to maximize the sum of the net present values of all the individual projects accepted. Similarly, $c_j t$ will be used to represent the capital outlay required for a unit of the jth project in period t, and C_t will equivalently stand for the total amount of funds available in the tth period. Our funds constraint for the tth year can thus be written as:

$$\sum_{j=1}^{n} c_j x_j \leqslant C_t.$$

The left-hand side of this inequality represents the sum of the outlays required by each of the possible projects in the tth period. The whole expression says that the sum of these outlays cannot be greater than the amount of funds available in period t (C_t). There will be one of these constraints for each period in which funds are limited. In our simple example, there were two such fund constraints.

In this general formulation, the non-negativity constraints can be amended so that multiple projects are disallowed by saying that x_j will not be negative and cannot be greater than one. This can be expressed in symbols, as:

$$0 \leqslant x_j \leqslant 1 \quad (j = 1 \ldots n).$$

Fractional projects are allowed by the above formulation (e.g. building only half a bridge). This can be avoided by amending the last constraint to $x_j = 0$, or 1, which says that a project can be undertaken only in its entirety ($x_j = 1$) or not at all ($x_j = 0$). However, programmes that deal only in whole projects (integer programmes) are often difficult to solve and the interpretation of their dual values is much more difficult than with simple linear programmes.

More generally, constraints can be placed on the multiples of any one identical project which can be undertaken. A new shadow price will be generated by the model for each such constraint which is binding. These dual prices indicate the incremental net present value obtainable if one more unit of each specific project could be found. Such shadow prices were not encountered in our earlier example for the number of vehicles that could be bought and hired out was limited only by the available funds.

The meaning of the shadow prices associated with scarce projects can be best appreciated by recalling that, under capital rationing, funds can be found for any new project only by robbing some other project. The incremental net present value obtained from another unit of the jth project is, therefore, not measured by its net present value (b_j) but rather by this less the net present value of the project(s) it displaces. This latter is measured by the opportunity cost (p_t) of the funds the new project employs in each year (c_{jt}). The incremental net present value of another unit of the jth project (U_j) is expressed in the formula below, where the project's net present value (b_j), defined in the normal way, is reduced by the total shadow price of the funds it uses in all years of its life. This latter is obtained by multiplying the funds used in each year (c_{jt}) by their shadow price in that year (p_t) and summing these items for all years of the project's life. The project's shadow price is, therefore, given by:

$$U_j = b_j - \sum_{t=1}^{m} p_t c_{jt},$$

where it is assumed that the firm's decision horizon encompasses m time periods. The jth project's shadow price will be positive if the number of times the project can be repeated is limited and if the project is relatively more profitable than the marginal project in the optimal solution. Thus the dual prices of projects give some indication of the type of investment opportunity which should be most actively sought by the firm. In our example, the U_js associated with cars and trucks would have a zero value for opportunities to purchase and hire out the vehicles were unlimited, given sufficient funds.

One interesting point that emerges out of all this is that the optimal programme may contain projects having negative net present values when their net cash flows are discounted at the external cost of capital. This is because such investments may produce relatively large net cash inflows in some years and thereby allow the acceptance of worthwhile projects which otherwise would have to be rejected. For this reason seemingly unacceptable projects may have positive shadow prices (U_js). These indicate that their negative net present values are more than compensated by those obtained from other projects undertaken because of the relaxation of fund constraints allowed by the acceptance of these 'unacceptable' projects. Thus a project's dual price reflects both its inter-relationship with all other investments and its impact on the firm's budget restrictions.

In our simple model we assumed that the cash flows from cars and trucks were all received at the end of the third year. This allowed us to abstract from the problem of the cash flows generated by projects during their life. Such flows may act to relieve the finance constraints of the year in which they occur. Most linear programming models that have been formulated assume that such 'throw-offs' are reinvested at the market cost of capital; that is, they are lent on the market at the going rate. However, it would normally be more profitable to use such money to relieve the capital-rationing situation. Our general model can be amended to allow for this by redefining the c_{jt}s associated with each project so that they no longer represent the cash outlay required by the project in the tth year. They are now defined so that they represent the cash flows from a project in year t, irrespective of whether these are positive (cash throw-offs) or negative (investment).

As a final example of how our model can be made more realistic, we can allow borrowing in each year up to some definite limit. Such borrowing means that the model's objective must be defined net of interest charges. Borrowing restrictions give rise to a new constraint in our model and, not surprisingly, an additional shadow price for each year in which such a constraint is binding.

The new constraints say that borrowing in each year must not exceed a specific amount. Letting B_t be the amount that can be borrowed in year t, and A_t be the number of pounds actually borrowed, this can be written as:

$$A_t \leqslant B_t.$$

The left hand element (A_t) is the sum of the amount of borrowed funds used on each project in year $t(a_{jt})$. Our funds constraint for each year will need to be slightly altered to take into account borrowing opportunities.

To avoid getting involved in the capital-structure debate, we will assume that the cash outlays required for every project will be financed by a constant mix of internal and borrowed funds. The funds constraint for any year can, with this assumption, be written as:

$$\sum_{=1}^{n} c_{jt} x_j + \sum_{=1}^{n} a_{jt} x_j \leqslant C_t + B_t.$$

The first expression on the left represents, as previously, the total amount of the company's own funds used on each project. The second expression on the left represents the sum of the borrowing required by each project in the tth year. The total expression says that the aggregate investment made in the tth year cannot exceed the company's total internal funds plus those it can borrow. The above constraint applies only to the tth year but there will be similar constraints for every other year in which borrowing is limited. For some projects, c_{jt} may be negative and represent a cash inflow. In this case, an additional instruction will have to be given to the model so that it does not borrow when there are net cash inflows.

This instruction could be incorporated in the expression which must be added to guarantee that each investment outlay is financed by a constant mix of internal and external funds. This latter expression will ensure that the amount of internal funds used on any project (c_{jt}) bears a constant proportion (say, $\bar{k}$, a number greater than unity) to the finance borrowed for the project (a_{jt}). Such an expression is:

$$\frac{a_{jt}}{c_{jt}} = \bar{k}, \quad \text{where } c_{jt} \geqslant 0,$$

$$\text{and} \quad a_{jt} = 0, \quad \text{where } c_{jt} \leqslant 0.$$

The second expression says that no borrowing is required where a project produces cash inflows (c_{jt} is negative or equal to zero). Gearing and its effects could be incorporated into the model by altering the above constraints, as could increasing costs of borrowing. However, the effects of such borrowing could be treated in a linear model only if the increased borrowing caused the cost of funds to rise in a direct and constant way. Similarly, the effects of gearing could be dealt with only if the firm's costs of capital varied linearly with leverage.

The introduction of limitations on the firm's ability to borrow will bring with them a new set of shadow prices. Each of these can be interpreted as the additional net present value which could be obtained if an extra pound of borrowed finance were available in any year.

This completes our review of some of the adjustments needed to make our simple model operational in the real world. The next and final section of this chapter summarizes the weaknesses and strengths of mathematical programming as a tool for capital budgeting.

Conclusions

Linear programming models would seem to have great promise for the future. They are very flexible and can incorporate many real-world problems. Examples of such cases are where resources, other than capital, are scarce; where projects are mutually exclusive or dependent on the existence of other projects; where funds can be carried over from one period to the next and where the intermediate cash flows from a project can be invested at a rate higher than the market cost of capital; where limited borrowing and lending is allowed, and where the cost of capital increases with increased borrowing. Many examples of the adjustments needed to render our simple model more realistic are contained in Quirin (1967, pp. 191–96), Peterson (1969, pp. 450–59), and Weingartner (1963, ch. 3, 8 and 9). For a good survey of the potential of programming models for capital budgeting see Amey (1972). Enough has probably been said to give some feel for programming models and their use for decision making.

Programming methods are not yet so free from criticism that the selection of optimal investment and financing policies is reduced to merely activating a linear programming model. An adequate theoretical definition of the discount rate remains a major problem.

Moreover, most of our discussion has been couched in terms of linear programming because adequate programming techniques do not exist for some situations where increasing or decreasing returns to scale are important. The computational techniques for non-linear programming lack generality, as do those for integer models. Special models often have to be built for each specific situation, and, often, the interpretation of the shadow prices generated by non-linear and integer models is by no means obvious.

For similar reasons we have not mentioned uncertainty in this chapter. Methods of coping with this in programming models are still in their infancy but an interesting attempt in the context of investment appraisal is contained in Peterson (1969, pp. 459–579). Weaknesses in dealing with uncertainty are probably not crucial in many applications of programming, but cannot be ignored in investment appraisal.

On a more practical level, the data requirements of the models may be a substantial obstacle; requiring as they do a complete specification of both the cash flows of all future projects and the financing conditions facing the firm for many years in the future. But whenever we are faced with uncertainty, all we can do is make the best estimates possible and be willing to re-think our ideas in the light of later information. One of the great strengths of programming methods is the ease with which optimal solutions can be recalculated to take account of changed conditions; though decisions taken on the basis of the old figures cannot be so easily changed.

However, even with all these difficulties there can surely be little doubt that the use of programming techniques for investment appraisal will expand. After all, such methods have only to produce sufficiently better results than existing methods to justify their incremental cost. It is by no means science fiction to expect that in ten years time, some firms will be using these techniques to generate their optimal investment and financing policies.

The remainder of this book surveys the analytical techniques which have been suggested to allow for uncertainty in investment appraisal.

12 Risk and Uncertainty – The Individual Project

So far in this book we have, in general, abstracted from one of the most crucial problems facing the decision-maker when practising investment appraisal – that of uncertainty, or risk. These terms will be used interchangeably throughout the remainder of this book, even though some writers draw a distinction between them. This chapter deals with the risk inherent in accepting an individual project and ignores the project's effect on the overall uncertainty associated with the firm. The overall riskiness of the firm is the subject of the last two chapters of the book. We will in this chapter review how far some of the techniques presently used to deal with uncertainty lead to the best selection of projects for shareholders. This chapter also suggests that the use of subjective probabilities gives the decision-maker a better picture of the possible consequences of the choices available to him than do the methods currently in use. The following chapter discusses various decision rules which utilize subjective probabilities.

No authoritative decision rules have yet been proposed which allow the decision-maker to deal fully with uncertainty in investment appraisal. However, many useful models and techniques have been suggested to aid him in dealing with this phenomenon. Space constraints mean that only a few of these proposals can be reviewed in this book.[1] Thus, for example, no reference will be made to the use of the theory of games, simulation methods and decision trees in the appraisal of uncertain projects. (For a

1. The literature on uncertainty is vast. One of the best elementary treatments is Grayson (1967, pp. 90–125); other good treatments of uncertainty in investment appraisal are Bierman and Smidt (1971, ch. 2) and Porterfield (1965, ch. 7). Van Horne (1968, ch. 4 and 5), and Quirin (1967, ch. 10 and 11), give a more rigorous treatment of this area. Two very useful treatments of the whole subject of uncertainty are Schlaifer (1959) and Raiffa (1968). More specialized references will be given as we progress.

discussion of these subjects see, respectively, Bennion (1956), Hertz (1964) and Magee (1964).) The next section explores the usual meaning given to risk and uncertainty in the capital-budgeting literature in the context of a single project considered in isolation.

The meaning of risk and uncertainty

A decision is normally said to be risky, or uncertain, if it has several possible outcomes. Such situations are legion, and range from the tossing of a 'fair' coin through gambling on horse races to investment on the stock exchange, and include the undertaking of industrial projects. Most of the literature either deals only with situations where all the possible outcomes from any risky decision are known or considers only those outcomes which the decision-maker can predict. We will follow this practice and therefore will not deal with the problem of ignorance about future outcomes.

Most treatments of risk and uncertainty assume not only knowledge of the possible outcomes from any decision but also that the decision-maker has some concept of the likelihood of each such outcome, that is, he can assign a probability of occurrence to each outcome.[2] This allows us to think of the risk and uncertainty associated with any particular decision in terms of the probability distribution of its outcomes.

Such a distribution is shown in Figure 24, where all the possible net incomes from an investment project of one year's duration are plotted along the horizontal axis, and the probabilities attached to these outcomes are shown vertically.

The horizontal axis indicates that the results of accepting the project may range from a loss of £1000 to a gain of £9000. The vertical axis allows us to assess the likelihood of any specific outcome. In our case, the result with the highest probability of occurrence is a gain of £4000. Probabilities are expressed as decimals and thus this gain of £4000 might have a probability of, say, 0·5. The total probabilities assigned to the outcomes of a project must sum to unity. This restriction flows from our earlier assump-

2. The theory of games was partially developed to deal with situations where such probabilities cannot be assigned. See Quirin (1967, pp. 243–8), and Bennion (1956). Reference should be made to Luce and Raiffa (1957) for a more rigorous treatment.

tion that we are considering all the possible outcomes from the project, only one of which will actually occur.

The above suggests that many uncertain or risky decisions can be described by the probability distribution of their possible outcomes. For example, a similar diagram to that shown below can be used to represent the possible net present values from a multiperiod project. Any point in the diagram now indicates the results of a given set of outcomes for each and every year of the project

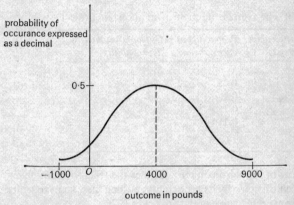

Fig. 24 Probability distribution of outcomes for an investment project

and is formed by combining those specific outcomes in every year which together yield a given net present value. The probability of any particular net present value will depend on the likelihood of the occurrence of each of the yearly incomes in the stream, or streams, of annual incomes which together yield this net present value. Thus, the formulation of a probability distribution of net present values requires us to predict the joint probability of all the annual incomes from a project.

With this background, we can explain the usual meaning ascribed to risk and uncertainty in the capital-budgeting literature. We can obtain the average[3] outcome for a project by

3. We shall later see that this measure has few of the usual attributes of an average.

weighting each possible outcome by its probability and adding together all such sums for every outcome.

The average net income of the project in our diagram is £4000. This average is a measure of the middle or the central tendency of the distribution, and is normally called the project's *expected value*. The table below gives a numerical example of the necessary calculation for a project with four possible outcomes (column 1), all of which are regarded as equally likely (column 2).

Table 30 The average outcome of an uncertain project

Possible outcomes (net incomes)	Probability of each outcome	Outcome weighted by its probability
£		£
10	0·25	2·5
20	0·25	5·0
40	0·25	10·0
60	0·25	15·0
	1·00	32·5

Each row of the third column indicates the result of multiplying one specific income by its probability; adding these sums together gives the expected value of the project as £32·5.

The risk associated with a project is normally seen in the capital-budgeting literature as being measured by the possible scatter of outcomes around this figure. This suggested measure of risk has intuitive appeal for many people, for measuring the spread or dispersion of the distribution from its expected value indicates the extent to which the actual outcome is likely to diverge from this 'best guess' estimate.

The meaning of this view of risk is probably most easily understood by looking at the diagram opposite, where the probability distributions of the outcomes for several different projects are plotted.

All three projects have the same expected value (£4000). Project C is the investment opportunity shown in the earlier diagram. Most people would regard Project B as less risky than C, for the former's extreme values are lower and there is a higher chance of

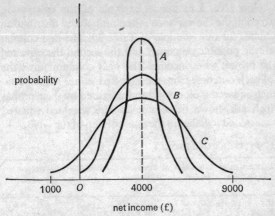

Fig. 25 Uncertainty measured by the dispersion of a project's outcomes around its expected value

obtaining the expected value of £4000. The same criterion suggests, similarly, that Project *A* is better than either *B* or *C*.

The usual measure of dispersion used in the literature is the variance (*V*) or the standard deviation (*σ*) of a probability distribution. The first step in computing the variance is to calculate the difference between each possible outcome and the probability distribution's expected value. These deviations are then squared and weighted by their probabilities. The final step is to total these sums for all deviations. The necessary computations are expressed in symbols below:

$$V = \sum_{1}^{n} p_i (O_i - E)^2,$$

where O_i represents a possible outcome, E the expected value of the probability distribution, and p_i, the likelihood of the outcome O_i. The sigma sign indicates that all the squared deviations weighted by their probabilities must be added for all possible deviations. The standard deviation (*σ*) of the probability distribution is found by calculating the square root of the variance; that is

$$\sigma = \sqrt{V} = \sqrt{\{\sum p_i (O_i - E)^2\}}$$

The table below gives a numerical example of the calculation necessary to compute the variance of the probability distribution of the outcomes for our example of Table 30. The first column indicates all the possible outcomes and the second the expected value of the project's net income. The next column shows the deviation of each outcome from the expected value. These deviations are then squared (column 4), and weighted by their probabilities, which are shown in column 5. The weighted squared deviations are added together in the final column of the table.

Table 31 The variance of a project

Possible outcomes (net incomes)	Expected value of net income	Deviation from E	Squared deviations from E	Probability of occurrence	Weighted squared deviations
(O_i)	(E)	$(O_i - E)$	$((O_i - E)^2)$	(p_i)	$p_i(O_i - E)^2$
1	2	$3 = (1 - 2)$	$4 = 3 \times 3$	5	$6 = 4 \times 5$
£	£	£	£		
10	32·5	−22·5	506	0·25	126
20	32·5	−12·5	156	0·25	39
40	32·5	7·5	56	0·25	14
60	32·5	27·5	756	0·25	189
					£368

Thus, the variance around the project's expected value is approximately £368 and the square root of this (approximately £19) is the standard deviation.[4]

The way in which the standard deviation or variance of a project's outcomes measures risk is particularly clear if we assume that the probability distribution involved is of the type described as *normal*. Such distributions are symmetrically bell-shaped, and resemble the curve shown in Figure 24, where the shape and location of the curve on the left of the average, or mean, of the distribution is a mirror image of that on the right. The variances and standard deviations of such distributions have special properties. For example, approximately 68 per cent of all the possible outcomes from a project will lie within the range defined by the mean

4. The above example is meant to give only an intuitive understanding of the calculation of measures of dispersion. The reader is referred to any elementary statistics book, such as Freund and Williams (1967, pp. 84–95), for a more rigorous exposition of calculations involved.

plus or *minus* one standard deviation. Similarly, over 95 per cent of all possible results will lie within *plus* or *minus* two standard deviations from the expected value. Again we see that the smaller the standard deviation of such a distribution, the lower is the project's riskiness. Project *A*, the least-risk project, illustrated in Figure 25, has the lowest standard deviation of all the projects shown.

The dispersion of the probability distribution of the outcomes from a project is the usual measure of risk used in the project-appraisal literature. The uncertainty associated with a project is normally quantified by computing either of our risk measures; the variance or standard deviation. The meaning of both of these depends on the interpretation we place on the probabilities used in calculating them. The next section examines briefly two possible interpretations of the probability concept.

Objective and subjective probabilities

The concept of probability used in statistics was, until recently, based on a frequency interpretation. That is, the usual 0·5 probability attached to obtaining a head or tail in a coin-tossing experiment was based on the finding that a head has an expected frequency of 50 per cent in a long series of trials with a 'fair' coin. The 1/6th probability of obtaining any one number on a six-sided die is similarly founded on the average result of a long series of experiments. Probabilities obtained in this way have been called objective, for the same results will be obtained by everyone who repeats these experiments with unbiased coins or dice.

However, frequency-based probabilities have little relevance to investment decisions which are not normally repeated many times. This difficulty led Savage (1954), and others, to seek a likelihood concept which was appropriate for such decisions. Such measures are called subjective probabilities. It is claimed that they share the same mathematical properties as frequency-based probabilities. This enables us to compute means and standard deviations for subjective probability distributions. However, this is the only similarity between the two probability concepts, for a subjective probability represents a specific individual's view about the likelihood of a given event. A high subjective probability reflects an individual's very strong belief that an event will occur. These degrees of belief are often heavily based on past experience, but may simply reflect intuitive feelings. For example, the eventuality of a specific team winning a football game may be assigned a 90 per cent probability following an intensive study of past performance or may simply reflect the beliefs of a supporter of the team.

One major difference between the classical and subjective concepts of probabilities is that the latter are likely to differ between individuals. This amounts to saying that people may take differing views about the prospects of a given investment. Similarly, an individual's subjective probability for a given event may change over time as he receives more information about the event. For example, at the beginning of a coin-tossing experiment, subjective probabilities may differ very considerably from those based on a frequency interpretation, but will tend to coincide with the latter as the experiment progresses.

The assumption that subjective probabilities can be manipulated in the same way as objective probabilities has not gone unchallenged.[5] A detailed review of the debate must lie outside the scope of this book for it requires intensive examination of the underlying philosophy of probability (see Edwards, 1961, pp. 71–4).

Some writers doubt whether people react equivalently to a subjective and objective probability of the same magnitude concerning the same event. There is some empirical evidence that subjective probabilities may be affected by the individual's view of the outcomes involved. Edwards conducted gambling experiments where both objective and subjective probabilities could be measured. He found that where the players could not lose, the subjective probabilities assigned to events tended to exceed the latter's objective probabilities. However, when losses could be made the two types of probability for any event were approximately equal. Thus, subjective probabilities may be affected by the pay-offs offered. This suggests that statistical theory based on

5. A full discussion of the difference between these two concepts of probability lies beyond the scope of this book. A good collection of readings in this area is Kyburg and Smokler (1964).

frequency concepts cannot necessarily be used unquestioningly with subjective probabilities.

This latter conclusion is reinforced by empirical studies which suggest that the subjective probabilities assigned to mutually exclusive events do not necessarily add to unity. A probability of 0·6 may be assigned to each of two mutually exclusive events, even though they are equally likely to occur, e.g. Edwards suggests that the answer to this problem is to think of subjective probabilities not as equivalent to objective probabilities, but rather as a system of weights assigned by the individual to uncertain outcomes.

We will ignore these difficulties in this and the next three chapters. Subjective probabilities will be used as if they conformed to rules of classical statistics. This approach is adopted partially because more evidence is needed about the generality of the difficulties associated with subjective probabilities. But, more importantly, if we abandon this approach in the face of these difficulties, it is not clear that we can even define and measure uncertainty, let alone produce any suggestions for its treatment in investment appraisal. The next section deals with less philosophical issues, and reviews critically the appraisal methods currently used in practice to deal with risk. Succeeding sections deal with some of the suggestions that have been made to improve current practice.

Risk adjustment in practice

In many cases businessmen virtually ignore risk, at least, in formal project analysis. All their sums are carried out in terms of single-valued estimates and risk is allowed for intuitively somewhere within the decision-making process. For example, a project may be expected to yield a net present value of £1000 but be rejected because discussion within a firm suggests that it is too risky. The essence of the single-valued approach is that no real attempt is made to quantify the uncertainty surrounding the project in any formal way (by, for example, calculating measures of dispersion).

There may be cases where the use of single-valued forecasts is all that can be done. For example, their use may be justified where management have no idea about the size and probable direction of deviations from their estimates. This view is based on the same reasoning as that which suggests it may be best to assume that a wobbly cyclist will continue straight on if there is no way of predicting the direction of his next wobble.

However, often management may have some idea of the 'cyclist's' direction. Incorporating such estimates into project evaluation may lead to better decisions, if only because they allow the decision-maker to consider more of the information relevant to the project. Moreover, the process of producing such information should force the firm to approach decisions in a more systematic manner.

A final disadvantage of the single-valued estimate approach is that it is not clear whether such estimates are forecasts of (a) the mean (the average) outcome, (b) the median result (which is the middle item of the distribution) or (c) the modal (the most likely value) outcome. These weaknesses have led some managements to seek other methods of dealing with uncertainty.

The payback method

With this approach, the required payback period for a potential project is shortened for more risky projects. This method makes allowances for uncertainty by concentrating on the short-term results from a project, and therefore on the liquidity of the firm.

Weingartner (1971, pp. 138–57) has suggested that the payback period may be a useful approximate measure of risk in situations where only a project's life span is uncertain. The chances that a given investment will make profits (or, at least, not yield a loss) increase the shorter is its payback period. Thus, all the decision-maker needs to do is weigh the chances that the project's life will continue long enough after the payback period for the investment to be worth while. Thus, the decision-maker is able to make complex decisions with but little information. He thus saves himself much time and money by using payback as a rule of thumb approach. However, against this must be set the net benefits from those neglected projects that he would have accepted if he had considered all the available information.

Whether the insistence on short payback periods for speculative ventures really reduces risk depends on how the funds returned by any project are used. The firm is safe for only a brief period if these latter are immediately reinvested in similar projects. The amount of capital the firm has at risk will depend on the time pattern over which investment opportunities reveal themselves to the firm. The company's capital will be completely safe at the end of the payback period provided that all its investment opportunities are of the same type, become available at the same time, and are all completed according to plan. Only part of its capital will be safe, at any specific time, if investment opportunities appear at different times. This transitory safety, obtained using short payback targets, may be bought at high cost if the method fails to select those relatively more-worthwhile projects which might be recommended by more sophisticated treatments of uncertainty.

Another advantage often claimed for the use of the payback period is that, with its emphasis on liquidity, it allows the firm to remain flexible and therefore enables it to take up more easily unexpected opportunities. This argument strictly has relevance only for firms under capital rationing, for otherwise opportunities could be financed by obtaining additional funds from the capital market. Even under capital rationing this need for flexibility suggests merely that part of the firm's overall capital should be kept in liquid form. There is no obvious reason why this requires that all the firm's projects fulfil some arbitrary payback criterion. (On this, see Byrne *et al*, 1967.)

Weingartner suggests another possible reason why firms may use payback as their criterion for risky projects. He argues that a project's payback period may be a crude index of the speed at which the uncertainty surrounding the proposal will be resolved. The firm may attach great importance to this factor, for the break-up value of a project may be far below its forecast present value. An investment's payback period is clearly only a partial measure of the speed of uncertainty resolution, but, in contrast to more comprehensive measures, is easily available to the decision-maker.

Adjustments to payback targets to allow for risk involves a major problem. The length of the target period is purely intuitive and has no analytical foundation, and may result in worthwhile projects being rejected.

Those using the payback method to cope with uncertainty should also understand the risk characteristics its use implies for projects. Normally, the net revenues used in the payback calculation are single-valued estimates, and are treated as certain up to the arbitrary payback date after which they are regarded as either nonexistent or unquantifiable. Such a state of affairs is unlikely; cash flows to be received during the payback period may be risky. Estimates of post-payback surpluses must enter into the decision process, for management should accept a project only if they believe that it will yield receipts after returning the necessary capital outlay. Later in this chapter we will consider methods that allow all the project's cash flows to be considered in a formal way.

Closely related to the payback method is the idea of setting a horizon for investment decisions. Possible receipts beyond this time are ignored on the grounds that these are too uncertain to be worthy of consideration. Receipts obtained before the horizon are usually regarded as certain and net present-value sums are done in the usual way. This method suffers from most of the disadvantages of the payback method and uses similar assumptions about risk. Along with payback, it may encourage subordinates to concentrate on high yielding short-term projects at the expense of more profitable long-term projects.

Conservative forecasts

These represent yet another way of treating uncertainties in practice. Here, the 'best' estimates of the project's annual outcomes are deflated by some intuitive correction factor. An arbitrary adjustment of, say, 20 per cent is made to all estimates used in project appraisal. This approach does not attempt to reflect the characteristics of the risk inherent in any given investment project.

The adjustment procedure may affect the behaviour of subordinate managers who may inflate their own estimates to allow for the application of the company's deflation factor. The major difficulty associated with the use of conservative forecasts is that because of their pessimism they may lead to the rejection of some good investments.

The above methods of coping with uncertainty are straightforward and simple to apply, but have little theoretical basis. The assumptions made about risk are unlikely to be of general applicability. They normally assume some arbitrary cut-off which cannot easily be related to any corporate goal. These methods are normally applied across the board without reference to the risk inherent in specific projects. Finally, they all encourage behaviour which is unlikely to lead to the maximization of share prices. Acknowledgment of these types of drawbacks has led some companies to look for more sophisticated methods of risk adjustment. This search normally ends in the use of some variant of the risk inflated discount rate.

The risk inflated discount rate

The shareholder in the market may be said to adjust for risk by increasing the cost of capital he charges to relatively more risky firms. If the rate at which the market discounts riskless government bonds is, say, 4 per cent, the equity-investor, when discounting uncertain future dividends, may be said implicitly to add to this a risk element. This discount rate serves, thus, to adjust for both time preference and risk. The actual risk premium used will vary between individual shareholders depending on their estimates of the intrinsic risk of a given firm's future dividends. Any actual market cost of capital derived from empirical data will be an average of the various discount factors used by individual holders of securities. Moreover, each investor may discount dividends to be received in various years in future by differing rates.

Many firms use a similar approach in allowing for risk by discounting risky projects using a cost of capital which includes a risk premium. Several different variants of the method are in use. All are subject to weaknesses.

Above, it was implicitly suggested that the firm cannot easily measure the cost of capital required by its equity-holders. Thus the firm would seem to have difficulty in using this rate in project appraisal. Even if such a figure could be obtained, it would seem to imply that the firm itself has access to the shareholder's second defence against risk – the diversification of investment holdings. The firm can diversify to some extent by accepting a mix of projects with differing degrees of risk. However, the final chapters of this book will suggest that it may not be in the shareholders' interests for the firm to attempt to do this.

The risk-inflated discount-rate approach often involves applying the same discount rate to all the firm's projects. Thus, the method does not deal with the risk involved in any specific project, and may ignore worthwhile information. This weakness is partially mitigated by a variant of the inflated discount-rate method which involves placing projects into risk classes and applying a different discount rate to each such class of risky investments. This procedure still ignores the differential risk of projects within the same class.

All variants of the risk-inflated discount-rate procedure seem to have three fundamental weaknesses. First, they use the same measure both to take account of risk and to allow for time preference. This may cause confusion in decision making.

The second weakness is best introduced by means of an example. Suppose that a given investment yields dividends ($D1$ and $D2$) of equal size and risk in two successive years. This amounts to saying that the probability distributions from which both dividends will come have the same mean and variance. Both sets of dividends should be given the same value by investors, prior to adjustment for their timing. Adjusting for risk, by adding to the normal discount rate (r) an additional constant element (k) which reflects the higher than normal uncertainty associated with the two sets of dividends, will not give the two dividends the same value. The value of $D1$ is found by discounting it by $(1 + r + k)$ and the value of $D2$ is similarly found by discounting it by $(1 + r + k)^2$: that is, the value of $D1$ equals $D1/(1 + r + k)$ and the value of $D2$ is given by $D2/(1 + r + k)^2$. This procedure does not treat the two dividends as of equal risk for $D2$ is discounted more heavily for risk than is $D1$.

Thus, applying a constant discount rate to equally risky cash flows received at different points in time will not, as may be supposed, give such cash flows the same value. Rather, the use of a constant discount rate to adjust for uncertainty can be shown to be consistent with a very large number of different risk functions.[6]

6. I am indebted to P. L. Watson of the London School of Economics for bringing this point to my attention.

It may well be less confusing for decision making to use other methods for dealing with risk which allow the individual's risk function to be taken into account explicitly. Some of these are explained in the succeeding pages of this book.

The final weakness of the inflated discount-rate method is that the size of the risk premium must be left to intuition. This may mean that different people in the firm will apply different risk allowances to the same proposal.

All the above methods of dealing with risk are used in practice partially because they are easy to understand, and partially because the academic world has not yet come up with methods which decision-makers regard as having practical superiority.

However, there exists a body of theory which attempts to tackle risk in a more formal way and can be more directly related to our goal of maximizing shareholders' welfare. These suggestions for coping with uncertainty will be examined in the remainder of this book. They have the advantage that they treat uncertainty using formal models which incorporate directly the concepts introduced in the first section of this chapter. Thus, these methods force us to think in a relatively precise way about project risk, and have led to considerable progress in isolating the crucial considerations in dealing with uncertainty.

Although the models examined below have yielded many techniques to help the decision-maker when dealing with uncertainty, they have not, as yet, provided any authoritative decision rules which allow him to resolve the problem fully. As will be explained in the next chapter, this is because the theory is still being developed and involves some rather abstract concepts which are not easy to quantify in a real world context. Thus, what follows should be regarded as a progress report on a field of academic endeavour.

Much has been written in this area and only the broadest trends can be outlined here. The interested reader is referred to the first footnote of this chapter which gives several references to more detailed treatments of the subject. The next section deals with the use of subjective probabilities in investment appraisal.

Subjective probabilities and business decision making
The use of subjective probabilities in investment appraisal

None of the above methods which are presently used in practice for treating uncertainty seems to make any formal attempt to estimate the riskiness inherent in the cash flows associated with a project. It is normal, when evaluating a project, to ask for estimates of the most likely cash flows for each year, but it may well be that management has some ideas about the likely deviations around these values. For example, the sales manager may believe that there is an 80 per cent chance that he will achieve annual sales of at least, say, 50 000 units of a product. This forecast may be used as the single-valued estimate in project evaluation, However, he may additionally feel that there is a 70 per cent likelihood that he will sell more than 70 000 units, but that if everything is against him he will obtain a sales volume of only 25 000 units per year. Many people would argue that such additional estimates are useful for decision making, and that they should be brought explicitly into the decision-making process.

The production manager of the same firm may have a very high degree of confidence (e.g. be 99 per cent sure) that the product can be manufactured at a unit cost of, say, £1·00. This latter figure would probably be used as the single-valued estimate for production costs. It may also be treated in decision making as identical in terms of risk to the sales manager's forecast even though, in a subjective sense, it is far more certain.

Management may obtain a much more graphic view of the uncertainty surrounding a project if it is provided with estimates of the likely outcomes for each of its revenue and expenditure items, and the degree of confidence associated with them by the executive involved. Management's attention is, in this way, drawn directly to the riskiness of each individual cash flow underlying the project. This should allow them to isolate the variables crucial to the project's acceptance.

This does not mean that we should ask each executive to both forecast all the possible outcomes for functions under his control, and to attach a probability to each possible occurrence. Even forecasts of the optimistic, average and pessimistic outcomes for any item associated with a project can give some guidance to the underlying probability distribution of this set of outcomes. Estimates which suggest that there is, say, a 5 per cent chance that the actual outcome from a project will lie outside the range covered by the optimistic and pessimistic forecast allow us to obtain some guide to the possible dispersion of the project's outcomes. Recall that with a normal curve there is a 95 per cent chance that all the actual results will lie within the range of the mean *plus* or *minus* two standard deviations. It is easy to estimate the standard deviation or variance of the project's outcomes using only our three forecasts if we assume that the distribution with which we are dealing is normal.

A detailed example of the use of subjective probabilities in decision making should help to understand the method. Consider a firm which is investigating whether to launch a new product which requires an immediate outlay of £4000 to cover advertising and capital assets. Management has assumed that the project will have a three year life and that the sales achieved in any one year will be independent of those for other years. The table below sets out both the forecast cash flow surpluses from the project in each year and the probabilities attached to each possible outcome.

The mean or expected value of the surplus in each year can be

Table 32 Possible outcomes from an uncertain project and their probabilities

Year 1		Year 2		Year 3	
Probability	Net cash flow	Probability	Net cash flow	Probability	Net cash flow
	£		£		£
0·10	2000	0·10	−1000	0·10	−2000
0·25	3000	0·25	0	0·25	−1000
0·30	4000	0·30	1000	0·30	0
0·25	5000	0·25	2000	0·25	1000
0·10	6000	0·10	3000	0·10	2000
Expected value	4000		1000		0

found by multiplying each possible outcome by its probability, and adding these sums over all outcomes. For example, the expected value of the outcomes in the first year is given by:

$0 \cdot 10 \times £2000 + 0 \cdot 25 \times £3000 + 0 \cdot 30 \times £4000 + 0 \cdot 25 \times £5000$
$+ 0 \cdot 10 \times £6000 = £200 + £750 + £1200 + £1250 + £600 =$
£4000.

The expected values of the net surpluses in the other two years are found in the same way and are shown respectively at the bottom of the second and third columns in the table.

The expected values of the surpluses in each year can be used to compute the project's expected net present value. This can be calculated by adding together the discounted expected values of the net cash flows for every year, for the result of any of the three years is independent of that obtained in either of the other years. We will use a risk-free rate of interest to discount these amounts; that is, our discount rate takes into account only the time value of money. This allows us to abstract from the difficulties associated with a discount rate including a risk premium.

The project has a positive *expected* net present value assuming a risk free rate of interest of 4 per cent. The project's *expected* net present value indicates the net present value of the cash flows which will be obtained if all three years yield their expected values. It is calculated thus:

$$\text{net present value} = \frac{4000}{(1 \cdot 04)} + \frac{1000}{(1 \cdot 04)^2} + \frac{0}{(1 \cdot 04)^3} - £4000$$

$$= £3848 + £925 - £4000 = £773$$

The expected net present value of a project is a useful summary measure, but it gives very little idea of the project's riskiness if possible losses are of concern.

One method of describing the uncertainty associated with a project in more detail is to calculate the entire probability distribution of the project's net present values. For example, our project would have negative net present value of £4779 if the worst possible outcomes for each of the three years occurred together. As the outcome for each year is independent of the other years, the probability of the project returning a net present value loss of this amount is found by multiplying together the probabilities of each year's worst cash flow.[7] These calculations indicate that there is only one chance in a thousand that the project will actually yield its worst possible outcome (net present value = −£4779). The complete probability distribution of a project's possible net present values obtained in this way gives a very useful picture of the project's risk. However, the calculations involved are rather tedious, for the net present value obtained when every possible outcome in the first year is combined with every outcome in each of the other two years has to be calculated.

This difficulty can be overcome if we are willing to assume that the probability distributions describing the project's possible cash flows in each year are approximately normal. With this approach, the first step is to calculate the standard deviation of the probability distribution of the project's net present value. This can be done by calculating firstly the variance of the probability distribution of the cash flows in each year using our earlier formula (pp. 239–40). These calculations give the variance of the possible net surpluses for our project in the first period as £1 300 000 (the σ is approximately equal to £1140). The cash flows of the other two years have the same dispersion around their expected value, and, therefore, have the same variance as for year one. The total risk of the project can be quantified by adding up the variances for each year, for the project's cash flows in each year are independent of those in either of the other periods.

These risk measures are expressed in money of the year in which the related cash flows are expected to be received and must be rendered comparable by discounting. This operation can be expressed in symbols as:

$$V_p = \sum \frac{V_i}{(1 + r)^{2i}}$$

where V_p is the variance of the project's net present values and V_i is variance of the project's cash flows in the ith year. The discount factor is squared so as to be in the same terms as the variance of cash flows. Plugging in our numbers gives:

7. See Freund and Williams (1967, pp. 116–17).

$$V_p = \frac{\pounds 1\,300\,000}{(1\cdot04)^2} + \frac{\pounds 1\,300\,000}{(1\cdot04)^4} + \frac{\pounds 1\,300\,000}{(1\cdot04)^6},$$

which yields $V_p = \pounds 1\,202\,500 + \pounds 1\,111\,500 + \pounds 1\,027\,000$
$= \pounds 3\,341\,000$

The standard deviation around the project's expected net present value – approximately £1828 – can be found by finding the square root of this number.

Given this information, and recalling that we are assuming that the probability distributions of each of the project's annual outcomes are normally distributed, we can calculate the probability of our proposal yielding a net present value below a specified amount. For example, assume we wish to know the probability that the project would yield a net present value lying between the expected value and a net present value of not more than £1000. This can be calculated by computing the difference between £1000 and the project's expected net present value of £773, and expressing this deviation of £227 in units of standard deviation. This yields a deviation of $+0\cdot124$ standard deviations (£227/£1828). We can compute the probability of any such deviation from the expected value of a project using the normal curve tables contained in most statistics books. Such a table tells us that there is less than a 5 per cent probability that our project will yield a net present value lying between the expected value and £1000. This is what we would expect for we are concerned with a small deviation from the expected value. Similar calculations would give us the probabilities attached to all the possible net present values from the project, provided that the probability distribution describing these can be thought of as being normally distributed. This allows us to draw the probability distribution of all the net present values which the project might return. The above techniques do not yield any decision rules but generate much important information about a project, summarizing the feelings of those involved with the project.

Mutual interdependence of cash flows

In the above example, it was assumed that the cash flows from our project in any year were unaffected by those obtained in other years. That is, the results of each year were affected by a completely different set of factors to those acting on the other years. Often, however, a new product is expected either to go well or badly in all the years of its life, depending upon whether the market is attracted by it. In this situation, there is a high degree of correlation between the results of different years. A full treatment of how this phenomenon should be taken into account is beyond the scope of this book and really requires an understanding of some quite complex mathematics which are best approached after reading the next chapter of this book. The most authoritative treatment is Hillier (1969, and 1971, ch. 1). What follows is but a brief sketch of the approach.

We shall firstly treat the case where the annual cash flows from a project are perfectly correlated in a positive way. In the context of our example, this means that any deviation from the expected value of the cash flow for any year will be accompanied by exactly similar deviations in the results for the other two years. The formula for the standard deviation of a perfectly correlated set of cash flow is:

$$\sigma_p = \sum_{i=1}^{n} \frac{\sigma_i}{(1 + r)^i}.$$

Thus, if the annual cash flows from our project are perfectly correlated, the standard deviation about the expected value of our project's net present value becomes:

$$\sigma_p = \frac{\sqrt{(£1\,300\,000)}}{(1\cdot04)} + \frac{\sqrt{(£1\,300\,000)}}{(1\cdot04)^2} + \frac{\sqrt{(£1\,300\,000)}}{(1\cdot04)^3} = £3165.$$

This suggests, as the next chapter explains, that a perfect and positive correlation of cash flows in each year, implies significantly higher risk than when cash flows are independent; remember we are defining risk in terms of deviations from a mean value. In this sense, a project is more risky the greater is the positive dependency between its annual cash flows.

Hillier (1963) has constructed a model which combines both independence between some cash flows and perfect correlation between others. He assumes, for example, that the annual production costs of his investment are independent of the results in other years, but that its yearly net marketing cash flows (sales minus the associated costs) are perfectly correlated. As an example of the approach, assume that the net cash flows for the first two years of our project are perfectly correlated, and those for the third are completely independent, perhaps, because the product is going to be transferred to a different market in that year.

In these circumstances, the standard deviation formula is a combination of (a) that used if the net cash flow for each year is completely independent of factors affecting the cash flows of the other years, and (b) that for situations when the net cash flows are assumed to be completely correlated. The general formula is:

$$\sigma_p = \sqrt{\sum_{p}^{s}\left(\sum_{i}^{n}\frac{\sigma^2{}_i}{(1+r)^{2i}}\right) + \sum_{k}^{m}\left(\sum_{j}^{n}\frac{\sigma_i}{(1+r)^i}\right)^2}.$$

The first term under the square root sign represents the sum of the variances for all items whose cash flow streams are independent. The right hand sigma sign in this expression indicates that the variance for each individual cash flow item is calculated firstly by adding together the discounted annual variances of the cash flows for each such revenue or cost item. The other sigma sign says that the overall variance for all such cash flow streams is found by adding together the discounted variances for all such elements making up the project. The second term in the formula is obtained by carrying out similar operations for all those elements of the project's cash flows which are perfectly correlated.

The first two years' net cash flows in our new product example are of the latter type, and their contribution to the project's total risk can be calculated using the second element of the above formula. The risk contribution of the third year's cash flows is found by using the first element of the formula. The total risk of our project can be quantified by plugging these cash flows into the above formula which gives:

$$\sigma_p = \sqrt{\frac{£1\,300\,000}{(1\cdot04)^6} + \left(\frac{£1140}{(1\cdot04)} + \frac{£1140}{(1\cdot04)^2}\right)^2}.$$

This yields a standard deviation of approximately £2430. As we would expect, this lies between that obtained when the new product's annual cash flows were assumed to be completely independent of each other, and that yielded when they were assumed to be perfectly correlated in a positive way.

The above model suffers from at least one severe defect. It can only cope with annual cash flows that are either perfectly correlated or completely independent. The relationship between the yearly results for many projects lies between these two extremes. There exist more sophisticated models for dealing with this situation (see Hillier, 1971). Basically, these require the use of the techniques of portfolio analysis which are reviewed in the last two chapters of this book.

Using subjective probabilities allows us to take risk into account in a much more precise way than did any of the practical methods outlined earlier. The decision-maker is given a much clearer picture of the project. With our project of Table 30, he can see that each of the four outcomes is thought equally likely. The risk measures which can be computed using these estimates indicate the uncertainty associated with the project in a quantifiable way. The method allows the decision-maker to utilize all the subjective feelings within the firm concerning the investment opportunity, which is a major advantage over the methods currently used in practice. Moreover, information about a project's expected net present value and the standard deviation around this value should help the decision-maker to assess whether the project's expected net present value justifies accepting its risk.

However, it is unlikely that businessmen are used to thinking in terms of the subjective probabilities and they may need help in using the concept. The next section describes several methods which have been suggested to help an individual to quantify his feelings about a project.

The practical derivation of subjective probabilities

The simplest method of obtaining such probabilities is to ask the forecaster to describe his feelings in terms of a probability distribution. Grayson used this method for exploration decisions in the oil and gas industry (1960). He found that after some practice, geologists accepted the idea of subjective probabilities and could describe their feelings about the likely results of a decision in terms of a probability distribution. An alternative method is to present the forecaster with a variety of probability distributions of different shapes and ask him to pick that which describes best his feelings about the project. However, many people feel uncomfortable when confronted with the task of describing their feelings in terms of probability distributions. In this case we can obtain some idea of the subjective probabilities which people assign to a given event by constructing a hypothetical situation which they feel is identical in terms of riskiness to the event under consideration. We can use the probabilities obtained in this way to describe those associated with the actual event, provided that the hypothetical situation is a reasonable replica of the real-world event concerned.

The procedure is to confront the forecaster with a choice between the actual event and a risky hypothetical event. If the former is chosen, the likely outcomes of the hypothetical event are altered until the individual is indifferent between the real world situation and its hypothetical counterpart.

For example, assume that we seek to quantify a sales manager's estimate of the likelihood that a new project will yield total sales revenue of £1 million. We can derive this probability by asking him whether he prefers either to gamble £5 for a known prize on the occurrence of sales of £1 million, or on a game of chance with known odds. Such a game of chance can be constructed by placing a known mixture of 100 red and white balls in a box and allowing the sales manager to select one ball. He is paid £10 if he selects a red ball and nothing if he chooses a white ball. He would normally prefer to invest in the hypothetical situation if the box were known to contain only red balls. Now imagine that we continue to offer him the choice of gambling either on the real-world situation or on the hypothetical game as we gradually increase the number of white balls in the box. At some stage in this process, the number of white balls in the box will be just sufficient to make him indifferent between investing his money in either the real-world or the hypothetical gamble. Increasing the number of white balls beyond this number will lead him to prefer the real-world gamble.

Let us assume that the manager is indifferent between the two gambles when there are seventy-five white balls in the box. In this situation there is a 25 per cent probability of selecting a red ball from the box and it can, therefore, be supposed that this is the subjective probability he assigns to selling one million pounds-worth of the new product. Similar experiments with different levels of demand should enable us to derive the sales manager's subjective probabilities for all levels of demand for the new product in any year. There are several difficulties associated with probabilities obtained using the above procedure. Some of these have been touched on earlier (see p. 241). For example, the probabilities assigned by the sales manager may be inconsistent; the subjective probabilities obtained may not add to unity even though the different levels of sales are supposed to be mutually exclusive. This difficulty can be solved by simply dividing each probability by the sum of the probabilities attached to all possible results. For example, if the probability assigned to both of two mutually exclusive events was 0·6, dividing each probability by 1·2 reduces the individual probabilities to 0·5 which, when added together, sum to unity. Such difficulties are likely to disappear gradually as the managers become more accustomed to the process.

A more serious disadvantage of the above process is that it may force a manager to choose a probability when really he has only rather fuzzy feelings about, at least, some outcomes. Such distorted probabilities may neither reflect his beliefs nor be acted upon by him. Some argue that, for similar reasons, findings based on the use of hypothetical gambles cannot accurately reflect the forecaster's feelings about a real-world gamble. These latter are said to become manifest only when he has to act on them in the real world. For example, there is no obvious way in which we can construct a hypothetical situation which simulates the risk that the sales manager may lose his job if his forecasts are incorrect by a certain margin.

A final problem is that such experiments are very time consuming and only capture the manager's feelings at specific times. New probabilities may be assigned to the same real-world operation if the experiments are repeated on a different day. Notwithstanding the above difficulties, many believe that the use of subjective probabilities represents a considerable improvement over current methods, if only because their use forces management to approach uncertainty in a systematic way.

The approaches outlined above do not give any indication of the best decision. The next chapter investigates some decision rules which are based on subjective probabilities and may lead to optimal decisions. None of these are, as yet, fully operational or free from criticism. However, some writers feel they hold considerable promise for the future.

13 Decision Rules for the Single Project based on Subjective Probabilities

Expected monetary value

One obvious candidate for use as an investment criterion in uncertain situations is the expected-value rule. This suggests that we should accept all those projects which yield a positive expected value. Our second example in the last chapter would be acceptable under this decision rule. The project in Table 32 generated an expected net present value of £773. This measure serves to summarize all the possible outcomes of a project in one figure – every possible outcome and its probability enters into the calculation of a project's expected value. Thus, the expected-value decision rule represents a considerable improvement over the currently-used methods reviewed in the previous chapter.

However, our new decision rule can be used without question in but a few situations. To understand this, recall that the project in Table 30 of the previous chapter (p. 238) could yield possible net incomes of £10, £20, £40 or £60, all with equal probability. The expected value of the project of £32·5 cannot, therefore, actually be obtained. The decision-maker may be affected by which of the four possible outcomes actually occurs. Thus a project's expected value does not fully measure all the uncertainty surrounding the project.

This is best explained using an example. Assume that an initial outlay of £30 was required to undertake our project. In this case, the actual outcome of the project could be either a loss of £10 or £20, or a gain of £10 or £30. Whatever happens, the expected value surplus of £2·5 after meeting the investment outlay (£32·5–£30) will not be obtained. Whether any specific individual is willing to accept the project depends on his attitude to the possible losses that may result from the project. Many people would probably be willing to accept the proposal for the loss involved, if the project does produce a loss, is not very great.

However, it is unlikely that many people would accept a new opportunity (project A) formed by multiplying all the figures for our project by 100. This new investment could yield possible gains of £1000 or £3000 but these would be obtained only at the cost of bearing potential losses of £1000 or £2000. Many writers argue that this vital piece of information is not conveyed by the amended project's expected net income of $+£250$.

As a final example of the difficulties associated with the expected-value decision rule, consider the choice between our amended project (A) and another with the same expected value. This latter (project B) offers outcomes of $+£3100$ or $+£3400$, both with a probability of 0.5 for an investment of £3000. The two proposals being considered yield the same expected value of $+£250$, but most people would opt for the latter project (B) for it involves no risk of a loss. Those individuals who prefer this latter proposal are willing to sacrifice the possibility of larger gains from our amended project (A) in order to avoid the possible loss of part of their investment. Such people are called *risk averters*. Those who would accept the more risky project are labelled *risk seekers*.

This failure of the expected-value rule to incorporate risk attitudes arises because it treats £1 of expected value as of equal worth irrespective of the risk of incurring losses associated with the project under consideration. Thus, the expected-monetary-value rule can be used unquestioningly only where the risk associated with any specific project is unimportant. Such a situation will arise when we are considering a combination of many relatively small but similar projects. This project portfolio should normally yield a total return equal to the aggregate of the expected values of all the projects. A below-average return from one project is likely to be offset by an above-average outcome for another. The possibility that any one proposal will yield a loss should not, therefore, be a problem to the firm. Today's multi-million companies may be able to use the expected-value criterion quite widely. Few proposals are of such a size that if they misfire they will seriously damage such a company and thereby cause large falls in equity values. However, this assumption may not be justified in some situations and here risk attitudes must, somehow, be taken into account.

Many writers have, therefore, sought to incorporate risk attitudes into decision making by suggesting the use of a measure which allows the value of £1 of income to depend on both the riskiness of its source and the risk attitude of the person whose welfare we have in mind. This involves measuring the uncertain outcomes of projects on a scale other than money where the unit of measurement used is called a 'utile'.

With the utility approach, it is possible to compute the expected net present utility of a proposal in the same way as we earlier calculated its expected net present value. Our decision criterion becomes: accept all projects which will yield an expected net present utility. Providing that utilities can be defined so as to reflect the individual's attitude to income relative to risk, this approach would seem to allow us to overcome the difficulties associated with maximizing monetary values. However, many problems remain to be solved before the expected utility model obtains general acceptance by the business world.

Some of these difficulties are outlined in the following sections, but prior to this it is necessary to review utility models in more detail. This can be done only briefly, and the interested reader is referred to Luce and Raiffa (1957, ch. 2). The best simple introduction is Grayson (1967, pp. 90–125). Other readable treatments are Baumol (1965, ch. 22), and Alchian (1953). The approach had its origin in a book written in 1953 by von Neumann and Morgenstern.

Expected utility[1]
Before proceeding to give an example of the use of the utility theory in decision making, it is necessary to see how a utility scale may be obtained for an individual. What we wish to do is obtain a curve, or function, like that shown in Figure 26, which relates possible monetary gains and losses to a utility index reflecting the decision-maker's attitude to these possibilities. This utility

1. The remainder of this chapter is based heavily on the existing literature, especially Luce and Raiffa (1957, ch. 2).

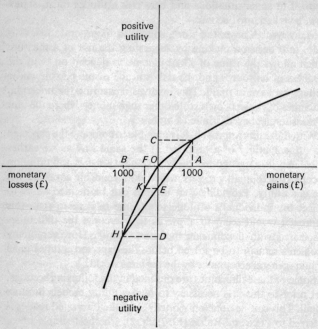

Fig. 26 A utility function

function serves merely to represent the individual's attitude to risky outcomes. Its importance in decision-making is based on the belief that it can be used explicitly as a guide to consistent decision making, both by the individual and by those to whom he has delegated the power to make investment decisions.

A brief examination of Figure 26 allows us to see precisely how an individual's utility function measures his attitude to risk. Imagine that the decision-maker is forced to participate in a gamble which offers the chance of winning or losing £1000 (outcomes A and B respectively) with equal probability. The expected-monetary-value rule would suggest that he should not mind this, for the gamble has a zero-expected value. However, the decision-maker whose risk preferences are charted in the diagram would prefer not to gamble. The utility he attaches to the gain (OC) is less than the negative utility (OD) which he associates with the possibility of an equivalent monetary loss (that is, $OD > OC$). As both outcomes are equally likely, he will expect to lose utility equal to one half of the difference between the utility of A and B $(OE$ in the diagram) if he is forced into the gamble. This can be shown by calculating the expected utility of the gamble by forming a weighted average of the utilities of the two possible outcomes using the probabilities of the two occurrences as weights. This gives:

$$\bar{U}(AB) = \tfrac{1}{2}U(A) - \tfrac{1}{2}(U)B,$$

where $\bar{U}(AB)$ is the expected utility of the gamble and $U(A)$ and $U(B)$ represent respectively, the utility of outcomes A and B.

Indeed, it can be shown using elementary geometry that the individual should be willing to pay to avoid entering into the gamble. The expected monetary value of the gamble can be found by finding the point on BA which divides BA in ratio to the probabilities of occurrence. As these are equal in our case, BA will be divided into two equal parts and the point on the horizontal axis which represents the expected monetary value of the gamble is the origin of the diagram $\left(\dfrac{(OB + OA)}{2} = 0 \right)$. Similarly, the point that bisects the straight line on which points H and E lie yields the expected utility of the gamble. At this point, (E), the vertical distance CD is divided into two equal parts and thus the distance between O and E represents the expected utility of the gamble (that is, $OE = \tfrac{1}{2}(OD - OC)$). The monetary value of this loss of utility can be found by drawing a horizontal line from E to the utility curve (point K) and finding the monetary amount that yields this level of utility. This can be done by drawing a vertical line from K to the horizontal axis. The equivalent monetary sum is shown by the distance OF. Our decision-maker should be willing to pay up to this amount to avoid the entering into the gamble. This is the type of reasoning that underlies the purchase of insurance.

Willingness to buy insurance implies risk aversion. This is clear from our diagram where the utility per extra pound declines as we move right from the origin. Each extra increment of money increases total utility, but at a diminishing rate. There is no reason why utility curves need be this shape. For example, they may be convex (i.e. saucer-shaped with their bases nearest the horizontal axis) and represent a willingness to gamble.

Friedman and Savage (1948) suggest that a utility curve may exhibit both concave and convex segments. Such a curve is shown opposite.

An individual whose risk preferences are correctly described by such a curve may both engage in small gambles when he is in a situation which is described by the convex segment of his utility function ($A - C$ in the diagram) and buy insurance in those situations which place him on the concave segments (see Alchian, 1953, pp. 144–9).

So far we have deliberately avoided saying how exactly the utility measure used in our diagram is defined. This matter is taken up in the next section.

The measurement of utility

The vertical axes of our diagrams measure utility in a very specific way. This concept of utility has little in common with the utility measures used in neoclassical economics which attempted to quantify the amount of pleasure or pain given by any commodity. This latter approach supposedly allowed us to say that a good which gave the decision-maker five units of satisfaction yielded exactly half as many units of pleasure as a commodity which generated ten units of utility.

The utility measure used in our diagrams has a far less ambitious aim. An outcome A which has a higher utility than some other possibility, B, is superior to B in a very restricted sense. The higher utility of the preferred outcome means that A would be ranked higher than B if we were ordering the outcomes on some scale.

However, our utility measures tell us a little more than this. If another outcome, say, C is inferior to B by the same number of utility units as A is superior to B, we can say that A is better than B by the same amount as B is better than C. This does not mean that we can say that A is worth 110 per cent of B and that C is only

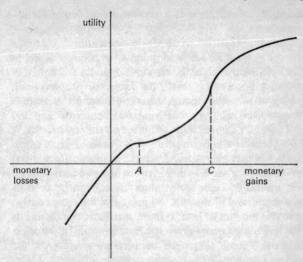

Fig. 27 A utility curve consistent with both gambling and insurance

90 per cent as valuable as *B*. Our utility index shares some of the characteristics of the fahrenheit scale of temperature measurement. This latter allows us to say both that a temperature of seventy degrees is hotter than one of fifty degrees, and that an object having a temperature of seventy degrees is as much hotter than one having a temperature of fifty degrees, as is this latter object relative to another with a temperature of thirty degrees.

Our utility measure has one final property which is that when the utilities of outcomes are weighted by their probabilities, the expected value obtained can be used to select the best action. That is, expected utilities allow us to rank sets of uncertain investments.

The above description of the properties of utility measurements means that we are quite restricted in the type of scale we can use for measuring utility. In fact, it can be shown that the utilities of all possible outcomes automatically follow once we assign numbers to any two specific outcomes. A rigorous explanation of this is beyond the scope of this book (see Markowitz, 1970, p. 215). This restriction basically follows from our requirement that the expected utility of outcomes is a good ordering device for uncertain prospects.

This requirement restricts us when selecting a utility scale to the same choices as we have when adopting a temperature scale. In this latter case, we can place the zero unit opposite any height of mercury and can similarly place the 100 degrees mark at any level. The spacing of the other temperature levels along this scale is determined by the arbitrary length interval between 0 and 100 degrees. Thus, fifty degrees must be placed on the scale so that it lies halfway between these two points. It is this scaling rule which allows us to say that the relative difference between fifty and 100 degrees is exactly the same as that between fifty and zero degrees. However, several different temperature indices can be used to describe a given level of warmth. All must give the same relative ranking to this amount of heat. It must, therefore, be possible to transform a reading on any given temperature scale into one on another scale. Thus a fahrenheit temperature reading can be converted into centigrade by applying a simple arithmetical rule.

Similarly, a given set of preferences described by a specific utility function ($u*$) can be equally well described by a restricted class of other functions. For example, an alternative scale can be obtained by multiplying the original function by b and adding a constant, a; that is, the utility attached to outcome i on the original scale (u_i*) can be transformed to $u_i*b + a$. Only linear transformations will maintain the original ordering of the outcomes on the new scale. This is why we are free to assign arbitrary utilities to only two outcomes. This restriction ensures that the rankings given to the outcomes will be maintained when the original utility scale is transformed in the above way. With this background, we can move on and see how utility functions can be used in project appraisal.

The expected-utility-decision rule

Our first task is to see how we can obtain a utility function which describes an individual's attitude towards risk and income. The usual method suggested is to offer the subject a series of choices between various hypothetical gambles. His utility function will emerge when his responses are plotted in a diagram like Figure 26.

Let us assume the individual is firstly offered the chance to participate in a lottery which will yield with equal probability either £0 or +£100000. It was indicated in the last section that we are free to assign utility values arbitrarily to any two outcomes. We shall, therefore, give utility values of zero and one, respectively, to these two outcomes. These two numbers can be used to derive utilities for every other uncertain result.

If our individual is indifferent between receiving, say, £40000 with certainty and a gamble yielding £0 and £100000 with an equal probability, the former sum must have the same utility as the gamble. This latter value can be obtained by computing the expected utility of the gamble. Thus, the utility of £40000 is equal to:

$$0{\cdot}5U(£0) + 0{\cdot}5U(£100000) = 0{\cdot}5(0) + 0{\cdot}5(1{\cdot}0) = 0{\cdot}5,$$

where the utilities of the two basic outcomes, $U(£0)$ and $U(£100000)$, are weighted by their probabilities. We now have three points on the utility function under consideration. The utility of other amounts of money can be found by proposing other gambles.

If we wish to place £50000 on the utility scale, we could ask the decision-maker whether he is indifferent between receiving this amount with certainty and, say, a 40 per cent chance of obtaining £100000 and 60 per cent chance of getting £40000. If he says he would choose the gamble, we can alter the probabilities attached to the two risky outcomes until indifference is achieved. We can obtain the utility of £50000 by calculating the expected utility of the gamble which produces this indifference. If indifference occurs with probabilities of 0·2 and 0·8 respectively, this gives the equation below:

$$U(+£50000) = 0{\cdot}2U(£100000) + 0{\cdot}8U(£40000).$$

Substituting on the right hand side the utilities we have already computed, we obtain:

$$U(+£50000) = 0{\cdot}2 \times (1{\cdot}0) + 0{\cdot}8 \times (0{\cdot}5) = 0{\cdot}2 + 0{\cdot}4 = 0{\cdot}6.$$

The utility of negative amounts of money can be obtained using the same procedure. Assume that the decision-maker is indifferent between receiving £50000 with certainty and indulging in a lottery with a 75 per cent chance of a gain of £100000 and a 25 per cent likelihood of losing £10000. This can be expressed in symbols as:

$$0.25U(-£10000) + 0.75U(+£100000) = U(+£50000)$$

By rearrangement and simplification, this yields:[2]

$$U(-£10000) = -0.6.$$

Plotting the above utilities in a diagram like Figure 26 would yield a curve of approximately the same shape as in that diagram. Such a curve would describe the attitude towards the uncertainty of a decision-maker who prefers less to more risk. It can be shown that the rational conduct for a decision-maker whose preferences are described by such a utility function is to accept all risky investment proposals which have a positive expected utility. This prescription has intuitive appeal, for the utility attached to any risky outcome reflects preferences towards both income and risk. It would, therefore, seem reasonable that the individual concerned would wish to maximize the utility he obtains from his actions.

There is a much more powerful argument to support this view. Von Neumann and Morgenstern (1953) have shown that a person will be acting according to his own tastes if he attempts to maximize expected utility, provided that he conforms to certain axioms or principles when choosing between risky alternatives. The reason why this argument is so powerful is that the assumed principles of choice which are presented in the next section are such as to commend themselves to most people (see Markowitz, 1970, pp. 225–42; and Luce and Raiffa, 1957, ch. 2). The proof that acceptance of these axioms of behaviour implies that the individual's objective should be to choose between uncertain projects so as to maximize expected utility is rather complex. This subject is therefore dealt with in an appendix to this chapter.

2. The original expression can be rearranged to become:
$$0.25U(-£10000) = -0.75U(£100000) + U(+£50000).$$
Substituting the known utilities of £100000 and £50000, we obtain:
$$0.25U(-£10000) = -0.75(1.0) + 0.60,$$
which equals:
$$U(-£10000) = \frac{-0.75 + 0.60}{0.25} = -0.6.$$

The assumptions (or axioms) of utility theory

These primary postulates, which are usually called axioms, serve the same purpose as those of geometry; their acceptance allows us to derive conclusions that are not intuitively obvious.

The axioms of rational behaviour

These have to be rigorously defined if they are to be of use in justifying utility maximization. However, the informal treatment below should give an idea of their general nature. The reader who wishes for a more rigorous treatment is referred to Luce and Raiffa (1957, pp. 23–31) or Markowitz (1970, ch. 10). The remainder of this section is quite difficult and many readers may prefer to skim through it briefly, foregoing the details.

To provide a context for the use of the assumptions, it is useful to imagine that they apply to an individual who is choosing between two gambles or uncertain prospects, both of which are composed of other gambles. That is, each outcome in one of the initial gambles entitles him to participate in a further gamble or lottery. It should be noted that the axioms set out below are far from the least restrictive that could be shown to lead to the expected utility rule. The postulates set out below are used in the appendix to derive the expected utility rule.

1 Given any pair of risky alternatives, the subject can say either that he prefers one to the other, or is indifferent between the two options.

2 The subject's preferences between the outcomes from gambles and the gambles themselves are transitive. That is, if lottery A is preferred to lottery B and B to C, the subject will prefer lottery A to C. Similarly, in any given gamble, outcome A will be preferred to outcome C if A is preferred to B and B to C.

3 If an uncertain prospect, Z, has as one of its outcomes a second uncertain prospect B, this outcome in the first option (Z) can be expressed using only the basic outcomes of prospect B. The odds to be attached to each of these basic outcomes from the secondary prospect (B) are the combined probabilities of the first (Z) yielding

the second (B) as its outcome and this latter yielding the outcome under consideration.

As an example, consider an uncertain prospect (Z) having two others (C and D) as prizes with probabilities g and $(1 - g)$, respectively. Prospect Z can be described by listing its constituent outcomes and their probabilities, i.e. Z can be expressed in symbols as:

$$Z = \{(g) \text{ gamble } C; (1 - g) \text{ gamble } D\}. \qquad 1$$

If C and D each comprise the same outcomes ($A1$, $A2$ to An), received with different probabilities, they may be written in the above notation as:

Lottery $C = (p_{1c}A1; p_{2c}A2; \ldots p_{nc}An)$ and
Lottery $D = (p_{1d}A1; p_{2d}A2; \ldots p_{nd}An)$, $\qquad 2$

where the subscripts indicate which of the gambles we are considering. Substituting these descriptions of our two secondary prospects into our definition of the basic option (Z), expression 2, gives:

Lottery $Z = ([g(p_{1c}A1; p_{2c}A; \ldots; p_{nc}A_n]; [(1 - g)(p_{1d}A; p_{2d}A2 \ldots; p_{nd}A_n)])$, $\qquad 3$

where the first expression in square brackets represents prospect C weighted by its probability in prospect Z and the second represents prospect D in the same way.

Prospect Z can now be restated using only the basic outcomes (the A_is) by combining the probabilities of each given outcome (A_i) in the two secondary prospects. This is done by calculating a weighted average of the probabilities in the two secondary prospects for each basic outcome using as weights the probabilities of obtaining either C or D as the outcome from prospect Z. Thus, the probability of obtaining the basic outcome A_1 if we indulge in the basic option (Z) depends on both the combined probability of the two secondary prospects returning this prize (A_1) and on the probabilities attached to the two secondary prospects in the basic option (Z). The chances of obtaining the prize A_1 if we undertake lottery Z are:

$$[g(p_{1c}A1)] + [(1 - g)(p_{1d}A1)]. \qquad 4$$

The second element in the first set of squared brackets indicates the probability of obtaining A_1 from prospect C, weighted by the chance of obtaining C as an outcome from Z (the first element in the first set of square brackets). The second set of square brackets represents the combined chances of obtaining D as the outcome of prospect Z and also obtaining A_1 as the outcome from D. The above expression can be simplified by collecting terms. This allows the probability of obtaining A_1 from prospect Z to be written as:

$$[g(p_{1c}) + \{(1 - g)(p_{1d})\}]A1. \qquad \textbf{5}$$

Similar operations for all the other basic outcomes of the two prospects allow us to describe the primary prospect (Z) using only the basic outcomes (the A_is) and their probabilities. This allows expression **1** to be written as:

$$Z = [(gp_{1c}) + \{(1 - g)p_{1d}\}]A1; [(gp_{2c}) + \{(1 - g)p_{2d}\}]A2; \ldots;$$
$$[(gp_{nc}) + \{(1 - g)p_{nd}\}]An. \qquad \textbf{6}$$

4 If the decision-maker is indifferent between two uncertain prospects (D and C), these are interchangeable in any compound lottery such as Z above. That is, if the individual is indifferent between our subsidiary prospect C and another gamble D, either can be used as the outcome in our basic prospect Z.

5 Of two prospects offering the same two outcomes, the decision-maker will prefer that which yields the preferred result with the highest probability.

6 If a basic outcome A_1 is preferred to two other basic outcomes A_2 and A_n, the decision-maker will be indifferent between A_2 and some prospect offering A_1 and A_n as possible outcomes. This latter gamble can be found by offering the subject a choice between A_2 and prospects involving A_1 and A_n with varying probabilities. There will be some set of probabilities associated with A_1 and A_n which will render him indifferent between A_2 and the gamble yielding A_1 and A_n. This can be stated in symbols as:

$$A_2 = \{uA_1; (1 - u)A_n\}, \qquad \textbf{7}$$

where u and $(1 - u)$ are the probabilities necessary to render the choice between A_2 and the gamble a matter of indifference and the equality sign signifies this indifference. This assumption allows us to state any basic outcome (A_i) in terms of lottery consisting of only the best and worst prizes, A_1 and A_n respectively. Axiom 4 says that such a prospect can be substituted for each of the outcomes in any gamble.

It is possible to show that if an individual's preferences are described by the above axioms, he should select risky investments as if he were maximizing expected utility. The general flavour of how this may be done is set out in the appendix to this chapter. The next section deals with some less abstract ideas and indicates how expected utility theory can be used in project appraisal.

Maximizing expected utility: an example

The expected utility of a project can be found by firstly assigning to each outcome a utility figure obtained from the decision-maker's utility function. Each outcome expressed in utility terms is then multiplied by its probability. The results of this calculation for every outcome are then totalled to give the expected overall utility of the project.

As an example, assume that an individual has to choose between the two projects shown below. The table shows, for each project, its possible outcomes, their probabilities and their utilities. These latter are measured on the utility scale used earlier.

Both projects have the same expected monetary value (see column 3), but our decision-maker will, if he wishes to maximize his expected utility, accept project 1 in preference to project 2. The utilities of the projects give a useful guide to the correct decision because they allow us to take into account explicitly the individual's preferences for income relative to risk. Once we have obtained his utility function, we can choose between projects without consulting him again. In our case, we know that he would not be willing to trade off the extra safety of project 1 for the greater chance of a larger return from project 2.

The above example brings out the advantages of using expected utility for the appraisal of risky investments. This procedure should help consistent decision making provided that the indivi-

Table 33 The expected utility of two projects

Discounted receipts net of original outlay	Probability (2)	(3) (1 × 2)	Utility (4)	(5) (2 × 4)
project 1 (£)		£		
100 000	0·03	3000	1·0	0·03
50 000	0·10	5000	0·6	0·06
40 000	0·70	28 000	0·5	0·35
0	0·17	0	0·0	0·00
	expected value	36 000	expected utility	0·44
project 2 (£)		£		
100 000	0·20	20 000	1·0	0·20
50 000	0·40	20 000	0·6	0·24
−10 000	0·40	−4000	−0·6	−0·24
	expected value	36 000	expected utility	0·20

dual's attitude to risk remains unchanged. The method ensures that the same utility is assigned to a given risky outcome whenever it occurs. When risk adjustment is carried out intuitively the value assigned to a given outcome may vary between projects and over time. It is unlikely that any intuitive procedure could easily simulate the rather complex calculations which were necessary to compute the expected utilities for our two projects.

More important is that utility theory gives us a formal structure for thinking about risk. For example, the feeling that various members of a firm's management have different risk attitudes can be tested by comparing their utility functions. This exercise might suggest that a specific function be adopted by them all in decision making. A similar approach could be employed if it were felt that subordinate managers are more conservative than their superiors wished.

Finally, in ideal circumstances, utility functions could be used to allow decision making to be delegated. Top management could provide subordinates with a utility function and instruct the latter to make decisions that were consistent with this utility function via calculations like those in Table 33. Prior to considering the criticisms that have been raised against utility theory, it is worth-while to look at the few attempts that have been made to apply the theory in a practical context.

Empirical evidence and criticisms

Grayson (1960) sought to obtain utility functions for executives concerned with exploration decisions in the oil industry. He found that some managers thought that these gave them some insight into how risk preferences affected both their own and other managers' decisions. In another company, Grayson found that the utility functions of the three top decision-makers represented very different risk preferences. The three executives involved had suspected this but the use of utility functions allowed the differences to be quantified more precisely. Swalm (1966) reports similar findings. However, Grayson does not claim that this approach to risk is taken up enthusiastically by executives, and is doubtful whether there is yet much direct use of utility theory in capital budgeting.

Most other empirical work relating to utility theory has been carried out in laboratory situations using students as subjects. Such work is too complex to describe in any detail, but does offer some evidence in favour of our model (see Edwards, 1961; Mosteller and Nogee, 1951; and Davidson *et al.*, 1957, ch. 2). Such tests normally offer the subject a choice between various simple gambles, the outcomes of which have known probabilities. It is claimed that by assigning utilities to two of these outcomes, it is possible, with many strong assumptions, to deduce utilities reflecting the subject's preferences among the other outcomes.

Mosteller and Nogee (1951) conducted such an experiment using as subjects a small number of students and national guards-men. They sought to obtain utility functions by offering choices between gambles with known probabilities of obtaining small sums of money. They then used the utility functions obtained in this way to predict how each of their subjects would choose between further uncertain prospects. Mosteller and Nogee claim that the number of correct predictions was such as to conclude that the subjects did choose among uncertain prospects as if they were attempting to maximize expected utility. They also found that utility functions differed considerably between individuals, and, indeed, between the two groups of subjects.

The Mosteller and Nogee experiments also suggest that attempts to derive utility functions in this way have to overcome many difficulties before they are successful. Indeed, Luce and Raiffa (1957) doubt whether anyone has yet successfully isolated an individual's utility function even under the most ideal and idealized experimental conditions.

A preference for a specific option results from an individual's estimates of both the probabilities of the events making up the option and the utility he attaches to each component event. The separate effects of these two factors may be exceedingly difficult, if not impossible, to unscramble empirically. This is indicated by the findings of Davidson *et al.* that their subjects did not assign a subjective probability of 0·5 to a coin coming up heads.

Laboratory studies suffer from what some writers regard as an overwhelming disadvantage. This is that, in general, they deal with trivial gambles and do not use businessmen as their subjects. Successful results obtained from such studies cannot automatically be used to explain the conduct of decision-makers involved in multi-million pound decisions. The next section deals with some of the related criticisms that have been made of utility theory.

Utility theory: some criticisms

The criticisms that have been made of the theory can be divided into two kinds. First, some researchers question the validity of the theory's assumptions and conclusions. These arguments will be briefly reviewed in the next section. The second set of critics argue that the theory is not yet operational in a business context. These views will be considered in this section.

The first practical difficulty associated with utility functions is the procedure used for generating them. Abstracting from the difficulty of getting top executives to indulge in time-consuming gambling situations, how can we be sure that responses obtained really describe their reactions when faced with actual risky decisions on which their own or the firm's future rests? Further, it has been found that inconsistent decisions are obtained even with relatively simple gambles (see Davidson *et al.*, 1957, and Mosteller and Nogee, 1951). Attempts to adjust for such inconsistencies may distort the utility function obtained. A similar difficulty is that an executive may feel forced to decide among several options even though he may not really be able to choose between them.

A final problem associated with generating a utility function for the individual is that this may be very sensitive to changes in the individual's circumstances. For example, the decision-maker's attitude to a very risky project may depend on the uncertainty associated with his existing project portfolio. Similarly, the individual's utility function may change over time reflecting his financial circumstances at any given time.

Thus, for these reasons, any utility function obtained is likely to be, at best, an approximation of the individual's preferences at a given time. This leads to a possible misuse in that the utility function obtained may, in time, be accepted without question because it is expressed in concrete numerical terms.

Even greater difficulties are associated with attempts to obtain a corporate utility function. There presently exists no obvious way of combining the utility functions of two or more members of a firm. Risk preferences may differ between the firm's shareholders and management if only because the former, owing to their ability to diversify, may be relatively more protected against the firm's liquidation. However, it is very likely that risk preferences will also differ among shareholders. The literature contains little which helps us in this situation. Grayson (1967) suggests that the utility function of the firm's top executive should be used. He bases this view on the suggestion that the top executive, to safeguard his position, will try to bear in mind the conflicting demands of all those involved with the firm when making decisions.

Criticisms of the theoretical framework of expected-utility theory

Some of these are aimed at the expected-utility rule itself, and are intended to show that its application leads to what most people would regard as inappropriate actions (see Markowitz, 1970, pp. 218–24). Proponents of this view normally set up a situation of choice between risky alternatives which leads to a contradiction between the best choice as selected in practice and that suggested by utility theory. However, it has been argued that individuals who act in conflict with the theory in these situations have preferences which are not only inconsistent with the above axioms but are also inconsistent between themselves.

Other critics have focused on the validity of the assumptions themselves. Several empirical studies suggest people often make intransitive choices. However, these choices are often corrected when such inconsistencies are pointed out. Persistent intransitivities would mean that most of the theoretical apparatus of economics and management science is of little use in practical decision making.

Another criticism of utility theory is that it does not allow for the pleasure or fun of gambling. This is because the theory assumes that any method of generating the actual outcome of an uncertain prospect is just as good as any other. However, some people get considerable pleasure out of betting on a horse race because of the suspense and surprise. Our axioms can be redrafted to allow for the excitement of betting. This may be unnecessary for most people do not spend much of their capital on such activities.

Also attacked have been the axioms (3, 4 and 6) which allow us to express any outcome in terms of a gamble using only the best and worst of the basic outcomes ($A1$ and An, in our case). It is considered unlikely that anyone will ever regard two prospects of equal utility if one involves an extreme outcome, such as death. However, we take just such a gamble every time we cross the road.

A similar difficulty is attached to axiom 5 which says that the decision-maker will choose that option having the highest probability of returning the most preferred outcome. If this were the case, no one would indulge in the dangerous sport of motor racing. That is, axiom 5 can be construed as saying that we should prefer not to race as this involves reducing the probability of living below its maximum level. This difficulty also arises from abstracting from the psychological effect attached to the way in which outcomes are generated.

In sum, it can be said that utility theory, as yet, does not lead to any practical decision rules for use in investment appraisal. However, the theory does seem to provide one of the best formal structures we have for thinking about uncertainty in capital budgeting. Further research in this area may well yield suggestions for substantial improvements to existing methods of capital budgeting under risk. Moreover, if we abandon utility theory, it is not at all clear what can take its place. The next two chapters discuss areas where utility theory has a very clear potential for improved decision making. The use of utility theory in portfolio theory has yielded many rewards, for the latter's area of concern is the individual equity-holder making decisions in a situation where the assumptions of utility theory are often reasonable.

This completes our review of the methods that have been suggested for analysing a single risky project in isolation from the rest of the firm's project portfolio. It is fair to say that no generally accepted decision rules have yet emerged.

However, much has been done to provide information helpful to the decision-maker and considerable progress has been made in isolating the crucial considerations in dealing with uncertainty. Utility theory seems to provide a good formal structure for thinking about risk, and may well have considerable potential for improving practical decision making.

All the above methods suffer from the disadvantage that they do not deal with the uncertainty attached to the firm as a whole. Corporate risk is some function of the uncertainty associated with the firm's individual projects. For example, the firm may be able to lower its overall risk by diversifying its activities. It thereby obtains benefits of the same type as a shareholder receives when he spreads his investment portfolio among different types of securities. The next two chapters of this book consider how such factors may impinge on project appraisal. Chapter 14 briefly reviews the concepts of portfolio theory, and the final chapter of the book considers how far the capital-budgeting models of earlier chapters need to be adjusted to allow for the findings of portfolio theory.

14 The Foundations of Portfolio Analysis

Introduction and overview

It is well-known that the overall uncertainty faced by an investor can on certain assumptions be lowered if he diversifies between securities.

Similarly, it is normally argued that the firm can lower its overall uncertainty by spreading its capital expenditure over several industrial sectors. With this view, the uncertainty caused by a project's acceptance depends on its effect on corporate risk. It is possible that projects which yield relatively low net present values but are affected by different factors to those acting on the firm's existing assets will be preferred to further investment in the firm's traditional area. This reasoning suggests that the capital-budgeting models presented earlier in this book should be modified to incorporate the change in corporate risk associated with the acceptance of any project.

However, it is unlikely that the shares of any specific company will form more than a small part of well-diversified portfolios. Thus, if we wish to follow those policies of maximum benefit to the firm's equity-holders, our decision rules for the firm must also allow for any alterations in the risks associated with security portfolios caused by the firm's capital-expenditure decisions. This necessitates building security-valuation models which incorporate the effects of project decisions on both the return received by investors from their security portfolios and the uncertainty associated with such returns.

These models can be constructed using the concepts of portfolio theory. This approach postulates that the market value of an individual security depends on the risk and return obtained when this share is held in combination with others. Using these models as a basis, it is possible to suggest project-appraisal models which allow for a project's effects on the overall risk and return of investors' portfolios.

The objective of this and the next chapter is to construct capital-budgeting models of this type. The remainder of this chapter reviews portfolio theory in an elementary way. In the following chapter, we utilize the concepts of the theory to build valuation models for investment portfolios and individual securities. Finally, we will review the characteristics of the decision rules implied by these models for capital budgeting.

Few specific decision rules for project appraisal can yet be derived from portfolio theory. Security-valuation models based on portfolio theory have developed only in, say, the last fifteen years, and there are, thus, many issues yet to be resolved. However, there is no doubt that important developments will occur in the future. Even in its present state, the approach serves to clarify many issues, and casts doubts on some 'popular' stock-market and capital-budgeting decision rules. For example, it will be suggested later that with this view the cost of capital concept becomes even more complex than it seemed in chapter 6 and may, when measured in the traditional way, give rise to incorrect decisions.

The next section begins our investigation of portfolio theory by looking at some of the important characteristics of share portfolios.

Portfolio characteristics

As with most recent theoretical advances in the business-finance area, a thorough review of the theory requires a considerable amount of abstract reasoning, and some knowledge of mathematics. Our presentation seeks to give only an intuitive understanding of the subject and uses a minimum of mathematics. As a first step, it is necessary to examine the assumptions used by the theory. We will start by setting out those about the individual investor.

The assumptions

The first of these is that the investor is making current decisions which will be binding until next time he reviews the disposition of his assets. The theory, as presented here, is therefore normally only relevant to one-period decisions.

The investor is assumed to be able to implement his decisions without incurring either transaction costs or tax liabilities. It is further assumed that any proportion of a security unit can be bought or sold; that is, share units are infinitely divisible. Additionally, it is supposed that all such units can be marketed with equal ease, that is, all securities are traded in an equally free market.

It is assumed that investors gauge the income benefits from a security by calculating the percentage return obtained on the original outlay. This return on investment is calculated by adding to the security's original purchase price any capital gains and dividends expected to accrue over the holding period, and expressing the result as a percentage of the original cost. Defining r_i as the rate of return, R_i as the forecast value of the security at the end of the period plus any dividends, and I_i as the cost of the original investment, the rate of return from the ith security can be represented in symbols as:

$$r_i = \frac{R_i - I_i}{I_i}.$$

It is further assumed that all investors have sufficient information to enable them to calculate the return promised by every security. Such returns are subject to uncertainty, and must therefore be defined more precisely.[1] Portfolio theorists assume that the return measure used by investors is the expected return from a security. Recall from chapter 12 that this value can be found by adding together all the possible returns weighted by their probabilities, that is, $\bar{r}_j = \sum_i^n p_i r_i$, where p_i is the probability of the ith return from the jth security. It is assumed that there are n possible outcomes. Portfolio theorists do not suggest that investors actually go through these calculations to obtain the expected return of any security. Rather, it is supposed that they act as if their 'best guess' concerning the return from any security is equivalent to its expected rate of return.

One of the most important assumptions used with portfolio models is that dispersion of a security's returns around their

1. The elements of the treatment of uncertainty are dealt with in chapters 12 and 13.

expected value serves as the investor's measure of that share's riskiness, when considered in isolation. This dispersion is measured by either the standard deviation (σ_j) or variance (V_j) around the security's expected return $(\bar{r}_j)$. Sometimes in this chapter we will express the variance as the square of the standard deviation $(V = \sigma^2)$. Again, the theory does not insist that all investors calculate these risk measures in any formal way, but rather that the risk measures actually used can be assumed to approximate to these concepts.

The way in which the standard deviation, or variance, of returns measures risk is especially clear if the distribution of possible returns is assumed to be bell-shaped (normal). In this situation, we can predict the chance of any given deviation from the expected return. For example, there is a 68 per cent chance that the actual outcome will be in the range defined by the expected return plus or minus one standard deviation $(\bar{r}_j \pm \sigma_j)$. Thus, a security with an expected return of 8 per cent and a standard deviation of 14 per cent will yield, with a 68 per cent chance, a return of between -6 per cent $(\bar{r}_j - \sigma_j = 8$ per cent $- 14$ per cent) and $+22$ per cent $(\bar{r} + \sigma_j = 8$ per cent $+ 14$ per cent).

It should be remembered that, as in the last two chapters, we are using classical statistical concepts based on the frequency concept to aid in decision making for the 'one-off' situation. Our probability distributions, again, reflect subjective degrees of beliefs about the likelihood of various outcomes. The expected, or mean, return for any security cannot therefore be treated as the most likely outcome over several periods. It is merely the central point of the probability distribution from which it is believed the actual outcome for the period will be obtained (assuming that the distribution of returns is of the normal type).

There are several other statistical concepts which could be used to measure the uncertainty attached to any security. Several writers have suggested that whilst an investor will welcome greater than average returns, he will measure risk in terms of the possibility of a return lower than some desired level (see, for example, Markowitz, 1970, ch. 9). It is therefore proposed that the semi-variance concept should be used as the risk measure in portfolio analysis. This measure is normally calculated using only returns below the mean and involves taking the expected value of the

squared negative deviations of these returns from the mean weighted by their probabilities. The semi-variance calculation can be represented in symbols as:

$$\text{semi variance} = \sum p_i \, (-r_{ij} - \bar{r}_j)^2.$$

In this formula, $-r_{ij}$ signifies that only those returns less than the expected value are included in the calculation.

The majority of the literature accepts the possible superiority of the semi-variance but continues to use the standard deviation or variance. This is, in part, because these latter measures facilitate computation when using portfolio theory in practice. In any case, provided that the probability distributions of returns are symmetric, the use of the semi-variance leaves unaltered most of the conclusions of portfolio theory. Other risk measures have been proposed, and each has at least one special advantage. These will not be discussed here, for most other elementary treatments of portfolio theory use either the variance or standard deviation of returns as their risk measure.

The limitations of these latter measures must be borne in mind when using portfolio theory. For example, they do not allow for the skewness, or lopsidedness, of probability distributions. This does not matter if distributions of returns are taken as normal, for such distributions are symmetric and are therefore completely specified once their variance, or standard deviation, and expected value are known. A complete description of other types of distributions requires the measurement of additional characteristics. However, portfolio theory becomes very complex when attempts are made to incorporate such characteristics. Only exceptional investors are therefore likely to use such refinements in their own valuation models. A further advantage of our chosen risk measures is that they are almost unique in having some common-sense meaning.

One further important assumption concerning risk is made by portfolio theorists. This is that all investors can estimate the degree to which the individual returns from every pair of shares are likely to move together. Investors are supposed to be able to predict how far a deviation from the mean return of one of a pair of securities is likely to be associated with a specific outcome from the other. More precisely, it is assumed that all investors can forecast the correlation between the returns from every pair of securities. Such estimates are likely to be beyond the ability of most people but we will see later that methods have been suggested that allow this assumption to be relaxed. However, in our initial review of portfolio analysis, we will use the proposition in its extreme form.

The most crucial supposition of portfolio theory is that our income and risk measures together provide a complete description of any security or portfolio; risk being defined here to incorporate an indicator of the association between the returns from each security and all other shares. This is reasonable for the assumptions of the theory serve to remove most of the other factors which might affect the attractiveness of any specific share or combination of securities.

For ease of understanding, the above assumptions are summarized below.

1 There are no transaction costs or taxes associated with buying or selling shares.

2 All investment decisions are being made for only one period in the future.

3 (a) Investors can forecast the expected value of the return from every security.
(b) They use this figure to measure the income benefits from each security.

4 (a) Investors can forecast the standard deviation of the distribution of the returns from every share.
(b) When considering any security in isolation, they treat this figure as if it were a complete measure of risk.
(c) They can forecast the correlation between the returns of every pair of shares.

5 The attractiveness of a security or portfolio of securities is completely measured by three variables:
(a) Its expected return;
(b) Its individual risk measured by the standard deviation (or variance) of its returns; and

(c) The correlation of its returns with those from all other securities or portfolios.

The use of the above assumptions (and others, which we shall need later) can be defended on the basis that they are necessary if we are going to begin to come to grips with investment decisions in conditions of uncertainty. With this background, we can begin our review of portfolio theory by looking at the objectives for investors implied by the above suppositions.

The criteria used in portfolio selection
Investors' preferences

The above postulates allow us to plot any portfolio in a diagram using only our income and risk measures. Figure 28 describes several portfolios in this way.

Portfolio A, which is represented by point A, yields the same expected return (S) as portfolio B, but the former's return is more

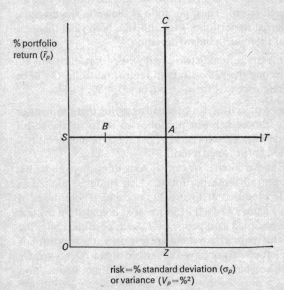

Fig. 28 Portfolios described by expected returns and standard deviations

likely to deviate from S; that is, A is more risky than B ($\sigma_A > \sigma_B$). That mix of shares represented by point C has the same risk (Z) as A but yields a greater expected return ($\bar{r}_C > \bar{r}_A$).

A knowledge of the preferences of the investor we have in mind is normally required before we can choose between portfolios described in this way. Portfolio theory, therefore, makes several reasonable assumptions about preferences between risk and return.

1 Investors are assumed to prefer more return to less, other things being equal.

2 They prefer lower to higher risk – that is, investors are assumed to be risk averse.

In combination, these two suppositions allow the derivation of two rules of behaviour:

3 First that the portfolio with the lowest standard deviation of returns will be selected from any two sets of securities offering the same expected return. Thus, portfolio B shown in the diagram, will be preferred to portfolio A for although both yield the same return, B has the lower standard deviation.

4 Second, the choice among two equally risky portfolios will fall upon that having the highest rate of return; portfolio C will be chosen in preference to A for $\sigma_C = \sigma_A$, but $\bar{r}_A < \bar{r}_C$.

These assumed objectives can be stated as saying that the investor will wish to choose between portfolios so as to maximize his expected return for a given degree of risk, or to minimize his risk for a given level of expected return.

Using the above criteria, we can say something more about the choice between all those portfolios which could be plotted in Figure 28 (reproduced as Figure 29 opposite). Those mixes of securities in Figure 29 which lie in the area bounded by the line SAC will be regarded as superior to A. Such portfolios offer the same or greater returns than A but are less risky (those portfolios lying to the left of AC) or have the same risk but offer a greater return (those combinations of securities which plot above A on AC).

Those portfolios which plot below and to the right of A will be

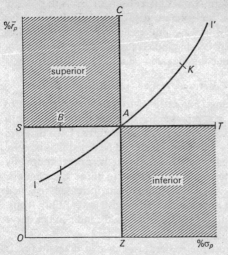

Fig. 29 Choice amongst portfolios

regarded as inferior to A by investors who conform to our assumptions. All those portfolios on, below or to the right of the line ZAT are either at least as risky as A but yield a lower return or yield the same return but involve a greater risk.

Our decision rules give us no real guidance in the choice between portfolio A and those plotting in the unshaded area of the diagram. Some of these may be preferred to A, but others may be regarded as inferior. For example, that mix of securities represented by point K yields a higher return than A but only at the cost of bearing greater risk. Portfolio L offers a lower return than A but is less risky. The choice between portfolios like A, L and K will depend on how the investor views risk relative to return, that is, on his trade-off between risk and return. This trade-off can be expressed as a ratio indicating how much extra uncertainty the investor is willing to bear to obtain an additional amount of expected return.

This rate of exchange between risk and return for any investor will depend on the characteristics of his utility function. As explained in the previous chapter, such functions allow the investor to rank the risky returns from different sets of assets in order of preference. Each investor's preferences for income relative to risk can be represented by drawing indifference curves, each of which links all those different combinations of expected return and risk that give his utility function the same value.

Investors' indifference curves for risk and return

The following diagrams (Figure 30 (a) to (e)) show several sets of indifference curves, each representing different assumptions concerning preferences for income relative to returns. Each diagram shows only a few selected curves. It should be noted that because of the convention used in labelling the axes, these curves normally slope upwards to the right, in contrast to those of economic theory.[2] Movements to the right represent increased risk and therefore, in contrast to economic theory, give lower utility. Thus, the highest level of utility is represented by the indifference curve labelled I in all the diagrams.

The individual whose preferences are shown in diagram (a), is assumed to be concerned only with the risk associated with any choice. He regards all portfolios having the same risk as equally valuable, irrespective of the different returns they may offer. The person whose tastes are represented in (b) has completely opposite preferences. He is unaffected by risk and judges all portfolios solely in terms of their expected returns. He follows the expected value rule introduced in the previous chapter in making his choice amongst portfolios.

Diagram (c) represents a halfway house between our first two diagrams. The individual whose tastes are charted in Figure 30(c) is concerned with both expected return and risk. The upward slope of his indifference curves indicates that he is risk averse and will only select an uncertain portfolio if the incremental return obtained compensates him for the risk involved. His trade-off between risk and return is measured by the slope of his indifference curves. He will select that portfolio indicated by *f* in preference to that shown by *g* only if he obtains an extra return of

2. Indifference curves of the conventional type used in economics can be obtained by plotting expected return on the horizontal axis, and risk on the other axis so that the highest risk lies nearest to origin.

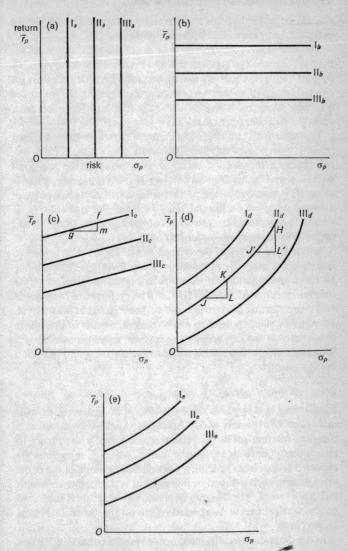

Fig. 30 Indifference curves characterizing different utility functions

fm. He believes that this will precisely compensate him for the extra risk (*gm*) associated with portfolio *f*.

The risk preferences represented in (c) are rather unusual for the rate of exchange between risk and return is constant. Another unit of risk (*gm*) will always be accepted provided that an increased return of at least *fm* is simultaneously offered. We would normally expect the individual's attitude to risk to depend, in part, upon the risk characteristics of his existing portfolio.

This situation is illustrated in Figure 30(d) where the individual starting from point *J* on curve II*d* is willing to accept *JL* extra risk to obtain an incremental return of *KL* owing to the low total return offered by his original holding. However, moving upwards along II*d* increases his expected return and will cause him to place a lower value on additional risky income. For example, he is willing to accept another increment of risk equal to *JL* ($J'L' = JL$) only if offered a large extra return (*HL'*).

Indifference curves of the type shown in Figure 30 allow us to specify completely the preferences of any investor. For example, all those combinations of securities in Figure 29 lying above the indifference curve through *A* (II'), will be preferred to portfolio *A* and those plotting below this curve will be rejected in favour of *A*. Thus, all available portfolios can be ranked in order of preference provided that we can specify the investor's indifference curves. The exact shape these take will depend on the utility function being assumed.

Investors' utility curves

Indifference curves which slope upwards at an increasing rate (as in Figure 30(d)) imply utility functions which when drawn in a diagram relating utility to return are concave with respect to return (bulge outwards from the $\bar{r}_p$ axis, where $\bar{r}_p$ represents the expected return from holding a portfolio). The slope of the curve representing such a function increases at a decreasing rate with increased return. The diagram opposite, where utility is measured on the vertical axis and expected return on the other, illustrates such a curve.

In the diagram, an extra increment of return equal to *ZX* has a utility of *PS*, but an equivalent amount of incremental return

($Z'X'$) received when the investor is already expecting an average return of OZ' increases utility by only $P'S'$ ($P'S' < PS$).

Different utility functions will yield differently shaped utility curves and will generate indifference curves of different shapes. For example, the investor whose tastes are represented in Figure 30(e) is less risk averse than the individual whose preferences are shown in 30(d). Moreover, the former's aversion to uncertainty increases more slowly. Thus, the slope of the utility curve on which 30(d) is based will increase more slowly with increased returns than that for Figure 30(e).

It is normally assumed by portfolio theorists that investors' preferences are described by a family of utility functions of the type described as quadratic. The title quadratic signifies that this type of function involves at least one squared term. Such functions have the advantage for portfolio theory that they allow utility to be specified solely in terms of expected return and the variance, or standard deviation, around this return. Such a function can be expressed, using symbols, as:

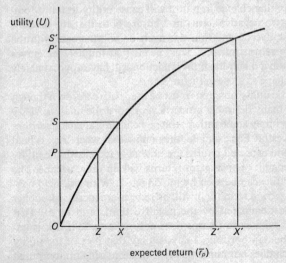

Fig. 31 Utility curve relating returns to utility

$$U = a + b\bar{r}_p - c\bar{r}_p^2, \tag{1}$$

where U represents utility and a, b, and c are constants. This general expression can be used to describe an individual's preferences by replacing the constants with numbers quantifying his attitude to risk.

The expression as set out does not directly include any risk measure. Section one of the Appendix to this chapter shows how such a term may be explicitly incorporated in the above expression. The appendix shows that this can be rewritten as:

$$\bar{U}_p = a + b\bar{r}_p - c\bar{r}_p^2 - cV_p \tag{2}$$

where $\bar{U}_p$ stands for the expected utility of portfolio p, $\bar{r}_p$, the expected return from the portfolio and V_p, the variance of this return.

Functions of this type fit well with our earlier assumptions (see p. 288) about investors' preferences. With risk held constant, an increase in expected return will cause utility to increase. Similarly, as our assumptions require, increasing the amount of risk without a compensating change in return will cause utility to fall. Moreover, the two negative terms in 2 ensure both that the investor will be risk averse, and that this aversion will increase with the size of the returns offered. This means that indifference curves derived from a quadratic utility function will have approximately the same shape as those in Figure 30(e).

Quadratic utility functions must be used with care, even though they have many desirable properties for portfolio analysis. They sometimes imply some rather strange behavioural characteristics for the investor. For example, they imply that where risk is held constant and expected returns are gradually increased, the utility yielded per unit of such extra returns will, in time, decline. The reason for this can be seen by looking at 2. With risk held constant, the second term ($b\bar{r}_p$) will, as returns are increased, sooner or later be dominated by the negative third term ($c\bar{r}_p^2$). That utility falls with extra returns does not make sense if risk is unaltered. Thus, in portfolio analysis, only that part of the utility curve which does not imply this type of decreasing utility is used (that is, we work in the range where $b\bar{r}_p > c\bar{r}_p^2$).

Quadratic functions also imply that as the investor becomes more wealthy – has more funds to invest – he will rearrange his security portfolio so that he is carrying less risk. Some writers have suggested that this is not a reaction they would intuitively expect (see Sharpe, 1970, pp. 200–201).

There is some evidence that the risk measure used in the above expression cannot be used in practice. Research suggests that empirical distributions of returns are not of the class described as normal. These observed distributions are fan-tailed; that is, their tails do not cross the horizontal axis. Such distributions do not have finite variances. This suggests that our risk measure cannot be quantified and therefore is not an operational tool. However, work by Fama indicates that our portfolio models can be extended to deal with such distributions (Fama, 1965a and 1965b). Many of the difficulties of infinite variances can be overcome by using variants of the index models referred to later and by re-defining our risk measure in an appropriate way. It can be shown that portfolio models extended in this way can deal with, at least, a class of distributions with infinite variances and have all the important properties of the portfolio models described in this book (see Fama and Miller, 1972, pp. 259–74).

The next section describes the results in terms of risk and return of combining individual securities into portfolios.

The results of combining securities

For ease of presentation, we will, in general, consider portfolios containing only two shares. The aim will be to describe the characteristics of portfolios made up of different amounts of these two securities (labelled j and s). The expected return from any combination of the two securities is a weighted average of the expected returns from the two securities ($\bar{r}_s$ and $\bar{r}_j$, respectively), with the proportions of the two shares in the portfolio (x_s and x_j, respectively) being used as weights. The expected return from any combination of the two shares is given by either of the expressions below:

$$\bar{r}_p = x_s \bar{r}_s + x_j \bar{r}_j \text{ or} \qquad\qquad 3$$

$$\bar{r}_p = x_s \bar{r}_s + (1 - x_s)\bar{r}_j \qquad\qquad 3a$$

where $\bar{r}_p$ is, as usual, the mean return from the portfolio, $\bar{r}_s$ and $\bar{r}_j$ are the mean returns from the two securities, and x_s represents the proportion that security s represents of the total value of the portfolio. The proportion of the portfolio not made up of s must be represented by j, and therefore x_j can be written as $(1 - x_s)$.

This expression for the expected return of a two security portfolio (3 and 3a) can be generalized to the situation where n shares make up the mix of securities. This can be done by writing:

$$\bar{r}_p = \sum_{j=1}^{n} x_j r_j. \qquad\qquad 4$$

Here, x_j represents the proportion which the jth share bears to the total portfolio. The above expression says that $\bar{r}_p$ can be found by multiplying the expected return from each security by its weight in the portfolio and totalling these sums for all securities.

Risk in portfolios

The uncertainty associated with any portfolio consisting of our two securities cannot be measured by taking a simple weighted average of their individual standard deviations or variances (σ_s, σ_j and V_s, V_j, respectively). The uncertainty of the portfolio will depend on the degree to which the returns from the two securities vary together. A portfolio made up of securities affected by the same influences will be more risky than one which combines securities subject to different factors. In this latter case, returns lower than the expected value for one security may be associated with results from the other which are better than its expected value. The importance of this effect will depend on three factors:

The relative proportions of the two securities in the portfolio;
The size of their respective variances or standard deviations; and
The degree of association between their returns.

We have already examined the first two factors, and we will now consider how the third factor may be quantified.

Correlation between the returns of the two securities

The coefficient of correlation is the usual statistical concept used to measure the degree of association between two variables. The returns from two securities are said to be positively correlated if large deviations above the expected value return for one security are associated with similar deviations in the returns of the other stock. The most extreme example of positive correlation of returns occurs where every deviation in the return of one security is uniquely associated with a similar deviation in the second share's return. In this case, the returns from the securities are said to be perfectly positively correlated, and knowledge of the return from one security enables us to predict exactly the return of the other security. Information about the return from one security will give us some idea of the likely outcome for the second even if the correlation between their returns is less than perfect.

The concept of correlation as used in portfolio analysis is illustrated in Figure 32 (p. 298), where the vertical axis measures possible deviations from the expected value of security s. These deviations are expressed as ratio to the standard deviation of its return (σ_s). The same ratio for share j is measured on the other axis. The possible deviations for each security are divided by the standard deviations of the distribution of returns from which they come so that our predictions of association can be expressed in multiples of standard deviations. With knowledge of the actual return for one security, we can predict the likely outcome for the other in terms of a number of standard deviations by which its return is likely to deviate from its expected value.

Each possible pair of associated deviations in the returns of two securities can be plotted as a point in the diagram. Thus, point A represents a deviation of P standard deviations for security s associated with one of Q standard deviations for the other share; each point in the diagram represents a pair of returns which may appear together. We would normally expect the correlation between returns to be imperfect and any deviation from the expected value of one security to be associated with a number of possible deviations for the other stock. Thus any deviation in the return of security s, like P, may occur in association with any of those outcomes for the other security plotting along a line like PAT. The number of outcomes on such a line will depend on the strength of correlation between the returns from the securities. If these outcomes were completely positively correlated, each return from s would be associated with only one outcome from j, and all the points in the diagram would lie along a line like LM.

The strength of correlation between the returns of the two securities can be measured by computing a correlation coefficient ($c\{s_j\}$). This coefficient can take values ranging from $+1$, signifying complete positive correlation, to -1, indicating complete negative correlation. This latter situation is represented in our diagram by a line like $L'M'$ which says that each positive deviation from one security's expected return will be associated with a given, negative outcome from the other.

The calculation of the correlation coefficient

For our purposes, this correlation coefficient can be found by taking a weighted average of all the points plotted in our diagram. Each point in our diagram represents a pair of deviations from the mean returns of the two securities expressed in standard

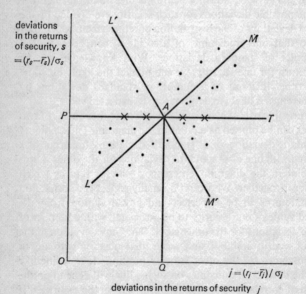

Fig. 32 The correlation of returns between two securities

deviations units. The correlation coefficient for the two securities is found by first multiplying together each possible pair of deviations $(r_s - \bar{r}_s/\sigma_s) \times (r_j - \bar{r}_j/\sigma_j)$. The result of this sum for each pair is then weighted by the probability of that pair of deviations occurring, together, and finally the results of this calculation for every possible pair of deviations are added together. This operation can be expressed in symbols as:

$$c(s_j) = \sum p_{sj} \left(\frac{r_s - \bar{r}_s}{\sigma_s} \right) \left(\frac{r_j - \bar{r}_j}{\sigma_j} \right) \qquad 5$$

The symbol $c(s_j)$ represents the correlation coefficient between the two stocks, and p_{sj} is the probability of occurrence of each pair of deviations from the respective means expressed in standard deviations units.

Portfolio theorists do not suggest that the average investor actually carries out the complex calculations necessary to obtain the correlation coefficient for every pair of securities that he may be considering. Rather, it is assumed that each investor can somehow make a guess about the association between the returns of any two stocks. It is further assumed that using such estimates in our models as if they were precise correlation coefficients enables us to make valid predictions about the investor's decisions.

The final step required before we can arrive at a measure of portfolio risk is to express the correlation coefficient in the same units as our other risk measures, that is, in units of return. The correlation coefficient can be stated in these terms by multiplying it by the product of the standard deviations of the two securities involved in its calculation. This measure of the association between the returns from a pair of securities is called the *covariance* between the two securities' rates of return ($\text{cov}(s_j)$) and in our case is given by:

$$\text{cov}(s_j) = c(s_j)\sigma_s\sigma_j. \qquad 6$$

A positive covariance indicates that a return greater than the mean for one security will be associated with similar deviation for the other. The exact strength of the association will depend on the correlation between the two sets of returns.

With this background, we can begin to investigate the meaning of portfolio risk. The uncertainty attached to each security considered in isolation is measured by the variance (or standard deviation) of its returns. The degree to which its returns are affected by the same influences as those acting on any other share is measured by the covariance of its returns with those of each of the other securities. Thus, each security brings to a portfolio its individual risk and its effect on the portfolio's overall uncertainty when it is combined with the other shares making up the portfolio.

Thus, the uncertainty produced by combining security s with security j is measured by $V_s + \text{cov}(_{js})$. The precise effect of combining the two securities will depend on the mix of the two securities in the portfolio. The risk of our two-security portfolio is found by taking a weighted average of variances and covariances of the two shares. The expression for this weighted average can be written as:

$$V_p = V_s x_s^2 + V_j x_j^2 + \text{cov}(sj)x_s x_j + \text{cov}(js)x_s x_j. \qquad 7$$

The final terms of this expression can be simplified, for the covariance between shares s and j must be identical for both securities $(\text{cov}(js) = \text{cov}(sj))$. The above expression can therefore be written as:

$$V_p = V_s x_s^2 + V_j x_j^2 + 2\text{cov}(sj)x_s x_j. \qquad 8$$

This formulation has some commonsense appeal; the uncertainty associated with a portfolio is the weighted average of both the variances and covariance of the securities involved, the weights being the proportion each share bears to the total portfolio. However, it is not obvious why the weights are squared for the variances and multiplied together for the covariances. An explanation of this requires some facility in handling symbols and is treated in section two of the Appendix to this chapter.

Our expression for the overall risk of a two-security portfolio can be generalized to encompass a portfolio made up of n different securities. Each share will contribute to overall portfolio risk, its variance weighted by the square of its proportion in the portfolio plus its covariance with all other securities weighted by the product of its weight in the portfolio and the weight of all other securities with which it covaries. The contribution of share i to portfolio risk can be written as:

$$x_i^2 V_i + \sum_{j=1}^{n} x_i x_j \operatorname{cov}(ij). \qquad \mathbf{9}$$

The overall risk of a combination of n securities can be found by adding together such risk effects for all securities; that is:

$$V_p = \sum_{i=1}^{n} x_i^2 V_i + \sum_{i=1}^{n} \sum_{\substack{j=1 \\ j \neq i}}^{n} x_i x_j \operatorname{cov}(ij). \qquad \mathbf{10}$$

The right hand sigma sign in the last term on the right indicates that the covariance effect of all n securities with security i must be added together. The second sigma sign says that such covariance effects for all securities must be added together. Our expression can be simplified because the variance of each stock is, in some sense, the covariance of its return with its own return. That is, in our expression for the covariance of a security's return, we may include its own variance. Thus, our expression for overall portfolio risk becomes:

$$V_p = \sum_{i=1}^{n} \sum_{j=1}^{n} x_i x_j \operatorname{cov}(ij). \qquad \mathbf{11}$$

This completes our review of the concepts that are necessary before we can begin to use portfolio analysis. The next section illustrates the meaning and usefulness of these concepts in the context of a two-security portfolio.

The two-security portfolio
Portfolio return

Earlier in this chapter (pp. 295–6) the expected return from a combination of securities such as s and j was given in **3** as:

$$\bar{r}_p = x_s \bar{r}_s + x_j \bar{r}_j.$$

The change in portfolio return as the mix of the two securities in a portfolio of a given monetary value is altered can be charted in a diagram (see Sharpe, 1970, p. 46). This is done below, where $\bar{r}_p$ is measured on the vertical axis and the proportion that security s (x_s) bears to the total portfolio is shown on the other axis. At the origin the whole of the investor's funds are invested in security j and he receives the expected return from j ($\bar{r}_j$) on his total investment. Movements along the horizontal axis represent increased investment in security s financed by reducing the amount of security j held. The investor holds only security s at the point labelled 1·00 and can therefore expect to earn $\bar{r}_s$ on all his funds.

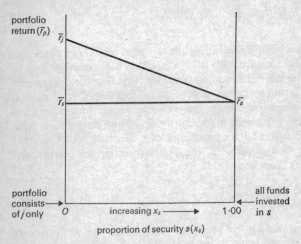

Fig. 33 Portfolio return

It can be seen from the diagram that the expected return from the portfolio is directly related to the proportion of funds invested in the two securities. An increase in the amount of s held will decrease the portfolio return by the difference between the return from j and s ($\bar{r}_j - \bar{r}_s$), weighted by the change in the proportion of s in the portfolio. Thus, those individuals interested only in maximizing their expected return will invest only in security j which offers the higher return ($\bar{r}_j > \bar{r}_s$). Preferences for a diversified portfolio must therefore arise because of attitudes to risk.

Portfolio risk

We can describe portfolio risk diagrammatically in the same way as we did expected return. However, only in exceptional cases will portfolio risk be linearly related to the amount held of any security. The horizontal axes of all the diagrams below, again, measure the proportion of security s in the portfolio. The vertical axes of the diagrams indicate portfolio risk in terms of the variance of

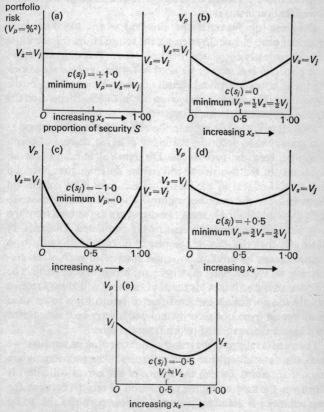

Fig. 34 Portfolio risk

portfolio returns. The diagrams plot the effect on portfolio risk of substituting security s for j under a variety of assumptions concerning the correlation between the two securities. For ease of understanding all the diagrams except (e) deal with the situation where both securities have the same variance of returns.

Diagram (a) deals with the simplest case, where both securities have identical variances and their returns are perfectly, positively correlated ($c\{sj\} = +1\cdot0$). For the present purposes, the two stocks can be regarded as identical. No advantage flows from diversification in this case.

Diagram (d) illustrates the situation where, although both securities have identical variances, the returns from the securities are not perfectly correlated ($c\{sj\} = +0\cdot5$). This diagram shows that portfolio risk may be reduced below the uncertainty associated with either individual security by a judicious mixing of the two stocks. The degree of reduction obtainable will depend on the strength of the correlation between the two securities.

Diagrams (a) to (c) indicate the effect of diversifying among two equally risky securities assuming differing degrees of correlation between the two stocks. Diagram (b) indicates that an equal mix of the two shares will reduce the minimum portfolio risk to half of that of the individual securities if no correlation exists between the securities' returns. The best case for diversification would intuitively seem to exist where the returns from the two securities are perfectly, negatively correlated. Diagram (c) illustrates that risk can be completely diversified away in these circumstances by holding an equal amount of each stock (remember we are assuming that the securities are of equal risk). The investor who distributes his funds in this way will always receive exactly the portfolio's expected rate of return for a lower than mean return from one security and will always be compensated by a higher than expected return from the other.

Diagram (e) suggests that most of our conclusions remain if we relax the assumption that both securities taken individually are equally uncertain, though the shapes of the curves will alter. It illustrates the case where the correlation of returns between the two securities is sufficiently small to allow portfolio risk to be reduced below that of either security considered in isolation. Even where this is not the case, diversification still allows the investor to obtain a higher return than that offered by the lowest yielding stock, subject to less risk than that of the most uncertain stock. Diagram (e) also indicates that equal investment in the two securities does not necessarily yield the minimum risk portfolio when the basic securities are of unequal individual risk.

The above diagrams can be constructed using our earlier expression for the uncertainty attached to combinations of securities. Section three of the Appendix to this chapter indicates how this is done.

It can be shown that the above findings are general and apply to portfolios containing more than two stocks, even though we used special, very restrictive, assumptions to derive our conclusions. These findings are summarized below:

1 Portfolios of securities whose returns are highly correlated will be of high risk. Portfolio uncertainty will be at its greatest where the returns from all component securities are perfectly, positively correlated.

2 Combining shares the returns from which are only partially correlated will reduce portfolio risk.

3 The minimum-risk portfolio is obtained by combining shares the returns from which are perfectly negatively correlated.

4 Diversification can sometimes reduce portfolio risk below that associated with any individual stock in the portfolio.

5 Diversification will allow the investor to obtain a higher income than can be obtained from the lowest yielding share without incurring that degree of uncertainty associated with the most risky share. The exact combination of securities chosen will depend on the investor's attitude to return relative to risk.

The next section indicates how the risk and return characteristics of any portfolio can be illustrated in one diagram.

The total characteristics of a portfolio

The diagram we used above to portray the changes in portfolio risk as the mix of the two securities altered can be combined with that which indicated the effects of such alterations on expected return. This enables us to summarize all the characteristics of an investment portfolio in one diagram. How this may be done is shown in the diagram below which has three parts. That section labelled 1 plots risk against differing combinations of the two securities. It is the same diagram as in Figure 34 but with the axes reversed. Risk is plotted horizontally and changes in security mix are measured downwards on the vertical axis. Section 1 corresponds to diagram 34(e) and assumes both that the returns from securities s and j are not perfectly correlated, and that security j is more risky than s ($V_j > V_s$).

Section 2 charts alterations in portfolio return against changes in portfolio mix. This diagram is the mirror image of Figure 33 with expected return still being measured on the vertical axis, but movements to the left along the other axis representing increases in the proportion of security s in the portfolio.

The final part of Figure 35 (3) combines the information contained in the other two sections. It measures expected return

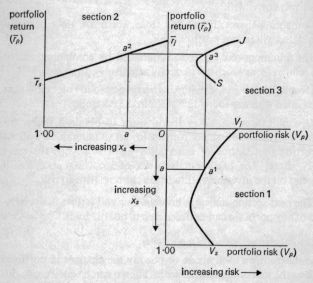

Fig. 35 Portfolio risk and return

and risk for all possible portfolios comprising securities s and j. The point labelled J in the section 3 shows the return and risk obtained from investing only in J. Similarly, point S indicates the results of concentrating all funds on the other security. Each point on the SJ curve in 3 measures the risk and return obtained from a specific combination of the two securities.

Each point on the curve can be obtained by choosing a specific mix (portfolio) of the two securities in, say section 1, and drawing from the vertical axis of this section a horizontal line ($a\ a^1$) to the risk curve, and then drawing a vertical line up to section 3 ($a^1\ a^3$). The point where this line is cut by its equivalent ($a^2\ a^3$) from section 2 will give one point on the SJ curve in section 3. All the other points in section 3 can be obtained in a similar way.

Section 3 of Figure 35, which is redrawn using a larger scale below, serves to describe completely every portfolio which can be obtained by combining our two securities.

The curve connecting the two points which represent investing entirely in either security j (J) or security s (S) measures the risk and return obtained from every possible combination of these two securities. The position and slope of this curve will depend on three factors: the individual returns from the two securities, their individual risk, and their covariance. If the returns from the two shares are perfectly positively correlated, the curve will have the minimum curvature. The lower is the positive correlation between the two securities, the more the curve will bow to the left. The slope of the curve at any point measures the amount of extra risk that must be accepted to achieve a given increment of return. For example, where the existing portfolio is composed mainly of security s bearing extra risk of PN yields a relatively large additional return of KN. However, accepting additional risk of PN ($P'N' = PN$) yields a much smaller increase in expected return (LN') where security j is the dominant stock.

The results yielded by combining any pair of securities can be plotted using curves similar to $J\ S$. For example, the SQ curve in Figure 36 represents the results of forming all possible portfolios of securities s and q. The new share q is assumed to have a higher expected return and variance than s. Similarly, the curve QJ represents the results of combining securities q and j. Thus, all the

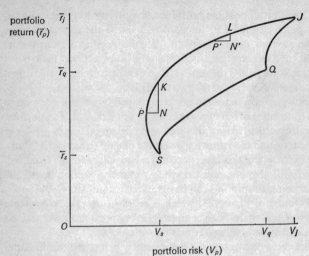

Fig. 36 The expected risk and return of every possible portfolio of securities S, J and Q

opportunities facing an investor can be plotted in the diagram as a set of curves like SJ. All possible combinations will plot within some area like SJQ which contains all the investment opportunities open to the investor. The exact shape of this feasible area will depend on the characteristics of stocks available to the investor and the constraints under which he must operate.

We have now completed our review of the foundations of portfolio theory, and have shown both how an investor's preferences can be characterized by indifference curves, and how the results generated by any portfolio of securities can be computed and represented diagrammatically in terms of only risk and returns. The first section of the next chapter uses these results to derive some investment decision rules.

15 Portfolio Analysis and Capital Budgeting

Portfolio analysis involves using the concepts of the previous chapter to obtain that mix of securities which best achieves the investor's objective. The formulation of decision rules that lead to this optimum requires a knowledge of the individual's utility function. However, it is possible to advise him that some portfolios are, in some ways, better than others, even without a detailed knowledge of his preferences.

These 'superior' portfolios can be isolated from all other available combinations of securities provided that the investor's preferences conform to our earlier assumptions. The characteristics of this set of 'best' portfolios, all of which are labelled *efficient*, are described in the next section.

Efficient portfolios

A mix of securities is regarded as efficient if:

It yields a higher expected return than any other combination of stocks having the same risk; and
It has a lower risk than any other portfolio having the same expected return.

The meaning of 'efficiency' can be seen in Figure 37 opposite which plots, in a similar way to Figure 36, the risk and return characteristics of all the portfolios available to an investor.

Considering only our second criterion above, it can be seen that portfolio L in the diagram is not efficient. All those combinations of securities lying along the line $A'L$ yield the same return as L and are less risky. In fact, of all the portfolios lying along this line only that mix of securities represented by A satisfies our second criterion. Investment in this latter portfolio minimizes the risk associated with obtaining the expected return common to all the

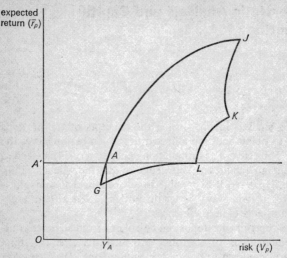

Fig. 37 Efficient portfolios

investment possibilities along $A'L$. Similar reasoning shows that each of those portfolios which plot along GJ offers the lowest risk method of obtaining a given expected return.

Moreover, only those portfolios which lie along GJ satisfy our first criterion. For example, A yields the highest return of all those portfolios having a risk equal to Y_A; that is, the expected return from A dominates that from all other available investment opportunities of the same risk quality (Y_A).

Thus, only these portfolios plotting along the left-hand boundary of the feasible area ($GLKJ$ in Figure 37), satisfy our two criteria for efficiency.[1] The investor should consider only this set of portfolios when buying and selling shares. All those other investments in the feasible area are inferior to the efficient set (GAJ). These inefficient portfolios yield either:

1. Strictly, the efficient portfolios will lie on the segment of this boundary which is vertical to the horizontal axis or slopes upwards away from the vertical axis. Thus, those portfolios lying below P in Figure 36 will be inefficient, for they are dominated by some other portfolio plotting on the section of PJ which slopes upwards away from the vertical axis.

A lower return for at least the same risk as a portfolio on the efficient boundary (GAJ); or
Involve accepting a higher risk to obtain a return no greater than that from an opportunity on the efficient boundary.

Efficient portfolios could be isolated by ranking all feasible portfolios along lines like $A'AL$ and Y_AA. However, this would be exceedingly costly and time-consuming and is also unnecessary, for there exists an easier method. This alternative procedure for isolating efficient portfolios involves using an advanced form of mathematical programming (see Sharpe, 1970, ch. 4). However, an elementary description of the method is given below. This should be sufficient to give an understanding of the ease with which portfolio theory can deal with the difficult problem of isolating efficient portfolios.

Each point on the efficient boundary of a feasible area ($GLKJ$ in Figure 37) will be tangential to a straight line drawn from the horizontal axis of a diagram like Figure 37. This is shown below:

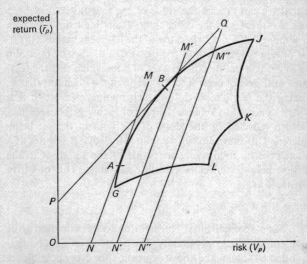

Fig. 38 Isolating efficient portfolios

For example, portfolio B is tangential to a line (PQ) drawn from the horizontal axis and A is tangential to a line (NM) of different slope.

Each point on the efficient boundary will be tangential to a straight line of a different slope. Thus, each point on the efficient boundary can be found by drawing a set of straight lines of a specific slope and observing where a line from this set becomes tangential to the left-hand boundary of the feasible area. For example, point A is tangential to a line from that set having a slope like NM. Similarly, point B is tangential to a straight line from that set having the same slope as PQ.

The tangential line from any set of straight lines of a given slope can be generated using mathematical programming. Any straight line can be written in mathematical terms as $Y = a + bx$. In this case, the symbol a represents the intercept with the horizontal axis, b indicates the slope of the line and measures the rate of exchange between risk and return, and x equals the rate of return measured on the vertical axis. Thus, the formula for each set of lines of a specific slope (b) is given by $V_p = a + b\bar{r}_p$, which indicates that we can predict the value of the fourth variable given numerical estimates of the other three. Each line from a set of a given slope will differ only because of the intercept variable (a).

The programming method for isolating an efficient portfolio works by finding that line from a set of lines which cuts the feasible area at the point nearest to the origin of the diagram; that is, by finding the feasible portfolio which minimizes the risk it is necessary to accept to achieve the rate of exchange between risk and return reflected by the slope of the lines in the set being considered. This portfolio can be found, for any set of lines of a specific slope, by minimizing the value of the intercept in the expression below, subject to certain constraints. This objective can be stated as:

$$\text{minimize } a = V_p - b\bar{r}_p,$$

where b has a specific value. The solution to this equation gives one point on the efficient boundary. The complete efficient boundary is found by solving the above expression for every possible set of lines, that is, for every possible value of b.

The investor's choice from the 'efficient' set of portfolios will depend on his preferences for expected return relative to risk. However, irrespective of the preferences of investors, the range of efficient portfolios which need to be considered can be reduced by making a few assumptions about the market in which securities are traded. These assumptions also allow us to begin to come to grips with the exceedingly difficult problem of share valuation in an uncertain world. The objective of the remaining sections of this chapter is to construct a model which can be used in such a situation.

Portfolio theory and the capital market
The capital market assumed in portfolio theory

The first of our new assumptions is that all investors, at least implicitly, practice portfolio theory when selecting their investments. Thus, each individual bases his decisions solely on his predictions about:

Expected returns;
The variances of such returns; and
Correlation between the returns of different securities.

Remember, we assumed earlier that no transaction costs or tax liabilities are associated with investment.

Secondly, it is assumed that the market is agreed about the prospects of every security traded. More precisely, the supposition is made that all investors make the same predictions concerning the above three variables for each and every security. This is manifestly not the case in the real world. However, it has been claimed that the theories obtained using this assumption allow us to explain much of the behaviour observed in the real world (see Sharpe, 1970, p. 113).

Another new assumption is that there exists a riskless asset which is free from the possibility of default. A perfect capital market for this asset is also assumed. Thus, everyone can borrow or lend as much as they wish of the riskless asset, provided that they are willing to pay, or receive, the going rate of interest for this security. In equilibrium, this rate will reflect only society's time preference and it is therefore called the 'pure' rate of interest.

It should be clearly understood that the security prices which will be derived using these assumptions are those which would obtain in equilibrium. Our first task is to amend our analysis to incorporate the existence of a riskless asset.

Portfolio theory with a riskless asset

Investing only in the riskless security will yield a specific return (r^*) with certainty. Transferring some funds from the riskless security to an uncertain portfolio will increase the investor's expected return but cause him to face some risk. This uncertainty can be calculated by weighting the risky portfolio's variance by the proportion it represents of his total investment. The risky portfolio will not covary with the riskless security. This is because the riskless security has a zero standard deviation and therefore our covariance formula will generate a zero covariance between the two investments.

The effects of incorporating the riskless asset into our earlier diagrammatic analysis are shown below. It should be noted that, in Figure 39, risk is measured in units of standard deviation rather

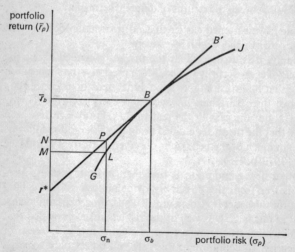

Fig. 39 Portfolio analysis incorporating a riskless security

than variance. This simplifies our work later, and its only effect at this stage is to lessen the degree of curvature of the efficient boundary, relative to that obtained when the variance is used as the risk measure.

To help understand the diagram, assume that an investor who holds only the riskless security is considering allocating a proportion of his funds to the purchase of portfolio B, a collection of risky securities. If he invests 10 per cent of his capital in B, he would expect a mean total return of:

$$\bar{r}_p = 0{\cdot}9r^* + 0{\cdot}1\bar{r}_b.$$

He would have to bear risk equal to $0{\cdot}10\,\sigma_b$ to obtain this return. Similarly, if he invests 50 per cent of his money in portfolio B, he should obtain an expected return of:

$$\bar{r}_p = 0{\cdot}5r^* + 0{\cdot}5\bar{r}_b,$$

and bear a risk equal to $0{\cdot}5\,\sigma_b$. The extra return per unit of risk obtained by investing in B can be found by dividing the change in overall return by the change in total risk. In our first case, these calculations give:

$$\frac{(0{\cdot}9r^* + 0{\cdot}1\bar{r}_b) - 1{\cdot}0r^*}{0{\cdot}1\sigma_b} \text{ which reduces to } \frac{\bar{r}_b - r^*}{\sigma_b}.\,^2$$

Similar calculations for our second case yield an identical incremental return per unit of extra risk. Indeed, this ratio will be constant for all combinations of the riskless security and the uncertain portfolio.

This is not surprising, for every mix of the two assets is obtained by swapping a given amount of one security for the same amount of the other. We sacrifice one unit of return from the riskless security (r^*) to obtain one unit of return from B ($\bar{r}_b$). Thus the net gain is $\bar{r}_b - r^*$. This gain is obtained at the cost of taking on one extra unit of risk, and thus the gain in return, relative to the extra risk, is

$$\frac{\bar{r}_b - r^*}{\sigma_b}.$$

1

2. The expression on the left is equal to $0{\cdot}1\bar{r}_b - 0{\cdot}1r^*/0{\cdot}1\sigma_b$ and simplifies to our expression by cancellation.

This constant ratio tells us the extra return over and above r^* obtained by taking on one extra unit of risk.

The total return obtained from any combination of the riskless security and portfolio B will depend on the amount of B's risk accepted; that is, the weight of B in the investor's portfolio multiplied by a measure of the risk of this security, σ_b. Each unit of risk accepted will be rewarded by a premium above the pure interest rate of $\dfrac{\bar{r}_b - r^*}{\sigma_b}$. Thus the portfolio's total return can be represented in symbols as:

$$\bar{r}_p = r^* + x_b \sigma_b \frac{\bar{r}_b - r^*}{\sigma_b}, \qquad\qquad 2$$

where x_b represents the proportion of portfolio B in the overall portfolio and σ_b, the risk attached to B. The rate of return for any portfolio can be found by plugging in the relevant numbers for any mix of the two investment possibilities. For example, assume that the investor spreads his funds equally between portfolio B and the certain security. In this case, his total expected return is given as:

$$\bar{r}_p = r^* + 0{\cdot}5\sigma_b \frac{\bar{r}_b - r^*}{\sigma_b} = 0{\cdot}5r^* + 0{\cdot}5\bar{r}_b,$$

which is the figure obtained earlier in a more direct way.

The above expression says that the total return obtained from any mix of the risky portfolio and the riskless asset will plot along a straight line in a diagram like Figure 39.[3]

This line is normally called the *capital market line*. Movements along this line increase both the investor's return and the risk which he bears. For example, that mix of the risky and certain securities represented by point P offers a greater return (N) than r^*, but involves risk of σ_n. That segment of the line beyond B represents the situation where the investor borrows funds at the riskless rate and uses these to purchase portfolio B.

3. This can be seen by rearranging the above expression for $\bar{r}_p$ and applying the formula for a straight line. This gives: $\bar{r}_p = a + bx$, where a is equal to r^*, b represents $\bar{r}_b - r^*/\sigma_b$ and x is the proportion of the risk attached to portfolio B accepted by the investor ($x_b\sigma_b$).

Those combinations of the two assets shown by the line $r*BB'$ are preferable to all those portfolios which lie along the efficient boundary (GJ). Each of these latter is dominated by a mixture of portfolio B and the riskless asset. For example, point L on the efficient boundary involves bearing the same risk as does that combination of portfolio B and the riskless asset represented by point P on $r*B$ but this latter investment (P) has a greater expected return. Similar reasoning indicates that all other risky portfolios in the diagram will be inferior to some combination of B and the riskless asset. This means that no investor will wish to hold any risky portfolio other than B.

Thus, with our very restrictive assumptions, the introduction of a riskless asset allows us to isolate the optimal portfolio from all those on the efficient boundary. Each investor needs to decide only:

The total amount of funds he wishes to invest; and
what proportion of his funds he will place in portfolio B.

The only decision which investors have to make is to choose that mix of portfolio B and the riskless asset which suits their risk preferences. In terms of the diagram, they have to decide their position on the $r*BB'$ line. Thus, all risky portfolios held by investors will contain the same mix of securities as portfolio B, and these portfolios will differ only in size.

That all investors will hold the same mix of risky stocks is a surprising conclusion.[4] However, an examination of the make-up of our optimal portfolio, which is normally referred to as the *optimal combination of risky securities, or the market portfolio*, may help to reduce the novelty of this suggestion. It can be shown that every security traded on the market will be represented in the optimal combination of risky securities. This is guaranteed because demand and supply considerations ensure that share prices

4. Sharpe considers that there could be several market portfolios; that is, the capital market line could be tangential to more than one point on the efficient boundary. He envisages that this position arises because the prices of securities not in the market portfolio will be depressed until someone wishes to hold them. However, the returns from all such portfolios must be perfectly positively correlated. Thus for our purposes we can proceed as if the market portfolio were unique; see Sharpe (1964) and Fama (1968).

will adjust so that in equilibrium, all the securities offered in the market which are forecast to offer a return will be bought by someone. However, we have just shown that investors who are described by our assumptions will hold only those securities which form part of the market portfolio. Thus, share prices must adjust so that all stocks are in the optimal combination of risky securities.

The proportionate weight of any specific firm's securities in the market portfolio must be equal to the aggregate value of these shares relative to the total value of all securities traded in the market. The total value of the market portfolio must equal the sum of the total values of all the individual securities it contains. This will occur only if the relative weight of each individual security contained in the optimal combination of risky securities reflects its total value relative to the aggregate value of all stocks traded.

In the next section, we use the above results to investigate the return required by investors from risky portfolios.

The return required from portfolios in an uncertain world

The first step is to determine the market's rate of exchange between risk and return. This trade-off between risk and return measures the market price of risk; that is, the amount of extra expected return which is required by investors for bearing one more unit of risk. Alternatively, it represents the price of risk reduction and reflects the amount of average return that must be sacrificed if risk is to be lowered by one unit. Any specific portfolio will only be held by investors if it yields this return per unit of risk.

We have already shown that, in equilibrium, only those portfolios plotting along the line (r^*BB') will be held by investors. The slope of this line reflects the incremental returns obtained by bearing the extra risk accruing from an increase in the proportion of funds invested in the market portfolio. Thus, in equilibrium, the slope of this line equals the market price of risk, which can, therefore, be written as:

$$\lambda = \frac{\bar{r}_m - r^*}{\sigma_m} \text{ (from expression 1)}$$

3

where the symbol λ stands for the market price of risk, $\bar{r}_m$ is the expected return from the market portfolio ($\bar{r}b$ in our diagram) and the standard deviation of this return is represented by σ_m (σ_b in the diagram).

Using this result and recalling our earlier expression for the expected return from any set of assets lying along r^*BB', the return ($\bar{r}_p$) required by investors before they will hold any mix of the riskless security and the market portfolio can be written as:

$$\bar{r}_p = r^* + \lambda\sigma_m x_m \text{ (from expression 2),} \qquad\qquad 4$$

where x_m equals the proportion the market portfolio represents of the investor's total funds. The return required from any combination of the two securities is given by adding to the pure interest rate a premium to cover the risk of holding that portfolio. This premium is obtained by multiplying the portfolio's uncertainty ($\sigma_m x_m$) by the market price of risk (λ). We can use this model to derive a valuation model for each individual security in the market portfolio. This task is undertaken in a non-rigorous way in the next section.

The valuation of individual securities under uncertainty

The construction of valuation models for a specific company's shares requires us to look at the overall return and riskiness which a unit of this security contributes to the market portfolio.

An understanding of the effects of any specific security on the market portfolio's risk and return requires some rather abstract reasoning; as does an appreciation of the relationship between the return expected from any specific security and that required from efficient portfolios. However, some knowledge of these relationships is crucial if the implications of portfolio theory for capital budgeting are to be understood. The aim of this section is merely to give an intuitive appreciation of the subject. We will begin our analysis by looking at the relationship between a security's return and that yielded by the market portfolio.

The contribution made by a specific security to portfolio return

This can best be isolated by considering the results of investing in a new portfolio which consists of two securities. One of these securities is the market portfolio itself (M) and the other is made up of additional units of some security, say the ith, over and above the amount of that security contained in the market portfolio. We will assume that an investor who holds only portfolio M is considering the effects of transferring some of his funds to security i. The change in his return $(\Delta \bar{r}_p)$ can be found using our formula for the return of a two-security portfolio (p. 295) and can be written in symbols as:

$$\Delta \bar{r}_p = \Delta x_i \bar{r}_i - \Delta x_i \bar{r}_m, \qquad\qquad 5$$

where Δx_i is the proportion the extra amount invested in security i bears to the investor's total funds.

The proportional effect on portfolio return of transferring funds from Mth to the ith stock is given by:

$$\frac{\Delta \bar{r}_p}{\Delta x_i} = \frac{\Delta x_i \bar{r}_i - \Delta x_i \bar{r}_m}{\Delta x_i}. \qquad\qquad 6$$

This yields the proportional amount of extra return obtained per unit of funds transferred to the purchase of the ith security. This expression can be simplified by cancellation to show that the change in overall portfolio return is the difference between the return from the ith stock and that of the market portfolio $(\bar{r}_i - \bar{r}_M)$. This latter serves as an approximate measure of the contribution our specific security makes to the total return of the market portfolio.

The portfolio risk contributed by individual securities

It can be shown that the uncertainty contributed by an individual share to the overall market portfolio is given by:

$$(\text{cov}(im) - V_m)/\sigma_m, \qquad\qquad 7$$

where $\text{cov}(im)$ is the covariance of the returns from the ith share with those from the market portfolio. The latter's variance and standard deviation are represented by V_m and σ_m respectively. The derivation of this expression is rather complicated and involves the use of calculus, and is therefore relegated to a footnote.[5] An easier, but non-rigorous, explanation is given below. However, even this is quite involved and those who are willing to take the above expression on trust should jump to the next section.

Our measure of the risk contributed to the market portfolio by an individual security is best approached by considering the effect on portfolio risk of a small increase in the amount of security i (Δx_i) financed by reducing the size of our investment in the market portfolio. We will call the portfolio, thus formed, portfolio Z. The variance of this new portfolio can be calculated using our formula for the variance of a two-security portfolio (see p. 300) which gives:

5. *Derivation of the formula for the contribution that the ith security makes to the overall risk of the market portfolio*

Let portfolio Z be any mix of the market portfolio, and security i, additional to its representation in the market portfolio. Let x_m and x_i be, respectively, the proportion of the market portfolio and security i in Z. The total uncertainty of portfolio Z can be written, using our expression for the overall risk of a two-security portfolio, as:

$$V_Z = x_i^2 V_i + x_m^2 V_m + 2x_i x_m \operatorname{cov}(im). \qquad \text{(a)}$$

(from expression 8 in ch. 14, p. 300)

Substituting $(1 - x_i)$ for x_m and multiplying out, this expression can be rewritten as:

$$V_Z = x_i^2 V_i + V_m + x_i^2 V_m - 2x_i V_m + 2x_i \operatorname{cov}(im) - 2x_i^2 \operatorname{cov}(im). \qquad \text{(b)}$$

Differentiating this expression with respect to x_i gives:

$$\frac{\partial V_Z}{\partial x_i} = 2x_i V_i + 2x_i V_m - 2V_m + 2\operatorname{cov}(im) - 4x_i \operatorname{cov}(im). \qquad \text{(c)}$$

Dividing through by σ_Z converts this into an expression for the change in the standard deviation of the returns of Z with respect to changes in x_i. This latter expression can be simplified by dividing throughout by two and collecting terms. These operations give:

$$\frac{\partial \sigma Z}{\partial x_i} = \frac{x_i(V_i + V_m - 2\operatorname{cov}(im)) + \operatorname{cov}(im) - V_m}{\sigma_Z}. \qquad \text{(d)}$$

However, we want an expression for the change in the risk of the market portfolio with respect to a small change in the amount of security i. If we let portfolio M be substituted for portfolio Z, the x_i term in the above expression will become equal to zero for, by definition, the market portfolio contains no additional amounts of security. The change in the market portfolio with respect to x_i is, therefore, given by:

$$\frac{\partial \sigma_m}{\partial x_i} = \frac{\operatorname{cov}(im) - V_m}{\sigma_m}. \qquad \text{(e)}$$

$$V_z = \Delta x_i{}^2 V_i + (1 - \Delta x_i)^2 V_m + 2\Delta x_i (1 - \Delta x_i) \operatorname{cov}(im). \qquad \textbf{7a}$$

When this expression is multiplied out in the usual way it becomes:

$$V_z = \Delta x_i{}^2 V_i + V_m + \Delta x_i{}^2 V_m - 2\Delta x_i V_m + 2\Delta x_i \operatorname{cov}(im) \\ - 2\Delta x_i{}^2 \operatorname{cov}(im). \qquad \textbf{7b}$$

The effect on portfolio Z of a small change in the amount held of security i can be isolated by looking at only those elements of the above expression which involve the Δx_i term. An approximate expression for the change in portfolio variance resulting from a small increase in the amount of the ith security held can be obtained by collecting these terms together and simplifying by dividing throughout by $2\Delta x_i$. These operations yield the following expression:

$$\Delta V_z = \tfrac{1}{2}\Delta x_i V_i + \tfrac{1}{2}\Delta x_i V_m - V_m + \operatorname{cov}(im) - \Delta x_i \operatorname{cov}(im). \qquad \textbf{7c}$$

This expression can be converted into one for the change in the standard deviation of the returns from portfolio Z generated by a small change in the amount held of security i. This can be written:

$$\Delta \sigma_z = \frac{\Delta x_i(\tfrac{1}{2}V_i + \tfrac{1}{2}V_m - \operatorname{cov}\{im\}) + \operatorname{cov}(im) - V_m}{\sigma_z} \qquad \textbf{7d}$$

The Δx_i term in the above expression becomes zero when portfolio Z is replaced by the market portfolio. The above expression (7d) is thus reduced to one containing only those terms not multiplied by Δx_i; that is:

$$\Delta \sigma_m = \frac{\operatorname{cov}(im) - V_m}{\sigma_m} = \text{expression 7}, \qquad \textbf{7e}$$

which is the expression we seek. With the background of the last two sections, we can now turn to considering in an elementary way the valuation model for individual securities implied by portfolio analysis.

The valuation of securities in an uncertain world

The return per unit of portfolio risk obtained from holding any security can be found by dividing the return contributed to the portfolio by the security $(\bar{r}_i - \bar{r}_m)$ by its effect on portfolio risk $(\operatorname{cov}\{im\} - V_m/\sigma_m)$.

That is, the return per unit of risk from the ith security (λ_i) is given by:

$$\lambda_i = \frac{\bar{r}_i - \bar{r}_m}{(\text{cov}(im) - V_m)/\sigma_m} = \frac{(\bar{r}_i - \bar{r}_m)\sigma_m}{\text{cov}(im) - V_m}. \qquad 8$$

In equilibrium, this trade-off between the return and risk offered by an individual security must be equal to the price of risk demanded by the market. We have already shown (expression 3) that this latter is measured by the slope of the capital market line $(\lambda = \bar{r}_m - r^*/\sigma_m)$. Thus, our equilibrium condition can be written as:

$$\lambda_i = \frac{(\bar{r}_i - \bar{r}_m)\sigma_m}{\text{cov}(im) - V_m} = \lambda = \frac{\bar{r}_m - r^*}{\sigma_m}. \qquad 9$$

The return required to induce investors to hold the ith security can be found by rearranging this equilibrium condition. This operation, which is described in a footnote below[6], yields the following expression:

$$\bar{r}_i = r^* + \frac{(\bar{r}_m - r^*)}{V_m} \text{cov}(im). \qquad 10$$

6. *Derivation of the return expected by the market from any individual security*

The first step is to cross-multiply the terms of our equilibrium condition of expression 9:

$$\frac{(\bar{r}_i - \bar{r}_m)\sigma_m}{\text{cov}(im) - V_m} = \frac{\bar{r}_m - r^*}{\sigma_m} \text{ to give } ((\bar{r}_i - \bar{r}_m)\sigma_m)\,\sigma_m = (\bar{r}_m - r^*)(\text{cov}\{im\} - V_m). \text{ (a)}$$

The second is to multiply out the expressions in brackets. This operation yields:

$$\bar{r}_i\sigma^2_m - \bar{r}_m\sigma^2_m = \bar{r}_m\text{cov}(im) - \bar{r}_m\sigma^2_m - r^*\text{cov}(im) + r^*\sigma^2_m. \qquad \text{(b)}$$

The second term on the left can be subtracted from the similar term on the right. The above expression can be further simplified by collecting on the left all those terms containing σ^2_m, and transferring to the right all those containing $\text{cov}(im)$. These operations give:

$$\bar{r}_i\sigma^2_m - r^*\sigma^2_m = \bar{r}_m\text{cov}(im) - r^*\text{cov}(im), \qquad \text{(c)}$$

which can be written as:

$$(\bar{r}_i - r^*)V_m = (\bar{r}_m - r^*)\text{cov}(im). \qquad \text{(d)}$$

When this latter expression is divided throughout by V_m, we obtain:

$$\bar{r}_i - r^* = \frac{(\bar{r}_m - r^*)}{V_m} \text{cov}(im) = \text{expression 10}, \qquad \text{(e)}$$

when the r^* element is transferred to the right-hand side.

Expression **10** says that the return required by the market from any security will be equal to the pure rate of interest plus a premium based on the covariance of the security's returns with those from the market portfolio. This risk premium is found by multiplying the security's risk (cov{im}) by the market price of risk expressed as the premium above the pure interest rate required per unit of risk $\frac{(r_m - r^*)}{V_m}$. This demonstrates, as we would expect, that in situations where diversification is feasible, the uncertainty flowing from holding any individual security is measured by the covariance of its returns with those of the market portfolio.

Some find it more helpful to think of the risk of the individual security as depending on the degree to which its returns vary systematically with the market; that is, in terms of the volatility of the security's return relative to that from the market portfolio. Our expression for a security's expected return can easily be recast in these terms. Recall that V_m measures the possible deviations from the expected return of the market portfolio, and cov(im) measures the degree to which the returns of an individual security are likely to be influenced by the same factors as those acting on the market portfolio. Thus, dividing the latter by the former gives a relative measure of the association between the returns from the market portfolio, and those from the specific stock. Thus, our expression for the expected return from a given security can be written, using this measure, as:

$$\bar{r}_i = r^* + (\bar{r}_m - r^*) \frac{\text{cov}(im)}{V_m} = r^* + (\bar{r}_m - r^*)b_i, \qquad \textbf{11}$$

where b_i is a measure of the volatility of a security's return with respect to the returns of the market portfolio.

Either of our two expressions for the equilibrium return required from an individual security by the market can be used to derive a valuation model for a company's shares. Share prices will adjust, in equilibrium, so that the investor will receive from each security in his portfolio just the required return generated using either of our two expressions.

The final step necessary before we can derive a valuation model

for individual securities is to rewrite our expression for the required return using aggregate cash flows rather than rates of
return. We will define $\bar{R}i$ as the average total cash return, net of
the necessary original outlay that the market requires from a
security before they will purchase all the available units of the
security. This cash return can be received either in the form of
cash dividends or capital appreciation. We will define $\bar{R}m$ as the
expected aggregate cash return from the market portfolio. The
risk measures we have so far used have been related to units of
return, and they too must be expressed in cash flow terms. The
footnote shows that the variance of a security's returns can be
converted into a cash flow measure by multiplying the variance of
a security's return by the square of the total market value of all
the issued units of that share (Vo_i).[7] This variance in cash flow

7. *The conversion of risk measures defined in terms of rates of returns into
measures based on cash flows*

(1) *The variance.* The expected return from the ith security $(\bar{r}i)$ can be
defined in cash flow terms as:

$$\frac{\bar{R}_i}{Vo_i},$$

where Vo_i is the total market value of the ith security at the beginning of the
period. Thus, our original definition of the variance in a security's return,
$(V_i = \Sigma\, p_i(r_i - \bar{r}_i)^2$ (see p. 239) can be written as:

$$V_i = \Sigma\, p_i \left(\frac{R_i}{Vo_i} - \frac{\bar{R}_i}{Vo_i} \right)^2 = \Sigma\, p_i \frac{(R_i - \bar{R}_i)^2}{Vo_i{}^2}.$$

The numerator of the expression on the right is the variance of the security's
cash flows and thus by rearrangement, we get:

$$V_i\, Vo_i{}^2 = \Sigma\, p_i(R_i - \bar{R}_i)^2.$$

(2) *The covariance.* The standard deviation of a security's returns can be
similarly expressed in cash flow terms by taking the square root of the above
expression. That is, the cash flow standard deviation of the ith security
returns (σf_i) is given by:

$$\sigma f_i = \sqrt{V_i\, Vo_i{}^2} = \sigma_i\, Vo_i, \tag{a}$$

where σ_i is, as usual, the standard deviation defined in terms of returns.
Recall that our original definition of the covariance of the ith stock with the
market portfolio was:

$$\mathrm{cov}(im) = \sigma_i \sigma_m c(im). \tag{b}$$

The correlation coefficient in this expression needs no adjustment for it is
already defined as an absolute number. Thus, the covariance between any

terms will be expressed as Vf_i and equals $V_i(Vo_i)^2$. (See footnote 7.) Similarly, a covariance measured in terms of return can be expressed in cash flow terms by multiplying our normal covariance concept by the product of the aggregate market values of the two securities involved, Vo_i and Vo_m (see Sharpe, 1970, p. 99). This measure of covariance in money terms will be represented by COV(im) and is equal to cov(im)Vo_iVo_m.

Our earlier expression for the return required by the market before it will hold the ith security ($\bar{r}_i = r^* + \{\bar{r}_m - r^*\}$ cov(im)/V_m) can, by substituting these new terms, be expressed in cash flow terms as:[8]

$$\frac{\bar{R}_i}{Vo_i} = \frac{Vo_ir^*}{Vo_i} + \frac{\bar{R}_m - r^*Vo_m}{Vo_m} \frac{\text{COV}(im)}{Vf_m}. \qquad 12$$

The required return ($\bar{R}_i$) is now defined in terms of the total value of the cash flows required by the market from the aggregate number of units of the security held. In this expression, the symbol Vo_ir^* is equal to the market value of the firm capitalized at the pure interest rate, and r^*Vo_m is the same figure for the market portfolio; $\bar{R}_m$ represents the total cash flows obtained from the aggregate market portfolio, COV(im) and Vf_m are our risk measures defined in terms of cash flows.

Our valuation model for the ith security can now be obtained by solving the above expression for the total value of the outstanding shares of the ith security (Vo_i) (see Lintner, 1965, especially section 4). This gives:

$$\left(\bar{R}_i - \left\{ \left[\frac{(\bar{R}_m - r^*Vo_m)}{Vf_m} \right] \text{COV}(im) \right\} \right) / r^* = Vo_i. \qquad 13$$

---

two stocks (i and m) can be written in cash flow terms (COV$\{im\}$) by substituting our expression for the cash flow standard deviations of each security, $\sigma_i Vo_i$ and $\sigma_m Vo_m$ respectively, into (b). This gives:

$$\text{COV}(im) = (\sigma_i Vo_i)(\sigma_m Vo_m)c(im), \qquad (c)$$

which can be written as:

$$\text{COV}(im) = Vo_i Vo_m\text{cov}(im).$$

This is the expression we seek.

8. A full treatment of this requires some complex mathematics and the presentation in this section is meant to give merely a general idea of the method.

The above expression says that value of the firm's shares on the market is given by capitalizing, using the pure interest rate, the difference between the total cash return from the firm and that required by the market to compensate investors for the effects of the security on overall portfolio uncertainty (see Lintner, 1965).

We are now in a position to see the implications of all this for capital budgeting and this subject is taken up in the next section. However, the utility of the decision rules discussed in the following section depends on the validity of the predictions of portfolio theory for the real world. This matter is considered in the final part of this chapter.

Capital budgeting and portfolio theory

Our valuation model for the firm can be used to evaluate whether a specific project should be accepted. A project will cause the value of the firm's shares to rise providing its expected cash flows are sufficient to cover:

The repayment of the funds needed for the project;
The pure interest rate on these funds; and
The cash flows the market requires to protect itself from the risk the project brings to the market portfolio.

The project should thus be undertaken if its effect on the right-hand side of our valuation expression (**13**) is non-negative (on all this, see Lintner, 1965). That is, project K should be accepted if:

$$\left(\bar{R}_k - \frac{(\bar{R}_m - r^* Vo_m)}{Vf_m} \text{COV}(km) \right) / r^* \geqslant 0. \qquad 14$$

This decision rule is not in the same form as those of earlier chapters, for it incorporates only with those cash flows that the project yields in excess of its capital outlay. The above accept/reject rule can easily be restated in a more usual form. Assume that the project is to be financed by equity funds, and let $\bar{H}_k$ be the expected value of the total equity cash flows from the project at the end of the period, assuming that the project is realized on the market at this time. Thus, $\bar{H}_k$ equals the mean net operating cash flows from the project, assuming these are paid out to shareholders, plus the project's value on the stock market at the end of the period.

Our decision rule can thus be rewritten as: accept if, and only if,

$$\bar{H}_k - \frac{(\bar{R}_m - r^*Vo_m)}{Vf_m} \text{COV}(km)/(1 + r^*) \geq I_k, \qquad \textbf{15}$$

where I_k stands for the capital outlay. This formulation of our decision rule says that an investment opportunity should be accepted only if its cash flows after meeting the required risk premium have a positive net present value when discounted at the pure rate of interest. It should be noted that this interest rate measures only time preference; uncertainty being taken separately into account.

This can be expressed more simply in terms of an accept/reject decision model using the usual rate of return as the decision variable. In these circumstances, our criterion can be stated as: accept the project if its expected return ($\bar{r}_k$) is equal to, at least, the pure interest rate plus the premium required by the market for assets of the project's uncertainty. This criterion can be expressed as: accept if, and only if,

$$\bar{r}_k \geq r^* + (\bar{r}_m - r^*) \frac{\text{cov}(km)}{V_m}. \qquad \textbf{16}$$

Implications for the cost of capital

It can be seen from this expression that the required rate of return concept used in portfolio theory $[(r^* + (\bar{r}_m - r^*)(\text{cov}(km)/V_m)]$ serves the same function as did the cost of capital in earlier chapters. However, it should be clear that the risk element in the above expression does not measure either the intrinsic riskiness of the project, or how its returns covary with the expected returns of the firm's existing project portfolio. Rather, the risk definition used in capital-budgeting models which incorporate portfolio theory takes into account the way in which the new project's returns covary with the returns of all other securities in the market portfolio.

This is because portfolio theory assumes that investors will be interested only in the expected return and risk associated with their individual portfolios. Such investors will appraise any project only in terms of its effects on these portfolio variables. The risk contributed to a combination of securities (j) by any given project (k) is the sum of:

$$x_k{}^2 V_k + x_k \sum x_j \, \mathrm{cov}(kj). \qquad\qquad 17$$

The x_k term in this expression is likely to be very small in any well-diversified portfolio. Thus the first element in the above expression is likely to be insignificant and its effect on portfolio risk completely dominated by the second term which will not tend to zero, even if we assume that x_k is very small.

Our capital-budgeting model suggests that estimating the cost of capital becomes an even more complex task than it seemed in earlier chapters. Correct estimates of the expected return required by the market from a given project require a knowledge of all the factors involved in our valuation models. It may, therefore, be easier to look directly at the project's impact on the firm's value in the market (see Lintner, 1965). Each of a firm's projects may have a different effect on portfolio risk and return and therefore the rate of return required by the market may be different for each project undertaken by the firm. Thus, the market cost of identical funds may differ between firms because of the different project opportunities available to them.

Portfolio theory suggests yet another reason for viewing with some doubt attempts to deal with risk by inflating the discount rate (see p. 248). Portfolio theorists would regard this practice as often being based on an incorrect concept of risk. The risk premiums used in practice are normally based on the uncertainty directly associated with a project (e.g. V_i or σ_i). However, projects which are regarded as risky according to this view may bring considerable risk-spreading benefits to investors' portfolios, and thus may be regarded as very valuable.

For example, it can be shown that investors would be willing to accept a project with returns that were perfectly negatively correlated with the returns from the market portfolio even though it yielded a return below the pure interest rate. A correct combination of such an asset and the market portfolio will yield the pure interest rate irrespective of the actual outcome from the market portfolio. The correct mix of the two assets will enable risk to be completely diversified away. This extreme example serves to emphasize that the traditional use of inflated discount rates may not lead to the best results for the firm's equity-holders.

The weaknesses of capital-budgeting models based on portfolio theory

This chapter has suggested a possible alternative approach to estimating risk premiums. However, many of the concepts involved cannot yet be made operational. This point will be taken up again later in this chapter (p. 334) when some of the more general criticisms of portfolio theory will be reviewed, but this does not mean that portfolio analysis has no lessons for the project analyst working in a firm whose shareholders are known to have well-diversified holdings. The first of these suggestions is that the analyst, if he wishes to do the best he can for the firm's shareholders, should not be concerned with the riskiness of any potential project considered in isolation. Rather, he should attempt to investigate how each project is likely to affect the risk and return associated with the portfolios held by the firm's equity-holders. This approach requires that the firm should attempt to estimate how the returns from each possible project will covary with the returns from existing portfolios. In addition, the firm will need to estimate its equity-holders' attitude to risk relative to return. The literature gives little guidance as to how this can be measured, even assuming that all investors have the same risk preferences. It is not clear whose risk preferences should be used in the presence of disagreement.

Similarly, the literature is of little help where investors have access to different information or draw different conclusions from the same information. Sharpe has suggested that one approach in these circumstances is to use some sort of weighted average of the different predictions used by shareholders in our models (Sharpe, 1970, ch. 6). However, even with its limitations, portfolio theory does suggest that a firm with its shareholders' best interests in mind should attempt to allow for the latter's ability to diversify.

The portfolio models in the literature are normally concerned with one period problems, though some attempts have been made to adapt the models for multi-period decisions (see Markowitz, 1970, and Mossin, 1968). Brown and Ball (1969) have pointed out that this single-period orientation of portfolio theory means that it sheds little light on the validity of splitting the decision period into several discrete periods when discounting.

Brown and Ball have also suggested that portfolio theory is not without difficulty even in its single-period framework. For example, the firm in seeking to use the theory has an impossible task in attempting to quantify the factors in our models. Introducing differing decision horizons between investors and the firm produces additional problems in that the manager must now also estimate his shareholders' decision horizon. If this span exceeds the possible lives of the projects available, he must plan to place the funds which will be released so that they earn the average return expected by the market, or must return the funds to the market.

Many people may find unacceptable portfolio theory's suggestion that a firm should not seek to diversify its own project portfolio. The theory suggests that investors can diversify and minimize the risk of holding securities. Thus, there seems little need for the firm to seek to spread its own risk. Investors would wish the firm to accept all projects which yield the market's required return for assets of their risk quality. Investors will be indifferent to the possible dispersion of any project's returns in so far as they can diversify away such risks. Thus, portfolio theory rigorously applied to capital budgeting would seem to advise the firm to accept projects, or combinations of projects, which could lead to the firm's liquidation, if events went badly. Firms with their shareholders' interests at heart should not seek to protect themselves from such disasters by diversifying their project portfolio. This is especially so as their attempts at diversification may be more inefficient than those of investors, given the difficulty of altering their existing project portfolio, and the possibility that the investment opportunities facing any firm tend to come in large discrete bundles which may be bunched over time.

This does not mean that firms should not diversify in search of higher 'profits'. Such activities may result because the possession of broad management skills allows the firm to locate successfully profitable opportunities in many fields. However, the conclusion that firms should not seek investment projects which allow them to avoid risk is of little help to those people associated with the firm who cannot protect themselves against the firm's liquidation. Such groups would include the firm's management, its work force, and members of its neighbourhood community. This concern with the uncertainty of the individual firm will be shared by investors whose holdings are not well diversified.

A firm which wishes to ameliorate the plight of any of the above groups may well try to diversify its capital-investment activities using the tools outlined earlier in this and the preceding chapter. Such behaviour by firms is likely, if, as has been argued earlier, management both dominate corporate decision making and take decisions with their own interests in mind (see chapter 2).

Several authors have implicitly accepted this view and formulated investment appraisal models which management can utilize in these circumstances (see Quirin, 1967, and Van Horne, 1968, pp. 90–99). We will not review these models in any depth for they merely involve the firm using those tools and models which we have already suggested for investors. The only major difference when firms use this approach is that the utility function used will now reflect the risk and return preferences of management, or whatever other group, whose welfare it is wished to maximize.

We have already suggested some reasons why diversification by the firm can only approximate to the results that could be achieved by investors. However, probably the greatest constraint on economy-wide diversification by any specific firm, is, at least in the short run, a lack of the specific managerial skills required for the various industrial sectors in which the firm may wish to have an interest.

This completes our summary of portfolio theory and the adjustments it makes necessary to the capital-budgeting models introduced in earlier chapters. It is clear that much work remains to be done before any really operational decision rules for project appraisal are obtained from the theory. However, even in its present state, the theory does cast severe doubts on current practice, and on the utility of some of the concepts that form the theoretical foundation of the capital-budgeting models examined in this book. To assess the validity of these doubts, it is necessary to consider whether the currently available empirical evidence refutes the predictions of portfolio theory, and to review some of the criticisms that have been levelled at the theory in its present stage of development. These subjects are reviewed briefly in the next section.

The empirical evidence and a critical review of the theory
The evidence

Most empirical investigations have attempted to test the theory's ability to explain stock-market behaviour. Such investigations normally involve the use of complex statistical techniques. However, a brief review of some of the current evidence may help us to appreciate the potential of future developments in this area for capital budgeting.

Sharpe (1970, p. 149) cites a study by Evans which suggests that the risk-reducing effect of diversification can be empirically observed. Evans looked at the historic variability in the overall rates of return of several security portfolios of differing degrees of diversification over the period 1958–67. He found that the mean standard deviation of the portfolios declined as a given amount of money was spread over a greater number of securities. He also found that the average risk of such combinations of securities tended to approach a definite limit ($\sigma_p = 11 \cdot 9$ per cent) as diversification was increased.

Evans also found that even a little diversification considerably reduced risk. For example, his study suggests that spreading funds equally over only, say, ten securities, will reduce portfolio risk to within 10 per cent of that associated with investing in the full market portfolio.

Finally, he found that over 50 per cent of the variance in a typical security's rate of return was explained by factors other than the correlation of the security's returns with those of the market portfolio. This finding was approximately confirmed by King who also suggests that the proportion of the variability in a security's rate of return that can be explained in this way increased over time (King, 1966). For example, the proportion of the variance in a typical share's rate of return explained by its relationship with the market as a whole, decreased from over 40 per cent for the period 1944–52 to 30 per cent for the period 1952–67. This seems to suggest, in a tentative way, that the risk-reduction possibilities of diversification have increased over time.

Work by Cohen and Pogue (1967) provides some evidence supporting the portfolio approach to risk. They used portfolio theory to select sets of widely diversified portfolios which had been efficient in a specific past period. They found that, in a later period, such portfolios out-performed sets of randomly selected portfolios, each consisting of forty shares held in equal proportion, drawn from a sample of 150 stocks. This finding supports the theory, but much more work is required before any general conclusion can be reached. This is especially so as Cohen and Pogue used historical data rather than the estimates of future returns and risk which form the foundation of the theory.

Other supporting evidence comes from Farrar (1962), who used the theory to calculate historically efficient portfolios. He found that the set of securities held by American mutual trusts (similar to unit trusts in the UK) closely approximated these portfolios. Those organizations who claimed to aim for high growth held high-risk, efficient portfolios, and those who sought to achieve well-balanced portfolios held mixes of securities similar to those he had calculated as low-risk, efficient portfolios. This finding, which has been supported by other studies, is important because it suggests that the theory may be a good predictor of actual behaviour.

The evidence presently available supports the view that portfolio analysis may represent a viable way to treat risk in, at least, stock-market decisions. In spite of these encouraging results, many criticisms have been made of the theory. These suggested practical and theoretical limitations of portfolio analysis are dealt with briefly in the next, and final, section of this chapter.

Some criticisms

Many of these concentrate on the validity of the assumptions underlying the theory. Others question the possibility of making the theory operational.

One major difficulty associated with the theory is the large data input required. The investor must forecast not only the return and variance of each security, but must also forecast the covariance of each security's returns with those from every other share on the market. Such estimates are necessary to forecast each security's covariance with the market portfolio. This is an impossible and uneconomic task for most investors. For example, if the investor is considering only one hundred securities, he must estimate one hundred expected returns together with the covariance for every pair of securities. He must make nearly 5000 separate estimates.

Markowitz (1970, especially pp. 97–101) and Sharpe (1964) have suggested that this exercise can be rendered manageable by seeking to estimate only how the return from a security covaries with some market index. This amounts to assuming that the sole relationship between the returns of any two securities results from the effect of market-wide influences. This means that only one covariance has to be estimated for each security. The covariance between each security and the market index can be used as a substitute for the former's covariance with the market portfolio in our earlier formulas without changing any of our conclusions.

One advantage of index models for portfolio analysis is that their use partially overcomes the objection that investors do not understand the complex concepts of the theory. Index models require investors merely to estimate how the return from each share will change in relation to changes in the index being used.

The adoption of a market index may be inappropriate in capital budgeting if the decision-maker wishes to protect the interests of those who are unable to use the stock market. Index models concentrate entirely on market-wide risk, and thus, this branch of portfolio theory may not be applicable to a firm which is attempting to diversify its portfolio of projects.

A major foundation stone of portfolio theory is the assumption that there exists a perfect capital market. It is impossible to derive any real theory of security values without this supposition for without this assumption, it is very difficult to analyse the effects of combining the riskless asset with the market portfolio. If individuals face different credit conditions, they will operate on different capital-market lines which will alter as credit conditions change. Similarly, if investors face different rates for borrowing and lending a curve will be introduced into the capital-market line (see Francis and Archer, 1971, pp. 126–32). However, the empirical evidence, which seems to support the theory's predictions, might suggest that a sufficiently large section of the market does operate in an approximately perfect capital market to allow the theory's predictions to explain real world behaviour. However, this is an empirical question, the resolution of which must await the results of further studies.

An associated point is that in the real world a completely riskless security is unlikely to exist. Government bonds may be default-free but holding them does not offer protection from inflation. As was shown in the preceding chapter, the efficient set of portfolios is represented by a curve if all the securities available to investors are risky. A market portfolio will still exist and will be found at the point on the curve representing efficient portfolios which is tangential to a line representing the borrowing or lending rate. But the security-market line (see expression 11, p. 324) will be indeterminate below the point indicating the expected return and risk of the market portfolio (Francis and Archer, 1971, pp. 130–31).

A more compelling reason for maintaining the assumptions of a perfect market and the existence of a riskless security is that their removal leaves us with very little in the way of a theoretical treatment of uncertainty. It is not clear that we should abandon portfolio theory until an alternative approach of, at least, equal promise is found.

Returning to the firm which wishes to practise portfolio analysis, it is unlikely that the assumption of a perfect capital market will apply to every firm wishing to diversify its project portfolio. However, it was argued earlier in this book that long-run capital rationing results mainly from managerial decisions. Thus, the wish to practise portfolio theory may provide yet another reason for management to review their capital-rationing policies.

Another assumption of the theory that has been criticized is that which says that all investors agree about the return and risk of any security. However, as was said earlier, Sharpe has suggested that most of the theory's conclusions remain intact when disagreement is allowed, providing that our models are appropriately adjusted. Without such alterations, our models would produce 'fuzzy' curves and lines become regions. This would mean that only major disequilibriums in the market would be corrected.

The firm which wishes to practise portfolio theory may, similarly, face considerable difficulties if individuals within the group whose welfare it has in mind, disagree amongst themselves about the prospects of various industrial sectors. It would seem that all management can do in these circumstances is follow policies that suit the majority of this group.

Portfolio theory shares, with most of this book, the assumption that investors obtain reasonable information about the firm's plans. Information lags and imperfections will distort the results of applying the theory. The use of portfolio theory by the firm wishing to maximize shareholder welfare must be founded on the faith that this will be given due recognition in the figures available to investors. It was suggested earlier that there is some evidence that the market does use to the full any information made available to it.

A final criticism of portfolio theory is that the variance and standard deviation of the returns from a security measure but part of the uncertainty which investors might incorporate into their utility functions. Alternative risk measures, such as the semi-variance of returns, were mentioned earlier. All such measures bring with them considerable difficulties which militate against their use in portfolio analysis. No one has yet suggested an alternative concept which has commanded general acceptance, though one such approach is agreed to have promise. This is the suggestion that portfolio analysis should recognize the desire to minimize the probability of 'catastrophe', where this latter is defined as a portfolio return falling below a level which the investor regards as disastrous. This alternative model has the additional advantage of simplifying the process of portfolio optimization. However, the details of the theory lie beyond the scope of this book (see Roy, 1952).

A more radical approach to uncertainty has been propounded by the supporters of the state-preference theory. This theory is very complex and still developing. However, basically the value of a security is seen as depending on the return it will yield in various possible states of environment. With this view, portfolio analysis requires the calculation of covariances between securities for each possible state of the environment. Thus, application of this approach is very complicated. However, it does suggest that the higher return required from a risky investment relative to a risk-free investment may not be due to risk aversion. The difference in returns is rather viewed as being due to the risky security providing relatively greater returns in some states of the world in which returns are regarded as of relatively high value (see Hirshleifer, 1966, and 1970, Part 2).

Finally, the equilibrium orientation of our theory should not be forgotten. Many investors hope to make their fortune by exploiting what they believe to be disequilibrium conditions in the market. Portfolio theory has little to offer those who believe either that they have better information than the market or that they can make relatively better deductions from widely available information. These 'more knowledgeable' investors, if correct in their beliefs, will maximize their wealth by concentrating their attention on those securities that they view as wrongly valued by the market.

Our review of portfolio theory and its implications for project appraisal is now complete. Some believe that the subject treated in the last two chapters may represent the beginning of a complete treatment of investment theory in conditions of uncertainty. Even in its present state, the theory does suggest that some current practices should be rethought. If nothing more, portfolio theory has gone some way towards isolating the crucial variables in any treatment of risk and suggests a few building blocks which may, in time, form the basis of a more complete model for security valuation and project appraisal under conditions of risk.

Appendix A to Chapter 13

Illustration that the axioms imply the maximization of expected utility as a decision rule

This appendix provides an informal and introductory demonstration that the axioms introduced in chapter 13 imply the maximization of expected utility by the rational individual whose beliefs can be assumed to be described by the axioms. The axioms and notation used in this appendix are those introduced in chapter 13.

The axioms allow the decision-maker to rank any pair of gambles, and ensure that all gambles can be restated in terms of an uncertain prospect involving outcomes expressed in terms of only the best and worst basic outcomes available, A_1 and A_n respectively.

For example, let C be a gamble involving outcomes A_1 to A_n with probabilities p_1 to p_n: that is:

$$\text{Lottery } C = (p_1 A_1; p_2 A_2; \ldots; p_n A_n). \qquad 1$$

By axioms 4 and 6, each A_i can be restated in terms of a gamble involving only the best outcome (A_1) and the worst (A_n). Using the same reasoning and the notation we used when explaining axioms 3 and 6, lottery C can be stated as:

$$C' = [(p_1 A_1); \{p_2(u_2 A_1), (1 - u_2)A_n\}]; \\ [p_3\{u_3 A_1\}, (1 - u_3)A_n\}]; \ldots; p_n A_n). \qquad 2$$

The u_is are the probabilities necessary to render the choice between each original A_i and a gamble consisting only of A_1 and A_n a matter of indifference.

Postulate 3 asserts that it is possible to state the above gamble (C') in more simple terms by summing the probabilities attaching to the two possible outcomes A_1 and A_n. Thus, the probabilities attached to the best outcome (A_1) in this variation of lottery C (C', expression 2) can be found by summing:

$$p_1 + p_2 u_2 + p_3 u_3, \ldots + p_n u_n = \sum_{i=1}^{n} (p_i u_i), \qquad 3$$
where $u_n = $ zero.

Similar calculations give the probabilities attaching to the worst outcome in lottery C' as:

$$\left[\sum_{i=1}^{n} (p_i(1 - u_i)) \right] = 1 - \left[\sum_{i=1}^{n} (p_i u_i) \right]. \qquad\qquad 4$$

Thus, the revised lottery which the decision-maker ranks as of equal utility to the original lottery C, can be written as:

$$\text{Lottery } C'' = \left[\sum_{i=1}^{n} (p_i u_i) A_1; \left(1 - \sum_{i=1}^{n} (p_i u_i) \right) A_n \right]. \qquad\qquad 5$$

Axiom 5 says that the decision-maker will choose between two lotteries expressed in this form on the basis of that which gives the highest probability of receiving the best outcome; that is, he will make his choices so as to maximize $\Sigma(p_i u_i)\, A_1$.

All we have to do now to show that our axioms imply the maximization of expected utility is to demonstrate that choosing out of a pair of projects that option which has the highest expected utility, is equivalent to opting for the proposal which, when stated in terms of only A_1 and A_n, yields the best outcome A_1 with the highest probability. The first step is to recall that the probabilities represented by the u_is in expressions 3, 4 and 5 were those which rendered the decision-maker indifferent between receiving a given outcome (A_i) or the result of a gamble consisting only of the best and worst outcomes, A_1 and A_n respectively. The individual must, therefore, assign equal utility to $A_i[U(A_i)]$ and to the gamble $(u_i)A_1; (1 - u_i)A_n$, where the upper case U represents a utility measure; that is,

$$U(A_i) = u_i U(A_1) + (1 - u_i)U(A_n), \qquad\qquad 6$$

Let us arbitrarily assign a utility of unity to A_1 and zero to A_n. The utility of A_i is therefore equal to:

$$U(A_i) = (u_i)(1) + (1 - u_i)(0). \qquad\qquad 7$$

This means that in our case the utility of A_i is equal to the probability assigned to the best outcome; that is $U(A_i) = u_i$.

Thus, with these assumptions, the utility of outcome A_2 in gamble C can be expressed as:

$$U(A_2) = u_2 U(A_1) + (1 - u_2)U(A_n). \qquad\qquad 8$$

Under our assumptions, the utility of A_1 is unity and that of A_n is zero. Plugging these assumed utility values into expression 8 gives:

$$U(A_2) = u_2(1) + (1 - u_2)(0) = u_2. \qquad\qquad 9$$

Similar calculations show that the utilities of the other basic alternatives in lottery $C(A_3, A_4, ..., A_{n-1})$ will be $u_3, u_4, ..., u_{n-1}$ respectively.

All that remains to be done is to substitute these utilities into the basic form of prospect C. Thus the expected utility of gamble C when expressed in its original form (expression 1), can be expressed as:

$$\bar{U}(C) = p_1(1) + p_2(u_2) + p_3(u_3) + \cdots p_n(0) = \sum p_i u_i, \qquad \textbf{10}$$

where $\bar{U}(C)$ is the expected utility of gamble C, p_i represents the probability attached to the basic outcome A_i in the original form of prospect C, and u_i is the utility for the individual of this outcome.

Thus, selecting those projects which maximize expected utility is the same thing as choosing those proposals which yield the highest $\sum p_i u_i$. We have already shown that the latter is a rational objective for a decision-maker whose preferences are described by our axioms, and follows directly from these postulates. The objective of maximizing expected utility is merely a way of restating this objective.

Appendix B to Chapter 14

Section 1: Derivation of a quadratic utility function explicitly incorporating a risk measure

The utility of any specific return (r_i) from a portfolio can be found by plugging this return into our general formula for a quadratic utility function (see p. 293). This operation gives:

$$U_i = a + br_i - c(r_i)^2,$$

where U_i is the total utility of the ith return (r_i) from the portfolio. The expected utility from the portfolio can be found by computing a weighted average of the utilities yielded by each possible return using the probabilities of the latter as weights. This expected utility can be expressed as:

$$\bar{U}_p = \sum_{i=1}^{m} p_i(a + br_i - c(r_i)^2).\qquad \textbf{1}$$

The symbol $\bar{U}_p$ stands for the expected utility of the portfolio.

By multiplying out the expression for the expected utility from a portfolio (**1**), we obtain:

$$\bar{U}_p = \sum_{1}^{m} p_i a + \sum_{1}^{m} p_i br_i - \sum_{1}^{m} p_i c(r_i)^2.\qquad \textbf{2}$$

The first term on the right of **2** reduces to a for the probabilities of all the possible returns sum to unity. The second term on the right is simply the portfolio's expected return multiplied by $b(b\bar{r}_p)$.

The meaning of the third term on the right is not so easy to make clear. It is easiest to begin by writing each possible return in this third term as the sum of the portfolio's expected return, *plus* the difference between this and the individual return under consideration; that is, each r_i is expressed as ($\bar{r}_p + \{r_i - \bar{r}_p\}$). Using this notation the third term of **2** can be written as:

$$\sum_{1}^{m} p_i c(\bar{r}_p + \{r_i - \bar{r}_p\})^2.\qquad \textbf{3}$$

Multiplying out the expression in brackets, we obtain:

$$-\sum_{1}^{m} p_i c((\bar{r}_p)^2 + \{r_i - \bar{r}_p\}^2 + 2\bar{r}_p\{r_i - \bar{r}_p\}).\qquad \textbf{4}$$

The first term in **4** after multiplying out becomes $-c\bar{r}_p^2$. The last term in **4** can be shown to be equal to zero.[1]

The second element in brackets in **4** when multiplied by the Σp_i outside the brackets is our earlier definition of the variance of a portfolio's return. Thus, remembering that the first element in brackets in **4** can be written as $c\bar{r}_p^2$ and that the second term is equal to V_p multiplied by c, **4** can be set out as:

$$-c\bar{r}_p^2 - cV_p. \qquad 4$$

Expression **2** can now be rewritten using only the portfolio's expected return and its variance. Recall that the first term on the right of **2** is equivalent to a, and the second term can be written as $b\bar{r}_p$. This means that, using the results of **4**, **2** can be set out as:

$$U_p = a + b\bar{r}_p - c\bar{r}_p^2 - cV_p \qquad 5$$

This is the expression we seek.

Section 2: Derivation of a formula for portfolio risk – the two-security case

The basic definition of the variance of the probability distribution of a random variable (r_i) is:

$$V_i = \sum p_i(r_i - \bar{r}_i)^2. \qquad \text{(a)}$$

The variance of our portfolio (V_p) can therefore be defined as:

$$V_p = \sum p_i(r_p - \bar{r}_p)^2, \qquad \text{(b)}$$

where r_p stands for each possible portfolio return. Each of these returns is a weighted sum of a given pair of individual returns from the two securities (s and j) which make up the portfolio; the weights being the proportions of j and s in the portfolio (x_s and x_j). Similarly, the expected value of the portfolio's return is a weighted average of the expected returns of the two stocks. Thus, **(b)** above can be written as:

$$V_p = \sum p_i((x_j r_j + x_s r_s) - (x_j \bar{r}_j + x_s \bar{r}_s))^2 \qquad \text{(c)}$$

1. Multiplying the term in brackets gives $2(r_i\bar{r}_p - \bar{r}_p^2)$, and multiplying by the element outside the brackets $\left(\sum^m p_i c \right)$ gives:

$$2c \left(\sum^m p_i\{r_i\bar{r}_p\} - \sum^m p_i\{\bar{r}_p\}^2 \right).$$

But the first element of the first term in brackets $\left(\sum^m p_i r_i \right)$ is equal to $\bar{r}_p$. Substituting this into the above expression gives:

$$2c \left(\sum^m p_i\bar{r}_p^2 - \sum^m p_i\bar{r}_p^2 \right),$$

which equals zero.

We can multiply this expression out using the $(x - y)^2 = x^2 + y^2 - 2xy$ rule. Expression (c) can thus be written:

$$V_p = \sum p_i [(x_j r_j + x_s r_s)^2 + (x_j \bar{r}_j + x_s \bar{r}_s)^2 \\ - 2(x_j r_j + x_s r_s)(x_j \bar{r}_j + x_s \bar{r}_s)]. \qquad \textbf{1}$$

The first term in brackets can be multiplied out to give:

$$(x_j r_j)^2 + (x_s r_s)^2 + 2(x_j r_j \, x_s r_s), \qquad \textbf{2}$$

and the second element in **1** can be similarly written as:

$$(x_j \bar{r}_j)^2 + (x_s \bar{r}_s)^2 + 2(x_j \bar{r}_j \, x_s \bar{r}_s). \qquad \textbf{3}$$

There is no simple rule that can be used to multiply out the third element of **1**. Each individual term in the second set of brackets has to be multiplied by each individual element in the first set of brackets. This calculation gives the third element of **1** as:

$$-2(x_j r_j x_j \bar{r}_j + x_j r_j x_s \bar{r}_s + x_s r_s x_j \bar{r}_j + x_s r_s x_s \bar{r}_s). \qquad \textbf{4}$$

Simplifying by collecting together those terms containing the same elements, using x_j and x_s as the basis for collection, we obtain:

$$-2x_j^2(r_j \bar{r}_j) - 2x_j x_s(r_j \bar{r}_s) - 2x_s x_j(r_s \bar{r}_j) - 2x_s^2(r_s \bar{r}_s). \qquad \textbf{5}$$

We have now broken the original expression **1** into its constituent elements. The first element of **1** is disaggregated in **2** and the results of similar operations on the other two elements of **1** are shown in **3** and **5** respectively. The next step is to collect like terms in the hope that these may yield expressions which have some definite meaning. Let us collect together all those terms in **2**, **3**, and **5** which contain x_j^2. This gives:

$$\underset{(1)}{(x_j r_j)^2} + \underset{(2)}{(x_j \bar{r}_j)^2} - \underset{(3)}{2x_j^2(r_j \bar{r}_j)}, \qquad \textbf{6}$$

where, (1) is the first element of **2**, (2) the first element of **3**, and (3) the first element of **5**. Collecting the x_j terms in **6** together gives:

$$x_j^2(r_j^2 + \bar{r}_j^2 - 2\{r_j \bar{r}_j\}), \qquad \textbf{7}$$

which by the $(x - y)^2$ rule can be written as the variance of security j ($\{r_j - \bar{r}_j\}^2$) multiplied by the square of its weight in portfolio.

Collecting all those terms from expressions **2**, **3** and **5** which contain xs^2 gives a similar expression for security s:

$$x_s^2(r_s - \bar{r}_s)^2, \qquad \textbf{8}$$

which represents the variance of security s multiplied by the square of its weight in the portfolio.

All that remains to be done is to collect together the remaining terms of 2, 3 and 5, and to see what meaning can be attached to the resulting expression. Collecting together the remaining terms yields:

$$2x_j x_s(r_j r_s) \quad + \quad 2x_j x_s(\bar{r}_j \bar{r}_s) \quad - \quad 2x_j x_s(r_j \bar{r}_s) \quad - \quad 2x_s x_j(r_s \bar{r}_j) \qquad 9$$
(2, 3rd term)   (3, 3rd term)   (5, 2nd term)   (5, 3rd term)

By collecting together all the terms in 9 which contain the term $2x_j x_s$, we obtain:

$$2x_j x_s(r_j r_s + \bar{r}_j \bar{r}_s - r_j \bar{r}_s - r_s \bar{r}_j). \qquad 10$$

The term in brackets is the result we would obtain if we multiplied together $(r_j - \bar{r}_j)$ and $(r_s - \bar{r}_s)$ and thus expression 10 can be written as:

$$2x_j x_s(\{r_j - \bar{r}_j\}\{r_s - \bar{r}_s\}). \qquad 11$$

However, the bracketed terms are our definition of the covariance between the returns of securities j and s, and thus 11 reduces to:

$$2x_j x_s \text{cov}(sj). \qquad 12$$

We have now succeeded in building an expression for the portfolio variance from its basic definition in terms of the individual variances of the securities (7 and 8) plus the covariances (12). Thus, portfolio risk can be written as:

$$V_p = x_s{}^2 V_s + x_j{}^2 V_j + 2x_s x_j \text{cov}(sj),$$

which is the expression we use in the text. This section also allows us to see how the weights in this formula are derived.

Section 3: Algebraic treatment of risk in a two-security portfolio

Recall that in the two-security case, portfolio risk can be quantified as:

$$V_p = x_s{}^2 V_s + x_j{}^2 V_j + 2x_s x_j(c\{sj\}\sigma_s \sigma_j), \qquad 1$$

where the expression with brackets is the covariance between the returns of the two securities broken down into its constituent parts. The proportion that the jth security represents of the whole portfolio can be written as $(1 - x_s)$ and, our expression becomes:

$$V_p = x_s{}^2 V_s + (1 - x_s)^2 V_j + 2x_s(1 - x_s)(c\{sj\}\sigma_s \sigma_j). \qquad 2$$

This is a general expression for the overall risk of a two-security portfolio. We can say quite a lot about portfolio risk using this formula. For example, this is at its greatest when the two securities are perfectly positively correlated. In this case, the correlation coefficient $c(sj)$ equals unity, and our expression for V_p reduces to:

$$V_p = x_s{}^2 \sigma_s{}^2 + (1 - x_s)^2 \sigma_j{}^2 + 2x_s(1 - x_s)\sigma_s \sigma_j, \qquad 3$$

and the application of the $(x + y)^2$ rule to **3** yields:

$$V_p = (x_s\sigma_s + (1 - x_s)\sigma_j)^2. \qquad\qquad\qquad 4$$

This is an expression for the maximum risk of any portfolio comprising two securities.

The risk of any portfolio consisting of two securities the returns of which are less than perfectly positively correlated will be less than that given by **4**. The third element on the right of **2** declines in importance as the degree of correlation tends to zero and disappears entirely when there is no correlation between the two securities $(c\{sj\}) = 0$. The risk of the portfolio in this situation will be given by $x_s^2 V_s + (1 - x_s)^2 V_j$.

The combination of the two securities which gives the minimum risk obtained will be achieved when the two stocks are perfectly, negatively correlated. In this case, V_p will equal $(x_s\sigma_s - (1 - x_s)\sigma_j)^2$.

Each diagram in Figure 34 is obtained by plugging a given correlation coefficient into **2** and tracing out portfolio risk as the proportion of security s is increased. Diagrams (a) to (d) illustrate the results of this operation where the returns of the two securities are assumed to have the same variance. As an example of the process, consider that point in diagram (d) which suggests that portfolio risk is minimized when funds are spread equally between s and j if the correlation coefficient of the returns from the two securities is $+0.5$. The uncertainty associated with this particular mix of shares can be found by plugging the assumed correlation coefficient into **2** above. This is done below:

$$V_p = (0.5)^2 V_s + (1 - 0.5)^2 V_s + 2(0.5)(1 - 0.5)(0.5)V_s,$$

where security s makes up half the portfolio ($x_s = 0.5$) and both $\sigma_s\sigma_j$ and V_j are written as V_s because the variance of the two securities are assumed to be equal ($V_s = V_j$ and $\sigma_s = \sigma_j$). The final 0.5 in the last element of the above expression represents the assumed correlation coefficient. Multiplying out the expression shows that, under our assumed conditions, the overall risk of the portfolio is equal to only 75 per cent of the risk associated with either individual security.[2] This can be demonstrated by plugging some numbers into **2**. For example, if both securities have a variance of 0.4, spreading funds equally between them will yield a portfolio risk of 0.3, if the correlation coefficient between the two stocks is $+0.5$. All other points in diagram (d) (and, indeed, in all the other diagrams) can be found in this way.

2. The above expression can be written as:

$$V_p = (0.5)^2 V_s + (0.5)^2 V_s + 2((0.5)(0.5)(0.5)V_s),$$

and multiplying this out gives:

$$V_p = 0.25 V_s + 0.25 V_s + 0.25 V_s = 0.75 V_s = 0.75 V_j.$$

Appendix C

Specimen Interest Tables prepared by Professor J. F. Flower and Mr K. N. Bhaskar

(reproduced with permission)

Note: Certain of the larger numbers in the tables are expressed as for example $0{\cdot}16641343\text{E}+09$; this is to be interpreted as $0{\cdot}16641343 \times 10^9 = 166413430$. With very small numbers, similarly, $0{\cdot}56546584\text{E}-07$ is to be interpreted as $0{\cdot}56546584 \times 10^{-7}$.

Rate of interest 2·50 per cent

n	$(1+r)^n$	v^n	s_n	$s_{\overline{n}}^{-1}$	a_n	$a_{\overline{n}}^{-1}$
1	1·02500	0·975609756	1·00000	1·000000000	0·97560976	1·025000000
2	1·05062	0·951814396	2·02500	0·493827160	1·92742415	0·518827160
3	1·07689	0·928599411	3·07562	0·325137167	2·85602356	0·350137167
4	1·10381	0·905950645	4·15252	0·240817878	3·76197421	0·265817878
5	1·13141	0·883854288	5·25633	0·190246861	4·64582850	0·215246861
6	1·15969	0·862290866	6·38774	0·156549971	5·50812536	0·181549971
7	1·18869	0·841265235	7·54743	0·132495430	6·34939060	0·157495430
8	1·21840	0·820746571	8·73612	0·114467346	7·17013717	0·139467346
9	1·24886	0·800728362	9·95452	0·100456890	7·97086553	0·125456890
10	1·28008	0·781198402	11·20338	0·089258763	8·75206393	0·114258763
11	1·31209	0·762144782	12·48347	0·080105956	9·51420871	0·105105956
12	1·34489	0·743555885	13·79555	0·072487127	10·25776460	0·097487127
13	1·37851	0·725420376	15·14044	0·066048271	10·98318497	0·091048271
14	1·41297	0·707727196	16·51895	0·060536525	11·69091217	0·085536525
15	1·44830	0·690465557	17·93193	0·055766456	12·38137773	0·080766456

n	$(1+r)^n$	v^n	s_n	s_n^{-1}	a_n	a_n^{-1}
16	1·48451	0·673624934	19·38022	0·051598989	13·05500266	0·076598989
17	1·52162	0·657195057	20·86473	0·047927770	13·71219772	0·072927770
18	1·55966	0·641165909	22·38635	0·044670081	14·35336363	0·069670081
19	1·59865	0·625527716	23·94601	0·041760615	14·97889134	0·066760615
20	1·63862	0·610270943	25·54466	0·039147129	15·58916229	0·064147129
21	1·67958	0·595386286	27·18327	0·036787327	16·18454857	0·061787327
22	1·72157	0·580864669	28·86286	0·034646606	16·76541324	0·059646606
23	1·76461	0·566697238	30·58443	0·032696378	17·33211048	0·057696378
24	1·80873	0·552875354	32·34904	0·030912820	17·88498583	0·055912820
25	1·85394	0·539390589	34·15776	0·029275921	18·42437642	0·054275921
26	1·90029	0·526234721	36·01171	0·027768747	18·95061114	0·052768747
27	1·94780	0·513399728	37·91200	0·026376872	19·46401087	0·051376872
28	1·99650	0·500877784	39·85980	0·025087933	19·96488866	0·050087933
29	2·04641	0·488661252	41·85630	0·023891268	20·45354991	0·048891268
30	2·09757	0·476742685	43·90270	0·022777641	20·93029259	0·047777641
31	2·15001	0·465114815	46·00027	0·021739002	21·39540741	0·046739002
32	2·20376	0·453770551	48·15028	0·020768312	21·84917796	0·045768312
33	2·25885	0·442702977	50·35403	0·019859382	22·29188094	0·044859382
34	2·31532	0·431905343	52·61289	0·019006751	22·72378628	0·044006751
35	2·37321	0·421371066	54·92821	0·018205582	23·14515734	0·043205582
36	2·43254	0·411093723	57·30141	0·017451577	23·55625107	0·042451577
37	2·49335	0·401067047	59·73395	0·016740899	23·95731812	0·041740899
38	2·55568	0·391284924	62·22730	0·016070118	24·34860304	0·041070118
39	2·61957	0·381741389	64·78298	0·015436153	24·73034443	0·040436153

n	$(1 + r)^n$	v^n	s_n	s_n^{-1}	a_n	a_n^{-1}
40	2·68506	0·372430624	67·40255	0·014836233	25·10277505	0·039836233
41	2·75219	0·363346950	70·08762	0·014267856	25·46612200	0·039267856
42	2·82100	0·354484829	72·83981	0·013728757	25·82060683	0·038728757
43	2·89152	0·345838858	75·66080	0·013216883	26·16644569	0·038216883
44	2·96381	0·337403764	78·55232	0·012730368	26·50384945	0·037730368
45	3·03790	0·329174404	81·51613	0·012267511	26·83302386	0·037267511
46	3·11385	0·321145760	84·55403	0·011826757	27·15416962	0·036826757
47	3·19170	0·313312936	87·66789	0·011406686	27·46748255	0·036406686
48	3·27149	0·305671157	90·85958	0·011005994	27·77315371	0·036005994
49	3·35328	0·298215763	94·13107	0·010623485	28·07136947	0·035623485
50	3·43711	0·290942208	97·48435	0·010258057	28·36231168	0·035258057
55	3·88877	0·257150518	115·55092	0·008654193	29·71397928	0·033654193
60	4·39979	0·227283588	135·99159	0·007353396	30·90865649	0·032353396
65	4·97796	0·200885574	159·11833	0·006284631	31·96457705	0·031284631
70	5·63210	0·177553576	185·28411	0·005397117	32·89785698	0·030397117
80	7·20957	0·138704569	248·38271	0·004026045	34·45181722	0·029026045
90	9·22886	0·108355788	329·15425	0·003038089	35·66576848	0·028038089
100	11·81372	0·084647368	432·54865	0·002311879	36·61410526	0·027311879

Rate of interest 3·00 per cent

n	$(1 + r)^n$	v^n	s_n	$s_{\overline{n}}^{-1}$	a_n	$a_{\overline{n}}^{-1}$
1	1·03000	0·970873786	1·00000	1·000000000	0·97087379	1·030000000
2	1·06090	0·942593909	2·03000	0·492610837	1·91346970	0·522610837
3	1·09273	0·915141659	3·09090	0·323530363	2·82861135	0·353530363
4	1·12551	0·888487048	4·18363	0·239027845	3·71709840	0·269027045
5	1·15927	0·862608784	5·30914	0·188354571	4·57970719	0·218354571
6	1·19405	0·837484257	6·46841	0·154597500	5·41719144	0·184597500
7	1·22987	0·813091511	7·66246	0·130506354	6·23028296	0·160506354
8	1·26677	0·789409234	8·89234	0·112456389	7·01969219	0·142456389
9	1·30477	0·766416732	10·15911	0·098433857	7·78610892	0·128433857
10	1·34392	0·744093915	11·46388	0·087230507	8·53020284	0·117230507
11	1·38423	0·722421277	12·80780	0·078077448	9·25262411	0·108077448
12	1·42576	0·701379880	14·19203	0·070462085	9·95400399	0·100462085
13	1·46853	0·680951340	15·61779	0·064029544	10·63495533	0·094029544
14	1·51259	0·661117806	17·08632	0·058526339	11·29607314	0·088526339
15	1·55797	0·641861947	18·59891	0·053766580	11·93793509	0·083766580
16	1·60417	0·623166939	20·15688	0·049610849	12·56110203	0·079610849
17	1·65285	0·605016446	21·76159	0·045952529	13·16611847	0·075952529
18	1·70243	0·587394608	23·41444	0·042708696	13·75351308	0·072708696
19	1·75351	0·570286027	25·11687	0·039813881	14·32379911	0·069813881
20	1·80611	0·553675754	26·87037	0·037215708	14·87747486	0·067215708
21	1·86029	0·537549276	28·67649	0·034871776	15·41502414	0·064871776
22	1·91610	0·521892501	30·53678	0·032747395	15·93691664	0·062747395
23	1·97359	0·506691748	32·45288	0·030813903	16·44360839	0·060813903

n	$(1+r)^n$	v^n	s_n	s_n^{-1}	a_n	a_n^{-1}
24	2·03279	0·491933736	34·42647	0·0 9047416	16·93554212	0·059047416
25	2·09378	0·477605569	36·45926	0·0 7427871	17·41314769	0·057427871
26	2·15659	0·463694727	38·55304	0·0 5938290	17·87684242	0·055938290
27	2·22129	0·450189056	40·70963	0·024564210	18·32703147	0·054564210
28	2·28793	0·437076753	42·93092	0·023293233	18·76410823	0·053293233
29	2·35657	0·424346362	45·21885	0·022114671	19·18845459	0·052114671
30	2·42726	0·411986760	47·57542	0·021019259	19·60044135	0·051019259
31	2·50008	0·399987145	50·00268	0·019998929	20·00042849	0·049998929
32	2·57508	0·388337034	52·50276	0·019046618	20·38876553	0·049046618
33	2·65234	0·377026247	55·07784	0·018156122	20·76579178	0·048156122
34	2·73191	0·366044900	57·73018	0·017321963	21·13183668	0·047321963
35	2·81386	0·355383398	60·46208	0·016539292	21·48722007	0·046539292
36	2·89828	0·345032425	63·27594	0·015803794	21·83225250	0·045803794
37	2·98523	0·334982937	66·17422	0·015111624	22·16723544	0·045111624
38	3·07478	0·325226152	69·15945	0·014459340	22·49246159	0·044459340
39	3·16703	0·315753546	72·23423	0·013843852	22·80821513	0·043843852
40	3·26204	0·306556841	75·40126	0·013262378	23·11477197	0·043262378
41	3·35990	0·297628001	78·66330	0·012712409	23·41239997	0·042712409
42	3·46070	0·288959224	82·02320	0·012191673	23·70135920	0·042191673
43	3·56452	0·280542936	85·48389	0·011698110	23·98190213	0·041698110
44	3·67145	0·272371782	89·04841	0·011229847	24·25427392	0·041229847
45	3·78160	0·264438624	92·71986	0·010785176	24·51871254	0·040785176
46	3·89504	0·256736528	96·50146	0·010362538	24·77544907	0·040362538
47	4·01190	0·249258765	100·39650	0·009960506	25·02470783	0·039960506

n	$(1 + r)^n$	v^n	s_n	s_n^{-1}	a_n	a_n^{-1}
48	4·13225	0·241998801	104·40840	0·009577774	25·26670664	0·039577774
49	4·25622	0·234950292	108·54065	0·009213138	25·50165693	0·039213138
50	4·38391	0·228107080	112·79687	0·008865494	25·72976401	0·038865494
55	5·08215	0·196767171	136·07162	0·007349071	26·77442764	0·037349071
60	5·89160	0·169733090	163·05344	0·006132959	27·67556367	0·036132959
65	6·82998	0·146413254	194·33276	0·005145813	28·45289152	0·035145813
70	7·91782	0·126297359	230·59406	0·004336625	29·12342135	0·034336625
80	10·64089	0·093977097	321·36302	0·003111746	30·20076345	0·033111746
90	14·30047	0·069927786	443·34890	0·002255560	31·00240714	0·032255560
100	19·21863	0·052032840	607·28773	0·001646666	31·59890534	0·031646666

Rate of interest 4·00 per cent

n	$(1+r)^n$	v^n	s_n	s_n^{-1}	a_n	a_n^{-1}
1	1·04000	0·961538462	1·00000	1·000000000	0·96153846	1·040000000
2	1·08160	0·924556213	2·04000	0·490196078	1·88609467	0·530196078
3	1·12486	0·888996359	3·12160	0·320348539	2·77509103	0·360348539
4	1·16986	0·854804191	4·24646	0·235490045	3·62989522	0·275490045
5	1·21665	0·821927107	5·41632	0·184627113	4·45182233	0·224627113
6	1·26532	0·790314526	6·63298	0·150761903	5·24213686	0·190761903
7	1·31593	0·759917813	7·89829	0·126609612	6·00205467	0·166609612
8	1·36857	0·730690205	9·21423	0·108527832	6·73274487	0·148527832
9	1·42331	0·702586736	10·58280	0·094492993	7·43533161	0·134492993
10	1·48024	0·675564169	12·00611	0·083290944	8·11089578	0·123290944
11	1·53945	0·649580932	13·48635	0·074149039	8·76047671	0·114149039
12	1·60103	0·624597050	15·02581	0·066552173	9·38507376	0·106552173
13	1·66507	0·600574086	16·62684	0·060143728	9·98564785	0·100143728
14	1·73168	0·577475083	18·29191	0·054668973	10·56312293	0·094668973
15	1·80094	0·555264503	20·02359	0·049941100	11·11838743	0·089941100
16	1·87298	0·533908176	21·82453	0·045819999	11·65229561	0·085819999
17	1·94790	0·513373246	23·69751	0·042198522	12·16566885	0·082198522
18	2·02582	0·493628121	25·64541	0·038993328	12·65929697	0·078993328
19	2·10685	0·474642424	27·67123	0·036138618	13·13393940	0·076138618
20	2·19112	0·456386946	29·77808	0·033581750	13·59032634	0·073581750
21	2·27877	0·438833602	31·96920	0·031280105	14·02915995	0·071280105
22	2·36992	0·421955387	34·24797	0·029198811	14·45111533	0·069198811
23	2·46472	0·405726333	36·61789	0·027309057	14·85684167	0·067309057

n	$(1 + r)^n$	v^n	s_n	s_n^{-1}	a_n	a_n^{-1}
24	2·56330	0·390121474	39·08260	0·025586831	15·24696314	0·065586831
25	2·66584	0·375116802	41·64591	0·024011963	15·62207994	0·064011963
26	2·77247	0·360689233	44·31174	0·022567380	15·98276918	0·062567380
27	2·88337	0·346816570	47·08421	0·021238541	16·32958575	0·061238541
28	2·99870	0·333477471	49·96758	0·020012975	16·66306322	0·060012975
29	3·11865	0·320651415	52·96629	0·018879934	16·96371463	0·058879034
30	3·24340	0·308318668	56·08494	0·017830099	17·29203330	0·057830099
31	3·37313	0·296460258	59·32834	0·016855352	17·58849356	0·056855352
32	3·50806	0·285057940	62·70147	0·015948590	17·87355150	0·055948590
33	3·64838	0·274094173	66·20953	0·015103566	18·14764567	0·055103566
34	3·79432	0·263552090	69·85791	0·014314772	18·41119776	0·054314772
35	3·94609	0·253415471	73·65222	0·013577322	18·66461323	0·053577322
36	4·10393	0·243668722	77·59831	0·012886878	18·90828195	0·052886878
37	4·26809	0·234296848	81·70225	0·012239566	19·14257880	0·052239566
38	4·43881	0·225285431	85·97034	0·011631919	19·36786423	0·051631919
39	4·61637	0·216620606	90·40915	0·011060827	19·58448484	0·051060827
40	4·80102	0·208289045	95·02552	0·010523489	19·79277388	0·050523489
41	4·99306	0·200277928	99·82654	0·010017377	19·99305181	0·050017377
42	5·19278	0·192574930	104·81960	0·009540201	20·18562674	0·049540201
43	5·40050	0·185168202	110·01238	0·009089886	20·37079494	0·049089886
44	5·61652	0·178046348	115·41288	0·008664544	20·54884129	0·048664544
45	5·84118	0·171199842	121·02939	0·008262436	20·72003970	0·048262456
46	6·07482	0·164613858	126·87057	0·007882049	20·88465356	0·047882049
47	6·31782	0·158282555	132·94539	0·007521885	21·04293612	0·047521885

n	$(1+r)^n$	v^n	s_n	s_n^{-1}	a_n	a_n^{-1}
48	6·57053	0·152194765	139·26321	0·007180648	21·19513088	0·047180648
49	6·83335	0·146341120	145·83373	0·006857124	21·34147200	0·046857124
50	7·10668	0·140712615	152·66708	0·006550206	21·48218462	0·046550200
55	8·64637	0·115655513	191·15917	0·005231243	22·10861218	0·045231243
60	10·51963	0·095060401	237·99069	0·004201845	22·62348997	0·044201845
65	12·79874	0·078132720	294·96838	0·003390194	23·04668199	0·043390194
70	15·57162	0·064219401	364·29046	0·002745062	23·39451498	0·042745062
80	23·04980	0·043384326	551·24498	0·001814075	23·91539185	0·041814075
90	34·11933	0·029308896	827·98333	0·001207754	24·26727759	0·041207754
100	50·50495	0·019800040	1237·62370	0·000808000	24·50499900	0·040808000

Rate of interest 5·00 per cent

n	$(1+r)^n$	v^n	s_n	s_n^{-1}	a_n	a_n^{-1}
1	1·05000	0·952380952	1·00000	1·000000000	0·95238095	1·050000000
2	1·10250	0·907029478	2·05000	0·487804878	1·85941043	0·537804878
3	1·15762	0·863837599	3·15250	0·317208565	2·72324803	0·367208565
4	1·21551	0·822702475	4·31012	0·232011833	3·54595050	0·282011833
5	1·27628	0·783526166	5·52563	0·180974798	4·32947667	0·230974798
6	1·34010	0·746215397	6·80191	0·147017468	5·07569207	0·197017468
7	1·40710	0·710681330	8·14201	0·122819818	5·78637340	0·172819818
8	1·47746	0·676839362	9·54911	0·104721814	6·46321276	0·154721814
9	1·55133	0·644608916	11·02656	0·090690080	7·10782168	0·140690080
10	1·62889	0·613913254	12·57789	0·079504575	7·72173493	0·129504575
11	1·71034	0·584679289	14·20679	0·070388891	8·30641422	0·120388891
12	1·79586	0·556837418	15·91713	0·062825410	8·86325164	0·112825410
13	1·88565	0·530321351	17·71298	0·056455765	9·39357299	0·106455765
14	1·97993	0·505067953	19·59863	0·051023969	9·89864094	0·101023969
15	2·07893	0·481017098	21·57856	0·046342288	10·37965804	0·096342288
16	2·18287	0·458111522	23·65749	0·042269908	10·83776956	0·092269908
17	2·29202	0·436296688	25·84037	0·038699142	11·27406625	0·088699142
18	2·40662	0·415520655	28·13238	0·035546222	11·68958690	0·085546222
19	2·52695	0·395733957	30·53900	0·032745010	12·08532086	0·082745010
20	2·65330	0·376889483	33·06595	0·030242587	12·46221034	0·080242587
21	2·78596	0·358942365	35·71925	0·027996107	12·82115271	0·077996107
22	2·92526	0·341849871	38·50521	0·025970509	13·16300258	0·075970509
23	3·07152	0·325571306	41·43048	0·024136822	13·48857388	0·074136822

n	$(1 + r)^n$	v^n	s_n	s_n^{-1}	a_n	a_n^{-1}
24	3·22510	0·310067910	44·50200	0·022470901	13·79864179	0·072470901
25	3·38635	0·295302772	47·72710	0·020952457	14·09394457	0·070952457
26	3·55567	0·281240735	51·11345	0·019564321	14·37518530	0·069564321
27	3·73346	0·267848319	54·66913	0·018291860	14·64303362	0·068291860
28	3·92013	0·255093637	58·40258	0·017122530	14·89812726	0·067122530
29	4·11614	0·242946321	62·32271	0·016045515	15·14107358	0·066045515
30	4·32194	0·231377449	66·43885	0·015051435	15·37245103	0·065051435
31	4·53804	0·220359475	70·76079	0·014132120	15·59281050	0·064132120
32	4·76494	0·209866167	75·29883	0·013280419	15·80267667	0·063280419
33	5·00319	0·199872540	80·06377	0·012490044	16·00254921	0·062490044
34	5·25335	0·190354800	85·06696	0·011755445	16·19290401	0·061755445
35	5·51602	0·181290285	90·32031	0·011071707	16·37419429	0·061071707
36	5·79182	0·172657415	95·83632	0·010434457	16·54685171	0·060434457
37	6·08141	0·164435633	101·62814	0·009839794	16·71128734	0·059839794
38	6·38548	0·156605365	107·70955	0·009284228	16·86789271	0·059284228
39	6·70475	0·149147966	114·09502	0·008764624	17·01704067	0·058764624
40	7·03999	0·142045682	120·79977	0·008278161	17·15908635	0·058278161
41	7·39199	0·135281602	127·83976	0·007822292	17·29436796	0·057822292
42	7·76159	0·128839621	135·23175	0·007394713	17·42320758	0·057394713
43	8·14967	0·122704401	142·99334	0·006993333	17·54591198	0·056993333
44	8·55715	0·116861334	151·14301	0·006616251	17·66277331	0·056616251
45	8·98501	0·111296509	159·70016	0·006261735	17·77406982	0·056261735
46	9·43426	0·105996675	168·68516	0·005928204	17·88006650	0·055928204
47	9·90597	0·100949214	178·11942	0·005614211	17·98101571	0·055614211

n	$(1 + r)^n$	v^n	s_n	s_n^{-1}	a_n	$a_{\overline{n}}$
48	10·40127	0·096142109	188·02539	0·005318431	18·07715782	0·055318431
49	10·92133	0·091563913	198·42666	0·005039645	18·16872173	0·055039645
50	11·46740	0·087203727	209·34800	0·004776735	18·25592546	0·054776735
55	14·63563	0·068326402	272·71262	0·003666864	18·63347196	0·053666864
60	18·67919	0·053535524	353·58372	0·002828185	18·92928953	0·052828185
65	23·83990	0·041946484	456·79801	0·002189151	19·16107033	0·052189151
70	30·42643	0·032866168	588·52851	0·001699153	19·34267665	0·051699153
80	49·56144	0·020176976	971·22882	0·001029623	19·59646048	0·051029623
90	80·73037	0·012386913	1594·60730	0·000627114	19·75226174	0·050627114
100	131·50126	0·007604490	2610·02516	0·000383138	19·84791020	0·050383318

Rate of interest 7·00 per cent

n	$(1 + r)^n$	v^n	s_n	s_n^{-1}	a_n	a_n^{-1}
1	1·07000	0·934579439	1·00000	1·00000000	0·93457944	1·070000000
2	1·14490	0·873438728	2·07000	0·483091787	1·80801817	0·553091787
3	1·22504	0·816297877	3·21490	0·311051666	2·62431604	0·381051666
4	1·31080	0·762895212	4·43994	0·225228117	3·38721126	0·295228117
5	1·40255	0·712986179	5·75074	0·173890694	4·10019744	0·243890694
6	1·50073	0·666342224	7·15329	0·139795800	4·76653966	0·209795800
7	1·60578	0·622749742	8·65402	0·115553220	5·38928940	0·185553220
8	1·71819	0·582009105	10·25980	0·097467762	5·97129851	0·167467762
9	1·83846	0·543933743	11·97799	0·083486470	6·51523225	0·153486470
10	1·96715	0·508349292	13·81645	0·072377503	7·02358154	0·142377503
11	2·10485	0·475092796	15·78360	0·063356905	7·49867434	0·133356905
12	2·25219	0·444011959	17·88845	0·055901989	7·94268630	0·125901989
13	2·40985	0·414964448	20·14064	0·049650848	8·35765074	0·119650848
14	2·57853	0·387817241	22·55049	0·044344939	8·74546799	0·114344939
15	2·75903	0·362446020	25·12902	0·039794625	9·10791401	0·109794625
16	2·95216	0·338714598	27·88805	0·035857648	9·44646860	0·105857648
17	3·15882	0·316574390	30·84022	0·032425193	9·76322299	0·102425193
18	3·37993	0·295863916	33·99903	0·029412602	10·05908691	0·099412602
19	3·61653	0·276508333	37·37896	0·026753015	10·33559524	0·096753015
20	3·86968	0·258419003	40·99549	0·024392926	10·59401425	0·094392926
21	4·14056	0·241513087	44·86518	0·022289002	10·83552733	0·092289002
22	4·43040	0·225713165	49·00574	0·020405773	11·06124050	0·090405773
23	4·74053	0·210946883	53·43614	0·018713926	11·27218738	0·088713926

n	$(1 + r)^n$	v^n	s_n	s_n^{-1}	a_n	a_n^{-1}
24	5·07237	0·197146620	58·17667	0·017189021	11·46933400	0·087189021
25	5·42743	0·184249178	63·24904	0·015810517	11·65358318	0·085810517
26	5·80735	0·172195493	68·67647	0·014561028	11·82577867	0·084561028
27	6·21387	0·160930367	74·48382	0·013425734	11·98670904	0·083425734
28	6·64884	0·150402212	80·69769	0·012391928	12·13711125	0·082391928
29	7·11426	0·140562815	87·34653	0·011448652	12·27767407	0·081448652
30	7·61226	0·131367117	94·46079	0·010586404	12·40904118	0·080586404
31	8·14511	0·122773007	102·07304	0·009796906	12·53181419	0·079796906
32	8·71527	0·114741128	110·21815	0·009072915	12·64655532	0·079072915
33	9·32534	0·107234699	118·93343	0·008408065	12·75379002	0·078408065
34	9·97811	0·100219345	128·25876	0·007796738	12·85400936	0·077796738
35	10·67658	0·093662939	138·23688	0·007233960	12·94767230	0·077233960
36	11·42394	0·087535457	148·91346	0·006715310	13·03520776	0·076715310
37	12·22362	0·081808838	160·33740	0·006236848	13·11701660	0·076236848
38	13·07927	0·076456858	172·56102	0·005795052	13·19347345	0·075795052
39	13·99482	0·071455008	185·64029	0·005386762	13·26492846	0·075386762
40	14·97446	0·066780381	199·63511	0·005009139	13·33170884	0·075009139
41	16·02267	0·062411571	214·60957	0·004659624	13·39412041	0·074659624
42	17·14426	0·058328571	230·63224	0·004335907	13·45244898	0·074335907
43	18·34435	0·054512683	247·77650	0·004035895	13·50696167	0·074035895
44	19·62846	0·050946433	266·12085	0·003757691	13·55790810	0·073757691
45	21·00245	0·047613489	285·74931	0·003499571	13·60552159	0·073499571
46	22·47262	0·044498588	306·75176	0·003259965	13·65002018	0·073259965
47	24·04571	0·041587465	329·22439	0·003037442	13·69160764	0·073037442

n	$(1 + r)^n$	v^n	s_n	s_n^{-1}	a_n	a_n^{-1}
48	25·72891	0·038866790	353·27009	0·002830695	13·73047443	0·072830695
49	27·52993	0·036324103	378·99900	0·002638529	13·76679853	0·072638529
50	29·45703	0·033947759	406·52893	0·002459850	13·80074629	0·072459850
55	41·31500	0·024204283	575·92859	0·001736326	13·93993881	0·071736326
60	57·94643	0·017257319	813·52038	0·001229226	14·03918115	0·071229226
65	81·27286	0·012304230	1146·75516	0·000872026	14·10993957	0·070872026
70	113·98939	0·008772746	1614·13417	0·000619527	14·16038934	0·070619527
80	224·23439	0·004459619	3189·06268	0·000313572	14·22200544	0·070313572
90	441·10298	0·002267044	6287·18543	0·000159054	14·25332794	0·070159054
100	867·71633	0·001152450	12381·66179	0·000080765	14·26925071	0·070080765

Rate of interest 10·00 per cent

n	$(1+r)^n$	s_n	s_n^{-1}	a_n	a_n^{-1}
1	1·10000	1·00000	1·000000000	0·90909091	1·100000000
2	1·21000	2·10000	0·476190476	1·73553719	0·576190476
3	1·33100	3·31000	0·302114804	2·48685199	0·402114804
4	1·46410	4·64100	0·215470804	3·16986545	0·315470804
5	1·61051	6·10510	0·163797481	3·79078677	0·263797481
6	1·77156	7·71561	0·129607380	4·35526070	0·229607380
7	1·94872	9·48717	0·105405500	4·86841882	0·205405500
8	2·14359	11·43589	0·087444018	5·33492620	0·187444018
9	2·35795	13·57948	0·073640539	5·75902382	0·173640539
10	2·59374	15·93742	0·062745395	6·14456711	0·162745395
11	2·85312	18·53117	0·053963142	6·49506101	0·153963142
12	3·13843	21·38428	0·046763315	6·81369182	0·146763315
13	3·45227	24·52271	0·040778524	7·10335620	0·140778524
14	3·79750	27·97498	0·035746223	7·36668746	0·135746223
15	4·17725	31·77248	0·031473777	7·60607951	0·131473777
16	4·59497	35·94973	0·027816621	7·82370864	0·127816621
17	5·05447	40·54470	0·024664134	8·02155331	0·124664134
18	5·55992	45·59917	0·021930222	8·20141210	0·121930222
19	6·11591	51·15909	0·019546868	8·36492009	0·119546868
20	6·72750	57·27500	0·017459625	8·51356372	0·117459625
21	7·40025	64·00250	0·015624390	8·64869429	0·115624390
22	8·14027	71·40275	0·014005063	8·77154026	0·114005063
23	8·95430	79·54302	0·012571813	8·88321842	0·112571813

n	$(1+r)^n$	v^n	s_n	s_n^{-1}	a_n	a_n^{-1}
24	9·84973	0·101525598	88·49733	0·011299776	8·98474402	0·111299776
25	10·83471	0·092295998	98·34706	0·010168072	9·07704002	0·110168072
26	11·91818	0·083905453	109·18177	0·009159039	9·16094547	0·109159039
27	13·10999	0·076277684	121·09994	0·008257642	9·23722316	0·108257642
28	14·42099	0·069343349	134·20994	0·007451013	9·30656651	0·107451013
29	15·86309	0·063039409	148·63093	0·006728075	9·36960591	0·106728075
30	17·44940	0·057308553	164·49402	0·006079248	9·42691447	0·106079248
31	19·19434	0·052098685	181·94342	0·005496214	9·47901315	0·105496214
32	21·11378	0·047362441	201·13777	0·004971717	9·52637559	0·104971717
33	23·22515	0·043056764	222·25154	0·004499406	9·56943236	0·104499406
34	25·54767	0·039142513	245·47670	0·004073706	9·60857487	0·104073706
35	28·10244	0·035584103	271·02437	0·003689705	9·64415897	0·103689705
36	30·91268	0·032349184	299·12681	0·003343064	9·67650816	0·103343064
37	34·00395	0·029408349	330·03949	0·003029940	9·70591651	0·103029940
38	37·40434	0·026734863	364·04343	0·002746925	9·73265137	0·102746925
39	41·14478	0·024304421	401·44778	0·002490984	9·75695579	0·102490984
40	45·25926	0·022094928	442·59256	0·002259414	9·77905072	0·102259414
41	49·78518	0·020086298	487·85181	0·002049803	9·79913702	0·102049803
42	54·76370	0·018260271	537·63699	0·001859991	9·81739729	0·101859991
43	60·24007	0·016600247	592·40069	0·001688047	9·83399753	0·101688047
44	66·26408	0·015091133	652·64076	0·001532237	9·84908867	0·101532237
45	72·89048	0·013719212	718·90484	0·001391005	9·86280788	0·101391005
46	80·17953	0·012472011	791·79532	0·001262953	9·87527989	0·101262953
47	88·19749	0·011338192	871·97485	0·001146822	9·88661808	0·101146822

n	$(1 + r)^n$	v^n	s_n	s_n^{-1}	a_n	a_n^{-1}
48	97·01723	0·010307447	960·17234	0·001041480	9·89692553	0·101041480
49	106·71896	0·009370406	1057·18957	0·000945904	9·90629594	0·100945904
50	117·39085	0·008518551	1163·90853	0·000859174	9·91481449	0·100859174
55	189·05914	0·005289350	1880·59142	0·000531748	9·94710650	0·100531748
60	304·48164	0·003284270	3034·81640	0·000329509	9·96715730	0·100329509
65	490·37073	0·002039273	4893·70725	0·000204344	9·97960727	0·100204344
70	789·74696	0·001266228	7887·46957	0·000126783	9·98733772	0·100126783
80	2048·40021	0·000488186	20674·00215	0·000048842	9·99511814	0·100048842
90	5313·02261	0·000188217	53120·22612	0·000018825	9·99811783	0·100018825
100	13780·61234	0·000072566	0·137796E + 06	0·000007257	9·99927434	0·100007257

Rate of interest 15·00 per cent

n	$(1+r)^n$	v^n	s_n	s_n^{-1}	a_n	a_n^{-1}
1	1·15000	0·869565217	1·00000	1·000000000	0·869565217	1·150000000
2	1·32250	0·756143667	2·15000	0·465116279	1·625708885	0·615116277
3	1·52087	0·657516232	3·47250	0·287970962	2·283225117	0·437976962
4	1·74901	0·571753246	4·99337	0·200265352	2·854978362	0·350265859
5	2·01136	0·497176735	6·74238	0·148315552	3·352155098	0·298315552
6	2·31306	0·432327596	8·75374	0·114236907	3·784482694	0·264236902
7	2·66002	0·375937040	11·06680	0·090360364	4·160419734	0·240360364
8	3·05902	0·326901774	13·72682	0·072850090	4·487321508	0·222850090
9	3·51788	0·284262412	16·78584	0·059574015	4·771583920	0·209574015
10	4·04566	0·247184706	20·30372	0·049252063	5·018768626	0·199252063
11	4·65239	0·214943223	24·34928	0·041068983	5·233711849	0·191068983
12	5·35025	0·186907150	29·00167	0·034480776	5·420618999	0·184480776
13	6·15279	0·162527957	34·35192	0·029110457	5·583146955	0·179110457
14	7·07571	0·141328658	40·50471	0·024688490	5·724475613	0·174688490
15	8·13706	0·122894485	47·58041	0·021017053	5·847370099	0·171017053
16	9·35762	0·106864770	55·71747	0·017947691	5·954234868	0·167947691
17	10·76126	0·092925887	65·07509	0·015366862	6·047160755	0·165366862
18	12·37545	0·080805119	75·83636	0·013186287	6·127965874	0·163186287
19	14·23177	0·070265321	88·21181	0·011336350	6·198231195	0·161336350
20	16·36654	0·061100279	102·44358	0·009761470	6·259331474	0·159761470
21	18·82152	0·053130677	118·81012	0·008416791	6·312462151	0·158416791
22	21·64475	0·046200589	137·63164	0·007265771	6·358662740	0·157265771
23	24·89146	0·040174425	159·27638	0·006278395	6·398837165	0·156278395

n	$(1+r)^n$	v^n	s_n	s_n^{-1}	a_n	a_n^{-1}
24	28·62518	0·034934283	184·16784	0·005429830	6·433771448	0·155429830
25	32·91895	0·030377637	212·79302	0·004699402	6·464149085	0·154699402
26	37·85680	0·026415337	245·71197	0·004069806	6·490564422	0·154069800
27	43·53531	0·022969858	283·56877	0·003526481	6·513534280	0·153526481
28	50·06561	0·019973790	327·10408	0·003057131	6·533508070	0·153057131
29	57·57545	0·017368513	377·16969	0·002651326	6·550876582	0·152651326
30	66·21177	0·015103054	434·74515	0·002300198	6·565979637	0·152300198
31	76·14354	0·013133091	500·95692	0·001996180	6·579112728	0·151996180
32	87·56507	0·011420079	577·10046	0·001732801	6·590532807	0·151732801
33	100·69983	0·009930503	664·66552	0·001504516	6·600463310	0·151504516
34	115·80480	0·008635220	755·36535	0·001306666	6·609098530	0·151306566
35	133·17552	0·007508887	881·17016	0·001134855	6·616607418	0·151134855
36	153·15185	0·006529467	1014·34568	0·000985857	6·623136885	0·150985857
37	176·12463	0·005677798	1167·49753	0·000856533	6·628814683	0·150856533
38	202·54332	0·004937215	1343·62216	0·000744257	6·633751898	0·150744257
39	232·92482	0·004293231	1546·16549	0·000646761	6·638045129	0·150646761
40	267·86355	0·003733244	1779·09031	0·000562085	6·641778373	0·150562085
41	308·04308	0·003246299	2046·95385	0·000488531	6·645024672	0·150488531
42	354·24954	0·002822869	2354·99693	0·000424629	6·647847541	0·150424629
43	407·38697	0·002454669	2709·24647	0·000369106	6·650302209	0·150369106
44	468·49502	0·002134494	3116·63344	0·000320859	6·652436704	0·150320859
45	538·76927	0·001856082	3585·12846	0·000278930	6·654292786	0·150278930
46	619·58466	0·001613984	4123·89773	0·000242489	6·655906770	0·150242489
47	712·52236	0·001403465	4743·48239	0·000210816	6·657310235	0·150210816

n	$(1+r)^n$	v^n	s_n	s_n^{-1}	a_n	a_n^{-1}
48	819·40071	0·001220404	5456·00475	0·000183284	6·658530639	0·150183284
49	942·31082	0·001061221	6275·40546	0·000159352	6·659591860	0·150159352
50	1083·65744	0·000922801	7217·71628	0·000138548	6·660514661	0·150138548
55	2179·62218	0·000458795	14524·14789	0·000068851	6·661145985	0·150068851
60	4383·99875	0·000228102	29219·99164	0·000034223	6·665910619	0·150034223
65	8817·78739	0·000113407	58778·58258	0·000017013	6·666290777	0·150017013
70	17735·72004	0·000056383	0·118231E + 06	0·000008458	6·666573753	0·150008458
80	71750·87940	0·000013937	0·478333E + 06	0·000002091	6·666643700	0·150002091
90	0·290272E + 06	0·344504E − 05	0·193514E + 07	0·516758E − 06	6·666660990	0·150000517
100	0·117431E + 07	0·851561E − 06	0·782875E + 07	0·127734E − 07		0·150000128

Rate of interest 20·00 per cent

n	$(1+r)^n$	v^n	s_n	s_n^{-1}	a_n	a_n^{-1}
1	1·20000	0·833333333	1·00000	1·000000000	0·833333333	1·200000000
2	1·44000	0·694444444	2·20000	0·454545455	1·527777778	0·654545455
3	1·72800	0·578703704	3·64000	0·274725275	2·106481481	0·474725275
4	2·07360	0·482253086	5·36800	0·186289121	2·588734568	0·386289121
5	2·48832	0·401877572	7·44160	0·134379703	2·990612140	0·334379703
6	2·98598	0·334897977	9·92992	0·100705746	3·325510117	0·300705746
7	3·58318	0·279081647	12·91590	0·077423926	3·604591764	0·277423926
8	4·29982	0·232568039	16·49908	0·060609422	3·837159803	0·260609422
9	5·15978	0·193806699	20·79890	0·048079462	4·030966503	0·248079462
10	6·19174	0·161505583	25·95868	0·038522757	4·192472086	0·238522757
11	7·43008	0·134587986	32·15042	0·031103794	4·327060071	0·231103794
12	8·91610	0·112156655	39·58050	0·025264965	4·439216726	0·225264965
13	10·69932	0·093463879	48·49660	0·020620001	4·532680605	0·220620001
14	12·83918	0·077886566	59·19592	0·016893055	4·610567171	0·216893055
15	15·40702	0·064905472	72·03511	0·013882120	4·675472642	0·213882120
16	18·48843	0·054087893	87·44213	0·011436135	4·729560535	0·211436135
17	22·18611	0·045073244	105·93056	0·009440147	4·774633779	0·209440147
18	26·62333	0·037561037	128·11667	0·007805386	4·812194816	0·207805386
19	31·94800	0·031300864	154·74000	0·006462453	4·843495680	0·206462453
20	38·33760	0·026084053	186·68800	0·005356531	4·869579733	0·205356531
21	46·00512	0·021736711	225·02560	0·004443939	4·891316445	0·204443939
22	55·20614	0·018113926	271·03072	0·003689619	4·909430370	0·203689619
23	66·24737	0·015094938	326·23686	0·003065258	4·924525309	0·203065258

n	$(1 + r)^n$	v^n	s_n	s_n^{-1}	a_n	a_n^{-1}
24	79·49685	0·012579115	392·48424	0·002547873	4·937104424	0·202547873
25	95·39622	0·010482596	471·98108	0·002118729	4·947587020	0·202118729
26	114·47546	0·008735497	567·37730	0·001762496	4·956322517	0·201762496
27	137·37055	0·007279581	681·85276	0·001466592	4·963602097	0·201466592
28	164·84466	0·006066317	819·22331	0·001220668	4·969668414	0·201220668
29	197·81359	0·005055264	984·06797	0·001016190	4·974723679	0·201016190
30	237·37631	0·004212720	1181·88157	0·000846108	4·978936399	0·200846108
31	284·85158	0·003510600	1419·25788	0·000704594	4·982446999	0·200704594
32	341·82189	0·002925500	1704·10946	0·000586817	4·985372499	0·200586817
33	410·18627	0·002437917	2045·93135	0·000488775	4·987810416	0·200488775
34	492·22352	0·002031597	2456·11762	0·000407147	4·989842013	0·200407147
35	590·66823	0·001692998	2948·34115	0·000339174	4·991535011	0·200339174
36	708·80187	0·001410831	3539·00937	0·000282565	4·992945843	0·200282565
37	850·56225	0·001175693	4247·81125	0·000235415	4·994121535	0·200235415
38	1020·67470	0·000979744	5098·37350	0·000196141	4·995101280	0·200196141
39	1224·80964	0·000816453	6119·04820	0·000163424	4·995917733	0·200163424
40	1469·77157	0·000680378	7343·85784	0·000136168	4·996598111	0·200136168
41	1763·72588	0·000566982	8813·62941	0·000113461	4·997165092	0·200113461
42	2116·47106	0·000472485	10577·35529	0·000094542	4·997637577	0·200094542
43	2539·76527	0·000393737	12693·82635	0·000078778	4·998031314	0·200078778
44	3047·71832	0·000328114	15233·59162	0·000065644	4·998359428	0·200065644
45	3657·26199	0·000273429	18281·30994	0·000054701	4·998632857	0·200054701
46	4388·71439	0·000227857	21938·57193	0·000045582	4·998860714	0·200045582
47	5266·45726	0·000189881	26327·28631	0·000037983	4·999050595	0·200037983

n	$(1 + r)^n$	v^n	s_n	s_n^{-1}	a_n	a_n^{-1}
48	6319·74872	0·000158234	31593·74358	0·000031652	4·999208829	0·200031652
49	7583·69846	0·000131862	37913·49229	0·000026376	4·999340691	0·200026376
50	9100·43815	0·000109885	45497·19075	0·000021979	4·999450576	0·200021979
55	22644·80226	0·000044160	0·113219E + 06	0·000008832	4·999779199	0·200008832
60	56347·51435	0·000017747	0·281733E + 06	0·000003549	4·999911265	0·200003549
65	0·140211E + 06	0·713213E − 05	0·701048E + 06	0·142644E − 05	4·999964339	0·200001426
70	0·348889E + 06	0·286624E − 05	0·174444E + 07	0·573250E − 06	4·999985669	0·200000573
80	0·216023E + 07	0·462914E − 06	0·108011E + 08	0·925828E − 07	4·999997685	0·200000093
90	0·133756E + 08	0·747632E − 07	0·668778E + 08	0·149526E − 07	4·999999626	0·200000015
100	0·828180E + 08	0·120747E − 07	0·414090E + 09	0·241493E − 08	4·999999940	0·200000002

Rate of interest 25·00 per cent

n	$(1+r)^n$	v^n	s_n	s_n^{-1}	a_n	a_n^{-1}
1	1·25000	0·800000000	1·00000	1·000000000	0·800000000	1·250000000
2	1·56250	0·640000000	2·25000	0·444444444	1·440000000	0·694444444
3	1·95313	0·512000000	3·81250	0·262295082	1·952000000	0·512295082
4	2·44141	0·409600000	5·76563	0·173441734	2·361600000	0·423441734
5	3·05176	0·327680000	8·20703	0·121846740	2·689280000	0·371846740
6	3·81470	0·262144000	11·25879	0·088819499	2·951424000	0·338819499
7	4·76837	0·209715200	15·07349	0·066341653	3·161139200	0·316341653
8	5·96046	0·167772160	19·84186	0·050398506	3·328911360	0·300398506
9	7·45058	0·134217728	25·80232	0·038756201	3·463129088	0·288756201
10	9·31323	0·107374182	33·25290	0·030072562	3·570503270	0·280072562
11	11·64153	0·085899346	42·56613	0·023492858	3·656402616	0·273492858
12	14·55192	0·068719477	54·20766	0·018447577	3·725122093	0·268447577
13	18·18989	0·054975581	68·75958	0·014543429	3·780097674	0·264543429
14	22·73737	0·043980465	86·94947	0·011500933	3·824078140	0·261500933
15	28·42171	0·035184372	109·68684	0·009116864	3·859262512	0·259116864
16	35·52714	0·028147498	138·10855	0·007240681	3·887410009	0·257240681
17	44·40892	0·022517998	173·63568	0·005759185	3·909928007	0·255759185
18	55·51115	0·018014399	218·04460	0·004586218	3·927942406	0·254586218
19	69·38894	0·014411519	273·55576	0·003655562	3·942353925	0·253655562
20	86·73617	0·011529215	342·94470	0·002915922	3·953883140	0·252915922
21	108·42022	0·009223372	429·68087	0·002327309	3·963106512	0·252327309
22	135·52527	0·007378698	538·10109	0·001858387	3·970485209	0·251858387
23	169·40659	0·005902958	673·62636	0·001484502	3·976388168	0·251484502

n	$(1 + r)^n$	s_n	s_n^{-1}	a_n	a_n^{-1}
24	211·75824	843·03295	0·001186193	3·981110534	0·251186193
25	264·69780	1054·79118	0·000948055	3·984888427	0·250948055
26	330·87225	1319·48898	0·000757869	3·987910742	0·250757869
27	413·59031	1650·36123	0·000605928	3·990328593	0·250605928
28	516·98788	2063·95153	0·000484508	3·992262875	0·250484508
29	646·23485	2580·93941	0·000387456	3·993810300	0·250387456
30	807·79357	3227·17427	0·000309869	3·995048240	0·250309869
31	1009·74196	4034·96738	0·000247833	3·996038592	0·250247833
32	1262·17745	5044·70979	0·000198227	3·996830873	0·250198227
33	1577·72181	6306·88724	0·000158557	3·997464699	0·250158557
34	1972·15226	7884·60905	0·000126829	3·997971759	0·250126829
35	2465·19033	9856·76132	0·000101453	3·998377407	0·250101453
36	3081·48791	12321·95164	0·000081156	3·998701926	0·250081156
37	3851·85989	15403·43956	0·000064921	3·998961541	0·250064921
38	4814·82486	19255·29944	0·000051934	3·999169233	0·250051934
39	6018·53108	24070·12430	0·000041545	3·999335386	0·250041545
40	7523·16385	30088·65538	0·000033235	3·999468309	0·250033235
41	9403·95481	37611·81923	0·000026587	3·999574647	0·250026587
42	11754·94351	47015·77403	0·000021269	3·999659718	0·250021269
43	14693·67939	58770·71754	0·000017015	3·999727774	0·250017015
44	18367·09923	73464·39693	0·000013612	3·999782219	0·250013612
45	22958·87404	91831·49616	0·000010890	3·999825775	0·250010890
46	28698·59255	0·114790E + 06	0·000008712	3·999860620	0·250008712
47	35873·24069	0·143489E + 06	0·000006969	3·999888496	0·250006969

v^n
0·004722366
0·003777893
0·003022315
0·002417852
0·001934281
0·001547425
0·001237940
0·000990352
0·000792282
0·000633825
0·000507060
0·000405648
0·000324519
0·000259615
0·000207692
0·000166153
0·000132923
0·000106338
0·000085071
0·000068056
0·000054445
0·000043556
0·000034845
0·000027876

n	$(1 + r)^n$	v^n	s_n	s_n^{-1}	a_n	a_n^{-1}
48	44841·55086	0·000022301	0·179362E + 06	0·000005575	3·999910797	0·250005575
49	56051·93857	0·000017841	0·224204E + 06	0·000004460	3·999928638	0·250004460
50	70064·92322	0·000014272	0·280256E + 06	0·000003568	3·999942910	0·250003568
55	0·213821E + 06	0·467681E — 05	0·855281E + 06	0·116921E — 05	3·999981293	0·250001169
60	0·652530E + 06	0·153250E — 05	0·261012E + 07	0·383124E — 06	3·999993870	0·250000383
65	0·199136E + 07	0·502168E — 06	0·796546E + 07	0·125542E — 06	3·999997991	0·250000126
70	0·607716E + 07	0·164550E — 06	0·243086E + 08	0·411376E — 07	3·999999342	0·250000041
80	0·565980E + 08	0·176685E — 07	0·226392E + 09	0·441712E — 08	3·999999929	0·250000004
90	0·527110E + 09	0·189714E — 08	0·210844E + 10	0·474284E — 09	3·999999992	0·250000000
100	0·490909E + 10	0·203704E — 09	0·196364E + 11	0·509259E — 10	3·999999999	0·250000000

Rate of interest 30·00 per cent

n	$(1+r)^n$	v^n	s_n	s_n^{-1}	a_n	a_n^{-1}
1	1·30000	0·769230769	1·00000	1·000000000	0·76923749	1·300000000
2	1·69000	0·591715976	2·30000	0·434782609	1·136046746	0·734782609
3	2·19700	0·455166136	3·99000	0·250626566	1·816112881	0·550628566
4	2·85610	0·350127797	6·18700	0·161629223	2·166240678	0·461629223
5	3·71293	0·269329074	9·04310	0·110581548	2·435569752	0·410581548
6	4·82681	0·207176211	12·75603	0·078394297	2·642745963	0·378394297
7	6·27485	0·159366316	17·58284	0·056873637	2·802112279	0·356873637
8	8·15731	0·122589474	23·85769	0·041915205	2·924701753	0·341915205
9	10·60450	0·094299595	32·01500	0·031235360	3·019001349	0·331235360
10	13·78585	0·072538150	42·61950	0·023463440	3·091539499	0·323463440
11	17·92160	0·055798577	56·40535	0·017728816	3·147338076	0·317728816
12	23·29809	0·042921982	74·32695	0·013454070	3·190260059	0·313454070
13	30·28751	0·033016910	97·62504	0·010243274	3·223276968	0·310243274
14	39·37376	0·025397623	127·91255	0·007817841	3·248674591	0·307817841
15	51·18589	0·019536633	167·28631	0·005977775	3·268211224	0·305977775
16	66·54166	0·015028179	218·47220	0·004577241	3·283239403	0·304577241
17	86·50416	0·011560138	285·01386	0·003508601	3·294799541	0·303508601
18	112·45541	0·008892414	371·51802	0·002691659	3·303691954	0·302691659
19	146·19203	0·006840318	483·97343	0·002066229	3·310532273	0·302066229
20	190·04964	0·005261783	630·16546	0·001586885	3·315794056	0·301586885
21	247·06453	0·004047526	820·21510	0·001219192	3·319841581	0·301219192
22	321·18389	0·003113481	1067·27963	0·000936962	3·322955063	0·300936962
23	417·53905	0·002394986	1388·46351	0·000720221	3·325350048	0·300720221

n	$(1+r)^n$	v^n	s_n	s_n^{-1}	a_n	a_n^{-1}
24	542·80077	0·001842297	1806·00257	0·000553709	3·327192345	0·300553709
25	705·64100	0·001417151	2348·80334	0·000425749	3·328609496	0·300425749
26	917·33330	0·001090116	3054·44434	0·000327392	3·329699612	0·300327392
27	1192·53329	0·000838551	3971·77764	0·000251776	3·330538163	0·300251776
28	1550·29328	0·000645039	5164·31093	0·000193637	3·331183203	0·300193637
29	2015·38126	0·000496184	6729·60421	0·000148929	3·331679387	0·300148929
30	2619·99564	0·000381680	8729·98548	0·000114548	3·332061067	0·300114548
31	3405·99434	0·000293600	11349·98112	0·000088106	3·332354667	0·300088106
32	4427·79264	0·000225846	14755·97546	0·000067769	3·332580513	0·300067769
33	5756·13043	0·000173728	19183·76810	0·000052127	3·332754241	0·300052127
34	7482·96956	0·000133637	24939·89853	0·000040096	3·332887877	0·300040096
35	9727·86043	0·000102798	32422·86808	0·000030842	3·332990675	0·300030842
36	12646·21855	0·000079075	42150·72851	0·000023724	3·333069750	0·300023724
37	16440·08412	0·000060827	54796·94706	0·000018249	3·333130577	0·300018249
38	21372·10935	0·000046790	71237·03118	0·000014038	3·333177367	0·300014038
39	27783·74216	0·000035992	92609·14053	0·000010798	3·333213359	0·300010798
40	36118·86481	0·000027686	0·120393E + 06	0·000008306	3·333241045	0·300008306
41	46954·52425	0·000021297	0·156512E + 06	0·000006389	3·333262343	0·300006389
42	61040·88153	0·000016382	0·203466E + 06	0·000004915	3·333278725	0·300004915
43	79353·14598	0·000012602	0·264507E + 06	0·000003781	3·333291327	0·300003781
44	0·130159E + 06	0·969377E − 05	0·343860E + 06	0·290816E − 05	3·333301021	0·300002908
45	0·134107E + 06	0·745674E − 05	0·447019E + 06	0·223704E − 05	3·333308478	0·300002237
46	0·174339E + 06	0·573596E − 05	0·581126E + 06	0·172080E − 05	3·333314213	0·300001721
47	0·226641E + 06	0·441227E − 05	0·755465E + 06	0·132369E − 05	3·333318626	0·300001324

n	$(1 + r)^n$	v^n	s_n	s_n^{-1}	a_n	a_n^{-1}
48	0·294633E + 06	0·339406E − 05	0·982106E + 06	0·101822E − 05	3·333322020	0·300001010
49	0·383022E + 06	0·261081E − 05	0·127674E + 07	0·783246E − 06	3·333324631	0·300000783
50	0·497929E + 06	0·200832E − 05	0·165976E + 07	0·602496E − 06	3·333326639	0·300000602
55	0·184878E + 07	0·540898E − 06	0·616258E + 07	0·162270E − 06	3·333331530	0·300000162
60	0·686438E + 07	0·145680E − 06	0·228813E + 08	0·437039E − 07	3·333332848	0·300000044
65	0·254870E + 08	0·392358E − 07	0·849565E + 08	0·117707E − 07	3·333333203	0·300000012
70	0·946313E + 08	0·105673E − 07	0·315438E + 09	0·317020E − 08	3·333333298	0·300000003
80	0·130457E + 10	0·766535E − 09	0·434857E + 10	0·229960E − 09	3·333333331	0·300000000
90	0·179846E + 11	0·556030E − 10	0·599488E + 11	0·166809E − 10	3·333333333	0·300000000
100	0·247934E + 12	0·403334E − 11	0·826445E + 12	0·121000E − 11	3·333333333	0·300000000

Rate of interest 40·00 per cent

n	$(1 + r)^n$	v^n	s_n	s_n^{-1}	a_n	a_n^{-1}
1	1·40000	0·714285714	1·00000	1·000000000	0·714285714	1·400000000
2	1·96000	0·510204082	2·40000	0·416666667	1·224489796	0·816666667
3	2·74400	0·364431487	4·36000	0·229357798	1·588921283	0·629357798
4	3·84160	0·260308205	7·10400	0·140765766	1·849229488	0·540765766
5	5·37824	0·185934432	10·94560	0·091360912	2·035163920	0·491360912
6	7·52954	0·132810309	16·32384	0·061260096	2·167974228	0·461260096
7	10·54135	0·094864506	23·85338	0·041922787	2·262838735	0·441922787
8	14·75789	0·067760362	34·39473	0·029074225	2·330599096	0·429074225
9	20·66105	0·048400258	49·15262	0·020344797	2·378999354	0·420344797
10	28·92547	0·034571613	69·81366	0·014323844	2·413570967	0·414323844
11	40·49565	0·024694009	98·73913	0·010127697	2·438264977	0·410127697
12	56·69391	0·017638578	139·23478	0·007182114	2·455903555	0·407182114
13	79·37148	0·012598984	195·92869	0·005103898	2·468502539	0·405103898
14	111·12007	0·008999275	275·30017	0·003632399	2·477501814	0·403632399
15	155·56810	0·006428053	386·42024	0·002587856	2·483929867	0·402587856
16	217·79533	0·004591467	541·98833	0·001845058	2·488521334	0·401845058
17	304·91347	0·003279619	759·78367	0·001316164	2·491800953	0·401316164
18	426·87885	0·002342585	1064·69714	0·000939234	2·494143538	0·400939234
19	597·63040	0·001673275	1491·57599	0·000670432	2·495816813	0·400670432
20	836·68255	0·001195196	2089·20639	0·000478651	2·497012009	0·400478651
21	1171·35558	0·000853712	2925·88894	0·000341776	2·497865721	0·400341776
22	1639·89781	0·000609794	4097·24452	0·000244066	2·498475515	0·400244066
23	2295·85693	0·000435567	5737·14232	0·000174303	2·498911082	0·400174303

n	$(1+r)^n$	v^n	s_n	s_n^{-1}	a_n	a_n^{-1}
24	3214·19970	0·000311119	8032·99925	0·000124487	2·499222201	0·400124487
25	4499·87958	0·000222228	11247·19895	0·000088911	2·499444430	0·400088911
26	6299·83141	0·000158734	15747·07853	0·000063504	2·499603164	0·400063504
27	8819·76398	0·000113382	22046·90994	0·000045358	2·499716546	0·400045358
28	12347·66957	0·000080987	30866·67392	0·000032397	2·499797533	0·400032397
29	17286·73740	0·000057848	43214·34349	0·000023140	2·499855380	0·400023140
30	24201·43236	0·000041320	60501·08089	0·000016529	2·499896700	0·400016529
31	33882·00530	0·000029514	84702·51324	0·000011806	2·499926215	0·400011806
32	47434·80742	0·000021082	0·118585E + 06	0·000008433	2·499947296	0·400008433
33	66408·73038	0·000015058	0·166019E + 06	0·000006023	2·499962354	0·400006023
34	92972·22254	0·000010756	0·232428E + 06	0·000004302	2·499973110	0·400004302
35	0·130161E + 06	0·768279E − 05	0·325400E + 06	0·307314E − 05	2·499980793	0·400003073
36	0·182226E + 06	0·548770E − 05	0·455561E + 06	0·219509E − 05	2·499986281	0·400002195
37	0·255116E + 06	0·391979E − 05	0·637787E + 06	0·156792E − 05	2·499990201	0·400001568
38	0·357162E + 06	0·279985E − 05	0·892903E + 06	0·111994E − 05	2·499993000	0·400001120
39	0·500027E + 06	0·199989E − 05	0·125006E + 07	0·799959E − 06	2·499995000	0·400000800
40	0·700038E + 06	0·142849E − 05	0·175009E + 07	0·571399E − 06	2·499996429	0·400000571
41	0·980053E + 06	0·102035E − 05	0·245013E + 07	0·408142E − 06	2·499997449	0·400000408
42	0·137207E + 07	0·728824E − 06	0·343018E + 07	0·291530E − 06	2·499998178	0·400000292
43	0·192090E + 07	0·520588E − 06	0·480226E + 07	0·208235E − 06	2·499998699	0·400000208
44	0·268926E + 07	0·371849E − 06	0·672316E + 07	0·148740E − 06	2·499999070	0·400000149
45	0·376497E + 07	0·265606E − 06	0·941242E + 07	0·106243E − 06	2·499999336	0·400000106
46	0·527096E + 07	0·189719E − 06	0·131774E + 08	0·758875E − 07	2·499999526	0·400000076
47	0·737934E + 07	0·135513E − 06	0·184484E + 08	0·542054E − 07	2·499999661	0·400000054

n	$(1+r)^n$	v^n	s_n	s_n^{-1}	a_n	a_n^{-1}
48	0·103311E + 08	0·967953E − 07	0·258277E + 08	0·387181E − 07	2·499999758	0·400000039
49	0·144635E + 08	0·691395E − 07	0·361588E + 08	0·276558E − 07	2·499999827	0·400000028
50	0·202489E + 08	0·493854E − 07	0·506223E + 08	0·197541E − 07	2·499999877	0·400000020
55	0·108904E + 09	0·918244E − 08	0·272259E + 09	0·367298E − 08	2·499999977	0·400000004
60	0·585709E + 09	0·170733E − 08	0·146427E + 10	0·682933E − 09	2·499999996	0·400000001
65	0·315009E + 10	0·317452E − 09	0·787521E + 10	0·126981E − 09	2·499999999	0·400000000
70	0·169419E + 11	0·590252E − 10	0·423548E + 11	0·236101E − 10	2·500000000	0·400000000
80	0·490053E + 12	0·204060E − 11	0·122513E + 13	0·816239E − 12	2·500000000	0·400000000
90	0·141750E + 14	0·705467E − 13	0·354375E + 14	0·282187E − 13	2·500000000	0·400000000
100	0·410019E + 15	0·243891E − 14	0·102505E + 16	0·975565E − 15	2·500000000	0·400000000

Rate of interest 50·00 per cent

n	$(1+r)^n$	v^n	s_n	s_n^{-1}	a_n	a_n^{-1}
1	1·50000	0·666666667	1·00000	1·000000000	0·666666667	1·500000000
2	2·25000	0·444444444	2·50000	0·400000000	1·111111111	0·900000000
3	3·37500	0·296296296	4·75000	0·210526316	1·407407407	0·710526316
4	5·06250	0·197530864	8·12500	0·123076923	1·604938272	0·623076923
5	7·59375	0·131687243	13·18750	0·075829384	1·736625514	0·575829384
6	11·39062	0·087791495	20·78125	0·048120301	1·824417010	0·548120301
7	17·08594	0·058527663	32·17187	0·031083050	1·882944673	0·531083050
8	25·62891	0·039018442	49·25781	0·020301348	1·921963115	0·520301348
9	38·44336	0·026012295	74·88672	0·013353503	1·947975410	0·513353503
10	57·66504	0·017341530	113·33008	0·008823783	1·965316940	0·508823783
11	86·49756	0·011561020	170·99512	0·005848120	1·976877960	0·505848120
12	129·74634	0·007707347	257·49268	0·003883606	1·984585307	0·503883605
13	194·61951	0·005138231	387·23901	0·002582384	1·989723538	0·502582384
14	291·92926	0·003425487	581·85852	0·001718631	1·993149025	0·501718631
15	437·89389	0·002283658	873·78778	0·001144443	1·995432683	0·501144443
16	656·84084	0·001522439	1311·68167	0·000762380	1·996955122	0·500762380
17	985·26125	0·001014959	1968·52251	0·000507995	1·997970082	0·500507995
18	1477·89188	0·000676639	2953·78376	0·000338549	1·998646721	0·500338549
19	2216·83782	0·000451093	4431·67564	0·000225648	1·999097814	0·500225648
20	3325·25673	0·000300729	6648·51346	0·000150410	1·999398543	0·500150410
21	4987·88510	0·000200486	9973·77019	0·000100263	1·999599028	0·500100263
22	7481·82764	0·000133657	14961·65529	0·000066838	1·999732686	0·500066838
23	11222·74146	0·000089105	22443·48293	0·000044556	1·999821790	0·500044556

n	$(1+r)^n$	v^n	s_n	s_n^{-1}	a_n	a_n^{-1}
24	16834·11220	0·000059413	33666·22439	0·000029703	1·999881194	0·500029703
25	25251·16829	0·000039602	50500·33659	0·000019802	1·999920796	0·500019802
26	37876·75244	0·000026401	75751·50488	0·000013201	1·999947197	0·500013201
27	56815·12866	0·000017601	0·113628E + 06	0·000008801	1·999964798	0·500008801
28	85222·69299	0·000011734	0·170443E + 06	0·000005867	1·999976532	0·500005867
29	0·127834E + 06	0·782264E − 05	0·255666E + 06	0·391135E − 05	1·999984355	0·500003911
30	0·191751E + 06	0·521510E − 05	0·383500E + 06	0·260756E − 05	1·999989570	0·500002608
31	0·287627E + 06	0·347673E − 05	0·575251E + 06	0·173837E − 05	1·999993047	0·500001738
32	0·431440E + 06	0·231782E − 05	0·862878E + 06	0·115891E − 05	1·999995364	0·500001159
33	0·647160E + 06	0·154521E − 05	0·129432E + 07	0·772608E − 06	1·999996910	0·500000773
34	0·970740E + 06	0·103014E − 05	0·194148E + 07	0·515072E − 06	1·999997940	0·500000515
35	0·145611E + 07	0·686761E − 06	0·291222E + 07	0·343381E − 06	1·999998626	0·500000343
36	0·218416E + 07	0·457841E − 06	0·436833E + 07	0·228921E − 06	1·999999084	0·500000229
37	0·327625E + 07	0·305227E − 06	0·655249E + 07	0·152614E − 06	1·999999390	0·500000153
38	0·491437E + 07	0·203485E − 06	0·982874E + 07	0·101742E − 06	1·999999593	0·500000102
39	0·737155E + 07	0·135657E − 06	0·147431E + 08	0·678283E − 07	1·999999729	0·500000068
40	0·110573E + 08	0·904377E − 07	0·221147E + 08	0·452189E − 07	1·999999819	0·500000045
41	0·165860E + 08	0·602918E − 07	0·331720E + 08	0·301459E − 07	1·999999879	0·500000030
42	0·248790E + 08	0·401945E − 07	0·497580E + 08	0·200973E − 07	1·999999920	0·500000020
43	0·373185E + 08	0·267964E − 07	0·746370E + 08	0·133982E − 07	1·999999946	0·500000013
44	0·559777E + 08	0·178642E − 07	0·111955E + 09	0·893212E − 08	1·999999964	0·500000009
45	0·839666E + 08	0·119095E − 07	0·167933E + 09	0·595475E − 08	1·999999976	0·500000006
46	0·125950E + 09	0·793966E − 08	0·251900E + 09	0·396983E − 08	1·999999984	0·500000004
47	0·188925E + 09	0·529311E − 08	0·377850E + 09	0·264655E − 08	1·999999989	0·500000003

n	$(1 + r)^n$	v^n	s_n	s^{-1}	a_n	a_n^{-1}
48	0·283387E + 09	0·352874E − 08	0·566775E + 09	0·176437E − 08	1·999999993	0·500000002
49	0·425081E + 09	0·235249E − 08	0·850162E + 09	0·117625E − 08	1·999999995	0·500000001
50	0·637622E + 09	0·156833E − 08	0·127524E + 10	0·784164E − 09	1·999999997	0·500000001
55	0·484194E + 10	0·206529E − 09	0·968388E + 10	0·103264E − 09	2·000000001	0·500000000
60	0·367685E + 11	0·271972E − 10	0·735369E + 11	0·135986E − 10	2·000000000	0·500000000
65	0·279211E + 12	0·358153E − 11	0·558421E + 12	0·179076E − 11	2·000000000	0·500000000
70	0·212026E + 13	0·471641E − 12	0·424051E + 13	0·235821E − 12	2·000000000	0·500000000
80	0·122265E + 15	0·817898E − 14	0·244529E + 15	0·408949E − 14	2·000000000	0·500000000
90	0·705039E + 16	0·141836E − 15	0·141008E + 17	0·709180E − 16	2·000000000	0·500000000
100	0·406561E + 18	0·245965E − 17	0·813122E + 18	0·122983E − 17	2·000000000	0·500000000

References

(For a more detailed annotated bibliography see Bromwich, 1970.)

ALCHIAN, A. (1953), 'The meaning of utility measurement', *Amer. econ. Rev.*, vol. 42, pp. 26–50; reprinted in Townsend (1971), to which cited page numbers refer.

ALEXIS, M., and WILSON, C. Z. (eds.) (1967), *Organisational Decision Making*, Prentice-Hall.

AMEY, L. R. (1972), 'Interdependencies in capital budgeting: a survey', *J. bus. Finan.*, vol. 4, no. 3.

ANSOFF, H. I. (1957), 'Strategies for diversification', *Harvard bus. Rev.*, vol. 35, pp. 113–24.

ANSOFF, H. I. (1968), *Corporate Strategy*, Penguin.

ARCHER, S. H., and D'AMBROSIO, C. D. (eds.) (1967), *The Theory of Business Finance: a Book of Readings*, Macmillan.

BALL, R., and BROWN, P. (1969), 'Portfolio theory and accountancy', *J. accountancy Res.*, vol. 7, no. 2, pp. 300–34.

BARGES, A. (1963), *The Effect of Capital Structure on the Cost of Capital*, Prentice-Hall.

BAUMOL, W. J. (1965), *Economic Theory and Operations Analysis*, Prentice-Hall (2nd edn.).

BAUMOL, W. J., and QUANDT, R. E. (1965), 'Investment and discount rates under capital rationing: a programming approach', *Econ. J.*, vol. 75, pp. 317–29; reprinted in Archer and D'Ambrosio (1967).

BAXTER, W. T., and DAVIDSON, S. (eds.) (1962), *Studies in Accounting Theory*, Sweet & Maxwell.

BENISHAY, H. (1961), 'Variability of earnings – price ratios of corporate equity', *Amer. econ. Rev.*, vol. 51, pp. 81–94.

BENNION, E. G. (1956), 'Capital budgeting and game theory', *Harvard bus. Rev.*, November–December; reprinted in Archer and D'Ambrosio (1967).

BIERMAN, M., and SMIDT, S. (1971), *The Capital Budgeting Decision*, Macmillan (2nd edn).

BODENHORN, D. (1959), 'On the problem of capital budgeting', *J. Finan.*, vol. 14, no. 4, pp. 473–92; reprinted in Archer and D'Ambrosio (1967).

BREALEY, R. A. (1969), *An Introduction to Risk and Return from Common Stocks*, MIT Press.

BROMWICH, M. (1969), 'Inflation and the capital budgeting process', *J. bus. Finan.*, vol. 1, Autumn.

BROMWICH, M. (1970), 'Capital budgeting: a survey', *J. bus. Finan.*, vol. 2, no. 3, pp. 3–26.

BYRNE, R., CHARNES, A., COOPER, W. W., DAVIS, O. A., and GILFORD, D. (eds.) (1971), *Studies in Budgeting*, North-Holland Publishing Company.

BYRNE, R., CHARNES, A., COOPER, W. W., and KORTANEK, K. O. (1967), 'A chance-constrained programming approach to capital budgeting', *J. finan. quantitative Anal.*, vol. 2, no. 4, pp. 339–64; reprinted in Byrne *et al.* (1971).

CARLETON, W. T. (1969), 'Linear programming and capital budgeting models', *J. Finan.*, vol. 25, pp. 825–53.

CARSBERG, B. V. (1969), *An Introduction to Mathematical Programming for Accountants*, Allen & Unwin.

CARSBERG, B. V., and EDEY, H. C. (eds.) (1969), *Modern Financial Management*, Penguin.

CLARKSON, G. P. E. (1965), *Portfolio selection: A Simulation of Trust Investment*, Prentice-Hall.

COASE, R. H. (1968), 'The nature of costs', in D. Solomons (ed.), *Studies in Cost Analysis*, Sweet & Maxwell (2nd edn).

COHEN, K. J., and CYERT, R. M. (1965), *Theory of the Firm: Resource Allocation in a Market Economy*, Prentice-Hall.

COHEN, K. J., and POGUE, J. A. (1967), 'An empirical evaluation of alternative portfolio selection models', *J. Bus.*, vol. 40, no. 2, pp. 166–93.

CYERT, R. M., DILL, W. R., and MARCH, J. G. (1958), 'The role of expectations in business decision making', *Admin. Sci. Q.*, vol. 3, no. 3, pp. 307–40.

CYERT, R. M., and MARCH, J. G. (1963), *A Behavioural Theory of the Firm*, Prentice-Hall.

DAVIDSON, D., SUPPES, P., and SIEGEL, S. (1957), *Decision-Making: An Experimental Approach*, Stanford University Press; parts of Chapter 2 are reprinted in Edwards and Tversky (1967).

DURAND, D. (1952), 'Cost of debt and equity funds: trends and problems of measurement', *National Bureau of Economic Research*, reprinted in Archer and D'Ambrosio (1967) and Solomon (1959).

DURAND, D. (1959), 'The cost of capital, corporation finance and the theory of investment: comment', *Amer. econ. Rev.*, vol. 49, pp. 639–54; reprinted in Archer and D'Ambrosio (1967).

DYCKMAN, T. R., SMIDT, S., and MCADAMS, A. K. L. (1969), *Management Decision Making Under Uncertainty*, Macmillan.

EDEY, H. C. (1963), 'Accounting principles and business reality', *Accountancy*, pp. 998–1002 and 1083–8; reprinted in Carsberg and Edey (1969).

EDWARDS, W. (1961), 'Behavioural decision theory', *Ann. Rev. Psychol.*, vol. 12, pp. 473–98; reprinted in Edwards and Tversky (1967).

EDWARDS, W. and TVERSKY, A. (eds.) (1967), *Decision Making*, Penguin.

ELTON, E. J. (1970), 'Capital rationing and external discount rates', *J. Finan.*, vol. 25, no. 3, pp. 573–84.

FAMA, E. F. (1965a), 'Portfolio analysis in a stable paretian market', *Manag. Sci.*, vol. 2, pp. 404–19.

FAMA, E. F. (1965b), 'The behaviour of stock market prices', *J. Bus.*, vol. 38, pp. 34–105.

FAMA, E. F. (1968), *Multi-Period Consumption – Investment Decisions.* Report No. 6830, Centre for Mathematical Studies in Business and Economics, University of Chicago, Ch. 15; see also Markowitz (1970), p. 311.

FAMA, E. F. (1970), 'Efficient capital markets: a review of the theory and empirical work', *J. Finan.*, vol. 25, pp. 383–417.

FAMA, E. F., FISHER, L., JENSEN, M. C., and ROLL, R. (1969), 'The adjustment of stock prices to new information', *Int. Econ. Rev.*, vol. 10, pp. 1–21.

FAMA, E. F., and MILLER, M. H. (1972), *The Theory of Finance*, Holt, Rinehart & Winston.

FARRAR, D. E. (1962), *The Investment Decision Under Uncertainty*, Prentice-Hall.

FRANCIS, J. C., and ARCHER, S. H. (1971), *Portfolio Analysis*, Prentice-Hall.

FREUND, J. E., and WILLIAMS, F. J. (1967), *Modern Business Statistics*, Pitman.

FRIEDMAN, M., and SAVAGE, L. J. (1948), 'The utility analysis of choices involving risk', *J. of polit. Econ.*, vol. 4, pp. 279–304; reprinted in Archer and D'Ambrosio (1967).

GORDON, M. J. (1962), *The Investment, Financing and Valuation of the Corporation*, Irwin.

GORDON, M. J. (1963), 'Optimal investment and financing policy', *J. Finan.*, vol. 18, pp. 264–72; reprinted in Archer and D'Ambrosio (1967).

GORDON, M. J. (1967), 'Some estimates of the cost of capital to the electrical utility industry 1954–57: comment', *Amer. econ. Rev.*, December; see also the reply by Miller and Modigliani in the same issue.

GOULD, J. R. (1962), 'The economist's cost concept and business problems', in Baxter and Davidson (eds.), *Studies in Accounting Theory*, Sweet & Maxwell.

GRAYSON, J. C. (1960), *Decisions Under Uncertainty: Drilling Decisions by Oil and Gas Operators*, Division of Research, Harvard Business School.

GRAYSON, J. C. (1967), 'The use of statistical techniques in capital budgeting', in Robichek (ed.), *Financial Research and Management Decisions*, Wiley.

HERTZ, D. B. (1964), 'Risk analysis in capital investment', *Harvard Bus. Rev.*, January–February; reprinted in Archer and D'Ambrosio (1967).

HILLIER, F. S. (1963), 'The derivation of probabilistic information', *Manag. Sci.*, vol. 9, pp. 443–57; reprinted in Archer and D'Ambrosio (1967).

HILLIER, F. S. (1969), *The Evaluation of Risky Interrelated Investments*, North-Holland Publishing Company.

HILLIER, F. S. (1971), 'A basic approach to the evaluation of risky interrelated investment', in Byrne *et al.* (eds.), *Studies in Budgeting*, North-Holland Publishing Company.

HIRSHLEIFER, J. (1958), 'On the theory of optimal investment decision', *J. polit. Econ.*, vol. 66, no. 4, pp. 329–52; reprinted in Archer and D'Ambrosio (1967) and Carsberg and Edey (1969).

HIRSHLEIFER, J. (1966), 'Investment Decisions Under Uncertainty: Applications of the State-Preference Approach', *Q. J. Econ.* 80 (May).

HIRSHLEIFER, J. (1970), *Investment, Interest, and Capital*, Prentice-Hall.

HORNE, J. C. VAN (1968), *Financial Management and Policy*, Prentice-Hall.

INFLATION ACCOUNTING COMMITTEE (1975), *Inflation Accounting, Report of the Inflation Accounting Committee*, Her Majesty's Stationery Office (Cmnd 6225) (the 'Sandilands' Report).

ISTVAN, D. F. (1961), *Capital Expenditure Decisions*, Indiana University.

JOHNSTON, J. (1963), *Econometric Methods*, McGraw-Hill.

KEENAN, M. (1970), 'Models of equity valuation: the great serm bubble', *J. Finan.*, vol. 25, pp. 243–73.

KING, B. F. (1966), 'Market and industry factors in stock price behaviour', *J. Bus.*, vol. 39, pp. 139–90.

KYBURG, H. E., Jr, and SMOKLER, H. E. (eds.) (1964), *Studies in Subjective Probability*, Wiley.

LERNER, E. M., and CARLETON, W. T. (1964), 'The integration of capital budgeting and stock valuation', *Amer. econ. Rev.*, vol. 54, no. 4, pp. 672–83; reprinted in Archer and D'Ambrosio (1967).

LINTNER, J. (1965), 'The valuation of risk assets and the selection of risky investments in stock portfolios and capital budgets', *Rev. econ. Stat.*, vol. 47, no. 1, pp. 13–37, reprinted in Archer and D'Ambrosio (1967).

LORIE, J. H., and SAVAGE, L. J. (1955), 'Three problems in capital rationing', *J. Bus.*, vol. 27; pp. 58–61 of Solomon (1959).

LUCE, R., and RAIFFA, H. (1957), *Games and Decisions*, Wiley.

MAGEE, J. F. (1964), 'How to use decision trees in capital budgeting', *Harvard bus. Rev.*, September–October; reprinted in Archer and D'Ambrosio (1967).

MARKOWITZ, H. M. (1952), 'The utility of wealth', *J. polit. Econ.*, vol. 60, pp. 151–8.

MARKOWITZ, H. M. (1970), *Portfolio Selection: Efficient Diversification of Investments*, Yale University Press.

MERRETT, A. J., and SYKES, A. (1963), *The Finance and Analysis of Capital Projects*, Longmans.

MILLER, M. H., and MODIGLIANI, F. (1961), 'Dividend policy, growth, and the valuation of shares', *J. Bus.*, vol. 34, pp. 411–33; reprinted in Archer and D'Ambrosio (1967).

MILLER, M. H., and MODIGLIANI, F. (1966), 'Some estimates of the cost of capital to electrical utility industry, 1954–57', *Amer. econ. Rev.*, vol. 56, no. 3, pp. 333–91; see also the comments in the December 1967 issue of this Journal.

MODIGLIANI, F., and MILLER, M. H. (1958), 'The cost of capital, corporation finance and the theory of investment', *Amer. econ. Rev.*, vol. 48, pp. 261–97; reprinted in Archer and D'Ambrosio (1967).

MODIGLIANI, F., and MILLER, M. H. (1959), 'The cost of capital, corporation finance and the theory of investment; reply', *Amer. econ. Rev.*, vol. 49, pp. 655–9; reprinted in Archer and D'Ambrosio (1967).

MODIGLIANI, F., and MILLER, M. H. (1963), 'Corporate income taxes and the cost of capital: a correction', *Amer. econ. Rev.*, vol. 53, pp. 433–42; reprinted in Archer and D'Ambrosio (1967).

MOSSIN, J. (1968), 'Optimal Multiperiod Portfolio Policies', *J. Bus.*, vol. 34, pp. 215–29.

MOSTELLER, F., and NOGEE, P. (1951), 'An experimental measurement of utility', *J. polit. Econ.*; reprinted in Edwards and Tversky (1967).

MUMEY, G. A. (1969), *The Theory of Financial Structure*, Holt, Rinehart & Winston.

NEUMANN, J. VON, and MORGENSTERN, O. (1953), *Theory of Games and Economic Behaviour*, Princeton University Press.

PENROSE, E. (1959), *The Theory of the Growth of the Firm*, Oxford University Press.

PETERSON, D. E. (1969), *A Quantitative Framework for Financial Management*, Irwin.

PORTERFIELD, J. T. S. (1965), *Investment Decisions and Capital Costs*, Prentice-Hall.

QUIRIN, G. D. (1967), *The Capital Expenditure Decision*, Irwin.

RAIFFA, H. (1968), *Decision Analysis*, Addison-Wesley.

ROBICHEK, A. A. (ed.) (1967), *Financial Research and Management Decisions*, Wiley.

ROBICHEK, A. A., and MYERS, S. C. (1965), *Optimal Financing Decisions*, Prentice-Hall.

ROY, A. D. (1952), 'Safety first and the holding of assets', *Econometrica*, pp. 431–49, July.

SAVAGE, L. J. (1954), *The Foundations of Statistics*, Wiley.

SCHLAIFER, R. (1959), *Probability and Statistics for Business Decisions*, McGraw-Hill.

SCHWAB, B., and LUSZTIG, P. (1969), 'A comparative analysis of the net present value and the benefit–cost ratio as measure of the economic desirability of investments', *J. Finan.*, vol. 24, no. 3.

SCHWARTZ, E. (1959), 'Theory of the capital structure of the firm', *J. Finan.*, vol. 14, no. 1, pp. 18–39; reprinted in Archer and D'Ambrosio (1967).

SIMON, H. A. (1959), 'Theories of decision making in economics and behavioural science', *Amer. econ. Rev.*, vol. 49, no. 3, pp. 262 ff.

SHARPE, W. F. (1964), 'Capital Asset Prices: A Theory of Market Equilibrium under Conditions of Risk', *J. Finan.*, vol. 19, pp. 10–18; reprinted in Archer and D'Ambrosio (1967).

SHARPE, W. F. (1970), *Portfolio Theory and Capital Markets*, McGraw-Hill.

SOLOMON, E. (ed.) (1959), *The Management of Corporate Capital*, Free Press.

SOLOMON, E. (1963), *The Theory of Financial Management*, Columbia University Press.

SOLOMON, E., and LAYA, J. C. (1967), 'Measurement of company profitability: some systematic errors in the accounting rate of return', in Robichek (ed.), *Financial Research and Management Decisions*, Wiley.

SOLOMONS, D. (ed.) (1968), *Studies in Cost Analysis*, Sweet & Maxwell (2nd edn).

STEWART, R. (1963), *The Reality of Management*, Heinemann.

STIGLITZ, J. E. (1974), 'On the irrelevance of corporate financial policy', *Amer. econ. Rev.*, vol. LXIV, no. 3, pp. 851–66.

SWALM, R. O. (1966), 'Utility theory – insights into risk taking', *Harvard bus. Rev.*, vol. 44, November–December, pp. 123–36.

TOWNSEND, H. (ed.) (1971), *Price Theory: Selected Readings*, Penguin.

WEINGARTNER, H. M. (1963), *Mathematical Programming and the Analysis of Capital Budgeting Problems*, Prentice-Hall; reprinted by the Markham Publishing Company (1966).

WEINGARTNER, H. M. (1966), 'Criteria for programming investment selection', *J. ind. Econ.*, vol. 15, no. 1.

WEINGARTNER, H. M. (1971), 'Some new thoughts on the payback period and capital budgeting decisions', in Byrne *et al.* (eds.), *Studies in Budgeting*, North-Holland Publishing Company.

WESTON, J. F. (1963), 'A test of the cost of capital proposition', *Southern econ. J.* reprinted in Archer and D'Ambrosio (1967).

WESTON, J. F. (1967), 'Valuation of the firm and its relation to financial management' in Robichek (ed.), *Financial Research and Management Decisions*, Wiley.

WILKES, F. M. (1972), 'Inflation and Capital Budgeting Decisions', *J. bus. Finan.*, vol. 4. Autumn.

WRIGHT, J. F. (1963), 'Notes on the marginal efficiency of capital', *Oxford econ. Papers*, New Series, vol. 15, p. 125.

Index

394 Index

More about Penguins and Pelicans

Penguinews, which appears every month, contains details of all the new books issued by Penguins as they are published. From time to time it is supplemented by *Penguins in Print*, which is our complete list of almost 5,000 titles.

A specimen copy of *Penguinews* will be sent to you free on request. Please write to Dept EP, Penguin Books Ltd, Harmondsworth, Middlesex, for your copy.

In the U.S.A.: For a complete list of books available from Penguins in the United States write to Dept CS, Penguin Books, 625 Madison Avenue, New York, New York 10022.

In Canada: For a complete list of books available from Penguins in Canada write to Penguin Books Canada Ltd, 41 Steelcase Road West, Markham, Ontario.

Some books on Business and Management published in Penguins

Some books on Business and Management published in Penguins